Monitoring and Assessment in Online Collaborative Environments:
Emergent Computational Technologies for E-Learning Support

Angel A. Juan
Open University of Catalonia, Spain

Thanasis Daradoumis
Open University of Catalonia, Spain

Fatos Xhafa
Open University of Catalonia, Spain

Santi Caballe
Open University of Catalonia, Spain

Javier Faulin
Public University of Navarre, Spain

INFORMATION SCIENCE REFERENCE

Hershey · New York

Director of Editorial Content:	Kristin Klinger
Senior Managing Editor:	Jamie Snavely
Assistant Managing Editor:	Michael Brehm
Publishing Assistant:	Sean Woznicki
Typesetter:	Michael Brehm
Cover Design:	Lisa Tosheff
Printed at:	Yurchak Printing Inc.

Published in the United States of America by
Information Science Reference (an imprint of IGI Global)
701 E. Chocolate Avenue
Hershey PA 17033
Tel: 717-533-8845
Fax: 717-533-8661
E-mail: cust@igi-global.com
Web site: http://www.igi-global.com/reference

Library of Congress Cataloging-in-Publication Data

Monitoring and assessment in online collaborative environments : emergent
computational technologies for e-learning support / Angel A. Juan ... [et
al.], editors.
     p. cm.
  Includes bibliographical references and index.
  Summary: "The book provides researchers and developers of online
collaborative systems with approaches for effective and efficient means that
would assist e-learning students and teachers with precise and relevant
information regarding the ongoing online learning activity at both individual
and group levels"--Provided by publisher.
  ISBN 978-1-60566-786-7 (hardcover) -- ISBN 978-1-60566-787-4 (ebook) 1.
Computer-assisted instruction--Evaluation. 2. Web-based instruction--
Evaluation. 3. Group work in education--Evaluation. I. Juan, Angel A., 1972-
  LB1028.5.M617 2010
  371.33'44678--dc22
                              2009007011

British Cataloguing in Publication Data
A Cataloguing in Publication record for this book is available from the British Library.

All work contributed to this book is new, previously-unpublished material. The views expressed in this book are those of the authors, but not necessarily of the publisher.

Table of Contents

Section 1
Tools and Applications for Monitoring in E-Learning

Section 2
Tracking, Feedback and Monitoring

Section 3
Assessment Approaches

Detailed Table of Contents

Section 1
Tools and Applications for Monitoring in E-Learning

This section contains four chapters which are focused on web-based tools that aim to monitoring learning processes, assist students in real-time and provide them with personalized feedback and support.

    F. Bellas, University of A Coruña, Spain
    O. Fontenla-Romero, University of A Coruña, Spain
    N. Sánchez-Maroño, University of A Coruña, Spain
    J. A. Becerra, University of A Coruña, Spain

The authors propose a methodology focused in monitoring both learning and resources. An application of web-based multimedia tools as a complement to the traditional e-learning materials to improve the quality of teaching is presented. The authors also show the advantages of providing the students with more familiar multimedia materials suitable for being transported and consulted in mobile devices.

    Sotirios Botsios, Democritus University of Thrace, Greece
    Dimitrios Georgiou, Democritus University of Thrace, Greece

The authors approach the adaptation and personalization of the information and instruction offered to the online learners and groups in online e-learning environments. They consider the Adaptive Educational Hypermedia Systems (AEHS) and address the need of standardization of user assessment in such environment. Thereafter, the authors provide a classification of some basic assessment aspects of an AEHS user as well as the basis for the development of a generic architecture for the retrieval of standardized Learning Objects.

Chapter 3

This chapter introduces the Virtual co Learner system aimed at using the behavior of a learning companion suitable to the user's cognitive and learning styles. The proposed collaborative system runs asynchronously and reuses digitized material in the system. The motivation behind the system is to increase matching of real and simulated learners who have similar cognitive characteristics so that learning procedure becomes more efficient and productive.

Chapter 4

This chapter considers online collaboration in a distributed e-learning environment. The authors describe the usefulness of web-based automated essay grading to provide extensive real-time data for monitoring and enhancing e-learning activities. By examining real data from student use of this software, it is evidenced that students take advantage of the proposed learning environment to revise and resubmit their work, which helped improving their final. The success of the proposed learning environment resides in its ability to provide detailed, personalized feedback to students in real time.

Section 2
Tracking, Feedback and Monitoring

This section contains several theoretical frameworks and practical models to monitoring both individual and collaborative activity in online scenarios, so that convenient feedback can be provided. Virtual teams' behavior is analyzed and main informational necessities for each different actor are highlighted.

Chapter 5

The author proposes Expertiza –a system for managing all kinds of communication that is involved in assessment of project work. Experimental studies showed that by using this system students are capable of producing work that can be used for teaching purposes.

Chapter 6

This chapter approaches the operation of virtual teams in organizations. The study is based on qualitative data collected by interviewing 20 virtual team managers and members of 20 different organizations. The objective is to analyze what projects virtual team participated in, how virtual teams operate and the difficulties virtual teams face.

This chapter focuses on the monitoring of students' activities in e-learning. To that end, the authors start from a socio-cultural approach to the notion of activity, which is conceived in terms of actions, which, in turn, are composed by operations. The definitions of activity, action and operation are then used in defining a model for monitoring activities in e-learning. The model accounts for indicators measure individuals' actions within a web environment. Moreover, the authors consider the application of Social Network Analysis to web interactions occurring in collective discussions within web environments.

This chapter introduces the reader in the new scenario defined by the recently created European Higher Education Area and by the increasing use of learning management systems in higher education worldwide. Then, authors discuss the importance of monitoring students' and groups' activity and performance, and review some of the monitoring tools already available in the market. Finally, they aim to identify which the informational necessities of online instructors and students are, and propose some graphs for the monitoring process.

This chapter deals with the issue of monitoring and evaluating CSCL processes. The approach is based on effective organization of information drawn through monitoring online courses. The authors present thereafter a general purpose model for organizing this information, which serves to make the monitoring, assessment and evaluation processes more systematic and effective.

Section 3
Assessment Approaches

In this final section, some works related to assessment processes in online collaborative learning are presented. Self-assessment importance is discussed and some real experiences regarding monitoring and assessment processes are introduced and analyzed.

The authors describe a learning scenario, situated in 3D Collaborative Virtual Environments, in which the user's graphical representation is the means to express nonverbal communications. The proposal aims at inferring indicators of collaborative interaction and their use to foster collaboration in a learning task situation. An exploratory study that consisted in the analysis of a real life situation during a collaborative task accomplishment exemplifies the proposed approach and its empirical analysis.

This chapter tackles the self-assessment as one of the crucial activities in e-learning. The authors present a recommender software system that aims at improving the effectiveness of self-assessment activities. The methodology for obtaining improvement of self-assessment is based on embedding knowledge management into the business logic of the e-learning platform. Techniques such as Naive Bayes Classifier are used for obtaining the learning resources that need to be further accessed by learners.

The author discusses collaboration between language learners while using computer-based tasks. Monitoring and assessment for the collaborative language learning are explored based on interview, observation and questionnaire data from both teachers and students at two UK university language centers. The results of the study indicate that collaboration in computer-based environments can help students to develop their language skills.

Chapter 13

Marta E. Zorrilla Pantaleón, University of Cantabria, Spain
Elena E. Álvarez Sáiz, University of Cantabria, Spain

This chapter motivates the need of suitable tools for the monitoring and follow-up of the students to facilitate the instructors' task. The authors propose a set of reports, designed from an educational point of view, to assist instructors to carry out the tracking and assessment task. An architecture software for the implementation of such monitoring tools is also presented.

Foreword

For centuries, the traditional model of education consisted of an instructor standing in front of a group of students with the aid of an overhead projector, chalk or dry-erase board, or lately perhaps a powerpoint presentation. The creation of the "cyber classroom" is a relatively new phenomenon that has enabled us to free ourselves from the restrictive mold of the traditional classroom. While the traditional educational institution will never be eliminated and while online education has its unique challenges, cyber classrooms present many attractive qualities such as accessibility, flexibility, and strengthening of students' technological and team-building skills, all of which explain the growing number of students electing to enroll in online classrooms rather than traditional classrooms.

I started teaching online graduate classes approximately ten years ago as part of the Masters in Business Administration (MBA) online program. This MBA online program can be taken in its entirety online or students can take individual online classes as part of their own curriculum. In the beginning, I, along with many of my fellow faculty members, were hesitant and had mixed feelings about the online approach. For one thing, the initial investment of money, time, and effort was tremendous. Faculty members were offered reduced teaching loads, cash incentives were provided to faculty members for the development of new online curriculum, and software companies were hired to assist with the technical aspects of the endeavor.

Faculty members have some degree of flexibility in designing the structure of their online class. My class is comprised of six modules. Each module covers a different topic and is released to the students every other week. In addition to these six modules, there is a one-week project, one week for a mid-term examination and one week for a final examination for a total of fifteen weeks or one semester. During the two-week period devoted to each module, students initially complete online reading consisting primarily of my notes and textbooks, they also engage in discussions, postings, and emails. The last four days of the two-week period are reserved for a quiz. Final grades are based on points earned for discussions (posting and commenting on other postings), quizzes, a project, and two examinations.

There are many advantages to online learning. First, and perhaps the most obvious, is the flexibility of online education where students can attend a course and access material at their own pace anytime and from any location. Students' ability to set their own schedule and access course material at a time and a place when and where they are able to focus best enhances their learning experience. Second, online study is time and cost-effective given that students need not spend any time or money commuting to the classroom. Third, online classes may have students from entirely different geographic locations with diverse cultural and social background and experiences. The increased diversity serves to enhance and enrich the learning environment. Fourth, the use of the Internet to attend class, research information and communication with other students teaches technology skills that are critical to workers in the 21st century business community. Fifth, online classrooms facilitate team-building and camaraderie by providing joint work, discussion boards, and chat rooms. Lastly, the anonymity of online learning is less intimidating than the traditional classroom environment. It provides even the most introverted student the opportunity to contribute as much as the most talkative student who may dominate the discussion.

While there are numerous benefits to online learning, there are some disadvantages. Online learning is not suited to all students but only to those who are disciplined and self-motivated enough to cover the material on their own. Although the absence of real-time live classroom discussion is somewhat of a disadvantage, it can be overcome by online discussion boards and chat rooms. For instructors, the biggest disadvantage is the requisite investment in developing online course material complete with links to other sites that students can access. Updating material is, of course, an ongoing challenge.

Another flaw of online programs is the inability to monitor student integrity and honesty. Without examination proctors, how can instructors be certain it is the students answering the examination and quiz questions? Student honesty is a huge issue in on-campus classes but is even more of an issue and nearly impossible to police in an online environment.

Despite the flaws of online learning, it is my opinion that online education is here to stay and will continue to augment on-campus education. During the next decade, we will continue to have regular on-campus programs along with online programs, as well as offering students a combination of both worlds. In fact, online education, which started in graduate programs, is quickly spreading to undergraduate programs, and I am certain it will continue to spread to other forms of education as well.

The popularity of on line teaching is recognized by many universities. The potential rewards of revenue, market share, and reputation encourages most universities to integrate on line teaching to their offerings. Eventually almost all educational institutes will join the band wagon. As time goes on, this medium will become more relevant and more acceptable. Recent Google search (January 15, 2009) on various terms yielded the following number of Web pages:

Term	Pages in millions
On line degree	196
On line education	180
On line master	82
e-learning	38
On line undergraduate	14
e-learning courses	10
On line MBA	6

This table is an indication of the strong global interest in online education.

I commend the editors of this book for publishing it and congratulate them for taking a leading role in online teaching and learning. The book and its content move us in the right direction of this new emerging field of education. Even though the technology has its imperfections, online education is, without a doubt, here to stay.

Benjamin Lev
The University of Michigan – Dearborn
Dearborn, Michigan 48126, USA
January 21, 2009

Dr. Benjamin Lev *is a Professor of Decision Science at the School of Management, University of Michigan – Dearborn where he was a Dean and a Department Chair. He earned a PhD in Operations Research from Case Western Reserve University, Cleveland, Ohio and an M.Sc in Industrial Engineering and B.Sc in Mechanical Engineering from the Technion, Israel Institute of Technology. Prof. Lev published five books, numerous articles and is the Editor-in-Chief of OMEGA-The International Journal of Management Science. He is also the Co-Editor-in-Chief of The International Journal of Management Science and Engineering Management, and is/was an associate editor of six journals: International Abstracts of Operations Research; Interfaces; Employee Responsibilities and Rights Journal; Institute of Industrial Engineering-Transactions; Journal of Operations Research. Dr. Lev served as INFORMS Vice President-Meetings and organized several conferences: ORSA/TIMS Philadelphia, 1990; INFORMS International, Israel, 1998 and IFORS Edinburgh 2002.*

Preface

With the fast development of Internet and other IT technologies, online learning is becoming a common approach in distance learning and teaching activity. The online distance learning is based on two fundamental fields: one the one hand, the computer supported collaborative learning (CSCL) theories and, on the other, the computational technologies that support the online learning activities aiming to achieve the learning goals. Nowadays, both fields have done considerable progress. CSCL theories are providing the online learning community with models and approaches that contribute to the success of online learning and teaching, while the maturity of Web technologies and the emergence of other large scale computational systems such as Web, Grid and P2P are enabling researchers and developers to put in practice online learning and teaching models. Despite the considerable progress in both fields, there are still plenty of issues to investigate on how to effectively put the emergent computational technologies to fully support online learning and teaching activity. Two such issues are monitoring and assessment in online learning environments.

Why monitoring and assessment? One big issue of real virtual campuses and online learning activities is to achieve the success in learning outcomes and academic goals. Put differently, this means to make the online collaborative system efficient and effective for the online students and teachers. Unlike traditional face-to-face learning and teaching where students *feel themselves* as part of the classroom, participate in the activities being carried out daily in the classroom and can have the advice and attention of their mates and/or the teacher who daily tracks students' activity, in online learning systems, students are faced to isolation, lack of feedback from their mates and/or the teacher, lack of knowledge about the learning progress, etc., which could eventually cause abandonment of the online learning studies. In fact, the situation becomes more complex if the learning activity is developed not only at online classroom level but also at group level; in this latter case, the interaction among members of the group plays an important role in achieving the learning goals. Further, difficulties arise to teachers in online collaborative learning systems. It is more difficult to assess the learning progress of the students, give them prompt support, identify problems, etc., especially when it comes to evaluate and assess not only the individual progress and learning outcomes but also the progress and learning outcomes of the online groups. Monitoring is thus a key approach to overcome such intrinsic difficulties in online collaborative learning systems.

In this book are presented up-to-date research approaches for monitoring and assessment on online collaborative learning systems. The book aims to provide researchers and developers of online collaborative systems with approaches for effective and efficient means that would assist e-learning students and teachers with precise and relevant information regarding the ongoing online learning activity at both individual and group levels. Moreover, approaches in the book appeal for the timely support to learners and teachers, that is, learners and teachers have to know both the group and individual activity performance as the learning process gets developed. The monitoring process is thus a means for groups and professors to act appropriately according to the group and individual performance.

Among the many features highlighted in the book, we could distinguish the following:

Conducting the learning activity through adaptation and personalization. Professors design the academic activities with concrete final learning goals, whose achievement require to continuously re-conduct the learning process as a way to assure that intermediate goals are successfully achieved. Adaptation and personalization of the information and instruction offered to the users in on-line e-learning environments are considered to be the turning point of recent research efforts.

Monitoring the progress. In collaborative learning activities that span over a long period of time, monitoring the group and individual progress is essential. Monitoring the progress, identifying all potential problems within groups or students and quickly resolving them will contribute to the successful achievement of the learning goals.

Scaffolding learners. In real complex online collaborative learning activities, groups are encountered with many difficulties that could be originated by the technical content of the learning exercise and/or by the intrinsic complex nature of the collaborative work developed inside small groups. Therefore, scaffolding learners whenever necessary is essential to the learning process. To do this, professors and groups involved in the learning activity need to continuously know "where they are", which members and/or groups need professors' intervention. Students can encourage their mates within a group and professors can encourage groups and/or students to collaborate in their activity.

Decision making and predictions. Activity planning is typical in long time learning exercises. However, achievement of final objectives could require using updates and strategies not initially planned, which may require taking new decisions. Clearly, groups can make better decisions if they are provided with critical information about their activity so that they can envisage "where they are headed to".

Tracking students' involvement. Two major related problems in real e-learning courses are: (a) assuring that students will reach a satisfactory level of involvement in the learning process, and (b) to avoid high abandonment rates. Tracking is thus very useful to identify non-attending students or groups and intervene to ensure student involvement in the collaborative learning process.

HOW THIS BOOK IS ORGANIZED

The chapters in this book have been divided into three key areas: (i) *Tools and Applications for Monitoring in e-learning,* (ii) *Tracking, Feedback and Monitoring,* and (iii) *Assessment Approaches.*

Tools and Applications for Monitoring in E-Learning

The chapters in this area are organized as follows:

In Chapter 1 "Web-based Multimedia Tools for Monitoring and E-learning" by Bellas et al., the authors propose a methodology focused in monitoring both learning and resources. An application of Web-based multimedia tools as a complement to the traditional e-learning materials to improve the quality of teaching is presented. The authors also show the advantages of providing the students with more familiar multimedia materials suitable for being transported and consulted in mobile devices.

Botsios and Georgiou, in Chapter 2 "Standardization in User Modeling and Learning Objects Retrieval: Recent Contributions," approach the adaptation and personalization of the information and instruction offered to the online learners and groups in online e-learning environments. They consider the adaptive educational hypermedia systems (AEHS) and address the need of standardization of user assessment in such environment. Thereafter, the authors provide a classification of some basic assessment aspects of an AEHS user as well as the basis for the development of a generic architecture for the retrieval of standardized learning objects.

Chapter 3, "Virtual co Learner: An approach against learner's isolation in asynchronous e-learning," by Georgiou et al. introduces the virtual co learner system aimed at using the behavior of a learning companion suitable to the user's cognitive and learning styles. The proposed collaborative system runs asynchronously and reuses digitized material in the system. The motivation behind the system is to increase matching of real and simulated learners who have similar cognitive characteristics so that learning procedure becomes more efficient and productive.

Brent et al., in Chapter 4 "Time-Shifted Online Collaboration: Creating Teachable Moments Through Automated Grading," consider online collaboration in a distributed e-learning environment. The authors describe the usefulness of Web-based automated essay grading to provide extensive real-time data for monitoring and enhancing e-learning activities. By examining real data from student use of this software, it is evidenced that students take advantage of the proposed learning environment to revise and resubmit their work, which helped improving their final. The success of the proposed learning environment resides in its ability to provide detailed, personalized feedback to students in real time.

Tracking, Feedback and Monitoring

The chapters in this area are organized as follows:

Chapter 5, "Expertiza: Managing Feedback in Collaborative Learning" by Gehringer, addresses the issue of providing feedback to students and work teams by assessing project work. The author proposes *Expertiza* – a system for managing all kinds of communication that is involved in assessment of project work. Experimental studies showed that by using this system students are capable of producing work that can be used for teaching purposes.

Shwarts-Asher, in Chapter 6 "Improving the performance of virtual teams through team dynamics," approaches the operation of virtual teams in organizations. The study is based on qualitative data collected by interviewing 20 virtual team managers and members of 20 different organizations. The objective is to analyze what projects virtual team participated in, how virtual teams operate and the difficulties virtual teams face.

In Chapter 7, "Monitoring Activity in E-Learning: A Quantitative Model Based on Web Tracking and Social Network Analysis" by Mazzoni and Gaffuri, the authors focus on the monitoring of students' activities in e-learning. To that end, the authors start from a socio-cultural approach to the notion of activity, which is conceived in terms of actions, which, in turn, are composed by operations. The definitions of activity, action and operation are then used in defining a model for monitoring activities in e-learning. The model accounts for indicators measure individuals' actions within a Web environment. Moreover, the authors consider the application of social network analysis to Web interactions occurring in collective discussions within Web environments.

Chapter 8, "Monitoring Students' Activity and Performance in Online Higher Education: A European Perspective" by Lera et al., introduces the reader in the new scenario defined by the recently created European Higher Education Area and by the increasing use of learning management systems in higher education worldwide. Then, authors discuss the importance of monitoring students' and groups' activity and performance, and review some of the monitoring tools already available in the market. Finally, they aim to identify which the informational necessities of online instructors and students are, and propose some graphs for the monitoring process.

Persico et al., in Chapter 9 "A Model for Monitoring and Evaluating CSCL," deal with the issue of monitoring and evaluating CSCL processes. The approach is based on effective organization of information drawn through monitoring online courses. The authors present thereafter a general purpose model for organizing this information, which serves to make the monitoring, assessment and evaluation processes more systematic and effective.

Assessment Approaches

In Chapter 10, "Nonverbal Communication as a means to support collaborative interaction assessment in 3D Virtual Environments for learning" by Pérez Negrón and de Antonio Jiménez, the learning scenario is situated in 3D collaborative virtual environments in which the user's graphical representation is the means to express nonverbal communications. The proposal aims at inferring indicators of collaborative interaction and their use to foster collaboration in a learning task situation. An exploratory study that consisted in the analysis of a real life situation during a collaborative task accomplishment exemplifies the proposed approach and its empirical analysis.

Burdescu and Mihăescu in Chapter 11, "Improvement of self-assessment effectiveness by activity monitoring and analysis," tackle the self-assessment as one of the crucial activities in e-learning. The authors present a recommender software system that aims at improving the effectiveness of self-assessment activities. The methodology for obtaining improvement of self-assessment is based on embedding knowledge management into the business logic of the e-learning platform. Techniques such as Naive Bayes Classifier are used for obtaining the learning resources that need to be further accessed by learners.

Chapter 12, "Computer-Supported Collaboration in Language Learning" by Zou, discusses collaboration between language learners while using computer-based tasks. Monitoring and assessment for the collaborative language learning are explored based on interview, observation and questionnaire data from both teachers and students at two UK university language centers. The results of the study indicate that collaboration in computer-based environments can help students to develop their language skills.

Pantaleón and Sáiz in the last chapter, "Proposal of a set of reports for Students' Tracking and Assessing in E-Learning Platforms," motivate the need of suitable tools for the monitoring and follow-up of the students to facilitate the instructors' task. The authors propose a set of reports, designed from an educational point of view, to assist instructors to carry out the tracking and assessment task. An architecture software for the implementation of such monitoring tools is also presented.

FINAL WORDS

Monitoring and assessment in online collaborative environments is a major research theme in CSCL research community. It aims at assisting e-learning students and professors with precise and relevant information regarding the ongoing individual and group activity. The monitoring process is thus a means for groups and professors to act appropriately according to the group and individual performance. The chapters collected in this book provide new insights, findings and approaches not only on analytical models for monitoring and assessment but also their achievement and use through emergent computational systems. Researchers will find in this book the latest trends in these research topics. On the other hand, teachers will find practical insights on how to use monitoring and assessment approaches in their daily task. Finally, developers from CSCL community can be inspired and put in practice the proposed models and evaluate them for the specific purposes of the online courses.

We hope the readers will find this book useful and share with us the joy!

Angel A. Juan
Open University of Catalonia, Spain
Thanasis Daradoumis
Open University of Catalonia, Spain
Fatos Xhafa
Open University of Catalonia, Spain
Santi Caballe
Open University of Catalonia, Spain
Javier Faulin
Public University of Navarre, Spain
February, 2009

Section 1
Tools and Applications for Monitoring in E-Learning

Chapter 1
Web–Based Multimedia Tools for Monitoring and E–Learning

F. Bellas
University of A Coruña, Spain

O. Fontenla-Romero
University of A Coruña, Spain

N. Sánchez-Maroño
University of A Coruña, Spain

J. A. Becerra
University of A Coruña, Spain

ABSTRACT

This chapter is devoted to the application of Web-based multimedia tools as a complement to traditional e-learning resources to improve the quality of teaching in two senses: adapting lesson contents to improving the understanding and increasing the motivation of the students. The authors present a set of practical tools that have achieved successful results in their courses and that, together, provide a more proactive teaching methodology based on interactive and mobile learning materials. These tools can be divided into two main groups: simulations and interactive videos, directly related to the process of studying, and quizzes and questionnaires, useful to adapt the teaching to the objective comprehension level. In addition, the authors point out the advantages of providing the students with more familiar multimedia materials suitable for being transported and consulted in mobile devices. A basic point of this methodology is that all these resources are available through a Web-based interface, so that the interaction does not depend on the physical presence of the students. Finally, the authors must point out that with their methodology they are focused on monitoring learning, which is achieved directly with online questionnaires, but they have also performed resource monitoring, in terms of degree of satisfaction and practical use. This is achieved, in this case, through the use of surveys and from the analysis of the statistics provided by the Web-based application.

DOI: 10.4018/978-1-60566-786-7.ch001

INTRODUCTION AND BACKGROUND

Nowadays, it is not usual to find on-line courses in which their contents and materials are only a "virtualization" of traditional classroom-based courses. In those on-line courses, the student reads from the computer monitor the same material that in traditional settings would be read on paper. These kinds of platforms are more "e-reading" than e-learning systems as commented in Reichert et al (2004). The goal of the latter should be to allow a more active and effective learning and, therefore, they must incorporate more advanced materials, resources and activities. As a consequence content design in an e-learning platform should be carried out following these main features:

- Adequately meeting the needs, capabilities and possibilities of the student.
- Clarity and quality of the information presented.
- An adapted structure for its correct understanding and assimilation.
- Interactivity with the student.

The first three points have been widely studied both in e-learning and traditional learning, but interactivity with the students becomes a extremely interesting topic in e-learning because traditional practices, based on physical interaction, are not applicable here. In this sense, we can find several examples in the bibliography of e-learning interactive systems that mainly use videos, simulations and games as interactive materials. Thus, we should highlight the LBA "Learning by asking" system presented in Shang et al (2001), where authors develop a multimedia based e-learning system that combines video lectures, PowerPoint slide presentations and lecture notes. This system promotes high levels of interaction by allowing learners to access individual video segments directly.

Another promising system has been developed in INETELE (Interactive and Unified E-Based Education and Training in Electrical Engineering) Project in Weiss et al (2004). . The objective of this project is to obtain an optimized lecture tool for teaching basic and some advanced topics of electrical engineering to a class of students, as well as a program for self-learning and distance-learning without direct presentation by a teacher. In this context, the authors use a web-based package presenting the information with interactive animations and simulations.

A third type of interactive material used in e-learning is computer games. Connolly et al (2006), have commented on their popularity in e-learning contexts, mainly through online games, over the past few years. . This kind of games range from text based ones to those that incorporate 3D graphics and virtual worlds (e.g., MUDs and MOOs) where the interaction takes place with many players simultaneously connected (Graven et al, 2005). Virtual communities that facilitate knowledge sharing and creation (edutainment) are very popular in this online game context as explained in De Freitas (2007). Examples of these learning environments are "Supercharged", used to teach high level physics concepts, "Savannah", a mobile game that introduces young learners to natural history concepts, or "The Racing Academy game", a racing car physics simulation designed to support learning communities in the field of engineering and science.

The work presented here is based on our experience (see Sanchez-Maroño et al, 2006 or Bellas et al, 2007) in the application of web-based multimedia software tools for e-learning with two main objectives: to monitor the learning of the students in a more realistic way and to improve the individual learning providing more motivating and familiar elements. All of these tools were accessible through the web-based e-learning platform Moodle.

The multimedia tools we have used are basically videos, simulations and on-line questionnaires. This way, we include two of the three typical materials that are present in the main interactive e-learning platforms, excluding games. In addition, we include questionnaires as interactive materials in our methodology in order to monitor the degree of understanding of the students in both traditional and e-learning courses. This kind of questionnaire allows the teacher to have more realistic feedback in real time to achieve a general overview.

As commented before, one of our main objectives is to find a way to obtain a higher motivation from students. Katzeff (2000) discusses how motivation is a crucial factor in many theories of learning. In the particular case of e-learning, we can find several classical empirical studies about motivation. Malone et al (1987) present a theoretical framework of intrinsic motivation in the design of educational computer games. Garris et al (2002) found that incorporating game features into instruction increased motivation and consequently produced greater attention and retention.

Our experience on motivating students is based on using elements that are familiar to them in the non-academic context (Duffy, 2008). Nowadays, students are used to web-based multimedia elements such as video clips (www.youtube.com) or podcasts (iPod player), which include both images and sound (or just sound), and to carry these elements with them using a portable multimedia player. As a consequence, we think that it is very important in this e-learning context to provide academic material in multimedia formats that can be stored, transported and used in mobile devices. The creation of multimedia elements is very easy with current software tools and the main course management systems. Moodle, for example, supports them as players and, naturally, allows them to be downloaded.

METHODOLOGY AND TOOLS

In this section, we will explain in detail the tools we have developed and applied in our courses to interact with students through more motivating

platforms and formats, mainly interactive videos and simulations and questionnaires and quizzes. But prior to elaborating these points, we are going to present a formal teaching organization methodology to structure the presented ideas.

Teaching Organization Plan

The first question we must answer in this section is: how to include these multimedia tools in the teaching organization plan of a course? It is obvious that it depends on the particular conditions of the course: subject and topics, level of the students, distance or presence learning, etc. However, we will present some general lines that can be applied to the teaching organization of an e-learning based course and that have been extracted from our experience during the last four years.

We can organize a course in the following seven consecutive stages:

1. **Master lessons:** in courses that combine e-learning with traditional learning (blended learning), this stage corresponds to the typical face-to-face lessons where the teacher presents the main contents of the subject or course, mainly theoretical contents. In distance learning courses, this stage corresponds to the study of e-reading materials. These lessons can include videos and simulations to improve the clarity of the explanations.
2. **In-class Quizzes:** in-class quizzes are very useful to adapt the master lessons to the real degree of understanding of the whole class.
3. **Interactive videos:** after a given lesson has been explained and can be considered generally understood, students can reinforce the concepts through interactive videos that imply a proactive relation with those concepts.
4. **Practical exercises:** in courses with practical contents, the previously explained concepts must be applied in real cases or situations. In

this stage, interactive videos and simulations can again be applied, in this case, with more practical objectives.

5. **Out-of-class quizzes:** at this point, students can test their comprehension level in the course through web-based quizzes as explained in the previous section.

6. **Portable videos and simulations:** this stage corresponds to the classical studying periods both for theoretical and practical materials. In this case, portable videos and simulations are very useful because they can be used in anywhere through portable devices.

7. **Questionnaires:** once a part of the course or the whole course is finished, questionnaires are introduced to plan the next course or the next lesson according to the student's feedback.

This is the organization plan we have applied in a subject called "Fundamentals of Computer Science" that is included in our University in the first course of the Industrial Engineering degree. It is a subject taught in the Spanish language with duration of four-months with 130 students per year on average. This high number of students implies that an individualized control of students is impractical and, in addition, we typically have to deal with students who are working while they are studying and with students from higher level courses. As we can see, although this is not an e-learning subject, we have a similar problematic due to the large number of students that cannot attend face-to-face lessons and we needed to develop tools like those presented here: questionnaires, to obtain general opinions and feedback from students, and videos or simulations that students can consult autonomously. Consequently, the use of a web-based platform like Moodle is essential within the presented methodology to minimize the need of a physical contact with teachers.

Figure 1 shows a screenshot of the course web page in Moodle during year 2008 where we can see that the items are organized by themes like:

general resources (with manuals, slides used in lessons, tutorials, contact information, etc), on-line quizzes, multimedia materials (videos, simulations), upload sections (to submit homework and assignments), etc.

We must point out that the use of this web-based tool is fundamental in our methodology. Thus, in the next two sections, we will explain in detail the practical application of the presented methodology and organization plan, focusing our comments on the use of multimedia tools and materials. The data collected to monitor the real use of these tools and the improvements in the students' learning are obtained through the web-based application Moodle.

Questionnaires and Quizzes

Giving and getting feedback is essential to the whole process of reflecting on learning. It is a two-way process. Teachers give learners feedback on their performance and learning, and learners reflect on their experience of learning and provide feedback to the teacher. There are immediate benefits for this feedback process, such as learners realizing what knowledge they have acquired and the teacher knows what he/she needs to improve for future teaching.

Questionnaires and quizzes have been broadly used to evaluate the teaching process. However, this evaluation is mostly performed at the end of the course. Therefore, the information provided by the questionnaire may be applied to improve subsequent course materials or activities, if required. However, it is well-known that, in most subjects, the complexity of lessons increases gradually and topics are related to each other. In these cases, if the initial lessons are not well understood, the subsequent ones can be incomprehensible, leading to high dropout rates. In "Fundamentals of Computer Science", besides explaining the main components of computers, we introduce students to programming in C language. Programming is a clear example of a subject of increasing complex-

Figure 1. Screenshot of the web-based application Moodle used in the course

ity; if any student does not understand loops or conditional sentences it is very difficult to move further. Therefore, considering the accessibility of Internet connections nowadays, online quizzes may be used for getting immediate feedback after a lesson is given to ascertain each and every student has achieved a certain level of understanding.

"Fundamentals of Computer Science" has both theoretical and practical classes. Practical classes last two hours and they are carried out in a computer laboratory where each student has a computer with Internet access. These laboratory classes are oriented to solving programming exercises and they are mandatory for students that are attending this course for the first time (approx. 50% of the students). Then, after some exercises about a specific topic are presented and solved, students are given 15 minutes to answer some short questions related to the topics explained to them. Students fill in the quiz individually and anonymously. In these in-class quizzes, a student

can only answer each question once. Anonymity is important because students are worried about the negative effect that a poor result in the quiz may have in their final grade. If anonymity is not guaranteed, they are predisposed to copying in order to ensure a good mark leading to unreliable results in the quiz. The goal of these in-class quizzes is twofold. First, the teacher will have an objective measure of the degree of understanding of the lesson. Second, students will perceive their knowledge acquisition. These quizzes are designed to measure comprehension, not simple memorization, although they should not be focussed on details that may require time for study because it is important to avoid discouraging the students. Consequently, these quizzes contain question types, such as true/false, that work well for assessing lower-order outcomes-knowledge or comprehension goals in Bloom's Taxonomy of cognitive levels (Bloom et al, 1956). The benefits of these in-class quizzes are:

- If a significant portion of the class has misunderstood a key point, then, this point may be clarified before moving on the other topics that build upon the misunderstood material (Bell, 1996).
- They may identify serious deficiencies in a teaching method or style. If a new method, such as collaborative exercise, has been employed during a lecture and the associated quiz has increased/decreased the level of success, it may indicate the suitability/unsuitability of this technique. The difficulty of the explained material has to be considered because it may also cause a low performance in the quiz.

"Fundamentals of Computer Science" students are subdivided into five groups to attend practical lessons. Figure 2 shows the results obtained for each one of these five practical classes in an eight questions quiz regarding arrays and dynamic memory allocation (both concepts are usually difficult to understand for students). The Moodle platform allows the teacher to see the quiz results graphically once the students complete it. This immediate feedback allows the teacher to correct possible errors in the questions and to assess the students about the misunderstood points. For example, the low rates achieved at question 2 for classes 1 and 2 were due to a mistake in the question, the teacher rewrote it after class 2 and better marks were achieved in the following classes. Similarly, question 5 was rewritten after class 1. However, the topic tackled at question 8 seems not to be comprehended by many students because 42% of them did not properly answer, specifically class 2 misunderstood this point. It was checked that this question was theoretically explained, but it was not included in any of the exercises. Then, it emphasizes the need of doing exercises for consolidating the topics explained. On the other hand, questions 1 and 4 with 88 and 92 percentage of success, respectively, were well understood.

Moreover, quiz results can also be downloaded as a text file where each line is a student record and his answers are separated by commas. A detailed analysis using this text file may reveal interesting information already suggested by Figure 2 such as differences between classes (see the mean mark in Table 1) and differences between students in the same class denoted by a high standard deviation in Table 1.

The main difficulty in designing those quizzes is to tackle all the important topics in a class considering the time restrictions. Doing the quiz must not take more than 10 minutes, so questions must be simple and easy to answer. Figure 3 shows an example of a question (true/false answer) used in "Fundamentals of Computer Science". These questions enable the teacher to check student understanding about the semantics of programming language structures. Learning the semantics of a programming language is an important part of programming knowledge in itself and it is also a prerequisite to acquiring higher-level programming skills as discussed in Brusilovsky & Sosnovsky (2005).

Despite the important benefits of those quizzes, the feedback provided is not enough for students. Student's feedback may be subdivided into many categories, three of which are the following: knowledge of results, knowledge of correct response, and elaborated feedback (Krause et al, 2008). Empirical findings show that elaborated feedback is more effective than mere knowledge of results or knowledge of correct response. By highlight-

Figure 2. Results from an in-class quiz

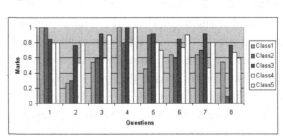

Table 1. Results per class for an in-class quiz

	Number of students	Mean mark (up to 10)	Standard deviation
Class 1	11	6.36	1.97
Class 2	10	6.25	1.05
Class 3	13	8.75	1.80
Class 4	15	6.75	1.30
Class 5	10	8.12	1.72

ing mistakes and offering explanations or other additional information, elaborated feedback helps students to reflect on the presented information and on their own knowledge and should thereby facilitate elaboration of the material, correction of misconceptions and filling of knowledge gaps. In-class quizzes provide knowledge of results and correct response, however, there is not sufficient class time to obtain elaborated feedback. Therefore, after the class, out-of-class self-assessment quizzes are provided. These quizzes must be accessible to the students through a web-based course management platform like Moodle.

Self-assessment questionnaires enhance motivation in students because of meaningful feedback. As indicated earlier, motivation is an important factor in learner's success and a lack of motivation can, according to Blanchard & Frasson (2004) produce a negative emotional impact. Self-assessment obliges students more actively and formally to evaluate themselves and may develop self-awareness and better understanding of learning outcomes. Those quizzes may include more complex questions and they may attend to the higher-order outcomes found Bloom's taxonomy: analysis, synthesis or evaluation goals (Bloom et al, 1956). Therefore, they should include open-ended questions like sentence completion, short answers, etc. that require students to formulate their own answers, which do not have to be pre-

Figure 3. Question of a quiz after a "C programming" class

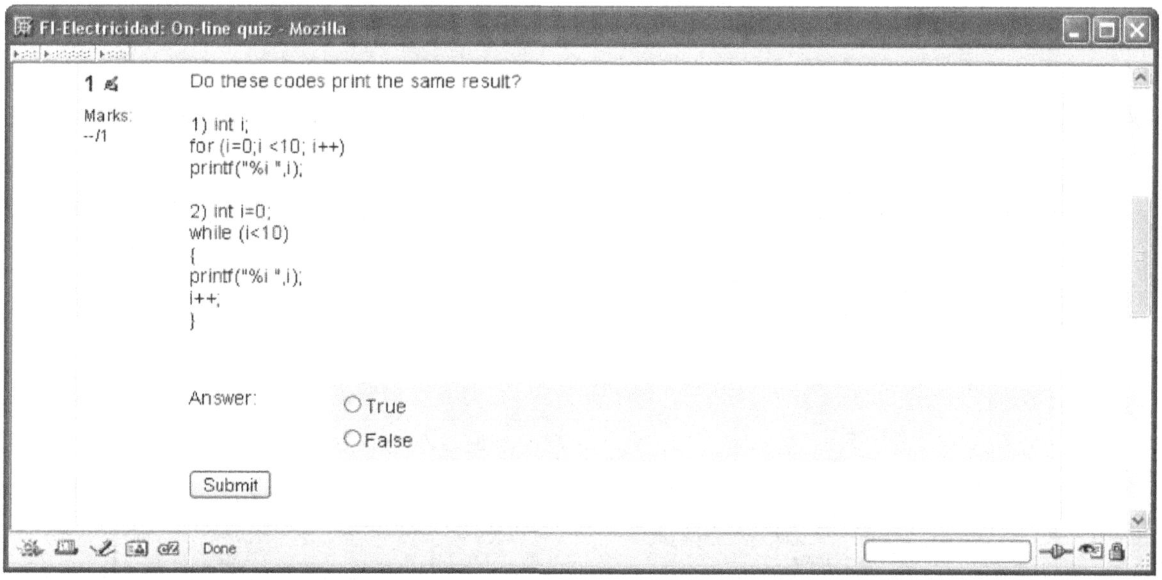

determined and unique. For certain domains like mathematics, physics or programming exercises, limited-choice questions might work for assessing higher-level objective because students have to apply their gained knowledge to complete the question. Moreover, out-of-class quizzes do not have time restrictions and the number of questions can be higher than for in-class quizzes, although long quizzes should be avoided (otherwise students may opt out of completing the quiz). Due to the fact that there is no time limitation for completing the quiz, an identification of the student is required so that his partial results can be saved and recovered for later use. Consequently, contrary to in-class quizzes, out-of-class quizzes are not anonymous. In those quizzes, special care has to be taken to design the messages when a wrong answer is given by a student, it is important to recognize positive aspects of the work and not only its shortcomings. Two different approximations may be considered:

- **Correct response:** The student gets immediate feedback obtaining the correct response to the question including a detailed explanation of it. There are some questions that are propitious to always making similar mistakes. Those mistakes have to be considered and focus the answer to highlight them.

- **Repeat last question:** The student gets the same question until he/she succeeds. In this case, the same question can be used again and again with different parameters, allowing every student to achieve understanding and mastery (Brusilovsky & Sosnovsky, 2005) and preventing them from merely guessing the proper answer after several attempts.

Figure 4 shows a question of a self-evaluation quiz for "Fundamentals of Computer Science". Again, the question is related to loops, but it includes more difficult issues combining loops and conditional sentences. Changing the values for variables x, j and k, the same question leads to different results.

Moodle has an option called "General feedback", other web-based course management platform have similar options, to provide feedback to

Figure 4. A question of a self-assessment quiz

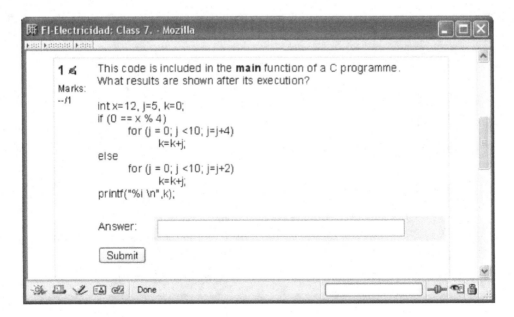

Figure 5. Error message for a wrong answer for question in Figure 4

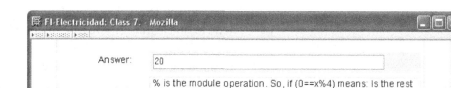

give students some background to what knowledge the question was testing or to give them a link to more information they can use if they did not understand the questions. Besides, in multiple answer questions, it allows the introduction of different answers with comments for each one, which turns out to be very useful for focussing on common mistakes. For example, Figure 5 illustrates a wrong answer for the question in Figure 4 derived from an inadequate interpretation of the "*if*" sentence.

An important fact of these in-class and out-of-class quizzes is that they do not affect student's grade. To assign marks, the environment has to be completely under control to discourage students from copying (notice that answering some questions, in the previous example, is a matter of executing the code). This is a difficult task for in-class quizzes with medium and large classes and completely impossible in out-of-class quizzes. The main drawback of this consideration is that student participation may be less than desired, mostly, in out-of-class quizzes. Moreover, two different ways of participation were detected for out-of-class quizzes. The first way corresponds to students that access the quiz and start it, but never finish it (unfinished quizzes in Figure 6). The other way includes the students that reply to all the questions in the quiz (finished quizzes). The rate of participation is much higher in the first case than in the second one (around 80% and

12%, respectively, of students attending practical classes). It was noticed that many students entered the quiz for copying the questions and later they try to solve them on their own using books, class notes or, if possible, the C language compiler. To motivate students and to enhance the participation, Brusilovsky & Sosnovsky (2005) suggest including questions related to forthcoming lessons. In spite of the low participation, Woit & Mason's (2000) study reflects the adequacy of on-line test, whereas White & Liccardy (2006) denote that 98% (of 113 students in hard applied sciences, such as engineering) said they would like more online tests, although students in hard pure subjects did not seem to prefer online tests.

Nevertheless, the quiz results automatically provided by the Moodle platform still represent students' complications as can be seen in Figure 6. This figure illustrates the results collected after doing a quiz that deals with conditional and iterative sentences. Specifically, questions 1-5 are related to conditionals while the others are devoted to loops. This quiz follows the approximation of repeating the last question until the student succeeds. Therefore, a correct answer values 1 point if it is provided at the first attempt and each new attempt decreases this marking by 0.1. Focusing our attention on finished quizzes, the two distinct parts of the quiz get significantly different marks. Therefore, it may be concluded that iterative sentences were not well compre-

Figure 6. Participation results of out-of-class quiz

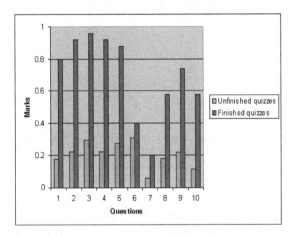

hended by students, specially the topic covered by question 7 that includes an iterative sentence inside another iterative sentence. The low marks accomplished by students with *Unfinished quizzes* are due to the fact that a zero mark is assigned to a non-answered question and most of the questions were blank.

Finally, another type of questionnaire is presented: a questionnaire measuring student satisfaction with class environment, materials, exercises, assessments and so on. In these questionnaires, at least one question should allow a free answer in order that students can express their opinions. Each student opinion may provide very interesting feedback about the teaching process, however, the teacher must be prepared to obtain negative feedback, even insults in some cases, and not be discouraged nor influenced by those responses. Moodle includes standard survey modules to facilitate this task for the teacher, such as a Constructivist On-line Learning Environment Survey (COLLES) developed by Taylor & Maor (2000) and Attitudes Towards Thinking and Learning Survey (ATTLS) developed by Galotti et al (1999). COLLES generates a measure of students' perceptions of both their preferred and actual on-line classroom environments. ATTLS is an instrument to measure the extent to which a

person is a 'connected knower' (CK) or a 'separate knower' (SK). People with higher CK scores tend to find learning more enjoyable and are often more cooperative, congenial and more willing to build on the ideas of others, while those with higher SK scores tend to take a more critical and argumentative stance to learning.

Quizzes have become so popular that there exist different tools that allow creating quizzes on the Web and using any Web browser to solve the generated quizzes. Examples of these tools are QuizCenter (http://school.discoveryeducation. com/quizcenter/quizcenter.html) or ClassMarker (http://www.classmarker.com/). Similarly, Quick-Composer (http://www.quizcomposer.dk/) is an Internet-based system for the creation and use of quizzes and questionnaires whose primary aim is to increase anyone's possibilities for understanding hard fact based subjects like mathematics and physics. However, in all of them, the teacher must create the questions and it is a time consuming and difficult task. Parameterized quizzes may facilitate this labour because the teacher only needs to create a question and many different questions may be generated from it by changing its parameters. In this sense, it is worth to mention QuizPACK created by Brusilovsky and Sosnovsky (2005) (http://www.sis.pitt.edu/~taler/ QuizPACK.html) or MacQTex (http://rutherglen. ics.mq.edu.au/~macqtex/). QuizPACK stands for "Quizzes for Parameterized Assessment of C Knowledge" and it is a system to author and deliver Web-based dynamic parameterized quizzes for programming-related courses. Mac-QTeX Randomised Quiz System developed at Macquarie University, Sydney, provides online quizzes in PDF format for mathematics, having randomised question parameters which allow students to practice many examples of the same quiz (Griffin, 2005).

Interactive Videos and Simulations

Video is an effective and meaningful non-textual way to gather and display information. It offers a multi-sensory learning environment to present information in an attractive and consistent way that may improve learners' capability to retain information (Syed, 2001). Video can improve learning outcomes due to practical and fascinating presentations via the combination of visual and auditory information. Several previous studies examined whether the learning process is affected by the concurrent presentation of visual and verbal information in video but they generated mixed results. Some studies reported little impact of video on learning outcome (Dillon & Gabbard, 1999; Mbarika et al, 2001). Nevertheless, the form of video used in those studies was non-interactive. Thus, one of the main problems with the use of this kind of material has been lack of interactivity. Although research suggests that instructional video increases learners' interest in subject matters and motivation (Wetzel et al, 1994), the linear nature of non-interactive video may severely reduce this potential effect. Academic reports have criticized the pedagogical approaches that focus on conveying fixed bodies of information and view students as passive recipients of knowledge (Alavi, 1994). If students can determine what to construct or create, they are more likely to engage in learning as commented in Shang et al (2001).

Interactive video increases learner-content interactivity, thus potentially motivating students and improving learning effectiveness. The term interactive video can be defined as the use of computer systems to allow proactive and random access to video content based on queries or search targets. Interactive video has not been widely used in e-learning until recently due to limitations of network bandwidth and multimedia technology. This kind of video can help learners to pay full attention to material through active interaction between learners and instructional contents (Agius & Angelides, 1999; Weston & Barker, 2001). It

provides valuable means to view actual objects and realistic scenes. The emergence of non-linear, interactive digital video technology allows students to interact with instructional video. This may enhance learner commitment and improve learning effectiveness. Moreover, interactive video in an e-learning environment not only provides visual and verbal hints, but also allows learners to view any video portion as many times as they want.

The influence of interactive video on learning outcome and learner satisfaction in e-learning environments was examined in recent studies (Zhang, 2005; Zhang et al, 2006). Results of the experiment showed that the value of video for learning effectiveness was based upon the provision of interactivity. Students in the e-learning environment that provided interactive video may lead to better learning performance and higher learner satisfaction than those in other settings. Interactivity is considered desirable and it is assumed that it can positively affect the effectiveness of education. Increasing interactivity in an e-learning environment can reinforce concepts learnt and provide the ability for on-demand learning.

Software simulation and interactive video afford different levels of interactivity with the user. In some of them the user is quite passive and in others he/she is almost as active and self-reliant as with a real system. The level of interactivity must match the knowledge and ability level of the user or he/she might become bored or confused. In general, four different types of simulation or video activities, along a scale of increasing interactivity and self-reliance, can be identified:

1. At the bottom of the scale is the *show me* simulation, in which the user just watches the simulated task being performed. This kind of video is usually referred as a demonstration or demo.

2. More interactive are *train me* simulations, which guide the user in performing the task themselves within the simulation.

3. Further up the scale are *test me* simulations, which measure the user's ability to perform the task on their own within the simulation.

4. At the top of the scale are *let me* simulations that have the user perform the task on their own with the real problem.

The significance of this scale is that it provides a roadmap to how the students can be educated. They start out at the bottom of the scale, because they know little about the simulated topic. For them to become productive, proficient users, however, must climb to the top level of the scale. Within each level of activity there are more specific levels of self-reliance. At this point, one interesting question is: what kind of specific activities can engage students as they progress through the various levels of simulation activities? Some options, following the previous scale of interactivity, are:

1. At the bottom of the scale of user self-reliance, at the foot of the *show me* activity, the user just watches a demonstration passively from beginning to end. Just above that, at the top edge of this level, the user controls the playback, typically by clicking a next or continue button each time the demonstration pauses.

2. At the bottom of the *train me* level, the user performs the simulated procedure, but is given explicitly prompts every step of the way. A more challenging *train me* activity might offer prompts but it requires the user to request them. Still more self-reliance is expected when the *train me* activity claims users to follow open-ended prompts that suggest what to do but not exactly how to do it. Further up the scale, *train me* activities provide no prompts, but let users request hints when needed. At the upper limit of the *train me* activity, users receive no assistance beyond hints that appear when they make mistakes.

3. *Test me* activities provide very little assistance other than feedback on errors. The feedback might occur immediately after an error at the bottom end of the *test me* level. At the upper end of the *test me* activity, the user might receive feedback only after completing the task or giving up.

4. *Let me* activities can be performed at two level of self-reliance. At the bottom level, the user performs a task prescribed by the instructor. In this case, the task must be structured to make it easier for the user. Some hints or cautions might also be included to keep the student on track. At the top end of the scale, at the most self-reliant end of the *let me* activity, the user performs a task of his/her own choosing for real. This level is indistinguishable from real usage and represents complete learner autonomy.

The notion of interactive videos and simulations is quickly gaining importance as a means to explore, comprehend and communicate complex ideas and concepts. For instance, how do the components of a four-stroke diesel engine work, what makes a bridge collapse, how does a virus spread, how is the communication between cell nerves achieved? These are just some examples out of a huge universe of questions that can be explored with simulations. The crucial combination of affordable computer hardware and software, high-resolution graphics, and Internet connectivity creates a rich environment, in which people can run, share and build interactive videos and simulations.

The main goals using these kinds of interactive materials in the learning process are:

• **Increasing student engagement and motivation:** there are many factors that contribute to students' interest and level of engagement in learning and instructors have little control over many of those factors. However, research (Wetzel et al, 1994;

Roblyer & Edwards 2001) has shown that they can influence student motivation, that certain practices do work to increase time spent on task and that there are ways to make learning activities more engaging and more effective for students at all levels. For example, using multimedia material that closes the gap between theory and theory's application to the real world may have a great positive effect in students. It is clear that students will try to keep their attention on a subject as long as they perceive its usefulness, while they may become distracted or desist learning something if they do not perceive any utility in understanding what is being explaining to them. Other important aspect to take into account is the added possibility of watching videos almost anywhere thanks to multimedia portable devices, which are very common nowadays. It is necessary to realize that there are many devices not specifically built as multimedia devices but with those characteristics incorporated (mobile phones, PDAs, digital TV receivers, portable USB storage devices, etc.), therefore the candidate playing devices number for videos is greater than expected at a first thought. In particular, the number of mobile phones with multimedia capabilities owned by young people is growing every day. To give the possibility of watching lessons whenever students want, not only when classes are scheduled, makes life easier for students, especially for those who divide their studies with a job, so having this portability in delivery is another point that favours their motivation.

- **Improving the understanding:** there are many situations where the learner must know about and comprehend the operation or behaviour of complex systems. In these situations, the use of text and static graphical information as the only mechanism for content delivery is not very fruitful and

intuitive. Interactive videos can enhance significantly the construction of knowledge, even those that can be classified at the *show me* level. In many areas, knowledge is presented in an accumulative way, therefore to understand a concept is necessary the understanding of the previous concepts. Teachers dealing with this kind of subjects usually experience the problem of having students that, for whatever the reason, lose or do not understand, at some point, a particular explanation and they are unable to continue following along the topic. Videos can be made in a way that they are linked between them, for example, if a video shows that "x" has a given property due to the already shown "y" and "z" properties, that video could have links, at that point, to other videos shown the explanations of "y" and "z". In this case, a student has the possibility of pausing the video showing "x" and watching videos to refresh the concept of "y" and "z". This could be useful if a student misses a lesson, the concepts being taught are hard to understand or, simply, that student did notunderstand something and he/she is too shy to ask for help or clarification from the instructor.

Nevertheless, besides these two main goals, there exist other benefits when using videos as learning material. First, they can smooth the integration of foreign students, as any video can have several audio tracks or subtitles. In addition, putting more than one audio track in a video is a way of exchanging learning material between teachers of different nationalities, which multiplies the possible sources of learning material and, therefore, it is a way of improving teaching quality. Second, videos can help students with handicaps. The capacity to use multiple media enables the provider to pick and mix resources to the needs of the individual in order to reach a broader set of learners. Thus, pupils with a disability (e.g., blindness or deafness) are not placed at a substantial disadvantage in comparison with students who are not disabled. For instance, hearing-impaired people can find videos with subtitles as a priceless tool for their learning and disabled people can employ videos for distance learning. In fact, videos are, due to their possibilities, one of the most useful tools for distance learning in general, which is always a welcomed feature, no matter how teaching is structured, as it makes learning for students more flexible.

From a functional point of view, these multimedia materials can be used in an e-learning platform or in a classroom for many proposes, for instance:

- Simulations of a real environment or process.
- Examples of the developing process of some product or design.
- Demonstrative examples of solving some problems or exercises.
- Animations to facilitate the comprehension of abstract concepts of some complex systems.
- Multimedia tutorials.

These educational resources can be used in almost all the disciplines and courses like, for example, Computer Science, Engineering, Biology, Architecture, etc. One of the most important features that can be included in these videos and simulations is the quiz that allows enriching them with interactive characteristics. These quizzes can be used to interact with the student during the learning process and to provide feedback about his/her comprehension of the concepts or topic of the lesson.

The recording and editing process of interactive videos is, in general, a simple task that can be done using some specific software. Two of the most popular are the "Camtasia Studio" and the "Adobe Captive" commercial solutions. These tools allow us to capture video from the screen, camera or a file and to include some kind of enrichment, like voice, call outs, hints, quizzes, menus, etc. These options enhance the quality, clarity and interactivity of the demonstrative video. Specifically, Camtasia Studio is a complete presentation recording solution for Microsoft Windows that allows the user to save streaming media from the internet by recording the computer screen, edit video and audio captures, and publish polished media in a number of file types for a wide variety of formats including Youtube and HD (High Definition) quality video. The Camtasia Studio workflow consists of four fundamental elements:

- Record: the user is able to capture a specified area or the whole screen using the screen recorder. The presenter carries out all steps of the demonstration in sequence and is able to jump from one application to another without interrupting the recording process
- Edit and enhance: after the presentation has been captured, the presenter is able to revise it by cutting and/or pasting different parts, as needed. In addition, he/she is also able to overlay voice, as well as sound effects or music onto the presentation
- Produce: it allows saving the presentation to the required format
- Share: it lets the generated video stream to be exported to common video formats which can be read by most computers

Camtasia Studio has the added feature to liven up presentations and videos using Flash hotspots and callouts. Callouts are attention-drawing graphic symbols that can spotlight an area of a recording using animated pointers, highlights and speech bubbles which are added with a simple drag-and-drop operation. Flash hotspots add interactivity to a video and they can be used to:

- Allow viewers to open a website page from a link within the movie.
- Allow viewers to re-view a section of the presentation.
- Enable downloads from within the video.
- Navigate through different sections of the recording.

There are also some free alternatives such as "CamStudio", which is also open source, or "Wink", although they are usually more limited than commercial ones in terms of integrated capabilities. The generated videos and simulations can be included in a web-platform in many ways. One of the most extended is the Flash format (.swf or .flv files). Flash technology has become a popular method for adding animation and interactivity to web pages. It is commonly used to create animation, advertisements, various web page components, to integrate video into web pages and, more recently, to develop rich Internet applications. However, other technologies and formats like QuickTime, Windows Media Video, Portable Document Format (PDF), etc. can also be used.

Figure 7. Example of a demonstrative video for a machine learning algorithm, (a) initial state of the video, (b) call-out employed to clarify some part of the simulation, (c) interactive multi-choice question about the algorithm and (d) response to the student's answer

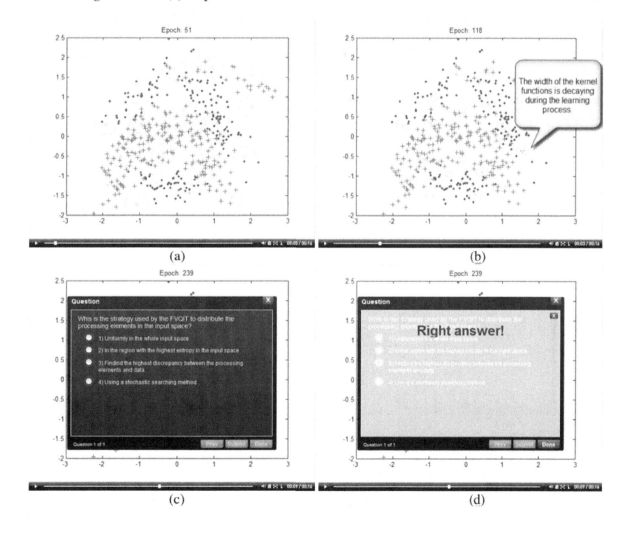

Figure 7 contains four screenshots of an illustrative example of a video containing a step-by-step simulation about the process performed by an algorithm from the machine learning field. The pictures at the top illustrate the information shown to the user and a call-out employed to clarify some complex issues. The pictures at the bottom show an example of one of the interactive questions included in the video, which can be answered by the student. These questions could be used to create more participatory material because the student has the opportunity of taking part in the process and he/she obtains feedback about the status of his/her knowledge and comprehension.

Another explanatory example is shown in Figure 8. It contains a screen capture for an instructional video employed to teach the use of functions in a programming language. This is part of the course entitled "Fundamentals of Computer Science" for industrial engineers. In this course, an

experimental study was conducted to measure the degree of usefulness for the employment of these kinds of interactive resources. In order to do this, a questionnaire was completed by the students. Figure 9 shows the most relevant results of this survey. As can be observed, almost all the pupils consider these resources as interesting materials to learn about the course topics.

FUTURE TRENDS

In-class quizzes have proven to be a successful tool for acquiring the level of comprehension of a specific topic from the students. Besides, quizzes may turn into an interesting cooperative learning technique by using group quizzes. Group quizzes can be used to promote discussion and peer teaching by structuring them so that students are given a minute or two to discuss the quiz before

Figure 8. Example of a demonstrative video for the course Fundamentals of Computer Science

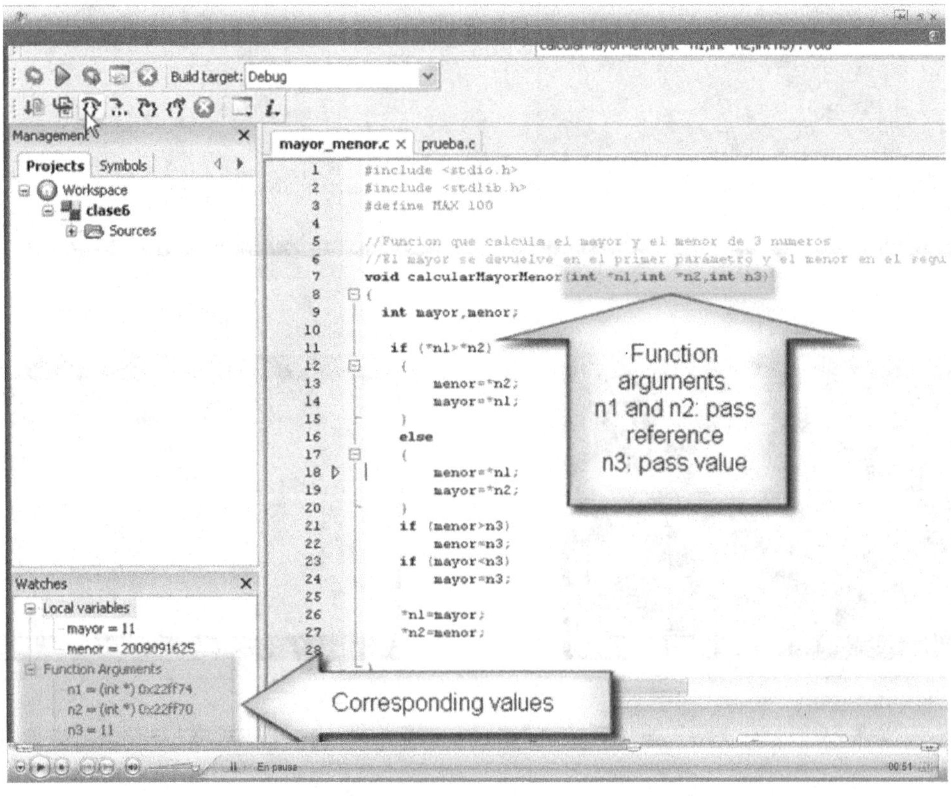

Figure 9. Results of the study regarding the usefulness degree of the students using the videos

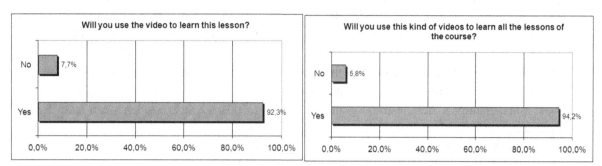

attempting a solution (Yokomoto & Ware, 1997). Group quizzes provide a natural transition from individual effort to collaborative effort because both teacher and students are already familiar with in-class quizzes and they can serve several purposes in the learning process. Clinton & Kohlmeyer (2005) study confirms that students taking group quizzes will provide higher student evaluation of teaching scores than students not taking group quizzes. In the future, we plan to use group quizzes only for advanced topics. Notice that this limitation is a consequence of time restrictions, group quizzes last longer than individual quizzes, so they cannot be done in every class. The idea would be that, first, students fill in the quiz individually and, later, after some time for discussion, they would do it in groups.

Despite the advantages of out-of-class quizzes, students do not use them as much as desired. Out-of-class quizzes utilization may be promoted by encouraging students to employ their idle time (for example, waiting for the bus) to carry out the quiz. Handled devices, such as mobile media players, multimedia cell phones and PDAs, offer great opportunities to access digital learning material and, therefore, many schools and universities have incorporated personal digital assistants (PDAs) into their teaching curricula in an attempt to enhance students learning experience and reduce instructors workload (Segall et al, 2005). In this work we proposed the utilization of such devices to watch interactive videos, however, they can also

be used to fill in out-of-class quizzes. Nowadays, there exist quiz generators that enable users to produce quizzes containing multiple-choice questions than can be displayed on portable devices (see Hürst et al, 2007, for example).

Two of the main trends in the development of new technological systems for education, training and e-learning are the following:

*   **Intelligent Tutoring Systems:** they can be defined as any system that is capable of emulating an instructor's behaviour in all aspects related to supporting students as they acquire knowledge. The teacher is not present and it is the system itself which guides the student as they learn different concepts. This idea, known as intelligent tutoring systems (ITS) or intelligent computer-aided instruction (ICAI), has been pursued for more than three decades by researchers in education, psychology and artificial intelligence. The goal of ITS is to provide the benefits of one-on-one instruction automatically and cost effectively. Like training simulations, ITS enables participants to practice their skills by carrying out tasks within highly interactive learning environments. However, ITS goes beyond training simulations by answering user questions and providing individualized guidance. Unlike other computer-based training technologies, ITS systems assess

each learner's actions within these interactive environments and develop a model of their knowledge, skills and expertise. Based on the learner model, ITS tailor instructional strategies, in terms of both the content and style, and provide explanations, hints, examples, demonstrations and practice problems as needed. The traditional ITS model contains four main components: the domain model, the student model, the teaching model and a learning environment. ITS projects can vary according to the relative level of intelligence of the components. For instance, a project focusing on intelligence in the domain model may generate solutions to complex and novel problems so that students can always have new problems to practice on, but it might only have simple methods for teaching those problems, while a system that focuses on multiple or novel ways to teach a particular topic might find a less sophisticated representation of that content.

- **Virtual Reality and Simulations:** many people associate virtual reality and computer simulations with science fiction, high-tech industries and computer games; however few associate these technologies with education. But virtual reality tools have been in use in educational environments for quite some time. Although they have mainly been used in applied fields such as aviation and medical imaging, these technologies have begun to edge their way into the classroom. Computer simulations and virtual reality offer students the opportunity of experiencing and exploring a broad range of environments, objects, and phenomena inside the classroom. Students can observe and manipulate normally inaccessible objects, variables and processes in real-time. These technologies have the ability to bridge the gap between the intangible world of concepts and models and the

concrete world of nature. This makes them an interesting alternative to the conventional study of many topics, like science and mathematics, which requires students to develop understandings based on textual descriptions and 2-D representations. In this scenario, students can learn by doing, in addition to learning by reading. This greatly facilitates the mastery of difficult and abstract concepts, for instance, the relation between distance, motion and time (Yair et al, 2001).

CONCLUSION

E-learning enables the distribution of quality education in an easier, faster, and convenient manner and facilitates content customization at the same time. We have presented our experience in a first year course of Industrial Engineering that presents very interesting features for the application of e-learning tools and principles. In this chapter, we have discussed the results obtained with a variety of online resources, such as quizzes, questionnaires and video, all of them made available through the web-based e-learning platform Moodle. As a general conclusion, we stress out that our experience when applying all the web-based multimedia tools we have presented here has been very successful. First of all, we have shown the use of on-line questionnaires to monitor the real understanding of students in our subject. They have provided us with immediate and objective feedback to further adapt the lessons according to the level of the students. In addition, the statistical results that can be derived from questionnaires indicate the difficulties that students to understand certain topics. Through the application of interactive videos, we have obtained a higher motivation level of the students when dealing with complex lessons, as we have shown with direct surveys. In the future we will continue in this line focusing on collaborative multimedia elements such as on-line games or activities, as students' overall participation in some activities was less than desired and it is necessary to make an effort to increase it.

REFERENCES

Agius, H. W., & Angelides, M. C. (1999). Developing knowledge-based intelligent multimedia tutoring systems using semantic content-based modelling. *Artificial Intelligence Review, 13*(1), 55–83. doi:10.1023/A:1006569626086

Alavi, M. (1994). Computer-mediated collaborative learning: An empirical evaluation. *MIS Quarterly, 18*(2), 159–174. doi:10.2307/249763

Bell, J. T. (1996). On the use of anonymous quizzes as an effective feedback mechanism in engineering education. *Chemical Engineering Education, 31*(1).

Bellas, F., & Alonso, A. (2007). Metodología de trabajo y experiencias de aprendizaje colaborativo y evaluación continua en la disciplina de sistemas multiagente. In *Proceedings of the Actas JENUI 2007.*

Blanchard, E., & Frasson, C. (2004). An autonomy-oriented system design for enhancement of learner's motivation in e-learning. In *Intelligent tutoring systems* (LNCS 3220, pp. 34-44). Berlin, Germany: Springer.

Bloom, B., Englehart, M., Furst, E., Hill, W., & Krathwohl, D. (1956). *Taxonomy of educational objectives: The classification of educational goals, handbook I: Cognitive domain*. New York: David McKay Company.

Brusilovsky, P., & Sosnovsky, S. (2005). Individualized exercises for self-asssesment of programming knowledge: An evaluation of Quiz-PACK. *ACM Journal of Educational Resources in Computing, 5*(3).

Clinton, B. D., & Kohlmeyer, J. M. III. (2005). The effects of group quizzes on performance and motivation to learn: Two experiments in cooperative learning. *Journal of Accounting Education, 23*, 96–116. doi:10.1016/j.jaccedu.2005.06.001

Connolly, T., & Stansfield, M. (2006). Using games-based elearning technologies in overcoming difficulties. *Teaching Information Systems . Journal of Information Technology Education, 5*, 459–476.

De Freitas, S. (2009). *Learning in immersive worlds: A review of game based learning report*. Retrieved from http://www.jisc.ac.uk/media/ documents/programmes/ elearninginnovation/ gamingreport_v3.pdf

Dillon, A., & Gabbard, R. B. (1999). Prepared to be shocked: Hypermedia does not improve learning! In *Proceedings of the Fifth Americas Conference on Information Systems*, Milwaukee, WI (pp. 369-371).

Duffy, P. (2008). Engaging the YouTube Google-eyed generation: Strategies for using Web 2.0 in teaching and learning. *The Electronic Journal of e-Learning, 6*(2), 119-130.

Galotti, K. M., Clinchy, B. M., Ainsworth, K., Lavin, B., & Mansfield, A. F. (1999). A new way of assessing ways of knowing: The attitudes towards thinking and learning survey (ATTLS). *Sex Roles, 40*(9/10), 745–766. doi:10.1023/A:1018860702422

Garris, R., Ahlers, R., & Driskell, J. E. (2002). Games, motivation, and learning: A research and practice model. *Simulation & Gaming, 33*(4), 441–467. doi:10.1177/1046878102238607

Graven, O. G., & MacKinnon, D. (2005). A survey of current state of the art support for lifelong learning. In *Proceedings of the ITHET 6th Annual International Conference.*

Griffin, F. (2005). The MacQTeX quiz project. In *Proceedings of the 7th International Conference on Technology in Mathematics Teaching (ICTMT7)*, Bristol, UK (pp. 242–249).

Hürst, W., Jung, S., & Welte, M. (2007). Effective learn-quiz generation for handled devices. In *Proceedings of the 9th International Conference on Human Computer Interaction with Mobile Devices and Services (Mobile HCI '07)*.

Katzeff, C. (2000). The design of interactive media for learners in an organisational setting – the state of the art. In *Proceedings of the NordiCHI 2000*.

Krause, U. M., Stark, R., & Madl, H. (2009). The effects of cooperative learning and feedback on e-learning in statistics. *Learning and Instruction*, *19*(2), 158–170. doi:10.1016/j.learninstruc.2008.03.003

Malone, T. W., & Lepper, M. R. (1987). Making learning fun: A taxonomy of intrinsic motivations for learning. In *Aptitude, learning and instruction. Volume 3: Cognitive and affective process análisis* (pp. 223-253).

Mbarika, V. W., Sankar, C. S., Raju, P. K., & Raymond, J. (2001). Importance of learning-driven constructs on perceived skill development when using multimedia instructional materials. *Journal of Educational Technology Systems*, *29*(1), 67–87.

Reichert, R., & Hartmann, W. (2004). On the learning in e-learning. In *Proceedings of the ED-MEDIA 2004 – World Conference on Education Multimedia, Hypermedia and Telecommunications* (pp. 1590-1595).

Roblyer, M. D., & Edwards, J. (2001). *Integrating educational technology into teaching*. Upper Saddle River, NJ: Prentice Hall.

Sánchez-Maroño, N., Fontenla-Romero, O., & Bellas, F. (2006). Aportaciones e ideas para el rediseño de la asignatura de fundamentos de informática al EEES. In *Proceedings of the Actas JENUI 2006*.

Segall, N., Doblen, T. L., & Porter, J. D. (2005). A usability comparison of PDA-based quizzes and paper-and-pencil quizzes. *Computers & Education*, *45*, 417–432. doi:10.1016/j.compedu.2004.05.004

Shang, Y., Shi, H., & Chen, S.-S. (2001). An intelligent distributed environment for active learning. *ACM Journal of Educational Resources in Computing (JERIC)*, *1*(2).

Syed, M. R. (2001). Diminishing the distance in distance education. *IEEE MultiMedia*, *8*(3), 18–21. doi:10.1109/MMUL.2001.939996

Taylor, P., & Maor, D. (2000). Assessing the efficacy of online teaching with the constructivist on-line learning environment survey. In A. Herrmann & M. M. Kulski (Eds.), *Flexible Futures in Tertiary Teaching. Proceedings of the 9th Annual Teaching Learning Forum*. Perth, Australia: Curtin University of Technology.

Weiss, H., Schmidhofer, A., & Schmid, A. (2004). Animated and interactive e-learning concept and realization. In *Proceedings of the IASTED Int Conf. Web-Based Education* (pp. 151-156).

Weston, T. J., & Barker, L. (2001). Designing, implementing, and evaluating Web-based learning modules for university students. *Educational Technology*, *41*(4), 15–22.

Wetzel, C. D., Radtke, R. H., & Stern, H. W. (1994). *Instructional effectiveness of video media*. Hillsdale, NJ: Lawrence Erlbaum Associates.

White, S., & Liccardy, H. (2006). Harnessing insight into disciplinary differences to refine e-learning design. In *Proceedings of the 36th ASEE/IEEE Frontiers in Education Conference*, San Diego, CA.

Woit, D., & Mason, D. (2000). Enhancing student learning through on-line quizzes. *ACM SIGCSE Bulletin, 32*(1), 367–371. doi:10.1145/331795.331887

Yair, Y., Mintz, R., & LiTVak, S. (2001). 3-D virtual reality in science education: An implication for astronomy teaching. *Journal of Computers in Science Education: An implication for Astronomy Teaching, 20*(3), 293-301.

Yokomoto, C. F., & Ware, R. (1997). Variations of the group quiz that enhance collaborative learning. In *Proceedings of the IEEE Frontiers in Education Conference* (pp. 552-557).

Zhang, D. (2005). Interactive multimedia-based e-learning: A study of effectiveness. *American Journal of Distance Education, 19*(3), 149–162. doi:10.1207/s15389286ajde1903_3

Zhang, D., Zhou, L., Briggs, R., & Nunamaker, J. (2006). Instructional video in e-learning: Assessing the impact of interactive video on learning effectiveness. *Information & Management, 43*, 15–27. doi:10.1016/j.im.2005.01.004

Chapter 2
Standardization in User Modeling and Learning Objects Retrieval:
Recent Contributions

Sotirios Botsios
Democritus University of Thrace, Greece

Dimitrios Georgiou
Democritus University of Thrace, Greece

ABSTRACT

Adaptation and personalization of the information and instruction offered to the users -individuals or groups- in on-line e-learning environments are considered to be the turning point of recent research efforts. The "one-size-fits-all" approach has some important drawbacks, from the educational point of view. Adaptive educational hypermedia systems (AEHSs) in World Wide Web became a very active research field and the need of standardization of user assessment, instruction material and e-learning environments arose, as the continually augmenting research efforts lacked the interoperability dimension. The main objective of this chapter is to provide a classification of some basic assessment aspects (adaptivity parameters) of an AEHS user, extracted from research work that refers to commonly accepted e-learning standards, such as SCORM. Also, the authors provide a starting point for the development of a generic architecture for the retrieval of standardized learning objects (LOs) from disperse learning objects repositories (LORs) to an e-learning environment, which can support collaboration activities. The retrieved LOs will comply with user assessment stored in the user model.

INTRODUCTION

The technologies that support the educational processes come closer to the traditional educational systems, as the Internet and the World Wide Web are developed. More and more teachers provide their teaching material to their students, groups and individuals, through simple or more sophisticated electronic means and experts in various fields continually provide knowledge to the public, usually in the from of web pages. A recent research by (Liaw, Huang, & Chen, 2007) demonstrated that instruc-

DOI: 10.4018/978-1-60566-786-7.ch002

tors have very positive perceptions toward using e-learning as a teaching assisted tool. From the learner's point of view, self-paced, teacher-led and multimedia instruction, are major factors to affect learners' attitudes toward e-learning as an effective learning tool. In their work Brusilovsky and Pyelo, (2003) mention that Adaptive and Intelligent Web-Based Educational Systems attempt to be more adaptive by building a model of the goals, preferences and knowledge of each individual student and using this model throughout the interaction with the system in order to be more intelligent by incorporating and performing some activities traditionally executed by a human teacher – such as coaching students, diagnosing misconceptions or motivating students to collaborate.

Among many different pedagogical approaches collaborative learning is considered to be an essential element of learning. In asynchronous systems one may not expect to fulfill the effective collaboration requirement for adaptive pairing of collaborative peers on real time. The idea of human – machine collaboration for educational purpose is not new (Doak & Keith, 1986). Such collaboration software has been addressed in literature as simulated student (Vanlehn, Ohlsson, & Nason, 1994), computational learner (Dillenbourg & Self, 1992) and learning companion (Chan & Baskin, 1990). An extensive definition was given by Chou et al: "*A learning companion is a computer-simulated character, which has human-like characteristics and plays a non-authoritative role in a social learning environment*" (Chou, Chan, & Lin, 2003).

According to Brusilovsky and Pyelo, existing AIWBES are very diverse. The "rules" that are used to describe the creation of such a system are not yet standardized, and the criteria that need to be used pedagogically effective rule-sets (i.e. adaptivity parameters) are, as yet, poorly mentioned (Brusilovsky & Pyelo, 2003). Many experimental AEH systems have been created – each to their own unique specifications. As yet, however, no combined effort has been made to

extract the common design paradigms from these systems. (Brown et al, 2005).

The scope of this chapter is to try to extract pedagogically effective rule-set suitable for adaptation and to provide a taxonomical classification of such adaptivity parameters, from research work that refers to commonly accepted e-learning standards, such as SCORM. Widely cited adaptivity parameters are considered to be among others: user knowledge and goals, learning style (LS), cognitive style (CS) (and cognitive abilities) and learning behavior. Assessment methods of the above adaptivity parameters and the connection of assessment results to e-learning standards are given.

This chapter also provides a starting point for the development of a generic architectuare for the retrieval of standardized Learning Objects (LOs) from disperse Learning Objects Repositories (LORs) to an e-learning environment. Rehak and Mason (2003) consider learning object as a digitized entity which can be used, reused or referenced during technology supported learning. The retrieved LOs will comply with user assessment stored in the user model. Practically, LOs acquisition is achieved by querying LOs repositories distributed over the internet with proper criteria. This LO's "journey" must comply with widely accepted standards. Properly adopted techniques and methods from the referenced work are suggested for application to the architecture's foundation to provide an open, modular and distributed solution, closely coupled to given standardizations. Also, a possible expansion of the architecture is examined, i.e. creation of a virtual-co-learner, to cover some collaboration needs that promotes the learning process. It is not in the authors intentions to address important aspects of this generic architecture such as validation, techniques for integration into existing architectures and integration on a service level.

The rest of the paper is structured as follows. In next chapter a background is provided concerning the most commonly used adaptivity parameters, assessment methods and pedagogical strategies from selected referenced papers. A chapter describing standards and specifications required in the proposed architecture, as well as suggested connections of adaptivity parameters with specific metadata elements follows. A first approach of the adaptive LO retrieval architecture is presented in the next section. This section closes with a conclusions chapter.

BACKGROUND

In this section a brief literature review is provided concerning the most commonly used adaptivity parameters. With the term adaptivity parameters we denote the criteria that a system should take under consideration to provide instructional material tailored to the user's needs. For each one of the parameters an assessment technique and specific rules describing the adaptation procedure are required. Other parameters can also be found in literature, such as any kind of impairments (visual, hearing, etc), technology, context of use (place, time, etc) and others.

Knowledge and Personal Goals

AH systems can be useful in any application area where a hypermedia system is expected to be used by people with different goals and knowledge and where the hyperspace is reasonably big (Brusilovsky, 1996). Users with different goals and knowledge may be interested in different pieces of information presented on hypermedia page, different levels of course material difficulty and may use different links for navigation. AH tries to overcome this problem by using knowledge represented in the user model to adapt the information being presented, limit browsing space and consequently minimize the cognitive load (Brusilovsky, 2003).

In (Hietala & Niemirepo, 1998) researchers conducted a research where two groups of users collaborated with agent co-learners of different competency levels. Their empirical data deals with young school children working on elementary mathematics and the group formation of the subjects was based on their IQ test results. Also, all students from both groups were marked as introvert or extrovert according to their answers in psychological tests. Their approach of providing several agents, some more knowledgeable and some slowly learning ones, turned out to be successful in keeping the learners' interest alive for collaboration. Some learners even preferred the weaker agents more at the end.

Experiments by Specht & Kobsa (Specht & Kobsa, 1999) and Brusilovsky & Rizzo (Brusilovsky & Rizzo, 2002), concluded that learners with higher previous knowledge seem to prefer non-restricting adaptive methods, while learners with low previous knowledge can profit from the guidance of more restrictive adaptive methods.

The idea of Baldoni et al (Baldoni, Baroglio, Patti, & Torasso, 2004) is to introduce the "prerequisites" and "effects" of each instruction material unit (LO). The term prerequisites denotes all the knowledge a user must already have in order to be taught the current instruction material unit and the term effects denotes the knowledge a user has gathered by successfully completing the current instructional material unit. Given a set of LOs, annotated by pre-requisites and effects, it is possible to compose reading sequences by using the standard planners based on graph algorithms. In their work, they also introduced some learning strategies, i.e. sets of rules for selecting those LOs which are the most suitable to the student, expressed only in terms of competences.

Chen et al (J. N. Chen, Huang, & Chu, 2005) proposed a system based on modified Item Response Theory which provides learning paths that can be adapted to various levels of difficulty of course materials and various abilities of learners. Experimental results indicated that their system can recommend appropriate course materials to learners based on individual ability, and help them to learn more effectively in a web-based environment.

Cognitive Style and Cognitive Abilities

The term "cognitive" roots on the Latin work cognisco, which in tern comes from the ancient Greek word "γιγνώσκω ~ gignosko". The meaning of this word is "I am aware of" or "I have the property of understanding". In literature one can find several models and theories regarding learning and cognitive characteristics. Although some authors do not distinguish between LSs and CSs (Rezaei & Katz, 2004), there are others who clearly do (Papanikolaou, Mabbott, Bull, & Grigoriadou, 2006), (Sadler-Smith, 2001). CS refers to an individual's method of processing information. The building up of a learning strategies repertoire that combine with CS, contribute to an individual's LS (see next subsection) (Riding & Rayner, 1998). In particular, LSs are applied CSs, removed one more level from pure processing ability usually referring to learners' preferences on how they process information and not to actual ability, skill or processing tendency (Jonassen & Grabowski, 1993). Cognitive Abilities are mechanisms that allow humans to acquire and recognize pieces of information, to convert them into representations, then into knowledge, and finally to use them for the generation of simple to complex behaviors (Lemaire, 1999).

Three main kinds of data can be used to measure CSs: behavioral, self-report, and physiological (Antonietti & Giorgetti, 1997). Behavioral data can be obtained by recording the final results of a given task or the procedure applied when performing the task. Most of the time, the task consist of filling out a paper-and-pencil test, a multiple choice test or a sorting test. Self-reports require that people evaluate themselves by describing introspectively the way they performed tasks by checking personal habits or preferences, or by endorsing statement about what they think of themselves (for example keeping diary). Finally, some physiological measures can be interpreted as hints of particular cognitive preferences in processing stimuli. Observations of physiological measures have indicated that, when someone is asked a question that requires some thinking, eyes make an initial movement to the left or right (Antonietti & Giorgetti, 1997).

There are many different classifications of CSs as different researchers emphasize on different aspects (Riding & Cheema, 1991). Field dependence/independence is probably the most well-known division of CSs and it refers to a tendency to approach the environment in an analytical, as opposed to global, way (Witkin, Moore, Goodenough, & Cox, 1977). It is indicated that field dependent learners are less likely to impose a meaningful organization on a field that lacks structure and are less able to learn conceptual material when cues are not available. For example, field dependent learners may find difficulties when freely navigating in hyperspace and shall prefer direct guidance. On the other hand field independent learners generally prefer to impose their own structure on information rather than accommodate the structure that is implicit in the learning material (Jonassen & Wang, 1993). For example, a menu from which learners can choose to proceed in the course in any order should be provided for field independent learners.

In (Karampiperis, Lin, Sampson, & Kinshuk, 2006) work, authors selected two cognitive characteristics, namely working memory capacity and inductive reasoning ability (available from the Cognitive Trait Model (Kinshuk and Lin, 2002)), to create adaptivity algorithms. According to Miller (1956), working memory is the cognitive system that allows us to keep active a limited amount of information for a brief period of time to temporarily store the outcome of intermediate computations during problem solving to perform further computations on these temporary outcomes. When the working memory capacity of the learner is low then a. the number of the paths and the amount of information presented to the learner should decrease to protect the learners from getting lost in the vast amount of information, b. the relevance of the information should increase to raise the possibility that the learners will get the most important information and c. the concreteness of the information should increase so the learner can grasp the fundamental rules first and use them to generate higher-order rules. The opposite should happen if the working memory capacity of the learner is high. Inductive reasoning skill is described by Heit (2000) as the ability to figure out the rules/theories/principle from observed instances of an event, described as working opposite to deduction, moving from specific observations to broader generalizations and theories. When the learner's inductive reasoning skill is poor then a. the number of paths and the amount of information in the learning system should increase to give the learner more opportunity for observation and thus promote induction, b. the relevance of paths should decrease, c. the concreteness of the information should increase so the learner can have more diverse observation to increase the possibility of induction. Obviously the opposite should happen when the learner's inductive reasoning skill is good. In their experiment they simulated different learner behaviors in navigating a hypermedia learning objects space, and measured the selection success of the proposed selection decision model as it is dynamically updated using the simulated learner's navigation steps. The simulation results provide evidence that the proposed selection methodology can dynamically update the internal adaptation logic leading to refine selection decisions.

Learning Style

Learning theories converge to the fact that students learn and acquire knowledge in many different ways, which has been classified as LSs. Students learn by observing and hearing; reflecting and acting or by reasoning logically and intuitively.

Students also learn by memorizing and visualizing; drawing analogies and building mathematical models. (Felder & Silverman, 1988) LS classifications have been proposed by D. Kolb (Kolb, 1999) and others (Honey & Mumford, 2000); (Dunn & Dunn, 1992), (Felder & Silverman, 1988). Most of the authors categorize them into groups and propose certain inventories and methodologies capable of classifying learners accordingly. Despite their efforts for classifications, most of the above authors notice that the LS variable is a continuous. That means that an effort for dichotomous classification of learners could be proved pointless. For example, (Coffield, Moseley, Hall, & Ecclestone, 2004) have tried to scientifically validate the main learning styles and showed that many of the test used to identify such styles suffer from the lack of reliability. As noted by Brusilovsky in his work in 2001, several systems that attempt to adapt to LS had been developed, however it was still not clear which aspects of LS are worth modeling, and what can be done differently for users with different styles. (Brusilovsky, 2001) Since then efforts have been made and a quite large number of surveys have been published that remark the benefits of adaptation to LS in the scope of providing tailored education.

It has been pointed out that LS effects e-learning more than traditional instructor based learning (Stathacopoulou, Magoulas, Grigoriadou, & Samarakou, 2005). Moreover, (Manochehr, 2006) among others suggests that e-learning becomes more effective for learners with a particular LS. LSs are considered relevant for the adaptation process in the user model, and have been used as a basis for adaptation in AEHS (E. Brown, Cristea, Stewart, & Brailsford, 2005), (Georgiou & Makry, 2004).

In their research, Graf and Kinshuk show how cognitive traits and LSs can be incorporated in web-based learning systems by providing adaptive courses. The adaptation process includes two steps. Firstly, the individual needs of learners have to be detected and secondly, the courses have to be adapted according to the identified needs. The LS estimation in their work is made by a 44-item questionnaire based on Felder-Silverman LS model (Graf & Kinshuk, 2007).

In another work, empirical studies were conducted on two educational systems (Flexi-OLM and INSPIRE) to investigate learners' learning and CS, and preferences during interaction (Papanikolaou, et al., 2006). The Index of Learning Styles questionnaire was used to asses the style of each participant according to the four dimensions of the Felder-Silverman LS model. It was found that learners do have a preference regarding their interaction, but no obvious link between style and approaches offered, was detected. Other examples which implement different aspects of the Felder-Silverman Index of Learning Styles are WHURLE (E. J. Brown & Brailsford, 2004), (Moore, Brailsford, & Stewart, 2001) and ILASH (Bajraktarevic, Hall, & Fullick, 2003). The development of an adaptive hypermedia interface, which provided dynamic tailoring of the presentation of course material based on the individual student's LS, was part of the research work by Carver Jr et al (Carver Jr, Howard, & Lane, 1999). By tailoring the presentation of material to the student's LS, authors believe students learned more efficiently and more effectively. Students determine their LS by answering a series of 28 questions. These forms were based on an assessment tool developed at North Carolina State University (B.S. Solomon's Inventory of Learning Styles). In iWeaver the Dunn and Dunn model is applied (Wolf, 2003).

Another approach tend to pursue adaptation according to generated user profile and its features which are relevant to the adaptation, e.g. the user's preferences, knowledge, goals, navigation history and possibly other relevant aspects that are used to provide personalized adaptations (Milosevic, Brkovic, Debevc, & Krneta, 2007). Researchers discuss lesson content's design tailored to individual users by taking into consideration user's LS and learning motivation. They also mention how LOs metadata can be used for LO retrieval

according to the specific needs of the individual learner. They relied on the Kolb's learning style model and suggest that every LS class should get a different course material sequencing.

Learning Behavior

In this paper with the term Learning Behavior we address the easily changeable psychological or emotional state of the learner while interacting with an e-learning system. Boredom, frustration, motivation, concentration, tiredness are emotional conditions that, among others, are considered important for the effectiveness of the learning process.

Tracing learner's behavior in real time is a quite challenging task. In her work, (Conati, 2002) address the problem of how an interactive system can monitor the user's emotional state using multiple direct indicators of emotional arousal. A Dynamic Decision Network was applied to represent the probabilistic dependencies in a unifying framework between possible causes and emotional states (anger, reproach, motivation, arousal) on one hand, and between emotional states and the user bodily expressions they can affect on the other hand (following the Ortony, Clore and Collins cognitive theory of emotions). Detection of user's body expressions, such as eyebrow position, skin conductance and heart rate, requires special sensors. The system was applied on computer-based educational games instead of more traditional computer-based tutors, as the former tend to generate a much higher level of students' emotional engagement.

Another approach that exploits novel methods of resolution for fine-grained user profiling based on real-time eye-tracking and content tracking information is presented in (Gutl, et al., 2005). The authors introduced the Adaptive e-Learning with Eye-Tracking System, a system that utilizes a monitor mounted camera that records the eye of the participant and trace the gaze in a scene through imaging algorithms. Real- time information of the precise position of gaze and of pupil diameter can be used for assessing user's interest, attention, tiredness etc.

Both of the above mentioned examples utilized a kind of sensors to capture users' behavioral indicators. In (J. N. Chen, et al., 2005) work, authors propose a Dynamic Fuzzy Petri Net inference engine that monitors "browsing time" and "browsing count" of users' interaction with their system. According to them, whenever the learner spends too much time on a specific section, either he/she is very interested in it or confused by it. Regardless, the auxiliary learning content should be provided. With fuzzy rules like this one, the engine provides an appropriate dynamic learning content structure and normalizes the exercise grade using a course intensity function.

(Milosevic, 2006) examined the users' motivation as a factor of learning efficiency. According to the author motivation is a pivotal concept in most theories of learning. It is closely related to arousal, attention and anxiety. Increasing learner's motivation during online course is one of the key factors to achieve a certain goal. For example, highly motivated students tend to learn faster and to accept learning material in larger quantities, while low motivators must be presented with smaller knowledge chunks with appropriate feedback, trying to increase their motivation. They propose a pre-course test to asses the user's motivation level, which they import it in user model to adapt the provided learning material.

A summary of adaptivity parameters is shown in Table 1.

STANDARDS

"Learning objects" is a term that originated from the object-oriented paradigm of computer science. The idea behind object-orientation is that components ("objects") can be reused in multiple contexts (Wiley, 2000). According to the Learning Technology Standards Committee, learning objects are defined as:

Any entity, digital or non-digital, that can be used, re-used or referenced during technology-supported learning. Examples of technology-supported learning applications include computer-based training systems, interactive learning environments, intelligent computer-aided instruction systems, distance learning systems, web-based learning systems and collaborative learning environments.

Learning object metadata can be defined as structured data used for the efficient description of learning objects and the effective support of educational functions related to those objects. In specific, Learning Objects Metadata is a data model:

- usually encoded in XML;
- to describe a LO to support learning;
- to support the reusability of learning objects;
- to aid discoverability of learning objects;
- to facilitate interoperability of learning objects: and
- is usually applied on online learning management systems (LMS).

There are several metadata standards, schemas and specifications available for the description of learning objects, such as SCORM (Shareable Content Object Reference Model), IEEE LTSC (IEEE Learning Technology Standards Committee), IMS (Instructional Management Systems), DC-ed (Dublin Core – Education) and AICC (Aviation Industry CBT Committee) have undertaken significant work on LOs schemas. The SCORM standard was developed by the Department of Defense's ADL (Advanced Distributed Learning) initiative.

Today SCORM is a widely accepted collection of standards in e-Learning applications. SCORM seeks to establish a collection of specifications and standards adapted from multiple sources to provide a comprehensive suite of e-Learning

Table 1. Summary of adaptivity parameters and pedagogical rules

research work	adaptivity parameter	adaptation rule		
		parameter value	adaptation strategy	
(Brusilovsky, 2003)	previous knowledge level	high	guidance of non-restricting adaptive methods (i.e. non-sequential links)	adaptive navigation
		low	guidance of restrictive adaptive methods (i.e. linear learning paths)	
(C. M. Chen, Lee, & Chen, 2005)	knowledge level θ from Item Response Theory	scale (-1,+1),	recommendation based on information function I(θ)	adaptive navigation
	course material difficulty b from Item Response Theory	scale (-1, +1)		
(Triantafillou, Pomportsis, Demetriadis, & Georgiadou, 2004)	cognitive style	field independent	navigation menu from which learners can choose to proceed in the course in their preferred order	adaptive navigation
		field dependent	hidden navigation menu, direct navigation	
(Tarpin-Bernard & Habieb-Mammar, 2005)	13 cognitive indicators (verbal/visual/musical working memory, form recognition, categorization, glossary, etc)	scale (0, 100) for each cognitive indicator	dynamic generation of modular web pages in order to increase memorization capacity and reduce cognitive load	adaptive presentation
(Karampiperis, et al., 2006)	working memory capacity from the Cognitive Trait Model	poor	- available path number + available path relevance - content amount + content concreteness and other	adaptive navigation
		good	+ available path number - available path relevance + content amount - content concreteness and other	
	inductive reasoning skill from the Cognitive Trait Model	poor	+ available path number - available path relevance + content amount + content concreteness and other	
		good	- available path number - content amount - content concreteness and other	

Table 1. continued

research work	adaptivity parameter	adaptation rule		
		parameter value	adaptation strategy	
(Carver Jr, et al., 1999)	learning styles sensing/intuitive visual/verbal sequential/global	scale (0, 100) for each dimension	heuristic rules describing the relationship of each LS dimension to each media tool	adaptive presentation
(Milosevic, et al., 2007)	learning styles	Assimilator	rules mapping teaching activities sequencing and optional links displaying with learning style	adaptive navigation and adaptive presentation
		Converger		
		Accommodator		
		Diverger		
	motivation	high	semantic density of learning object: 5	
		moderate	semantic density of learning object: 3 and 4	
		low	semantic density of learning object: 1 and 2	
(J. N. Chen, et al., 2005)	browsing time and browsing count as learning behavior indicators	high	auxiliary learning content provided	adaptive navigation
		little		

capabilities that support the interoperability, accessibility and reusability of web-based learning content (SCORM, 2004) ((ADL), 2006). It can be considered as a collection of "technical books" which are presently grouped under three main topics: a. Content Aggregation Model (CAM), b. Run-time Environment (RTE) and c. Sequencing and Navigation (SN).

SCORM CAM defines how learning resources are defined with the XML metadata. Learning resources in SCORM are assets, Sharable Content Objects (SCOs) and Activities. Assets are electronic representations of media that can be collected together to build other assets. If this collection represents a single launchable learning resource that utilizes SCORM RTE to communicate with an LMS, it is referred to as an SCO. An Activity is a meaningful unit of instruction that may provide learning resources (assets or SCOs) or be composed of several subactivities. SCORM CAM consists of three different parts: a. Content

Model which describes the low level components of instruction (assets, SCOs and content aggregations), b. Metadata, i.e. information describing the instruction material, and c. Content Packaging ((ADL), 2006).

SCORM RTE defines the communication procedures between a Learning Management System and the instruction material. It consists of three parts: a. Launch, which defines a common way for LMS to start Web-based learning resources, b. Application programmable interface, which is the communication mechanism for informing the LMS of the state of the learning resource and c. a standard set of elements used to define the information being communicated, the Data Model ((ADL), 2006).

SCORM Sequencing and Navigation (SN) defines a method for representing the branching and flow of learning activities in any SCORM conformant LMS. The learning resources flow could be both predefined by the content author and run-time created by user interactions with content objects ((ADL), 2006).

IMS Learner Information Package specification LIP is a collection of information about a learner (individual or group learners) or a producer of learning content. The specification addresses the interoperability of internet based Learner Information systems with other systems that support the Internet learning environment. Storing information regarding recording and managing learning-related history, goals, preferences and accomplishments is described in LIP specification ((IMS), 2001).

Adaptivity Parameters and Standards

As mentioned in the introduction, this paper's basic contribution is to provide a classification of research efforts that connect adaptivity parameters and standards (see table 2). Connecting adaptivity parameters and standards means creating pedagogically effective connections between users' behavior assessment results with LOs' metadata annotation values. As an example one can mention the connection between the cognitive characteristic "working memory capacity" (Miller, 1956) with metadata nodes "interactivityType", "interactivityLevel", "semanticDensity" and "Difficulty" described in SCORM RTE following the IEEE Learning Objects Metadata Standard. This connection is described in (Karampiperis et al, 2006). When the assessment result for a specific user is "working memory capacity = low", queries to LOR are created in order to retrieve Los which are annotated as "interactivityType = Expositive", "interactivityLevel = Very low or low", "semanticDensity = Very low or low" and "Difficulty = Very easy or easy".

Each paper examines adaptivity parameters which appear in the second column and adaptivity types (adaptive presentation, navigation, content retrieval) which are placed in the third column. The forth column provides the reference to given standardizations and specifications and the fifth column provides some information about the assessment method used to capture the adaptivity parameter. Specific, properly adopted, methods and techniques from research efforts of table 2 are selected to underlie the generic architecture, which is described in the next section.

One can notice that some of the referenced scientific work is annotated as standards extension proposals. Authors of these papers propose certain standards additions in order to create adaptive courses. In specific, Ray-Lopez et al (2008) (Rey-Lopez, Fernadez-Vilas, Diaz-Redondo, Pazos-Arias, & Bermejo-Munoz, 2006) argue that current standards do not fully support content personalization. They study the adaptation possibilities of the SCORM standard and present an extension to permit the instructors to create adaptive courses with flexible structures, as well as to define the rules that permit the system to decide which activities are the most appropriate for a particular student. The adaptivity is provided at two levels: SCO level and activity level. Adaptivity at SCO level is achieved by defining a new type of SCO: the self-adaptive SCO, which self-configures based on a set of user's characteristics. Adaptivity at activity level consists in offering different combinations of subactivities to achieve the objective of the parent activity.

Other examples of standard extension proposals are the Rumetshofer et al (2003) (Rumetshofer & Wo, 2003) work, where the parent element <Psychological> is suggested to be added in IEEE LOM, and Sampson's et al (2002) (Sampson, et al., 2002) effort, where extensions over the IMS content packaging specification are suggested.

Table 2. Classification of recent research which reference to standardization and adaptivity parameters

paper	adaptivity parameter	assessment method	reference to standardization	adaptivity type
(Milosevic, et al., 2007)	learning style	Kolb Learning Style Inventory	<learningResourceType>	adaptive navigation
	motivation	pre-, post- tests	<SemanticDensity>	adaptive presentation
(Watson, Ahmed, & Hardaker, 2007)	knowledge level	SCO performance assessment	SCORM interaction elements	adaptive content retrieval
(Karampiperis, et al., 2006)	cognitive style > working capacity	monitoring navigation steps	<aggregationLevel> <interactivityType> <interactivityLevel> <semanticDensity> <difficulty> <typicalLearningTime> <learningResourceType>	adaptive content retrieval
(C. M. Chen, Liu, & Chang, 2006)	knowledge level	modified Item Response Theory	<description> <keyword> <difficulty>	adaptive content retrieval
(J. N. Chen, et al., 2005)	learning behavior	Dynamic Fuzzy Petri Net	Activity Tree of <organization> SCORM Rollup Rules	adaptive content retrieval
(Baldoni, et al., 2004)	knowledge level	-	<purpose> <taxon>	adaptive navigation
(Yahya & Yusoff, 2008)*	learning style knowledge level	-	<learningStyles> <history> <pastHistory> <relatedSubjects>	-
(Rey-Lopez, et al., 2008)*	dependent to each LMS	dependent to each LMS	<adaptation> <organization> <item>	adaptive content retrieval adaptive presentation
(Rumetshofer & Wo, 2003)*	cognitive style learning strategy skill	assessment center (questionnaires)	<psychological> <cognitive style> <learning strategy> <learning modality> <skills>	adaptive content retrieval, presentation, navigation
(Sampson, Karagiannidis, & Cardinali, 2002)*	learner profile (general)	questionnaire to create an IMS LIP based profile	<rules> <domain ontology> <LO meta-data> <questions & tests> <competencies> <user profiles>	adaptive content retrieval

*standards extension

GENERIC ARCHITECTURE: A FIRST APPROACH

Description

In this section a brief description of the proposed generic architecture is given (figure 2). The model describes a solution to the scenario of distributed LOs adaptive retrieval and presentation from a web-based Learning Management System (LMS), as it seems to be the dominant practice. Practically, LOs acquisition is achieved by querying LORs distributed over the internet, using LOs metadata standards. The database queries must have solid structure with strictly defined parameters.

The criteria of the retrieval, presentation and

navigation (sequencing of the LOs) are in accordance with the adaptivity parameters examined in section 3.

- Cognitive Style, cognitive abilities
- Learning Style
- Learning Behavior, motivation
- Knowledge level

The above parameters are considered independent to each other, by the means of absence of influence. The values of these parameters are resulted from separate modules, accordingly.

The numbered list which follows, describes the most important aspects of the architecture's modules. The "x" symbol in the corner of some boxes implies that the module could be disabled or not present, without disturbing the LO's retrieval, but, of course, disabling some, or all, of these modules the system becomes less parametric or less "intelligent".

1. Learning Management System (LMS). The beginning and the end of the e-learning experience. The LMS captures user interactions and forwards them to next modules. Also, the LMS is responsible to receive and display the returned LOs. Of course, both captured user interactions and received LOs must be standardized.

2. According to visited LO (in figure 2: current state) and user interactions –information

Figure 1. A first approach of the generic architecture

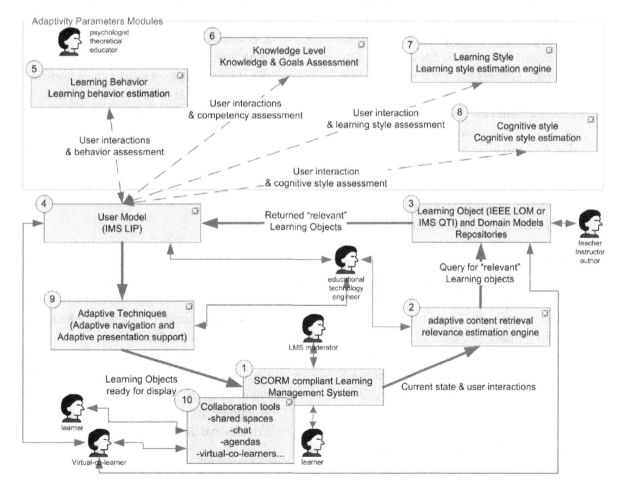

that is send from the LMS- the relevance estimation engine is responsible to create the appropriate query to "ask" LORs for "relevant" LOs. Algorithms proposed by Chen et al (C. M. Chen, et al., 2006) or Watson et al (Watson, et al., 2007) could be applied to provide a taxonomy of "relevant" LOs. Taking under consideration user interactions and LOM, these algorithms are inference engines that provide selection rules to filter LOs from disperse and vast LORs.

3. Learning Objects and Domain Models Repositories receive a query and return a number of "relevant" LOs. A catalogue of some large LORs with sharable LOs can be found in Nash' work (Nash, 2005).

4. The User Model is responsible to store (keep personal user data, preferences data and history related data) and forward user interactions to adaptivity parameters modules (see 5, 6, 7 and 8), receive their assessments and export a final filtered taxonomy of the Learning Objects that have received from 3.

5. Learning Behavior. This module is dedicated to learning behavior diagnosis. A suggestion for estimating learning behavior from user's interaction is proposed by Chen et al (J. N. Chen, et al., 2005) or Milosevic et (Milosevic, et al., 2007) (see table 2).

6. Competence Level. This module supports the assessment of user's knowledge and goals. The modified item response theory from Chen et al (C. M. Chen, et al., 2006) or SCO performance assessment from Watson et al (Watson, et al., 2007) are two alternatives for this purpose (see table 2).

7. Learning Style. Similarly to 5 and 6, this module produces results for user's LS. Milosevic et al (Milosevic, et al., 2007) developed a solution that "connects" user's LS to specific LOM (see table 2).

8. Cognitive Style. This module is dedicated to estimate the user's CS. The module receives user interaction related data and exports an assessment. An example application is the Karampiperis et al (Karampiperis, et al., 2006) work. Data about user navigation is used to export LOM (see table 2).

9. All the algorithms to provide adaptive navigation and adaptive presentation services are the last stage of this architecture. This module receives user model information and produces a filtered taxonomy of learning objects, applies the appropriate algorithms and forwards the data to be displayed in the interface of the LMS.

10. Tools which support collaboration provided by the LMS. We focus on asynchronous collaborative problem-solving technique where participants could be both humans and virtual learners. The agent should take under consideration the information stored in the user model and adjust so as to become a co-learner with a "compatible profile". With the term "compatible profile" we denote all those human-like characteristics the agent should have in order to promote collaboration with the real learners. Also, VcL requires access to the LO and Domain Model repositories. More information about the design of VcL one can find in (Botsios, Mitropoulou, Georgiou, & Panapakidis, 2006).

We must also mention that our model, as an AEHS, is created in favor of the learner, but it should be supported by others, such as:

- Instruction material providers (educators, teachers, authors etc)
- System moderators
- Cognitive Psychologists (assessment engines)
- Administrators
- Educational Technology Engineers

Relations to Other Architectures

The proposed architecture has some similarities to components of other architectures one can find in literature. As already mentioned, one of this paper's objectives is to gather, formalize and generalize other research efforts on this field. In referenced work, researchers seek to create an architecture which meets specific needs, but the basic aspects of their efforts can be considered as the following:

- A pool, database, repository of the instruction material and the domain models (possible relation to instruction material) $\rightarrow$ (3)
- An assessment method: An engine that tries to capture some user characteristics $\rightarrow$ (5, 6, 7, 8)
- A user model generation process: Techniques that gather results from the assessment engines and create a dynamic user "instance" which is used throughout the e-learning experience $\rightarrow$ (4)
- An adaptation process: Techniques based on rules that map user model to the instruction material $\rightarrow$ (4 to 9)
- A user interface generator: An engine which produces the final screenshot of the e-learning experience which is displayed to the user's screen $\rightarrow$ (9 to 1)
- Agents that capture user interactions with the interface $\rightarrow$ (1 to 2)

Note that agents or society of agents function between each component.

In his work, Oliveira (Oliveira, 2002) presents a generic architecture for AEHSs, which is resulted from known AEHS architectures' analysis and other adaptive systems, as well. In our paper we refer to the very significant parameter of standards, which has not been included in his work.

Some of the above modules can be found in Bernard & Mammar (Tarpin-Bernard & Habieb-Mammar, 2005) work. Authors present an environment called "Cognitive User Modeling for Adaptive Presentation of Hyper-Document". The proposed environment is based on four components, namely a cognitive user model, a hyper-document generator, an adaptive engine, and a generic style sheet to present the adapted hyper-documents. Adaptive presentation is viewed as a process of selection of the most suitable combination of multimedia items (text, images, audio and video) that describe a concept. The best combination is the one that better fits the user cognitive abilities.

A generic architecture is also described in Karampiperis et al (Karampiperis & Sampson, 2005) work. It follows a two layer architecture: a Runtime Layer and a Storage Layer. The Runtime Layer consists of an Educational Content Presenter, a Behavior Tracker and an Adaptation Rule Parser. The Storage Layer consists of a User Model, an Adaptation Model, the Educational Resources (LOs) themselves and a Domain Model, where the connections of Educational Resources with concepts are held. These connections are represented in the <classification> element of the IEEE LOM standardization. An interesting part of that work is the use of the IMS LIP specification for representing User Model elements. For example user's LS is represented with Accessibility/Preference/typename and Accessibility/Preference/prefcode IMS LIP elements.

Another example that utilizes some of the above mentioned modules is found in Chen et al work (C. M. Chen, et al., 2006). The modular system architecture consists of a courseware analysis module, a courseware recommendation agent, which is responsible to match user interaction with course material, and finally a learning interface agent.

CONCLUSION

There exist a wide variety of diverse Adaptive and Intelligent Web-Based Educational Systems. The 'rules' that are used to describe the creation of such systems are not yet fully standardized, and the criteria that need to be used pedagogically effective rule-sets (i.e. adaptivity parameters) are, as yet, poorly mentioned (E. Brown, et al., 2005). In this paper we provide a starting point for the development of a generic architecture for the retrieval of LOs from disperse LORs. This LO "journey" must comply with widely accepted standards. The model is based on a distributed architecture. Interoperability, information sharing, scalability and dynamic integration of heterogeneous expert fields are considered as the major advantages of the proposed model. a. Interoperability: support for available standards, technology and platform independent. b. Information Sharing: user information, learning objects, services and assessment tools. c. Scalability: continuous update of each module's functionality (Learning Objects, monitoring tools, cognition and learning style theories, sequencing and navigation algorithms). d. Integration of heterogeneous expert field: independent module development and dynamic adaptation to the latest criteria.

The scope of this chapter is to gather recent research work concerning adaptivity parameters, investigate their connection with widely accepted LO standards and provide suitable methods and techniques from the literature which can be applied in a generic architecture for the retrieval of learning objects from disperse LORs to an e-learning environment. Further development and validation of the above described generic architecture will be conducted, focused in each module separately. Also, a wider literature review will be conducted to discover the most recent approaches in adaptivity parameters diagnosis.

ACKNOWLEDGMENT

This work is supported in the frame of Operational Programme "COMPETITIVENESS", 3rd Community Support Program, co financed.

75% by the public sector of the European Union – European Social Fund.

25% by the Greek Ministry of Development – General Secretariat of Research and Technology.

REFERENCES

(ADL), A. D. L. (2006). *SCORM 2004 3rd edition, sharable content object reference model*. Alexandria, VA: Advanced Distributed Learning.

Antonietti, A., & Giorgetti, M. (1997). The verbalizer-visualizer questionnaire: A review 1. *Perceptual and Motor Skills*, 86(1), 227–239.

Bajraktarevic, N., Hall, W., & Fullick, P. (2003). *ILASH: Incorporating learning strategies in hypermedia*. Paper presented at the Fourteenth Conference on Hypertext and Hypermedia.

Baldoni, M., Baroglio, C., Patti, V., & Torasso, L. (2004). *Reasoning about learning object metadata for adapting SCORM courseware*. Paper presented at the EAW'04.

Botsios, S., Mitropoulou, V., Georgiou, D., & Panapakidis, I. (2006). *Design of virtual co-learner for asynchronous collaborative e-learning*. Paper presented at the Sixth International Conference on Advanced Learning Technologies, ICALT 2006.

Brown, E., Cristea, A., Stewart, C., & Brailsford, T. (2005). Patterns in authoring of adaptive educational hypermedia: A taxonomy of learning styles. *Educational Technology and Society*, 8(3), 77–90.

Brown, E. J., & Brailsford, T. (2004). *Integration of learning style theory in an adaptive educational hypermedia (AEH) system*. Paper presented at the ALT-C Conference.

Brusilovsky, P. (1996). Methods and techniques of adaptive hypermedia. *User Modeling and User-Adapted Interaction, 6*(2-3), 87–129. doi:10.1007/BF00143964

Brusilovsky, P. (2001). Adaptive hypermedia. *User Modelling and User-Adapted Interaction, 11*(1-2).

Brusilovsky, P. (2003). Adaptive navigation support in educational hypermedia: The role of student knowledge level and the case for meta-adaptation. *British Journal of Educational Technology, 34*(4), 487–497. doi:10.1111/1467-8535.00345

Brusilovsky, P., & Pyelo, C. (2003). Adaptive and intelligent Web-based educational systems. *International Journal of Artificial Intelligence in Education, 13*(2-4), 159–172.

Brusilovsky, P., & Rizzo, R. (2002). Map-based horizontal navigation in educational hypertext. *Journal of Digital Information, 3*(1).

Carver, C. A. Jr, Howard, R. A., & Lane, W. D. (1999). Enhancing student learning through hypermedia courseware and incorporation of student learning styles. *IEEE Transactions on Education, 42*(1), 33–38. doi:10.1109/13.746332

Chan, T. W., & Baskin, A. B. (Eds.). (1990). *Learning companion systems*. New Jersey: Ablex Pub. Corp.

Chen, C. M., Lee, H. M., & Chen, Y. H. (2005). Personalized e-learning system using item response theory. *Computers & Education, 44*(3), 237–255. doi:10.1016/j.compedu.2004.01.006

Chen, C. M., Liu, C. Y., & Chang, M. H. (2006). Personalized curriculum sequencing utilizing modified item response theory for Web-based instruction. *Expert Systems with Applications, 30*(2), 378–396. doi:10.1016/j.eswa.2005.07.029

Chen, J. N., Huang, Y. M., & Chu, W. C. C. (2005). Applying dynamic fuzzy petri net to Web learning system. *Interactive Learning Environments, 13*(3), 159-178. doi:10.1080/10494820500382810

Chou, C. Y., Chan, T. W., & Lin, C. J. (2003). Redefining the learning companion: The past, present, and future of educational agents. *Computers & Education, 40*(3), 255–269. doi:10.1016/S0360-1315(02)00130-6

Coffield, F., Moseley, D., Hall, E., & Ecclestone, K. (2004). *Should we be using learning styles? What research has to say to practice*. London: Learning and Skills Research Centre (LSRC).

Conati, C. (2002). Probabilistic assessment of user's emotions in educational games. *Applied Artificial Intelligence, 16*(7-8), 555–575. doi:10.1080/08839510290030390

Dillenbourg, P., & Self, J. (1992). *People power: A human-computer collaborative learning system*. Paper presented at the Second Int'l Conf. Intelligent Tutoring Systems.

Doak, E. D., & Keith, M. (1986). Simulation in teacher education: The knowledge base and the process. *Tennessee Education, 16*(2), 14–17.

Dunn, R., & Dunn, K. (1992). *Teaching elementary students through their individual learning styles*. Boston: Allyn and Bacon.

Felder, R. M., & Silverman, L. K. (1988). Learning and teaching styles in engineering education. *English Education, 78*(7), 674–681.

Georgiou, D. A., & Makry, D. (2004). *A learner's style and profile recognition via fuzzy cognitive map.* Paper presented at the IEEE International Conference on Advanced Learning Technologies.

Graf, S., & Kinshuk. (2007). *Considering cognitive traits and learning styles to open Web-based learning to a larger student community.* Paper presented at the International Conference on Information and Communication Technology and Accessibility.

Gutl, C., Pivec, M., Trummer, C., Garcia-Barrios, V. M., Modritscher, F., Pripfl, J., et al. (2005). AdeLE (adaptive e-learning with eyetracking): Theoretical background, system architecture and application scenarios. *European Journal of Open, Distance and E-Learning (EURODL).*

Hietala, P., & Niemirepo, T. (1998). The competence of learning companion agents. *International Journal of Artificial Intelligence in Education, 9*, 178–192.

Honey, P., & Mumford, A. (2000). *The learning styles helper's guide.* Maidenhead, UK: Peter Honey Publications.

(IMS), I. M. S. (2001). *IMS learner information packaging information model specification.* Instructional Management Systems.

Jonassen, D. H., & Grabowski, B. L. (1993). *Handbook of individual differences: Learning and instruction.* Hillsdale, NJ: Lawrence Erlbaum Associates.

Jonassen, D. H., & Wang, S. (1993). Acquiring structural knowledge from semantically structured hypertext. *Journal of Computer-Based Instruction, 20*(1), 1–8.

Karampiperis, P., Lin, T., Sampson, D. G., & Kinshuk, . (2006). Adaptive cognitive-based selection of learning objects. *Innovations in Education and Teaching International, 43*(2), 121–135. doi:10.1080/14703290600650392

Karampiperis, P., & Sampson, D. (2005). Adaptive learning resources sequencing in educational hypermedia systems. *Educational Technology and Society, 8*(4), 128–147.

Kolb, D. A. (1999). *Learning style inventory - version 3: Technical specifications.* TRG Hay/McBer, Training Resources Group.

Lemaire, P. (1999). *Psychologie cognitive.* Bruxelles, Belgium: De Boeck Universite.

Liaw, S. S., Huang, H. M., & Chen, G. D. (2007). Surveying instructor and learner attitudes toward e-learning. *Computers & Education, 49*(4), 1066–1080. doi:10.1016/j.compedu.2006.01.001

Manochehr, N. N. (2006). The influence of learning styles on learners in e-learning environments: An empirical study. *CHEER, 18*, 10–14.

Milosevic, D. (2006). Designing lesson content in adaptive learning environments. *International Journal of Emerging Technologies in Learning, 1*(2).

Milosevic, D., Brkovic, M., Debevc, M., & Krneta, R. (2007). Adaptive learning by using SCOs metadata. *Interdisciplinary Journal of Knowledge and Learning Objects, 3*, 163–174.

Moore, A., Brailsford, T. J., & Stewart, C. D. (2001). *Personally tailored teaching in WHURLE using conditional transclusion.* Paper presented at the ACM Conference on Hypertext.

Nash, S. S. (2005). Learning objects, learning object repositories, and learning theory: Preliminary best practices for online courses. *Interdisciplinary Journal of Knowledge and Learning Objects, 1*, 217–228.

Oliveira, J. M. P. d. (2002). *Adaptation architecture for adaptive educational hypermedia systems.* Paper presented at the World Conference on E-Learning in Corporate, Government, Healthcare, and Higher Education.

Papanikolaou, K. A., Mabbott, A., Bull, S., & Grigoriadou, M. (2006). Designing learner-controlled educational interactions based on learning/cognitive style and learner behaviour. *Interacting with Computers, 18*(3), 356–384. doi:10.1016/j.intcom.2005.11.003

Rey-Lopez, M., Dvaz-Redondo, R. P., Fernandez-Vilas, A., Pazos-Arias, J. J., Garcva-Duque, J., Gil-Solla, A., et al. (2008). An extension to the ADL SCORM standard to support adaptivity: The t-learning case-study. *Computer Standards & Interfaces.*

Rey-Lopez, M., Fernadez-Vilas, A., Diaz-Redondo, R. P., Pazos-Arias, J. J., & Bermejo-Munoz, J. (2006). Extending SCORM to create adaptive courses. In Innovative approaches for learning and knowledge sharing (LNCS 4227, pp. 679-684). Berlin, Germany: Springer.

Rezaei, A. R., & Katz, L. (2004). Evaluation of the reliability and validity of the cognitive styles analysis. *Personality and Individual Differences, 36*(6), 1317–1327. doi:10.1016/S0191-8869(03)00219-8

Riding, R., & Cheema, I. (1991). Cognitive styles - an overview and integration. *Educational Psychology, 11*(3), 193–215. doi:10.1080/0144341910110301

Riding, R., & Rayner, S. (1998). *Cognitive styles and learning strategies.* London: David Fulton Publishers.

Rumetshofer, H., & Wo, W. (2003). XML-based adaptation framework for psychological-driven e-learning systems. *Educational Technology and Society, 6*(4), 18–29.

Sadler-Smith, E. (2001). The relationship between learning style and cognitive style. *Personality and Individual Differences, 30*(4), 609–616. doi:10.1016/S0191-8869(00)00059-3

Sampson, D., Karagiannidis, C., & Cardinali, F. (2002). An architecture for Web-based e-learning promoting re-usable adaptive educational e-content. *Educational Technology and Society, 5*(4), 27–37.

Specht, M., & Kobsa, A. (1999). *Interaction of domain expertise and interface design in adaptive educational hypermedia.* Paper presented at the Second Workshop on Adaptive Systems and User Modeling on the World Wide Web.

Stathacopoulou, R., Magoulas, G. D., Grigoriadou, M., & Samarakou, M. (2005). Neuro-fuzzy knowledge processing in intelligent learning environments for improved student diagnosis. *Information Sciences, 170*(2-4), 273–307. doi:10.1016/j.ins.2004.02.026

Tarpin-Bernard, F., & Habieb-Mammar, H. (2005). Modeling elementary cognitive abilities for adaptive hypermedia presentation. *User Modeling and User-Adapted Interaction, 15*(5), 459–495. doi:10.1007/s11257-005-2529-3

Triantafillou, E., Pomportsis, A., Demetriadis, S., & Georgiadou, E. (2004). The value of adaptivity based on cognitive style: An empirical study. *British Journal of Educational Technology, 35*(1), 95–106. doi:10.1111/j.1467-8535.2004.00371.x

Vanlehn, K., Ohlsson, S., & Nason, R. (1994). Applications of simulated students: An exploration. *Journal of Artificial Intelligence in Education, 5*(2), 135–175.

Watson, J., Ahmed, P. K., & Hardaker, G. (2007). Creating domain independent adaptive e-learning systems using the sharable content object reference model. *Campus-Wide Information Systems, 24*(1), 45–71. doi:10.1108/10650740710726482

Wiley, D. A. (2000). Connecting learning objects to instructional design theory: A definition, a metaphor, and a taxonomy In *The Instructional Use of Learning Objects*.

Witkin, H. A., Moore, C. A., Goodenough, D. R., & Cox, P. W. (1977). Field-dependent and field-independent cognitive styles and their educational implications. *Review of Educational Research*, *47*(1), 1–64.

Wolf, C. (2003). *iWeaver: Towards 'learning style'-based e-learning in computer science education*. Paper presented at the Fifth Australasian Computing Education Conference on Computing Education 2003.

Yahya, Y., & Yusoff, M. (2008). Towards a comprehensive learning object metadata: Incorporation of context to stipulate meaningful learning and enhance learning object reusability. *Interdisciplinary Journal of E-Learning and Learning Objects*, *4*, 13–48.

Chapter 3
Virtual Co Learner:
An Approach Against Learner's Isolation in Asynchronous E-Learning

Dimitrios Georgiou
Democritus University of Thrace, Greece

Sotirios Botsios
Democritus University of Thrace, Greece

Georgios Tsoulouhas
Democritus University of Thrace, Greece

ABSTRACT

Adaptation and personalization of the information and instruction offered to the users in on-line e-learning environments are considered to be the turning point of recent research efforts. Collaborative learning may contribute to adaptive and personalized asynchronous e-learning. In this chapter authors intend to introduce the Virtual co Learner (VcL) that is a system designed on a basis of distributed architecture able to imitate the behavior of a learning companion who has suitable to the user's cognitive and learning style and behavior. To this purpose an asynchronous adaptive collaborating e-learning system is proposed in the sense of reusing digitized material which deployed before by the users of computer supported collaborating learning systems. Matching real and simulated learners who have cognitive characteristics of the same type, one can find that learning procedure becomes more efficient and productive. Aiming to establish such VcL, one faces a number of questions. An important question is related to the user's cognitive or learning characteristics diagnosis. Other questions are examined too.

INTRODUCTION

Collaborative learning provides an environment to enliven and enrich the learning process and so, it has well known benefits. The presence of interactive partners into an educational system creates more realistic social contexts, and increases the effectiveness of the system. As Vygotsky (1978) pointed out, "in a collaborative scenario, students interchange their ideas for coordinating when they working for reaching common goals. When dilemmas arise, the discussion process involves them in learning". When the learners work in groups they reflect upon their ideas (and those of their colleagues'), explain their

DOI: 10.4018/978-1-60566-786-7.ch003

opinions, consider and discuss those of others, and as a result, learn. In this way, each learner acquires individual knowledge from the collaborative interaction. A collaborating environment would help sustain the learner's interests and would provide a more natural learning habitat. Collaborative learning deals with instructional methods that seek to promote learning through collaborative efforts among learners working on a given learning task. As the importance of collaborative learning is widely accepted in learning theorists, implementation of collaborative learning in Learning Management Systems (LMSs) arises as of crucial interest. The three basic factors in collaborative learning are: the tutor, the learner and his/her co learner. The role of the late is crucial. Many students emerge from basic science courses with inabilities to apply the scientific concepts or principles that they ostensibly learned, with significant misconceptions, and with poor problem solving abilities. They need to, and they use to address questions and so they expect to get answers. Tutors respond to their questions with accuracy and their responses are also characterized for their educational value. This is not the case when the learner addresses questions to his co learner. A co learner responds inaccurately and in many cases gives fault answers. Even so, the presence of a co learner is meaningful. Therefore, it is crucial for researchers to focus their attention on the design of systems capable to integrate a simulated co learner. The goal of building a computerized Simulated Student (VanLehn et al. 1994) is to facilitate the learner's own efforts at learning by employing cooperative learning techniques.

Computer Supported Collaborative Learning (CSCL) offers students many advantages and so delivers a collaborative environment that deals with "learning". Such system can take an active part in analysing and controlling collaboration. Learners exchange ideas and reflect upon other points of view. A **CSCL** usually is supported by a system of simulated learners that play various roles in collaborating learning. In fact, simulated learner can be simultaneously an expert and a co learner, scaffolding and guiding the humans' learning in subtle ways. It also provides an attractive environment for learning skills of problem solving. To Polya (28), problem solving was a major theme of doing mathematics and "teaching students to think" was of primary importance. "How to think" is a theme that underlies much of genuine inquiry and problem solving in mathematics. Collaboration experience can also facilitate planning and problem solving. Blaye et al. [Blaye et al. 1990, Blaye1989] showed that children who had previously worked as collaborative pairs on the task of planning and problem solving were twice as successful as children who had had the same amount of experience working alone. In CSCL students involved in planning and problem solving tasks, interact to each other asking questions and explaining answers. Based on the above remarks, a new question arises: Is there any way the digitized material formed from all the questions and explanations produced by the CSCLs' users, to be reused?

The scope of this chapter is to provide a starting point for the development of a system capable to collect and to store digitized material (in question above) produced by CSCLs' users to the purpose of reuse it. Furthermore, the proposed system should be able to manage such material in the best possible way in favor of real learners. Therefore, the proposed system has to be adaptive to learner. It also has to make use standards in order to classify and retrieve the stored material in the best possible way.

There are several points of view to look at such an issue. In what follows, a Virtual co Learner (VcL) capable to collaborate by asking questions or by responding in the form of explanations to questions posed by the real learner is presented. Research over the last fifteen years has provided solid evidence that generating explanations can lead to deeper understanding when learning new material. There remain however, many unanswered questions about the factors that influence the effectiveness of an explanation. One of those factors is the presence of a learning partner. The main problem the proposed VcL tries to solve is the establishment of a flexible dialogue between real co learner and VcL that will help keep the real learner's exploration going, by occasionally prompting with questions or responding to questions posed by real learners.

A secondary goal of this work is to explore ways in which VcL can be adaptive. Learning partner's contribution on learning procedure becomes more efficient in the presence of identically same to the real learner's cognitive characteristics. As we consider adaptivity as an important issue, we focus our attention on a number of properties that VcL should have in order to be adaptive to the real learner's needs in the CSCL environment. Among other properties, the VcL should appear to be cognitively similar to the collaborating real co learner. That is, the adopted learning profile, i.e. the learning style, the cognitive style and learning behavior, should match to the real learner's learning profile.

This chapter has a number of sections. In order to design the VcL we describe in the chapter's first section the background one can rely on. The background shows mainly how attractive the idea of introducing a virtual classmate is, and the different approaches on the collaborative asynchronous e-learning that appeared so far.

The following section exposes a suggested distributed architecture capable to store and manage digitized material (items in the form of questions and responses or explanations appeared in CSCL systems).

Detailed information about the form and the functionality of VcL's data bases are given in the next section of this chapter. Data bases are spread in varius spots of the distributed system's architecture. In the sequence data bases will be referred as VcL's items repositories. Learning companion's contribution on learning procedure gains added value if it responds to the student's learning needs as they governed by his/her cog-

nitive characteristics. This should be considered as an additional dimension that can add value on the computerized simulated learner design. As it appeared in the next chapter's section, once a suitable learning behavior is chosen, the VcL is called to response to a great number of different questions or to suggest various actions. Taking under consideration the great deal of differences between tutor and co-learner, the system tunes the second, allowing even a small number of wrong answers and suggestions. In this way VcL combines roles of learning companion and trouble maker. VcL's responses can be withdrawn adaptively from a VcL's

Finally, aiming to increase the VcL's influence in the learning process, efforts have been done to discuss the proposed system's monitoring and evaluation issue. The evaluation issue of VcL and its influence to the learning procedure will be discussed. Taking advandage of the evaluation's feedback, VcL becomes able to apply simple control techniques that result on the fine tuning of its functionality. This last part of the proposed architecture aims to the optimization of VcL's contribution to the learning procedure.

BACKGROUND

As the Internet and World Wide Web are rapidly developed, the technologies that support the educational processes come closer to the traditional educational systems. Taking advance of technological evolution, asynchronous e-learning shows an accelerating progress in adapting methods capable to introduce functionalities such as adaptivity, reusability or interoperability. On the other hand asynchronous e-learning faces a number of questions on certain pedagogical issues that strongly influences its efficiency. Among such issues we focus on the isolation of learner in front of an interface. Crucial issues posed by educators, such as the boredom effect, the absence of socialization and the luck to self confidence has to be faced as researchers put efforts to develop LMSs. Taking an extensive look at related to the theme bibliography one may see the increasing interest researchers show. VanLehn et al (1993) proposed for a single episode of learning a simulated learner that was given two inputs: (a) a formal representation of the relevant parts of real learner's knowledge prior to the episode (b) a formal representation of the instructions given to the real learner. The model produces two outputs: (a) a formal representation of the real's knowledge just after the instruction and (b) a formal representation of the student's behavior during the learning episode. Before this effort many simulated learners appeared in bibliography. A suitable classification along two dimensions: the granularity of their knowledge and processes and the extent to which their model of learning is table-driven (Anderson 1988, Dillenburg and Self 1992, VanLehn 1988).

Collaboration is rather unanimously considered as one of the most important qualities of meaningful and effective learning (Jonassen, 1995; DeCorte, 1993) and it is often suggested that computer-support for learning should include also supports for collaborative action. In many Intelligent Tutoring Systems (ITS) developments of a cooperative approach between the learner and the system simulated various forms of collaborating partners such as the learning companion and the trouble maker, which are called pedagogical actors, (Frasson et al (1996); Frasson & Aimeur 1997). Simulated learners have only recently become available, even though the idea is not new Doak and Keith, 1986). Vizcaino introduced a type of agent that simulates a learner's behavior and interacts with others in a group as if it were a real learner. Vizcaino's simulated learner mission is the detection and avoidance of negative situations that decrease the benefits of the collaborative learning. The model was designed for synchronous and distributed collaboration, thus enabling learners to collaborate at the same time although they are in different geographical places. Goodman B. et.al. (1998) introduced ITS equipped with modules

to support cooperative activities. Their Learning Companion supports collaboration between two real learners. Since then a vast number of research papers appeared presenting technical approaches to the question of the Co-learner functionality. Authors restrict their work on synchronous e-learning as they required at least two participants willing to learn thought collaboration. Chan and Baskin (1988) proposed a simulated co-learner acted as a peer in an intelligent tutoring environment that ensured the availability of a collaborator. The goal of their work was to promote more effective instructional exchanges between a student and an ITS. The proposed system provides a simulated peer as a partner for the student in learning and problem solving.

Chan and Baskin (Chan & Baskin, 1988; Chan, 1991) implemented a collaborative learning environment called *Integration-Kid* for the domain of symbolic integration. In *Integration-Kid* the learner collaborates with a simulated *companion* to learn integration. The system provides more dimensions of learning, higher motivation, and better attitude toward learning through collaboration. According to P. Brusilovsky (2003), this is a main issue in developing AEHS. A simulated learner that operates adaptively to the real learner contributes significantly to the functionality of AEHSs.

According to Brusilovsky and Pyelo (2003), Adaptive and Intelligent Web-Based Educational Systems (AIWBES) provide an alternative to the traditional 'just-put-it-on-the-Web' approach in the development of Web-based educational courseware. In their work mention that AIWBES attempt to be more adaptive by building a model of the goals, preferences and knowledge of each individual student and using this model throughout the interaction with the system in order to be more intelligent by incorporating and performing some activities traditionally executed by a human teacher – such as coaching students or diagnosing misconceptions. One step further, activities performed by collaborating learners may be transferred and executed by intelligent educational systems. Hadiana and Kaijiri (2006) introduced an asynchronous web based system equipped with a kind of white board where students can act as questioners who ask some questions collaboratively to acquire additional knowledge, or act as respondents who answer questions posed from other students.

DISTRIBUTED SYSTEM'S ARCHITECTURE

VcL's functionality is based on a distributed system of servers, the associated databases, and a society of collaborating agents capable to imitate the behavior of a real co-learner. In a separate section we intend to present technical solutions that contribute to the functionality of the system. Interoperability, information sharing, scalability and dynamic integration of heterogeneous expert fields are considered as the major advantages of the proposed model.

a. Interoperability: support for available standards, technology and platform independentancy.
b. Information Sharing: user information, Learning Objects (LOs), services and assessment tools.
c. Scalability: continuous updating of each module functionality (questions related to Learning Objects, answers adoption, monitoring tools, cognition and learning style theories, sequencing and navigation algorithms).
d. Integration of heterogeneous expert field: independent module development and dynamic adaptation to the latest criteria.

As it said before, VcL's functionality is based on a system of collaborating servers. Each server hosts two repositories. One to store questions related to certain Learning Object (LO/Q) and the second

one to store the related to LO/Qs given answers (LO/A). The conceptual framework for creating distributed digital repositories of entries such that LO/Q and related to LO/A has been based on the DIENST system which provides the necessary specifications for the implementation of a protocol distributed storing and searching of multiple types (multi-format) data in an Internet environment. The DIENST servers accessed through ports from any Web Server that supports CGI (Common Gateway Interface). Applications to DIENST Protocol are placed inside the HTTP Hyper Text Transfer Protocol). In this way, DIENST exploits all the current features of the Internet and has the ability to support user authentication, and data classification standards (Lagoze C., Davis J.R., 1995, Lagoze, C., Shaw, E., Davis J. R., Krafft D. B., 1995)

The system's architecture is consisting of a number of distributed nodes (LO/Q and LO/A) able to present their data to the rest of the system's nodes (see figure 1). The more the system spreads in the worldwide academic environment; the biggest becomes the number of such nodes. In order to gain speed of LO/retrieval the systems architecture defines regions of grouped vertices. We may define an entire university with all its networked computers as a region facing the World Wide Web through a certain web server that serves as the regional server. It is a matter of the system's administrator strategic plan to decide the distribution of regions.

The VcL's framework is based on a protocol for service communication within the proposed architecture altogether with a software system that implements that protocol.

Major components of this architecture are:

*   A model for entries based on IEEE, LOM standards that incorporate unique naming, logical structuring, and multiple content-type disseminations.
*   A set of individually defined services that expose their operational semantics through an open protocol.

Figure 1. Connected basic elements in suggested distributed architecture

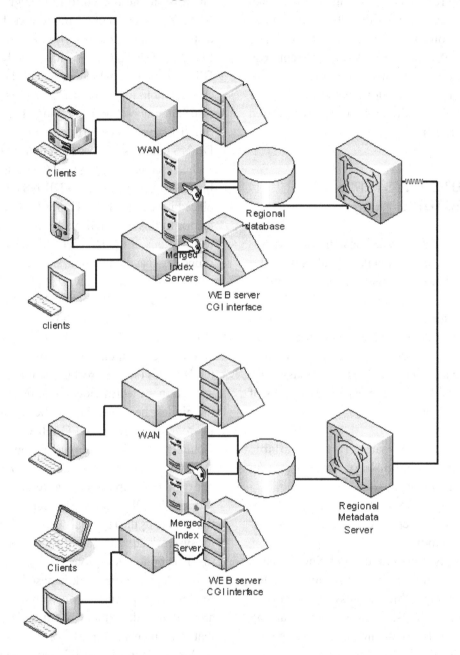

- A mechanism for combining services and entries into multiple collections.
- A mechanism for distributing collections among regions to facilitate global distribution.

The entries model allow for storage of both Q&As in text form. It also supports their dissemination of the A/LO in multiple variations. Main features of the entries model are:

- Bijective assigning metadata to entries using the IEEE's Learning Object Metadata following SCORM. Metadata to be assigned consist of a number of labels and its identity string.

- Logical structuring of entries with the following features:
  - Types of descriptive metadata associated with the LO that the entry concerns.
  - Hierarchical Conceptual structuring of each entry, such as keyword, subject, theme, area, that drives the aforementioned LO.

These features may easily be logically exposed through the protocol requests that provide access to Q&As entries. In the frame of VcL a categorisation of local servers has been done according to the major regions they provide services in the web topography. To support such an organizational schema, VcL introduces two kinds of servers: a server processing service area called Regional Metadata Server (RMS) and a server of merged directories called Merged Index Server (MIS). An area (region) consists of a server processing service (RMS), one or more servers merged indexes (MIS) and from normal servers standard sites). All the VcL servers belonging to a region acquire the metadata from the server processing service area (RMS). This in turn has modified meta-data which distributes every search directories on servers in the region.

VcL'S ITEMS REPOSITORIES

On the basis of the described system's architecture design, all of the Q&As full collections indexes are essentially stored on servers within the region. This can be achieved through MIS. MISs are responsible for collecting all indexes from other servers that do not belong in their own region and are supplied with functional **CSCL** systems. Thus the usual VcL servers in a region is responsible for indexing and support queries (A/LOs) coming through the area, while servers are merged indexes

support searches in the A/LO texts belonging to servers in other regions.

According to the above architectural shape, searches do not take place outside from the boundaries of a region. It is necessary a central Master Metadata Server (MMS). This is responsible for the complete definition of a collection of texts and for the meta-data exchange between RMS. In return, we consider as a system bondage the need for storing multiple copies of directories on several merged indexes servers in different regions. On the other hand, this can be considered to be an advantage, since it represents a method of replication to insure data loss protection. In this way it improves system reliability, especially in regard the performance of the network.

The VcL is designed so as to outline the questions tutors address to learners during the CSCL learning module (questions may be addressed by tutors as well, in case they consider question's instructive value of high importance)., to record the questions learners use to ask, and finally to store any given answer. It aims to the creation of Questions and Answers (Q&A) repositories capable to provide elements contributing to the activation of collaborative learning.

Therefore, it is necessary to supply the system with a number of data bases (VcLIRs) necessary for the storage of questions associated to learning objects in use, and answers provided by students at each question. In order to store Q&A in the system's VcLIRs, a window allows the entrance to the assorted «discussion's room». Questions or answers posted in the discussion's room window are stored in the regional Q&A repositories. In order to improve the effectiveness of Q&A storage, the need arises to supply questions or answers with special arrays of metadata. XML based metadata carry information that allows questions and answers to be managed, searched, used and reused by multiple applications for different purposes including some that are learning-procedure-critical. Thus they need to ensure that their storage technology can respond appropriately and quickly enough to meet the demands of their different learners.

Questions are stored as such in VcLIR. Each one of them is accompanied with a metadata array that adopted automatically. IEEE-LOM standards based metadata carry all the necessary pieces of information that make the question identifiable. Such information are: information describing the instruction material the given question refers to, its character, a short description, keywords, e.c. ..... . Due to their metadata every single question can be retrieved in first demand and can be reused in future time. Q&A retrieval achieved by collaborating agents. The system reuses questions in such a way that gives the impression that it has been posed by an on line real co-learner. Thus, every learner willing to make use of the LMS in the future (and under predefined conditions) will find an asking the question simulated co-learner ready to collaborate with.

It is expected that a number of submitted questions to be irrelevant, or of minor relevancy to the LO in use. The relevance of a question to the LO's main concept, determines the priority of its choice. Among the set of questions that are linked with a degree of relevancy to a certain LO, first priority of choice have the questions with the larger number of keywords, traceable in the LO's metadata. As of high priority also are considered questions that got larger numbers of answers before. Nevertheless, even the questions of low relevancy to LO, are eligible to be chosen, since they contribute in a way to the picture of a co-learner.

Every respond to a question that is stored to an A VcLIR, has an appended sequence of metadata that includes an inclusive three dimensional code vector, representing the regional server's code number (where the A VcLIR), the code number of the question to which is corresponded, and the number it has in the sequence of the given answers for the question in hands. Every learner who makes use of a LMS that includes a VcL system, is candidate to face questions related to the LO's concepts on real time.

Metadata standards in use are the LOM/IEEE standards. Therefore, a certain standards manipulation (see Botsios and Georgiou 2008) allows the implementation of the proposed Q&A recognition.

In figure 2 the suggested system is presented. There are four main parts in the picture:

1. the learning style recognition engine,
2. the group of regional servers were the learning object repositories are located altogether with Q&A VcLIRs
3. The relevance estimation engine installed in the system's MMS that governs Q&A retrieval and metadata's exchange.
4. The adaptive content provider. This module provides LO's and Q&A's as well. Its functionality is tailored to the user's learning style. That is, in order to adapt learning style, the system applies online diagnostic methods based either on Bayesian networks (Botsios S., Georgiou D., Safouris N.(2007): or on Fuzzy Cognitive Maps (Botsios S., Georgiou D., Safouris N. (2008)). Using such tools VcL becomes capable to recognize the learner's learning style and to adjust on it. As far as the system recognizes the learner's learning profile it becomes capable to synthesize the VcL's learning profile following a list of pre given rules. The system also monitors the learner's learning behavior (i.e. knowledge level evaluation, response time, e.t.c.) and interfere whenever is necessary. According to visited LO and user learning style –information that is send from the Learning Style recognition Engine- the relevance estimation engine is responsible to create the appropriate query to "ask" Q/LO or A/LO repositories for "relevant" entries (Qs or As). Algorithms proposed by Chen et al, (2005), and Watson et al (2007) could be applied to provide a taxonomy of "relevant" Q&A. More points of view about adaptivity

parameters and SCORM compliant LO repositories the reader will find in table 1. Crucial role in this taxonomy will also have the number of existing key words that are common to those that can be found in LO's metadata, and the number that shows how many times the answer reused successfully. Taking under consideration user learning styles and LOs metadata, these algorithms are inference engines that provide selection rules to filter Q&A/LOs from disperse and vast Q&A/LOs. SCORM compliant Q or A/ LO repositories receive a query and return a number of "relevant" Q or A/LO.

Items Repository (VcLIR) Q or A/LO using the IEEE/LOM standards. Table 1 contains a number of published results that deal with this issue. The Learner's Learning Profile data base (Figure 2) contains any information concerns learner's cognitive characteristics. Moreover it may keeps additional data such as personal user data, preferences data and history related data. It forwards user interactions to adaptivity parameters modules, receive their assessments and export a final filtered taxonomy of the Q or A/LO it have received.

5. Learning Style Recognition Engine. This module is dedicated to LS diagnosis. A suggestion for estimating learning style from user's interaction is proposed by Botsios S., and Georgiou D., (2008), (see table 1).

Figure 2. Relevance estimation engine retrieve data from a number of Q&A repositories

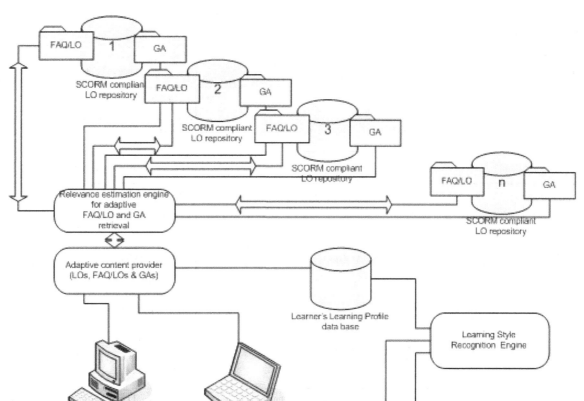

6. Competence Level. This module supports the assessment of user's knowledge and goals. The modified Item response theory from Chen et al, (2005) and SCO performance assessment from Watson et al (2007) are two alternatives for this purpose (see table 1).

7. Learning Style. Similarly to 5 and 6, this module produces results for user's LS. Milosevic et al (2007) developed a solution that "connects" user's learning style to specific learning objects metadata (see table 1).

8. Cognitive Style. This module is dedicated to estimate the user's CS. The module receives user interaction related data and exports an assessment. An example application is the Karampiperis et al (2005). Data about user navigation is used to export LOs metadata values (see table 1).

9. All the algorithms to provide adaptive navigation and adaptive presentation services are the last stage of this architecture. This module receives the filtered taxonomy of LOs, applies the appropriate algorithms and forwards the data to be displayed in the interface of the LMS.

MONITORING AND EVALUATING THE SYSTEM: RATE OF VcL ACTIVATION

The degree of the VcL's role contribution in a-synchronous an e-LMS is measured by the rate of its activation index. Each user of the system may ask or may not ask VcL for help. In the most of the bases, an increasing interest for collaboration is obseved. The system is supplied with a counter of the times a learner asks for help. The

Table 1. Adaptivity parameters and standards

Paper	adaptivity parameter – adaptivity type – assessment method	reference to standardization
Milosevic et al (2007)	learning style - adaptive navigation - Kolb Learning Style Inventory	\<LearningResourceType\> \<NavigationRules\>
	motivation - adaptive presentation - pre-, post-tests	\<educational\> \<semantic density\>
Watson et al (2007)	knowledge level - adaptive content retrieval - SCO performance assessment	SCORM interaction elements
Karampiperis et al (2006)	cognitive style - adaptive content retrieval - monitoring navigation steps	\<general\> \<structure\> \<aggregation_Level\> \<educational\> \<InteractivityType\> \<InteractivityLevel\> \<SemanticDensity\> \<Difficulty\> \<typicallearningtime\> \<learningresourcetype\>
Chen et al (2005)	knowledge level - adaptive content retrieval - modified Item Response Theory	\<general\> \<Description\> \<Keyword\> \<educational\> \<Difficulty\>
Chen et al (2005)	learning behavior - adaptive content retrieval - Dynamic Fuzzy Petri Net	Activity Tree of \<Organization\> SCORM Rollup Rules

system also keeps records about the time relative frequency a user activates VcL. Both, are useful to modulate the rate of VcL activation index and the average rate of VcL activation index as well. The first concerns the rhythm an individual learner stimulates the system, as the second concerns the total updated output one gets from all the users of the VcL. Such indices give update information about the acceptance of the system. VcL's system administrators may intervene to "clear" Off-Topic or irrelevant Q&As that may disturb the system's reliability.

It is expected that in real time applications of the system, suitable "filters" may be applied to the purpose of excluding annoying Q&As from recording in Q&A repositories. The idea is to make use of the previously described indices in order to energize the filters.

Monitoring and Evaluating the System: Evaluation of VcL's Influence on Learning

One role of the VcL is to help the real learner to understand better some concepts or to overcome certain misunderstandings whenever he/she is lost on problem solving situations. Whenever this happened the VcL supported learners by asking questions or giving answers. The evaluation of the VcL's effectiveness can be done in many ways. The simpler one can be by the installation of a counter that keeps track of the number of times a learner ask he VcL for help. It would be more valuable if such inputs can be combined with evaluations of the learner's knowledge level referring a certain concept, or on a learning module. A schema for keeping tracks on the above mentioned multivariable index has been defined by a sequence of questions such as:

- How many times a learner working on certain LO's concept ask VcL for help?
- How many answers on each specific question the learner rejects before the final

acceptance?
- Did the VcL intervention help learner to understand the specific concept in LO? Evaluation of a Q or A comes out from the evaluation of the learner's progress on the related concept.
- What is the percentage rate of learners who influenced positively by VcL's intervention?

A second role of the proposed system concerns the detection of the Off-Topic Q&A. This ability of the VcL is based on the relevancy measure i.e. the number of LO's keywords included in the question and the number of rejections an answer counts. Using such indices the system reevaluate the Q&As relevancy to the LO's concept and rearrange their ranking.

Monitoring and Evaluating the System: VcL's Optimization Based on Evaluation Results

Educators, who have professional points of view on stored Q&A and may have system administrator's rights, are eligible to offer their support to the VcL's functional optimization. It is recommended that experts should intervene to the system whenever the average rate of VcL activation tends to decline, or even whenever the evaluation index of influence on learning shows that the system increases the boredom effect on user.

CONCLUSIONS AND FUTURE WORKS

It is the author's strong intention was and remains to keep working on the problem of collaborative learning in asynchronous e-learning environments. To the best of the authors' knowledge, there is a lack in this research area. Moreover, the demand to apply such systems in adaptive environments makes the problem more interesting. The proposed architecture shows that such attempts are possible. In the future more sophisticated architectures will appear and simulated learners will act more efficiently supporting other areas of collaborative learning, such as the problem solving situation. Authors believe that the proposed architecture will add some ideas to approach the problem more efficiently in the very next future.

The VcL system's implementation in laboratory, allows us being very optimistic for its real www application. The educational platform that has been used is the e-Class. It would be convenient to add an explanation about the integration of VcL and e-Class or any other LMS platform used by the consortium of Greek Universities GUnet. E-Class version 1.7.2 or any other LMS. E-Class is an open source code program and easily one may append new systems. The system should also be included in other LMS platforms, to collaborate with. It is expected that bugs that may appear in such large scale application will easily be eliminated.

In specific, the proposed chapter contains basic knowledge gained in the in-lab application and it lacks of any experience from large scale application. All of the system's parts and techniques described are applicable in an on-line learning environment. It remains to see working as a whole as it works in lab applications. Also, in the description of the proposed VcL, one can find some important principles that can add value to the design of a distributed and modular LMS. These principles can be extended in groupware systems in e-learning environments. The example of a virtual-co-learner that triggers user's interest in the learning process is presented.

ACKNOWLEDGMENT

This work is supported in the frame of Operational Programme "COMPETITIVENESS", 3rd Community Support Program, co financed by the public sector of the European Union – European Social Fund and 25% by the Greek Ministry of Development – General Secretariat of Research and Technology.

REFERENCES

A.D.L. (2006). *SCORM 2004 3rd edition, sharable content object reference model*. Alexandria, VA: Advanced Distributed Learning.

Anderson, J. R. (1988). The expert module. In M. Polson & J. J. Richardson (Eds.), *Foundations of intelligent tutoring systems*. Hillsdale, NJ: Lawrence Erlbaum Associates.

Botsios, S., & Georgiou, D. (2008). Recent adaptive e-learning contributions towards a standard ready architecture. In *Proceedings of the 5th International Conference on Adaptive Hypermedia and Adaptive Web-Based Systems*, Hannover, Germany

Botsios, S., Georgiou, D., & Safouris, N. (2007). Learning style estimation via Bayesian networks. In *Proceedings of the WEBIST 2007*, Barcelona, Spain.

Botsios, S., Georgiou, D., & Safouris, N. (2008). Contributions to adaptive educational hypermedia systems via on-line learning style estimation. [IEEE]. *Journal of Educational Technology & Society, 11*(3), 322–339.

Botsios, S., Mitropoulou, V., Georgiou, D., & Panapakidis, I. (2006). *Design of virtual co-learner for asynchronous collaborative e-learning*. Paper presented at the Sixth International Conference on Advanced Learning Technologies, ICALT 2006.

Brusilovsky, P. (2003). Developing adaptive educational hypermedia systems: From design models to authoring tools. In T. Murray, S. Blessing, & S. Ainworth (Eds.), *Authoring tools for advancing technology learning environment* (pp. 377-409). Dordrecht, The Netherlands: Kluwer Academic Publishers.

Brusilovsky, P., & Miller, P. (2001). Course delivery systems for the virtual universities. In T. Tschang & T. Della Senta (Eds.), *Access to knowledge: New information technologies and the emergence of virtual university* (pp. 167-206). Amsterdam: Elsevier Science.

Brusilovsky, P., & Pyelo, C. (2003). Adaptive and intelligent Web-based educational systems. *International Journal of Artificial Intelligence in Education, 13*(2-4), 159–172.

Chan, T. W., & Baskin, A. B. (1990). Learning companion system. In C. Frasson & G. Gauthier (Eds.), *Intelligent tutoring systems: At the crossroad of artificial intelligence and education* (pp. 6-33). Norwood, NJ: Ablex.

Chen, C. M., Lee, H. M., & Chen, Y. H. (2005). Personalized e-learning system using item response theory. *Computers & Education, 44*(3), 237–255. doi:10.1016/j.compedu.2004.01.006

Chen, J. N., Huang, Y. M., & Chu, W. C. C. (2005). Applying dynamic fuzzy petri net to Web learning system. *Interactive Learning Environments, 13*(3), 159-178. doi:10.1080/10494820500382810

Dillenbourg, P., & Self, J. (1992). A framework for learner modeling. *Interactive Learning Environments, 2*(2), 111–137. doi:10.1080/1049482920020202

Dillenbourg, P., & Self, J. (1992). People power: A human-computer collaborative learning system. In *Proceedings of the Second Int'l Conf. Intelligent Tutoring Systems* (pp. 651-660). Berlin, Germany: Springer Verlag.

e-Class. (2008). *Open eClass portal*. Retrieved December 10, 2008, from http://www.openeclass.org/

Frasson, C., & Aimeur, E. (1997). Lessons learned from a university-industry cooperative project in tutoring systems. *Int. J. Failures and Lessons learned in Information Technology Management, 1*(2) 149-157.

Frasson, C., Mengelle, T., Aimeur, E., et al. (1996). An Actor-based architecture for intelligent tutoring systems. In C. Frasson, G. Gauthier, & A. Legold (Eds.), *Proceedings of the ITS'96 Conference, Third International Conference on Intelligent Tutoring Systems* (LNCS 1086, pp. 57-65). Berlin, Germany: Springer.

Goodman, B., Soller, A., Linton, F., & Gaimari, R. (1998). Encouraging student reflection and articulation using a learning companion. *International Journal of Artificial Intelligence in Education, 9*(3-4).

Hadiana, A., & Kaijiri, K. (2002). The construction of asynchronous Q&A support system. In *Information Technology Letters Forum on Information Technology* (pp. 249-250).

Hadiana, A., Zhang, T., Ampornaramveth, V., & Ueno, H. (2006). WEB e-learning based on concept of online whiteboard. *WEBIST, (2)*. 387-391.

(IMS), I. M. S. (2001). *IMS learner information packaging information model specification*. Instructional Management Systems.

Jonassen, D. (1995). Supporting communities of learners with technology: A vision for integrating technology with learning in schools. *Educational Technology*, (July/August): 60–63.

Karampiperis, P., & Sampson, D. (2005). Adaptive learning resources sequencing in educational hypermedia systems. *Educational Technology and Society, 8*(4), 128–147.

Kolb, D. A. (1999). *Learning style inventory - version 3: Technical specifications.* TRG Hay/McBer, Training Resources Group.

Lagoze, C., & Davis, J. R. (1995). Dienst: An architecture for distributed document libraries. *Communications of the ACM, 38*(4), 47. doi:10.1145/205323.205331

Lagoze, C., Shaw, E., Davis, J. R., & Krafft, D. B. (1995). *Dienst: Implementation reference manual* (TR95-1514). Cornell University, USA.

Milosevic, D. (2006). Designing lesson content in adaptive learning environments. *International Journal of Emerging Technologies in Learning, 1*(2).

Milosevic, D., Brkovic, M., Debevc, M., & Krneta, R. (2007). Adaptive learning by using SCOs metadata. *Interdisciplinary Journal of Knowledge and Learning Objects, 3,* 163–174.

Safouris, N., Botsios, N., & Georgiou, D. (2007). Some approaches in learning style diagnosis. In *Proceedings of the ICICTE 2007,* Patras, Greece.

Vanlehn, K. (1988). Student modeling. In M. Polson & J. J. Richardson (Eds.), *Foundations of intelligent tutoring systems.* Hillsdale, NJ: Laurence Erlbaum & Associates.

Vanlehn, K., Ohlsson, S., & Nason, R. (1994). Applications of simulated students: An exploration. *Journal of Artificial Intelligence in Education, 5*(2), 135–175.

Vygotsky, L. S. (1978). *Mind in society: The development of higher psychological processes.* Cambridge, MA: Harvard University Press.

Watson, J., Ahmed, P. K., & Hardaker, G. (2007). Creating domain independent adaptive e-learning systems using the sharable content object reference model. *Campus-Wide Information Systems, 24*(1), 45–71. doi:10.1108/10650740710726482

Chapter 4

Time–Shifted Online Collaboration:
Creating Teachable Moments Through Automated Grading

Edward Brent
Idea Works, Inc., and University of Missouri, USA

Curtis Atkisson
Idea Works, Inc., and University of Missouri, USA

Nathaniel Green
Idea Works, Inc., USA

ABSTRACT

This chapter examines online collaboration in a distributed e-learning environment. The authors describe the emerging technology of Web-based automated essay grading that provides extensive real-time data for monitoring and enhancing e-learning activities. They examine data from student use of this software service in a large introductory social science class. Using information routinely collected by the system, the authors find that students take advantage of this learning environment to revise and resubmit essays, dramatically improving their final grade by an average of 20% or two letter grades. They conclude the essential components of this learning environment that makes it so successful are its ability to provide detailed, personalized feedback to students immediately after they submit their work along with the opportunity to revise and resubmit. This transforms an automated assessment tool into a powerful collaborative learning environment. Instead of waiting days or weeks for instructor comments, that feedback is time-shifted to occur at the time it can be most effective for students. Changing the timing of feedback creates a powerful teachable moment when students have motivation, information, opportunity, and feedback. They are motivated to improve their grade, they are told what they did right or wrong while the relevant information is fresh in their minds, and they have the opportunity to revise and resubmit. The chapter ends with consideration of how those same elements can be, and sometimes already are, used in other instructional strategies such as podcasting to create effective learning environments that take advantage of the teachable moment.

DOI: 10.4018/978-1-60566-786-7.ch004

INTRODUCTION: STUDENT – INSTRUCTOR COLLABORATION

The relationship between students and instructors takes many forms. In traditional large lecture course communication is mostly one-way with very little interaction. Most class time is devoted to the instructor lecturing passive students. Then, a few times a semester student performance is evaluated in tests. The role of the instructor is primarily to lecture and evaluate student performance. There is little or no two-way communication between instructor and student. In contrast, the constructivist classroom (Jonassen et al., 1999) provides a collaborative learning environment in which the instructor's role is guiding students, coaching them to help them learn. In such a classroom there is repeated interaction between instructor and student as the student benefits from instructor feedback to enhance their understanding and, not incidentally, improve their grade. The constructivist environment is a collaborative learning environment in which students learn from repeated instructor feedback.

Increasingly, that collaboration takes place online. Distributed online environments provide the benefits of space-shifting: students and instructors need not be in the same place to interact effectively. This dramatically expands learning opportunities for many, increasing access and reducing travel costs and time. However, some of these new online environments have the ability to provide not only space-shifting but also *time-shifting*. "Many times learners are more interested in time-shifting capabilities provided by technology-based distance education systems than they are in the location-shifting capabilities of the systems" (Major & Levenburg, 1999). Unfortunately, synchronous collaboration which is the most effective is often impractical, while asynchronous collaboration is much easier to arrange but less effective for learning.

Synchronous collaboration (as exemplified by traditional classrooms, telephone conversations, or chat rooms) requires students and instructors to engage in interaction at the same time. The importance of interaction in learning is widely recognized from many perspectives, though it may often be described as "engagement," "participation," or "collaboration." It is widely agreed that "learning rarely takes place solely through unidirectional instruction. The social process of interaction is required for optimal learning (Lave & Wegner, 1991)." Many studies have found that some form of participatory interaction by students is critical to their success in face-to-face and in distance education courses (Kearsley, 1995); (Sutton, 2001). This engagement is illustrated by what it must have been like for Plato and Socrates to participate in a Socratic dialogue[1]. There the instructor and student are simultaneously focused on the learning task. The student can ask questions and immediately receive a response from the instructor. The instructor can gauge the student's progress and decide when she is ready to go on to more advanced material. If the student makes a mistake, the instructor can immediately point out the problem and explain what they did wrong.

Synchronous interaction encourages such engagement. But it does so at a cost. Merely putting instructor and student in the same room at the same time does not assure effective collaboration. Synchronicity requires students to learn on the same schedule that instructors teach, something that can be inconvenient or impossible for students whose work schedule causes them to miss classes. Worse yet, it may impose a schedule for learning on students that does not fit their optimal learning times (witness students sleeping in class, doodling, or surfing the web with their laptops). Likewise, it can impose a schedule on instructors that conflicts with other activities (e.g., when students all submit papers at the same time just before a holiday, or call the instructor's home at night with questions).

Asynchronous collaboration, typified by email or discussion group postings, does not require that everyone participate at the same time and is often easier to arrange, but may require long waits for a response from the instructor/collaborator. This reduces the interactive dynamic of the collaboration and may render learning less effective. For example, in large classes it often takes days or weeks to grade papers and students may have forgotten many of the key points in their essay. Often there is a "breakdown in conversational 'flow' due to the lack of continuity in the discussion over an extended timescale" (Hewson & Laurent, 2008); (Bowker & Tuffin, 2004); (Murray & Sixsmith, 1998). Because grading essays is a time-consuming and often onerous process for instructors, students are rarely given the opportunity to revise their essays. Instead of a learning environment in which students learn through collaborative interaction with the instructor, it is primarily an assessment environment in which students get one chance to achieve their grade. There is a temporal gap, and often a large one, between when students are primed to learn and when they have the guidance they need to benefit from that feedback. Even when they receive the feedback there may be no opportunity to capitalize on it through revisions.

This breakdown in interaction between student and instructor threatens learning. This chapter describes how an automated essay grading system, SAGrader™, can be used to implement a collaborative learning environment for e-learning that has the *convenience* of asynchronous collaboration and the *power* of synchronous collaboration. This method of collaboration in effect *time-shifts* instructor responses and assessments of student work. It allows the instructor to specify assistive knowledge to the student at a time convenient for the instructor. Then it allows the student to interact with the instructor-provided materials through assessments on the student's time frame. In this learning environment, students submit essays and immediately find out their grade, receive detailed feedback, and have the opportunity to revise their work. Students just received their grade and are motivated to improve it. They see detailed

feedback to guide that revision. They have just completed the previous draft and have the necessary information in their grasp. For instructors, automated grading makes it possible to permit students to revise multiple times with little or no additional effort for the instructor. Together, these elements—motivation, information, feedback, and opportunity—create a uniquely powerful "*teachable moment*" analogous to the teachable moment for smoking cessation when someone is diagnosed with lung cancer (Gritz et al., 2006).

In this chapter we describe how SAGrader™ works, compare it to other automated essay grading programs less suitable for this task, and show how it can be used to implement a collaborative learning environment. We examine data from a classroom application of SAGrader™ and show how it creates a collaborative relationship between instructor and students, examining how students take advantage of that opportunity, showing how their performance improves as a result, and reporting student assessments that reflect on the collaborative aspects of the course made possible by SAGrader™. In the process we address two of the themes of this book: how to provide for ongoing assessment in collaborative learning environments and how to effectively and efficiently manage computing resources in the distributed systems over which the collaborative learning system is implemented.

USING SAGrader™ TO ENHANCE THE COLLABORATIVE LEARNING ENVIRONMENT

Computer-supported collaborative learning is learning that takes place through computer-assisted dialogue among students and between students and instructors (Findley, 1988). While the term is most often used to describe systems in which student peers collaborate to produce a joint product, instructors are inevitably involved to assess learning and the collaboration between student and instructor is of equal importance. When the opportunity for repeated feedback is available this collaboration between student and instructor can be extensive. SAGrader™ is an online automated essay grading service developed by Idea Works, Inc (Brent et al., 2006); (Brent & Townsend, 2007). SAGrader™ permits students to submit essays at any time over the world-wide-web using standard web browsers. Once their essay is submitted, SAGrader™ employs a number of artificial intelligence strategies to automatically grade the essay. Students receive immediate feedback indicating their grade along with detailed comments indicating what they did well and what needs further work. Since SAGrader™ grades essays automatically it is practical to permit students to revise their work and resubmit it for grading as often as instructors will allow. The effect for students is something analogous to immediate collaboration with the instructor while they are writing and rewriting their paper. SAGrader™ is currently in use in both on-site and online courses in several disciplines and at a range of educational institutions.

SAGrader™ can interface seamlessly with other more broadly collaborative systems since it can be accessed through an Application Programming Interface or can be "skinned" (made to appear like other applications). SAGrader™ addresses one of the major concerns of this book -- there are no standard models to monitor and perform efficient assessment of activity in online collaborative working and learning environments to guide and support the development of efficient collaborative projects. SAGrader™ provides one such mechanism for assessing performance in collaborative environments. It provides assessments of writing and hence can assess higher-level reasoning (Bloom, 1956) instead of the rote memory and recall assessed by multiple choice tests. It is also more objective, faster, and more economical than human scorers (Rudner & Gagne, 2001); (Yang et al., 2001), hence suitable for larger populations.

RELATED WORK: AUTOMATED ESSAY GRADING

SAGrader™ is one of several commercially available programs for automated essay grading, including the Intelligent Essay Assessor (Landauer et al., 2000), the Electronic Essay Rater developed by Burstein and her colleagues at the Educational Testing Service (Burstein, 2003), and the Intellimetric program (Elliot, 2003). These programs are playing an increasing role in assessment and instruction; however, SAGrader™ differs in important ways from most of those other programs.

Many automated essay grading programs are based on statistical models, judging essays by how they compare to other good and bad essays. Criterion, Vantage, and IEA all employ a statistical model for developing and assessing the automated grading model. In each case human graders must first grade many (usually several hundred) essays. Those overall grades are then used as the "gold standard" to fit or "train" statistical models predicting scores assigned by human graders from features of essays measured by the programs (Yang et al., 2001). Once trained, the resulting model can then be used to assign grades to papers in the test set without human graders. Unfortunately, while these programs can determine if an essay looks more like good essays than bad ones, they have difficulty providing useful feedback to tell students how they could improve their score. Other early essay grading programs (Page, 1994) emphasized writing style over substance (Deane, 2006) and often measured proxies that correlated with good writing rather than features of good writing.

However, both of these approaches are often found wanting. Chung and Baker (Chung & Baker, 2003) review the literature assessing the reliability and validity of automated essay grading programs and conclude that where there is a correct answer or a range of correct answers, the sensible "gold standard" for judging good writing is not whether it displays indirect measures that correlate with human readers' scores (Page, 1966; Page, 1994) or whether it matches documents having similar scores (Landauer et al., 1998); (Landauer et al., 1997). The important issue is not *consistency* with human graders who, after all, are notoriously inconsistent in their grading (Bejar & Mislevy, 2006) but the *validity* of the scores as measured by the fit of student essays to the knowledge that must be expressed in good essays. Valid measures will have the added advantage of providing *informative feedback* that can be used by teachers and students to improve, and to detect differences in writing as a result of instruction (Chung & Baker, 2003). To be effective at creating a collaborative learning environment an essay grading program must focus on substantive content rather than writing style (Deane, 2006) and must provide informative feedback to guide student revisions. SAGrader™ does both of these things.

These programs use a wide range of natural language processing strategies (Cole, 1997) for recognizing important features in essays. Intelligent Essay Assessor (IEA) by Landauer, Foltz and Lahm (1998) employs a purely statistical approach, latent semantic analysis (LSA). This approach treats essays like a "bag of words" using a matrix of word frequencies by essays and factor analysis to find an underlying semantic space. It then locates each essay in that space and assesses how closely it matches essays with known scores. E-rater uses a combination of statistical and linguistic approaches. It uses syntactic, discourse structure, and content features to predict scores for essays after the program has been trained to match human coders. SAGrader™ uses a strategy that blends linguistic, statistical, and AI into a computational intelligence approach. It uses *fuzzy logic* (Zadeh, 1965) to detect key features in student papers, a *semantic network* (Sowa & Borgida, 1991) to represent the semantic information that should be present in good essays, and *rule-based expert systems* (Benfer et al., 1991); (Braun et al., 2006) to compute scores based on how well a student's constructed responses match explicit standards of semantic content for good essays.

The operation of SAGrader™ is illustrated in Figure 1. The instructor first specifies the task or assignment in a prompt. Then the instructor creates a rubric identifying "desired features"—key elements of substantive knowledge that should be included in a good response, along with relationships among those elements. For example, one SAGrader™ assignment asks the student to describe important characteristics of two well-known sociologists. The rubric specified that students should include several *desired features* in their essay, including the sociologist's name, the dates they were born and died, the country or countries in which they lived, the name of a theory for which they are known, one or more key concepts they first defined as part of that theory, and the title of an important publication of theirs related to that theory. The *desired relationships* students should express include correctly linking each sociologist to the correct theory, concept, publication, and so on. That rubric is then expressed in SAGrader™ as a semantic network or concept map. A partial semantic network for this essay showing information for a single sociologist is illustrated in Figure 2.

Figure 1. SAGrader™ logic

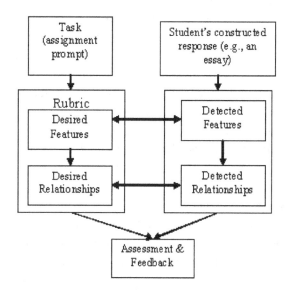

Figure 2. A partial semantic network (© 2008, Idea Works Inc. Used with permission.)

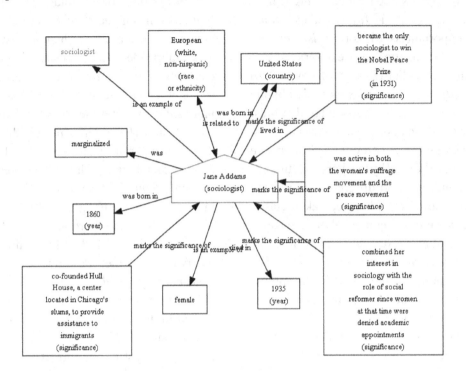

A number of computational intelligence strategies, noted above, are used by SAGrader™. Fuzzy logic permits the program to recognize literally thousands of word combinations that can be used to detect desired features in the student's essay, including not just concepts but also forms of reasoning and argument important for that discipline. Next, desired features based on the assignment and represented in the semantic network are compared to those detected in the student essay. Finally, an expert system using procedural rules scores student essays based on the similarities and differences between the desired and observed features. Detailed feedback for the student indicates what they did right and wrong, and provides a detailed breakdown of how points were assigned along with their overall score for the assignment.

SAGrader™ is suitable for a wide range of problems, problems with more than one good answer, and problems of varying difficulty. As-signments can ask about virtually any substantive knowledge instructors might want to assess. Even though SAGrader™ compares desirable features of good answers with features found in student essays, that still leaves great flexibility. These desired features can assess more abstract rhetorical goals as well as specific substantive knowledge. These features can be extensive, with many options, and considerable diversity. Assignments can permit students to include any of several possible correct answers, and question difficulty can be varied by giving students more or fewer options and requiring only some of the many possible correct answers. SAGrader™ has been used in sociology, psychology, English, biology, business, journalism, and several other disciplines. It could be used in any discipline where the instructor can specify the kinds of learning objectives students should meet in their essays.

Different instructors and different institutions use SAGrader™ in different ways. Not all of these create collaborative learning environments that take advantage of the teachable moment. Assignments may be required for credit or optional self-study exercises. Instructors may permit only a single draft, a specific number of drafts, or unlimited drafts of an assignment. The program's grade may be the final student grade or instructors may review the final draft and have the option of changing the student's grade. Feedback can be configured to provide informative guidance to students for further revision, or it can provide the final detailed summary suitable for self-study. How instructors configure SAGrader™ to work has a good deal to do with the kind of learning environment created. This chapter examines the use of SAGrader™ where students complete writing assignments *for credit*, receive *immediate feedback designed to guide* students as they make revisions while not telling them everything they will ultimately need to learn, and students are given the *opportunity* to revise their essays as many times as they wish. Together these three conditions fulfill the requirements for a teachable moment.

EFFICIENTLY MANAGING COMPUTER RESOURCES

A second major concern of this book is the efficient management of computer resources in the distributed systems over which collaborative groupware learning systems are implemented. This poses a significant issue for SAGrader™ because in order to effectively time-shift it is important that feedback be immediate. The specific time required to provide feedback in one recent class ranged from between six and eight seconds for five simpler assignments to between 19 and 26 seconds for the five most complex assignments. The overall mean response time for all assignments was 19 seconds.

However, students often wait until the last minute to submit their assignments and in very

busy times students might have to wait until other essays are graded before theirs is graded. Even when that happened in this course 99% of all essays were graded within one minute and the longest wait time was 81 seconds. So at this time the program is able to provide a very quick response even during peak time periods that effectively time-shifts instructor feedback to students to capture the teachable moment.

As use of SAGrader™ scales up, bursts of activity can be handled by the Amazon Cloud, a grid computing technology permitting SAGrader™ to automatically adjust the number of available microprocessors devoted to grading as a function of load. Only a few processors are in use all the time for essay grading and as student submissions increase additional processors are cloned and put into operation.

THE ROLE OF FEEDBACK IN CREATING A COLLABORATIVE LEARNING ENVIRONMENT

A key aspect of SAGrader™ that makes it a collaborative learning environment is the design of feedback. This feedback is *assistive*, not *exhaustive*. Rather than showing students a complete answer, this feedback tries to point students in the direction of a complete answer, leaving it up to students to review the study materials and determine how to address the critique. In effect, the feedback is designed so that students could paste the feedback into their essay and still not improve their score.

This feedback strategy can be illustrated with a specific example. In this assignment students were asked to (among other things) read a hypothetical life history, identify six concepts related to social stratification, and define each concept.[2] Here is an example of the kind of feedback one student received regarding identifying the concepts:

You received partial credit for identifying 4 items that are illustrated in Janice's autobiography: "working class," "welfare," "meritocracy," "working poor," and "structural mobility." You should also identify 2 more.

Notice the student is told the specific items they got right, while they are only told the kind of items they missed, but not the specific items. The student must identify the missing items themselves.

Next the student received detailed feedback regarding definitions of the concepts. Note that feedback is only provided for concepts students have *already identified*.

You received no credit for identifying 0 items that define meritocracy. You should identify 1. You received full credit for identifying 2 items that define structural mobility: "changes in a society's occupational structure including the disappearance of some jobs and the appearance of other new ones" and "mobility resulting from a change in the occupational structure or stratification system."

Here again, students are told the definitions they identified correctly, while they are only told which concepts lack definitions, not the definitions themselves.

As assignments become more complex and students are asked to identify a series of interrelated items the feedback continues to provide supportive information reinforcing correct answers while providing guidance for incorrect or missing items. As students improve their essays and correctly identify more items the feedback shifts accordingly, always trying to guide them in that next step to successfully completing the assignment. This feedback is designed to help students throughout the learning process while keeping the responsibility for learning squarely on the student's shoulders. In this manner the program provides a collaborative learning environment in which instructors (assisted by the program) collaborate with students to improve student learning.

COLLABORATING TO IMPROVE INSTRUCTION THROUGH STUDENT CHALLENGES

Clearly, the collaborative learning environment created by SAGrader™ assists students with feedback time-shifted from instructors. Less evident, but also important, students assist instructors with their own feedback in the form of challenges facilitated by SAGrader™'s built-in challenge and communication system. When students view feedback for their submission, if they believe the program graded them incorrectly they can challenge their grade. For example, here is a challenge one student entered for an assignment where they were asked to use sociological concepts and principles to interpret a description of a hypothetical community.

My example of sector theory is: "With Interstate 494 running north to south through the center of the city, Hwy. 55 bisecting the city east to west and Hwy. 169 running along the eastern border, people who live and work in Rockford have easy access to Twin Lakes and area suburbs."

When challenging their result, students are asked to identify what item or items they believe the program missed and indicate how they expressed those items. The instructor then reviews the challenge and may resolve it in any of several ways, including a) explaining to the student why they are wrong and the program is correct, b) overriding the program's score and acknowledging the student's correct response, or c) acknowledging the student's response is correct and at the same time sending a communication to a developer to correct the program. For example, here is a response by the instructor to that student challenge.

The quotes you used were a good start, but think about what the terms mean, and what they are associated with. Sector theory is associated with growth, and urban decline is about the decline, not just the current state. --- This challenge was resolved by explaining to the student.

Challenges help instructors further collaborate with students to help students learn and assure they are graded fairly. Equally important, challenges help students collaborate with instructors to improve the grading of the SAGrader™ program by pointing out any potential weaknesses in the program. Instructors can also, at their own initiative, review a student's assignment and then provide additional helpful feedback or even override the grade assigned by the program.

ASSESSING STUDENT COLLABORATION USING SAGRADER™

To get an idea of how SAGrader™ contributes to a collaborative learning environment and how it affects student performance, we examined data from student essays submitted to assignments in a large introductory sociology course offered at the University of Missouri at Columbia. During Spring Semester of 2008, one hundred and seventy two (172) students submitted essays as a major part of the requirement for their grade. This course had 16 required writing assignments over the semester along with 7 optional extra-credit assignments. Assignments varied from several short-answer questions to moderate sized (1 or 2-page assignments) to a full-blown 3-part 15-page term paper. The SAGrader™ computer program graded all of these assignments. Students were permitted to revise their essays as many times as they wished based on this feedback from the SAGrader™ program.

Students Use the Opportunity to Revise

To make the case that a collaborative learning environment facilitates learning it must be shown that there is collaboration and it results in improved learning. In the SAGrader™ learning environment collaboration occurs as students use feedback to improve their learning and increase their grades. Students submitted a total of 1,193 distinct essays to the assignments and 2,863 separate submissions, for a mean of 2.4 submissions (one first draft and 1.4 revisions) per assignment. When given the opportunity to revise their essays, students clearly took advantage of the opportunity for collaboration, revising their essays one or more times for 71% of the assignments. In most cases a relatively few revisions are made. In ninety percent of the essays, students submitted three or fewer revisions for an assignment. Eighty-four percent made two or fewer revisions.

Revisions Improve Grades Significantly

Given that students take advantage of the collaborative learning environment provided by SAGrader™ to revise their papers, the next question is "Does that collaboration lead to improved learning and higher scores?" Table 1 compares initial score and final score means and standard deviations for all essays, essays having first drafts not followed by revisions, and essays including one or more revisions.

For all essays across all assignments, the average performance for the first draft is 69% and the average for the last draft is 90%, for a change of 21% or approximately two letter grades on the 4.0 grading scale typically used in American universities. This is quite an improvement. It is statistically significant (t=34.42, df=5730, p<.0001) and produces an effect size (Glass, McGaw, & Smith, 1981) of 0.77 (the difference in means is .77 times the standard deviation)[3]. To put this

Table 1. Mean score and standard deviation for initial draft and final draft

	Number	Initial Score (%)		Final Score (%)	
	Number	Mean	Standard deviation	Mean	Standard deviation
All essays	2,866 (100%)	69	27.76	90	18.08
Essays with first drafts only	820 (29%)	87	20.92	87	20.92
Essays including one or more revisions	2,046 (71%)	61	26.72	91	16.67

in perspective, Cohen (Cohen, 1969) describes an effect size of .8 as "grossly perceptible and therefore large" and comparable to the differences between the average heights of 13 year old and 18 year old girls (Coe, 2002). In comparison, most educational interventions have effect sizes that are often around 0.2 (Coe, 2002) or what Cohen calls "small" effect sizes.

However, in 29% of the cases (N=820) first drafts were not followed by revisions. The initial and final performance for those essays is the same -- 87%. So those 820 essays that show no change make the improvement due to revisions appear lower than it really is. To better understand the impact of revisions we look only at essays having one or more revisions. For essays having one or more revisions, the average performance on the first draft is 61% and for the last draft, 91%, resulting in *a change of 30%, or a three-letter grade jump from a D- to an A-*. This is an even more impressive improvement. It is statistically significant (t=42.84, df=4090, p<.0001) and produces an effect size of 1.12 (this being the most conservative estimate of effect size). That is, by using feedback from SAGrader™ and revising their work, students improved their grade by 30 percentage points or three letter grades—even before the instructor examined their essay. In fact, students who revise, on average, ultimately outperform students who do not revise, even though the non-revisers began with an average of 87% compared to a beginning average of 61% for revisers.

HOW SUCCESSFUL IS THIS COLLABORATION?

In a successful collaborative learning environment we would expect students to continue with the learning process until they reach a level of performance that meets their personal standard. In an unsuccessful collaborative learning environment we might expect to find large numbers of students who quit in frustration before reaching an acceptable level of performance. In the figure below, the performance scores for students for each essay are broken down by the number of revisions made by that student for the assignment. For example, there were 820 essays where students submitted no revisions and had an average score of 87%. There were 611 essays where students submitted one revision. Their initial score was 70.6% and their final score was 90.4%.

Notice that the average of scores for the last submission, whether it is the second, the eighth, or any in between, is essentially 90% or a bit higher. Thus it appears that for most essays, students seem to quit revising when their average approaches 90%, regardless of how many revisions it takes to achieve that average. Some students achieve a personally acceptable score with their first draft; others take one, two, or more revisions to reach that score. If final scores for essays with more revisions were substantially lower than the scores for essays with few revisions, this would suggest some of the students were giving up on some of the essays rather than being satisfied with their score. In fact, this does not appear to happen for most essays. This suggests students are getting the help they need during this collaborative learning process to enable them to perform up to their standard.

While the final scores on essays are very much the same regardless of numbers of revisions, at each step there is a large gap between scores for students who stop revising and those where students continue revising. Generally, there is a difference of at least 12 percentage points and as much as 26 percentage points. Students who

continue revising have mean scores on their latest submission from 61% to 79%, while students who decide to quit have mean scores between 87% and 94%. These results suggest students are both rational and tenacious, continuing to work on their papers when they are not satisfied with their score, quitting only when they achieve what they regard as a "good" or at least "acceptable" score. The decision about when to stop working on their papers appears to be determined primarily by their current grade and has little or no relationship to the number of revisions they have submitted.

Table 2. Average scores for all submissions with final submissions highlighted

Number of Essays	Number of Revisions	Submission Number							
		1	**2**	**3**	**4**	**5**	**6**	**7**	**8**
820	0	87.2*	.	.	.	.	.	.	.
611	1	70.6	90.4*	.	.	.	.	.	.
425	2	65.1	79.3	90.1*	.	.	.	.	.
314	3	61.8	76.4	83.8	91.9*	.	.	.	.
187	4	60.2	73.7	80.3	84.4	91*	.	.	.
127	5	60.4	72.3	78.8	83.9	85.9	93.4*	.	.
97	6	49.7	63.1	70.5	75.1	80.9	83	89.8*	.
75	7	47.7	60	67.6	74	80	84.7	88.6	93.6*

Figure 3. Performance at each submission by number of revisions

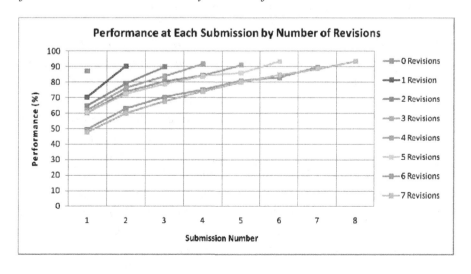

ARE THEY REALLY LEARNING, OR ARE THEY JUST GAMING THE SYSTEM?

This improvement in scores from 61% to 91% for essays that are revised based on SAGrader™'s feedback is impressive. But could it be overestimated? It might be argued that the improvement by students from first to last drafts is overestimated to the extent that students submit very poor first essays and then use feedback from SAGrader™ to modify their essay. That is to say, perhaps they are letting SAGrader™ do more of the work for them. It is *possible* that students do sometimes exercise less care with their first drafts and rely more heavily on SAGrader™'s feedback to improve their final drafts. However, if this was widespread, one would expect most early drafts to be poor ones. Instead, the average score on first drafts (including students who do not do subsequent drafts) is 69%. The fact that, for 29% of essays, students stop after the first draft is also consistent with the view that students make a reasonably good effort on their first drafts and do not rely exclusively on advice from SAGrader™ to improve their scores. Finally, it is also possible that the improvements made by using SAGrader™ are underestimated to the extent that original essays receive good scores. For essays that are less difficult where initial average scores are already high, there is little room for improvement, no matter how helpful the SAGrader™ program's advice might be. So any biases that might lead to overestimating learning with SAGrader™ may be countered somewhat by biases that underestimate learning.

A CASE STUDY

Further evidence that students are indeed learning is provided by examining a specific case. We can illustrate this general trend of dramatic improvement from first draft to final draft, when essays are revised, by examining a specific case. This student submitted her essay three times. The first submission was at 7:59 PM on February 23rd, and the student received a score of 27%. The second submission occurred 6 minutes later and the student received a much-improved score of 71%. She made her third submission for this assignment at 8:09 PM and received a perfect score of 100%. In the course of three submissions and ten minutes, this student went from a score of 27% to a score of 100% – a 73% improvement – all occurring long before an instructor could have graded and provided feedback on any of the essays. In fact, all of this improvement by the student occurred before an instructor even saw her essay.

This case illustrates the general trends found above. In this case the student submitted three times (the average is 2.4 submissions). The student's initial grade was less than 70% (27% in this case). The student stopped revising the paper when they achieved a grade near 90% or higher (100% in this case). We believe that this is due to a student's natural tenacity and desire to maximize her grade. It is interesting to note that dramatic improvements such as this are facilitated by systems that provide an opportunity for students to continue working in a collaborative learning environment to improve their understanding.

In Figure 4 is a screen shot from SAGrader™ showing the student's first draft at the top and the last draft at the bottom for an essay addressing the following prompt:

In your readings about interaction, you found that the elements shaping most social interaction are social statuses and roles. Each of us has a multitude of statuses and roles that direct the ways we interact in various contexts. In this assignment, use your own sets of statuses and roles to discuss some of the major issues associated with the two concepts. For example, which of your statuses are ascribed or achieved? Have you ever experienced role segregation, distance, or conflict? Be sure to define all of these terms in your answer. In addition, you should discuss the major forms of social interaction. We have all experienced these varying forms of interaction to some degree, so make sure to pick examples that illustrate each type. Explain what each type is.

Differences between the two drafts are highlighted. The display has been anonymized and displays a number instead of the student's name.

The first draft score was 27%, for an effort that was clearly a serious attempt to answer the prompt. This shows that getting even a 27% on an essay is not a trivial matter and requires some effort and knowledge. We can see clear improvements in the essay. The student's initial draft had 330 words. The last draft was considerably longer, with 452 words. The final draft was more developed, with

Figure 4. Comparison of first and third drafts of a student's essay (© 2008, Idea Works Inc. Used with permission.)

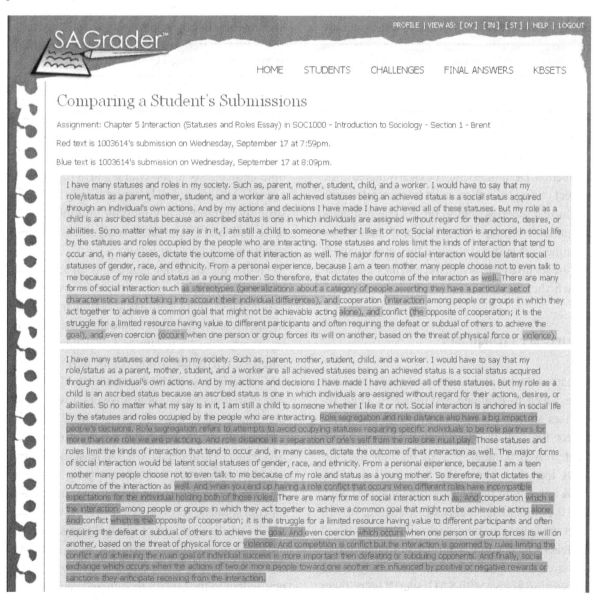

greater coverage of important topics and more precise language. Among other changes, it adds definitions of role conflict, role segregation, and role distance; and it adds several common types of social interaction not discussed earlier.

SAGrader™ is designed to insure that the correspondence between scores and knowledge found in this example is likely to be found in general. To begin with, constructed responses or essays are much harder to "fool" than fixed-choice tests, and the process of constructing essay responses itself often fosters learning. The way in which SAGrader™ assesses essays makes it hard to "game" the system and get a high score. Good essays must not only include appropriate concepts and terms, but must also express relationships among them consistent with the knowledge underlying the learning objectives. In the student excerpts above, for example, mentioning concepts such as competition or conflict alone is not enough to get full credit. Students must also indicate that those are both examples of social interaction. Definitions must be clearly linked to the correct concepts; authors must be associated with the correct theories; and so on. As one instructor said at an SAGrader™ workshop, if students are "gaming" the system the game they are playing is the one set up by the instructor, and they are learning whether they realize it or not.

STUDENT OPINIONS

As part of the normal course evaluation, students were asked to evaluate SAGrader™. Their responses along with their open-ended comments reflect the collaborative learning environment created by SAGrader™. Tops on their list, students like the opportunity to redo their work (95% agree with that, 89% strongly agree), they love the immediate feedback (93% agree, 76% of them strongly agree) and the detailed personalized feedback (82% agree, with 65% of them agreeing strongly). Students overwhelmingly agree that writing essays with SAGrader™ helps them

learn (78% agree, 44% of those strongly agree). These responses reflect the importance to students of SAGrader™'s ability to take advantage of the teachable moment to provide a collaborative environment that facilitates learning.

Students overwhelmingly like the fact that SAGrader™ grades everyone's essays without bias (86% agree, with 57% of those strongly agreeing)—no trivial matter in social science courses where students sometimes express concern instructors are biased and unfair in their grading. Most agree the program grades their essays fairly" (63% agree and 29% of those strongly agreed). Students also like the opportunity to challenge their grade (80% agree, with 53% strongly agreeing). This sends the message to students that we are concerned with fairness and accuracy and gives them an opportunity to voice any concerns they might have about having a computer program grade their work. When whether they prefer to have only SAGrader™ assignments and no multiple choice tests in the course, 56% of students agreed (44% strongly). In contrast, only 10% (6% strongly) preferred having only multiple choice tests and no SAGrader™ assignments. These results are diplayed in Figure 5.

While these results suggest an effective collaborative learning environment is created by SAGrader™, there were a few cautionary results. In open-ended comments students occasionally say things like "Sometimes I feel that my examples do fit the description of the definition, but SAGrader™ says that it does not." "SAGrader™ was extremely picky about answers. I would say the right thing, just not the perfect way." or "You had to have pretty much the exact definition for SAGrader™ to understand it." At least some of the students sometimes think the program is asking for greater precision from them than is necessary. Of course that level of precision may be appropriate. Every discipline has technical terms students are expected to employ correctly, and a student's use of the phrase, "differentiation of labor" is *not* equivalent to the widely recognized sociological

Figure 5. Student opinions

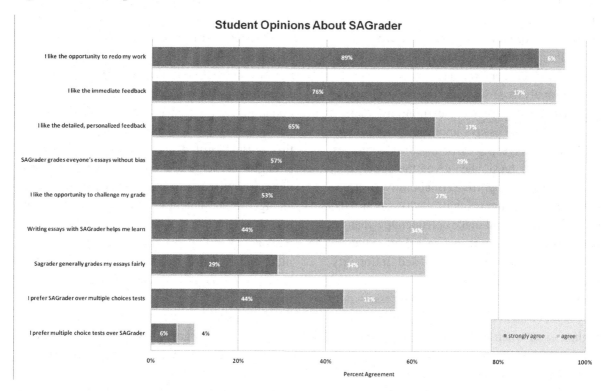

Student Opinions About SAGrader

I like the opportunity to redo my work — 89% | 6%
I like the immediate feedback — 76% | 17%
I like the detailed, personalized feedback — 65% | 17%
SAGrader grades eveyone's essays without bias — 57% | 29%
I like the opportunity to challenge my grade — 53% | 27%
Writing essays with SAGrader helps me learn — 44% | 34%
Sagrader generally grades my essays fairly — 29% | 34%
I prefer SAGrader over multiple choices tests — 44% | 12%
I prefer multiple choice tests over SAGrader — 6% | 4%

strongly agree   agree

0%   20%   40%   60%   80%   100%
Percent Agreement

DISCUSSION AND CONCLUSION

When instructors grade essays, each submission incurs a substantial commitment of time, money, or both to grade. This encourages instructors to limit writing assignments and to restrict the number of times students can revise their work or prohibit revisions altogether. As a result, writing assignments are few and far between and when they do occur they are used primarily to evaluate students rather than as a learning experience. Because of the time required for grading, that evaluation often comes long after the essay is written. Writing-across-the-curriculum programs at many universities try to overcome this by making more resources available for selected courses to make it possible to have

term, "division of labor". This is a mistake by the student, and the TAs or instructor would mark it wrong as well.

more writing assignments, to have enough graders to shorten the wait for grading, and to permit multiple revisions and learning through writing. Those writing programs have often not been extended to online learning environments at least in part because of the difficulties of achieving the level of interactivity and collaboration so crucial for effective writing assessment.

In contrast, SAGrader™ automates the grading of essays, creating an environment in which assessments of student revisions are nearly free. Once the initial essay assignment is constructed, the incremental cost of grading multiple drafts by each student is hardly more than the cost of grading a single draft (Brent et al., 2006a). Thus, SAGrader™ provides both an assessment tool and a collaborative learning environment where students can submit essays, receive detailed, personalized feedback immediately while the issues are still fresh in their minds, and revise and resubmit their work. We have shown in this study that, when SAGrader™ is used in such an environment, students take advantage of this learning opportunity to revise their work based on feedback from the program, often dramatically improving their performance.

This analysis of students' use of SAGrader™ finds it to be a very effective learning environment in which revised essays improve by an average of 30 percentage points or three letter grades. Students work hard when given the opportunity to do so in this supportive collaborative learning environment. Students submit each essay an average of 2.4 times and make considerable changes between the first draft and last draft. Students display considerable tenacity and rationality, taking advantage of this learning opportunity by continuing to revise and resubmit their essays until they achieve an average grade of roughly 90% or higher, even when their initial grades may have been quite low. Students who revise many times generally end with average scores much like those of students who submit only once or a few times. This suggests that these students are not finally giving up and settling for lower scores, but instead are persisting with revisions until they perform up to the standard they have set for themselves. The dramatic improvement in scores from first draft to final draft does not appear to be an artifact of artificially low first draft scores or artificially high last draft scores. Students are making changes in their essays that show evidence of learning and improved writing. The case study illustrates how this large change in scores chronicles a true improvement in understanding and communication that is reflected in increased length, quality of writing, coverage of topics, and writing precision. Remarkably, students make all this progress largely unattended by instructors.

Students may be unattended, but they are not unassisted. By providing the feedback and opportunity to revise at that crucial time, SAGrader™ in essence time-shifts interaction with the instructor to fit the student's schedule. The feedback to the student is crucial for this process. By being able to view detailed comments and advice on how to improve their essay immediately after each revision, students are in essence collaborating with the instructor. This is not synchronous collaboration because the instructor does not participate at the same time as the student. Nor is it asynchronous collaboration in which the student must wait days or weeks for feedback from the instructor. Instead, this is time-shifted collaboration in which the strength of synchronous collaboration is delivered without requiring student and teacher to be actively engaged at the same time. It is as though students had an instructor looking over their shoulder responding to their work, providing encouragement and direction for improvement, permitting students to take advantage of the teachable moment to achieve significant learning.

It is interesting to note that there are a number of other pedagogical solutions that provide approximations of time-shifting – even though they don't use that terminology. There are also many learning environments that fail to incorporate time-shifting. We know of no existing literature that examines the time-shifting aspect of pedagogical solutions. It is our hope that this article will stimulate such work so that we can better understand how time-shifting can be used to enhance existing educational strategies. We argue that those educational environments that fail to provide time-shifted interaction are missing out on important ways to facilitate student learning.

Some teaching tools capture many of the aspects of time-shifting but not all aspects. One of the oldest and most widely used educational tools – the textbook – in effect time-shifts information. What the textbook does is take the knowledge of the author, and time-shifts that knowledge to the moment in time that the student desires to learn from the author. The textbook fulfills a number of the requirements to be a student-directed teachable moment, but fails in one respect – feedback. In order to take maximum advantage of the moment when students are most ready to learn, the textbook would need to provide feedback on how the students are performing. Some learning environments that do a better job of capturing the teaching moment are computer-based multiple choice assessments and fill-in-the-blank lecture notes. Some common practices that fail to take advantage of the teachable moment are hand-graded essays, lectures, and optically scanned tests, each of which typically provides feedback to students days or even weeks after they complete their work. On the positive side, there are some technologies that have started moving closer to taking advantage of teachable moments including podcasts, clickers, and online chat and discussion groups.

The key to determining whether or not a technology will take full advantage of time-shifted interactions is to identify whether the technology has all of the features needed to create teachable moments. In order for these teachable moments to be attained, the student needs to be motivated, have the relevant information in hand, receive feedback on their work, and have an opportunity to revise. All of this needs to be available in a span of minutes or seconds. We argue that only by providing access to those teachable moments, and taking advantage of them, can teachers realize the full potential of their students. The results from this study show that students exposed to such a teachable moment will take full advantage of it.

ACKNOWLEDGMENT

We'd like to thank Matthew Wood and James Barton who helped program the reporting interface for SAGrader™ that provided much of the information reported here. We also wish to thank the anonymous reviewers who raised important issues that greatly strengthened this work.

REFERENCES

Bejar, I., & Mislevy, R. (2006). Automated scoring of complex tasks in computer-based testing: An introduction. In D. Williamson, R. Mislevy, & I. Bejar (Eds.), *Automated scoring of complex tasks in computer-based testing*. Mahwah, NJ: Erlbaum.

Benfer, R., Brent, E., & Furbee, L. (1991). *Expert systems*. Newbury Park, CA: Sage.

Bloom, B. (1956). *Taxonomy of educational objectives: The classification of educational goals*. Susan Fauer Company, Inc.

Bowker, N., & Tuffin, K. (2004). Using the online medium for discursive research about people with disabilities. *Social Science Computer Review*, *22*(2), 228–241. doi:10.1177/0894439303262561

Braun, H., Bejar, I., & Williamson, D. (2006). Rule based methods for automated scoring: Application in a licensing context. In D. Williamson, R. Mislevy, & I. Bejar (Eds.), *Automated scoring of complex tasks in computer based testing*. Mahwah, NJ: Erlbaum.

Brent, E., Carnahan, T., & McCully, J. (2006a). *Students improve learning by 20 percentage points with essay grading program, SAGrader™*. Columbia. MO: Idea Works, Inc.

Brent, E., Carnahan, T., McCully, J., & Green, N. (2006). *SAGrader™: A computerized essay grading program, version 2*. Columbia, MO: Idea Works, Inc.

Brent, E., & Townsend, M. (2007). Automated essay grading in the sociology classroom: Finding common ground. In P. Frietag Ericsoon & R. Haswell (Eds.), *Machine scoring of student essays: Truth or consequences?* Logan, UT: Utah State University Press.

Burstein, J. (2003). The e-rater® scoring engine: Automated essay scoring with natural language processing. In M. Shermis & J. Burstein (Eds.), *Automated essay scoring: A cross-disciplinary perspective*. Mahwah, NJ: Erlbaum.

Chung, G., & Baker, E. (2003). Issues in the reliability and validity of automated scoring of constructed responses. In M. Shermis & J. Burstein (Eds.), *Automated essay scoring: A cross-disciplinary approach*. Mahwah, NJ: Erlbaum.

Cohen, J. (1969). *Statistical power analysis for the behavioral sciences*. New York: Academic Press.

Cole, R. (1997). *Survey of the state of the art in human language technology*. Cambridge, UK: Cambridge University Press and Giardini.

Deane, P. (2006). Strategies for evidence identification through linguistic assessment of textual responses. In D. Williamson, R. Mislevy, & I. Bejar (Eds.), *Automated scoring of complex tasks in computer-based testing*. Mahwah, NJ: Erlbaum.

Elliot, S. (2003). Intellimetric™: From here to validity. In M. Shermis & J. Burstein (Eds.), *Automated essay scoring: A cross-disciplinary perspective*. Mawah, NJ: Lawrence Erlbaum Associates, Inc.

Findley, C. (1988). *Collaborative networked learning: On-line facilitation and software support*. Burlington, MA: Digital Equipment Corporation.

Glass, G., McGaw, B., & Smith, M. (1981). *Analysis in social research*. London: Sage Publications.

Gritz, E., Fingeret, M. C., Vidrine, D. J., Lazev, A. B., Mehta, N. V., & Reece, G. P. (2006). Successes and failures of the teachable moment: Smoking cessation in cancer patients. *Cancer, 106*(1), 17–27. doi:10.1002/cncr.21598

Hewson, C., & Laurent, D. (2008). Research design and tools for Internet research. In N. Fielding, R. M. Lee, & G. Blank (Eds.), *Online research methods*. London: Sage Publications.

Jonassen, D. H., Peck, K., & Wilson, B. (1999). *Learning with technology: A constructivist perspective*. Upper Saddle River, NJ: Merrill.

Kearsley, G. (1995). *The nature and value of interaction in distance learning*. Paper presented at the Third Distance Education Research Symposium.

Landauer, T., Foltz, P., & Laham, D. (1998). Introduction to latent semantic analysis. *Discourse Processes, 25*, 259–284.

Landauer, T., Laham, D., & Foltz, P. (2000). The intelligent essay assessor. *IEEE Intelligent Systems, 15*, 27–31.

Landauer, T., Laham, D., Rehder, B., & Schreiner, M. (1997). *How well can passage meaning be derived without word order? A comparison of latent semantic analysis and humans*. Paper presented at the Cognitive Science Society, Mahwah, NJ.

Lave, J., & Wegner, E. (1991). *Situated learning: Legitimate peripheral participation*. Cambridge, UK: Cambridge University Press.

Major, H., & Levenburg, N. (1999). Learner success in distance environments: A shared responsibility. *The Technology Source*.

Murray, C., & Sixsmith, J. (1998). Mail: A qualitative research medium for interviewing? *International Journal of Social Research Methodology: Theory and Practice, 48*(12), 103–121.

Page, E. (1994). Computer grading of student prose, using modern concepts and software. *Journal of Experimental Education*, •••, 62.

Rudner, L., & Gagne, P. (2001). An overview of three approaches to scoring written essays by computer. *ERIC Digest*.

Sowa, J., & Borgida, A. (1991). *Principles of semantic networks: Explorations in the representation of knowledge*. San Francisco: Morgan-Kaufmann.

Sutton, L. (2001). The principle of vicarious interaction in computer-mediated communications. *International Journal of Educational Telecommunications, 7*(3), 223–242.

Yang, Y., Buckendahl, C., & Juskiewicz, P. (2001). *A review of strategies for validating computer automated scoring*. Paper presented at the Midwestern Educational Research Association.

Zadeh, L. (1965). Fuzzy sets. *Information and Control, 8*(3), 338–353. doi:10.1016/S0019-9958(65)90241-X

ENDNOTES

[1] Participating in a Socratic dialogue, as discussed here, should not be confused with reading a Socratic dialogue. In the latter case, time-shifted learning is not occurring and there is no feedback from the instructor to students.

[2] Admittedly, this assignment does not involve the highest level of reasoning we like to encourage in students (Bloom, 1956), but we want to keep this example simple enough to clearly illustrate feedback.

[3] Effect sizes were estimated conservatively by dividing mean differences by the largest standard deviation of the two groups.

Section 2
Tracking, Feedback and Monitoring

Chapter 5
Expertiza:
Managing Feedback in Collaborative Learning

Edward F. Gehringer
North Carolina State University, USA

ABSTRACT

Educators and accrediting agencies demonstrate a growing awareness that students learn better when they work in groups, and on projects that are more similar to those encountered on the job, where their contributions are used by others to add value to the operations of the enterprise. However, it is very time consuming to assess project work; the only scalable way to accomplish this is to have students assist in the assessment. Expertiza is a system for managing all kinds of communication that is involved in assessment: double-blind communications between authors and reviewers, assessment of teammate contributions, evaluations by course staff, and surveys of students to assess the assignment and the peer-review process. This chapter places Expertiza in context among other electronic peer-review systems, algorithms, and methodologies. It relates the results of three experiments showing that through the peer-review process, students are capable of producing work that can be used as teaching materials in later classes.

INTRODUCTION

Summative assessment, in the form of exams and standardized tests, has long been a mainstay of our educational system. But the shortcomings of basing student evaluations on "high-stakes" testing are well known. Among other things, it disadvantages students (e.g., nontraditional students) who lack

DOI: 10.4018/978-1-60566-786-7.ch005

self-confidence, and it focuses students' attention on passing tests, rather than honing their skills in communication and collaboration—which will be much more important to them on the job.

Nonetheless, in most American college courses, the majority of the grade is determined by exams. The situation is even more extreme in other areas of the world, where the *entire* grade is often based on exams, with homework being assigned, but not counting in assessment (Gehringer 2008a). Why do university faculty continue to rely on such a flawed system? By and large, it is a question of resources. The effort required to assess performance on hour-long exams, where each student answers the same question, is much less than needed to determine project grades, where each student (or team of students) comes up with a different solution after spending many hours on the task. It is also more difficult to grade fairly when there are many correct, and partially correct, solutions. Certain kinds of exam questions can even be graded by computer, which is not possible for projects.[1]

An important challenge, then, is to facilitate the grading of project work. A concomitant need is to provide formative assessment—feedback to help students *improve* their work, instead of just assigning a score. Formative assessment has been shown to "level the playing field" among all kinds of students. In a survey of 250 research papers on Classroom Assessment, Black and Wiliam (1998) concluded,

While formative assessment can help all pupils, it yields particularly good results with low achievers by concentrating on specific problems with their work and giving them a clear understanding of what is wrong and how to put it right. Pupils can accept and work with such messages, provided that they are not clouded by overtones about ability, competition, and comparison with others.

The only *scalable* way to provide this feedback is to get peers involved in the act. If each student is asked to assess a few (say, one to five) other students or student teams, the task requires a reasonable amount of effort; and that effort does not increase as the class gets larger. Thus, each student gets the same amount of feedback whether the class consists of 10 students or 100.

Team projects are an important form of collaboration. However, few if any other online peer-review tools support them. At the minimum, members of a team must have access to a single submission area, so that any team member can modify the group's submission. Team members are asked to review each other's contribution after the projects are finished. The instructor can modify the grade assigned to the team for each member, based on teammate evaluations. While students submit as teams, they review as individuals. This has important benefits, including increasing the amount of feedback and reducing the need for teams to meet.

Our Expertiza system (Gehringer et al. 2007) supports several kinds of evaluation.

Instructors/TAs ("tutors") as well as other students can review students. The instructor might, for example, do the first review to tell the student reviewers what to watch out for. Authors can give feedback to their reviewers at any time. This too helps to mitigate the problem of "rogue" reviews, since it gives author and reviewer a double-blind method for resolving conflict. Reviewers can update their reviews after communication with authors. In fact, authors are also allowed to update their submissions at any time, even during a review period. We have developed rules for canceling review scores when they are not applicable because of a resubmission.

Expertiza is designed to allow the production of reusable learning resources through peer review of student work. Large projects (e.g., devising exercises or case studies for each chapter in a textbook, creating a glossary of terms used in a course, annotating a semester's worth of lecture notes with hyperlinks to related material) can be parceled out to individuals or teams, each of which signs up for a chunk of the project. This is done by allowing them to select from a set of tasks listed on a Web page. Only a limited number of students/teams are allowed to select each choice. This allows the instructor to assure that multiple creators choose each chunk.

The rest of this chapter is organized as follows. The next three sections (Reviewing, Teamwork, and Distributing Work) discuss various interactions required in project-based collaborative learning. "Distributing work" (page 13) means how small pieces of large projects are assigned to groups of students. Each of these sections is divided into two parts: The first subsection introduces the interaction, and describes how Expertiza accomplishes it. The second subsection discusses related work, contrasting the Expertiza approach with how other systems have tackled the same problem. Following this, we describe (starting on page 15) three experiments that demonstrate the efficacy of the Expertiza approach: student-authored exercises included in a textbook; peer review found more effective than other means of evaluating wiki contributions; and student-generated active-learning exercises shown to be useful in teaching subsequent classes in the same subject. The final section (page 18) summarizes the chapter, and discusses several exciting extensions of the present work.

REVIEWING

Rubric-Based Reviewing

Submissions to Expertiza may be in various forms, depending on the assignment. Three kinds of submissions are supported: files, URLs, and wiki pages.[2] Any file type may be submitted (Figure 1); currently, Expertiza does not attempt to read the file or interpret its contents. Multiple files may be submitted; if so, the reviewer will be presented with a list of the files. If many files are to be submitted, it is convenient to "zip" or "tar" them first; in this case, the submitter may specify whether the files should be "unzipped" after upload. Sometimes it makes sense to unzip (e.g., if a small Web site is to be submitted and most of the files are included graphics), and sometimes it does not (e.g., when the files represent source code for the classes in a computer program that is to be reviewed).

Figure 1. Submitting a file

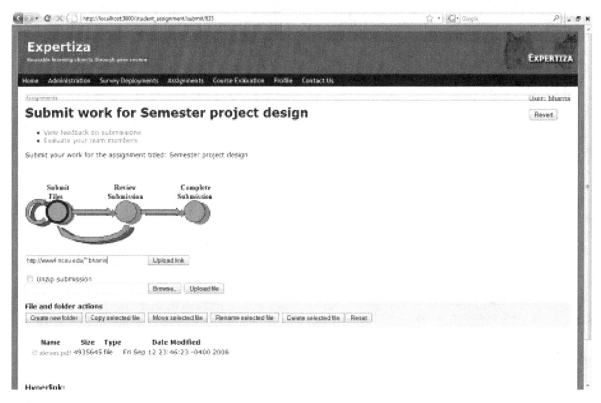

If a URL is being submitted, the user should fill in the text box to the left of the "Upload link" button. Wiki pages are not submitted explicitly; instead, when setting up the assignment, the instructor specifies a "base URL," and the wiki is "spidered" for all pages whose address begins with the base URL and which were edited by the user since the beginning of the current assignment. Thus, any wiki page that the user has edited during that period is, in effect, submitted to the user's reviewers (Figure 2). Diffeent code is required to support each type of wiki. Currently, MediaWiki and DokuWiki are supported.

As seen in Figure 2, reviews are rubric based. For each question, the reviewer can assign a score from m to n; typically 1 to 5 or 0 to 5. The reviewer may also give a text comment. At the end of the review form, there is a free-form box for additional comments.

Review rubrics are one of several kinds of rubrics in Expertiza. There are also author-feedback, teammate-feedback, assignment-survey, and global-survey rubrics. Any of these types may be created by an instructor (see Figure 3), and it may be designated as public (so it is available to other instructors) or private.

Figure 2. Reviewing a wiki submission

Figure 3. Creating a rubric

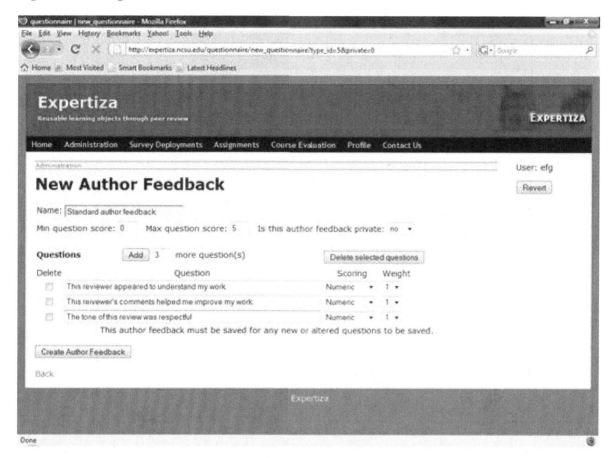

Since multiple rounds of review are supported, students are forced to use the feedback they receive from their reviewers to improve their work. Frequently, the instructor will do the first round of review, followed by one or two rounds of review by other students. This helps the students see what a good review is like, and as authors, they gain experience responding to feedback from multiple sets of reviewers. In a large class, though, instructor review compromises the scalability of the system, so it might be provided only for one assignment during the semester, or the instructor might instead do metareviews (see Section 2.2.3), which takes less time than reviewing students' submitted work.

Whenever a review is received, the author is notified by e-mail. An example is shown in Figure 4. Similarly, an author's reviewers are e-mailed whenever the author resubmits work that they have reviewed.

An assignment in Expertiza can be configured to use static or dynamic reviewer assignment (called a "reviewer mapping" in Expertiza, to distinguish it from the "assignment" for which students are submitting their work). The dynamic strategy is similar to the Banker's algorithm for resource allocation. Each time a reviewer is assigned ("mapped") to review a particular submission, before the mapping is performed, a check is made to assure that the remaining mappings can be performed without requiring any student to review his/her own work. A slightly more intricate version of the algorithm is used for metareviews (see Section 2.2.3). The algorithm is described

Figure 4. E-mail notification that a review has been submitted for an author's work

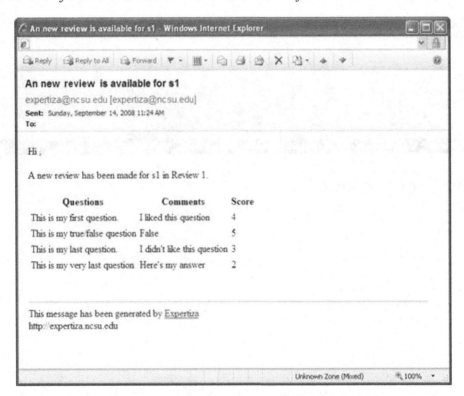

by Gehringer and Cui (2002), and in more detail and generality by Wang (2002).

To insure that students take reviewing seriously, Expertiza employs two quality-control mechanisms. The first is *metareviewing*, or "reviews of reviews," where after the end of the review-and-revision process, the reviews themselves are presented to a reviewer—either the instructor or another student (Figure 5). Students are not assigned to review their own reviews, or reviews of their own work. Scores assigned during metareviewing count for some fraction of a student's grade on the assignment, typically 20% or 25%.

The second quality-control tool is some sort of feedback from the author on review helpfulness. Like other feedback in Expertiza, author feedback is based on a rubric (Figure 6). The author may give feedback at any time, and reviewers can update their reviews at any time during the review period. Before this feature was added, authors would complain to the instructor about "rogue" reviews. If time permitted, the instructor would look up the reviewer and convey the author's concern. Now, author and reviewer have the ability to carry on a double-blind conversation throughout the review period. In addition to resolving misunderstandings, this has saved the instructor considerable work.

Figure 5. A metareview

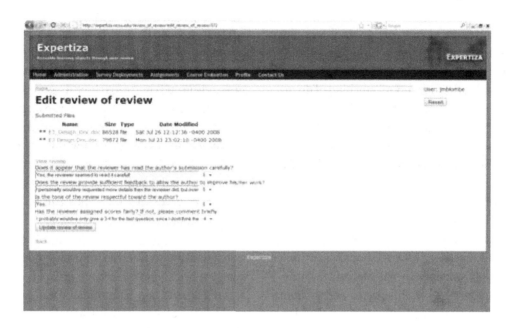

Figure 6. How an author gives feedback to a reviewer

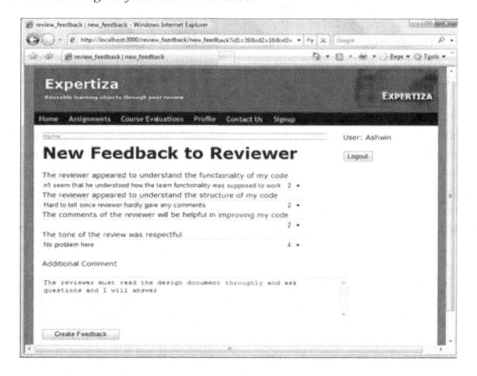

Related Work

The first commercial peer-review tool was the Daedalus Integrated Writing Environment, introduced in 1997. The current version (Daedalus 2008) allows students to submit any kind of document (e.g., a Microsoft Word file) and provides pre-created rubrics that guide students through the peer-review process. Rubric-based review is also available in Blackboard (Blackboard 2008); reviews can be made anonymous or not. Sakai (Sakai 2008) allows an instructor to let students read and fill out an evaluation form on other students' submissions. Moodle (Moodle 2008) supports the creation of "workshops," in which instructor and student can fill out rubric forms on other students' work. Instructor and student feedback can be weighted differently in calculating final grades.

Calibrated Peer Review (Chapman and Fiore 2000, Carlson and Berry 2003) (CPR) is perhaps best known of the peer-review systems used in higher education. It has been used by nearly 5,000 courses and 160,000 students. Its key innovation is *calibration* of students' reviews to the instructor's standards. The instructor provides three sample submissions for a writing assignment. One, known as the *exemplar*, demonstrates the standard that the instructor wants the students to achieve. Two other submissions are provided, to illustrate common errors and misconceptions. The instructor creates a rubric, and rates each of these three essays using the rubric.

Before being allowed to review his/her peers, the student must review each of these three essays. The student's agreement with the instructor on these ratings is used to compute a "reviewer competency index," which determines the impact that this student's review will have on the scores of the students being reviewed. Students may need to repeat this calibration process multiple times in order to "get it right." Before students are allowed to see scores given to them by their peers, they must complete a self-assessment. If the self-assessment matches the scores given them by their peers, they are given full credit for their self-assessment. Peer reviews and self-assessment are factored into the student's final grade.

Currently, all submissions to CPR are typed (or cut-and-pasted) into a text box. This means that no formatting, or equations, etc., can be included. It is possible to type the URL of a file into the text box (instead of the essay itself), but if the URL points to the student's account, anonymity is broken. So classes that submit files usually work with an auxiliary server to which files can be uploaded without compromising anonymity.

The effort of creating a CPR assignment is considerable, so libraries of assignments, exemplars, rubrics, etc. have been created. However, it is difficult to take a pre-created assignment and use it in a course without adapting it, because coverage of material and expectations differ from one class to the next. Individual instructors (Keeney-Kennicutt et al. 2008) report that it is difficult to get a class to appreciate the benefits of CPR, but with persistence, favorable results can be obtained.

Lightweight Preliminary Peer Review (LPPR) (Denning et al. 2007) is an add-on to Ubiquitous Presenter (Griswold and Simon 2006) designed for peer review within a classroom. Students submit their work to Ubiquitous Presenter during class; UP makes it available to other students, who rate it quickly along various dimensions. Students are encouraged to rate many other students' work, as many as they can analyze in the time allotted. They rate it primarily by clicking on buttons, though comments may also be supplied.

LPPR has been used in computer-science classes, although it could be used in other fields where problem-solving exercises can be carried on in class. A few tools have been designed specifically for review of code. One of these is Praktomat (Zeller 2000), which shows submitted program code to other students in the class, and asks them to rate it along various dimensions. To prevent plagiarism, students only review other students who were assigned to write code for different problems. The system tries to even out the number of reviewers for each student's code, and it also attempts to assign reciprocal reviews (i.e., if student A reviews student B, then there is a good likelihood that student B will be assigned to review student A as well). Another such system is PCR (Peer Code Review) (Wang et al. 2008b). Their review-and-revision process is very similar to Expertiza's, but they used a non-blind e-mail review process, with metareviewing (see Section 2.2.3) performed by the instructor.

Validity and Reliability of Reviews

Students come to the table with less experience in the subject matter than the instructor. Additionally, because of their relative immaturity, they have less familiarity with the review process. So the question naturally arises, Are student peer reviews as useful as "expert" (instructor or TA) reviews in assessing student performance? However, Cho et al. (2006) note that there are also reasons to doubt that the instructor would necessarily do a better job: Instructors are more pressed for time because they have to grade everyone's work, and they are not as expert in grading the first student submission examined as they are in grading the last. Instructor ratings can be idiosyncratic, since they are generated by just one person; peer reviews are the average (somehow computed) of several observers' perceptions.

Cho et al. (2006) differentiate between validity (did the students know what to look for?) and reliability (did they give similar scores to the same work?). Their study was larger (708 students) than previous studies. It used the SWoRD peer-review system (Cho and Schunn 2007). They found that the single-rater reliability of peer reviewers ranged from 0.17 to 0.56 for the various courses studied, which compared favorably with a student of single-rater reliability for professional journals (0.27). They also found that three to four peer reviews produced "middling effective reliabili-

ties," while six peer reviews yielded "excellent effective reliabilities."

Reviewer Assignment

The question of how to assign peer reviewers in a class is very similar to how to assign reviewers for a professional conference. In both cases, assignments need to be made quickly, and if some reviewers do not perform their assigned tasks, new reviewers need to be located quickly. Several groups of researchers have addressed this issue (Dumais and Nielsen 1992, Merelo-Guervós and Castillo-Valdivieso 2004, Wang et al. 2008a, Rodriguez and Bollen 2008). Pesenhofer et al. (2008) consider the problem as one part of the task of automating conference management. Though the problem of assigning student peer reviewers is similar, the students' expertise is usually more uniform than professional referees'; hence, it is much less important that students' expertise be taken into consideration when assigning reviewers. On the other hand, especially at the beginning of the term, students drop out of the course (and hence, drop out of the process) at a much greater rate than professional reviewers. For this reason, it is desirable to have a backup plan for assigning additional reviewers until a student's submission has been reviewed by "enough" peers.

Quality Control

The validity of peer reviews by students depends heavily on whether there is some mechanism to insure review quality. This means that the students must know how to do a good review, and have some incentive to do a careful job. Otherwise, they will rationally allocate their time toward activities that help their final grade more than reviewing. The result will be review scores that are unrealistically high, and review comments that offer little, if any, guidance on how to improve.

In any case, the students should be given clear instruction on what constitutes a good review, and should be shown examples of good reviews. Beyond that, the simplest sanction is simply to give a 0 to any student who fails to do all assigned reviews (Kerr et al. 1995). The study that used that approach reported that almost all students completed their assigned reviews. But, of course, that does not demonstrate that the reviews were valid, simply that they were completed. The *calibration* process in Calibrated Peer Review helps insure that reviews are competent.

One incentive toward careful reviewing is *reciprocal reviews* (Zeller 2000). As mentioned in Section 2.1.1, if student *A* reviews student *B*, it is likely (not certain) that student *B* will also be assigned to review student *A*. In our experience, we have observed reciprocity not only in careful reviewing, but also in "reciprocal backbiting," where a student who receives a harsh review attempts to retaliate against his/her reviewers by downgrading their submissions.

In an *algorithmic* quality-control strategy, an algorithm is used to compute a reviewer's reliability, based on his/her reviews. The first such strategy was proposed by Hamer et al. (2005). Their strategy weights reviews more heavily roughly in inverse proportion to the distance between the scores assigned by this reviewer and the grade ultimately assigned to the student. That is, reviewers who give scores that are much different from other reviewers of the same material have their scores weighted less heavily.

In the version used by SWoRD (Cho & Schunn 2007), a reviewer's reliability is based on *systematic differences* (whether a reviewer tends to give low or high scores), *consistency* (how well the reviewer's scores agree with others who reviewed the same work), and *spread* (the distance between the lowest and highest scores given by the reviewer). These metrics are used to construct a review-accuracy score; reviews from reviewers with higher scores count more in determining a student's grade. Moreover, the review-accuracy score itself can influence a student's grade; students thus compete to increase their review-accuracy scores.

Another algorithmic approach is given by Lauw et al. (2007). They propose a *differential model* for determining review quality. They determine the *quality* of a submission and the *leniency* of a reviewer. The quality of a submission is determined by the scores given by reviewers, and the leniency of those reviews. Similarly, the leniency of a reviewer is determined by the scores given by other reviewers to the same submission. Quality and leniency are thus mutually dependent, and must be solved for simultaneously, e.g., by solving a system of linear equations.

The final piece in quality control is some sort of feedback from the author on review helpfulness. SWoRD (Cho et al. 2006) has each author rate the helpfulness of each review on a scale of 1 to 7. This feedback is given once the student has uploaded the revision of his/her original work. Expertiza's author feedback carries this a step further by using a rubric to allow authors to rate the usefulness of a review along several dimensions.

TEAMWORK

Expertiza's Support for Teams

Team assignments add another dimension to collaboration. Expertiza supports team assignments as well as individual assignments. Teams may be formed by the instructor (Figure 7), or by the students themselves, who may issue invitations (Figure 8) to other students through the system to join their team. In order to be added to the team, a student must accept the invitation through Expertiza. Any member of the team may submit or modify the team's submission.

Individuals can be assigned to review teams, so that each team gets several times as many reviews as each student is required to do. For example, with three-member teams and two reviews per student, each team would get six reviews. Individual reviewing is beneficial, first, because it avoids the

Figure 7. An instructor adds a member to a team

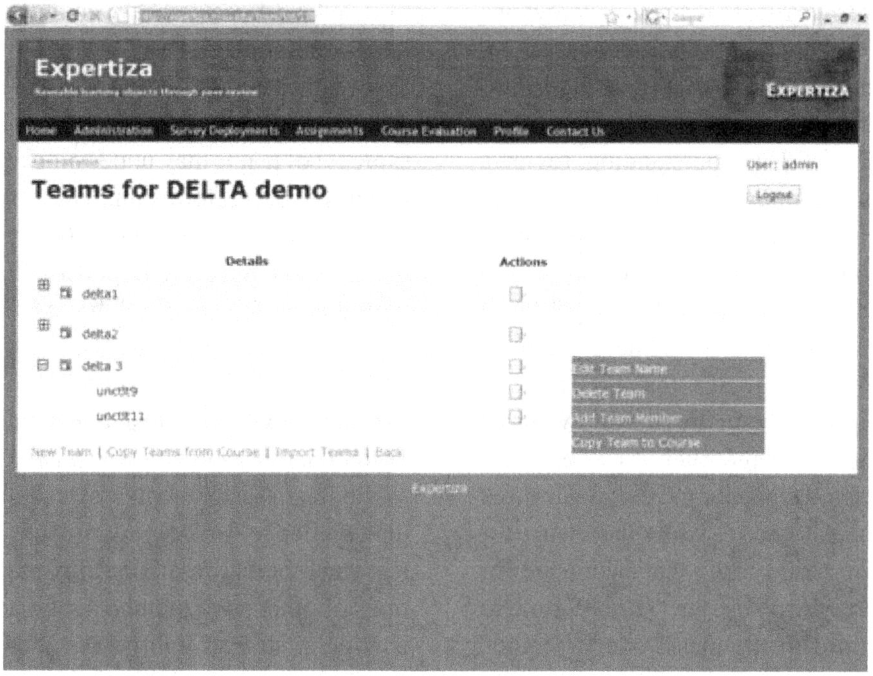

Figure 8. A student invites another student to join a team

need for teams to meet to do a review, and also because it makes it easier to reach the six reviews required for excellent reliability (Section 2.2.1).

Our dynamic reviewer-mapping algorithm will "automatically" assign a student to review the team with the least outstanding reviews (subject to constraints, e.g., that no individual may review his/her own team). However, there are many situations where dynamic mapping is not the most desirable approach. One of these is a case in which teams (or students) choose different assignment topics (as described in Section 4). Suppose the instructor allows three teams to select each topic; then it makes sense to assign the same students to review all three of these teams. Another is when the instructor wants to assign reviewers so that each team (or individual) is reviewed by one "strong" student in the upper third of the class, one "average" student, and one student from the bottom third of the class.

We hope eventually to automate these strategies, but we do not yet have enough experience to know what strategies instructors desire. Nor do we know which strategies will be counterproductive. Assigning the same set of students to review the same set of teams may undermine reviewer-competency scoring, for example. For these reasons, we allow instructors to enter (or upload) review mappings directly into Expertiza. Figure 9 shows how this is done. A CSV file can be uploaded, with each line specifying the reviewers for one submission. The "Contributor" in each line refers to a team or an individual, depending on whether or not the assignment is a team assignment.

For team assignments, "slackers" are a perennial challenge. In order to mitigate the problem, team members are assigned to assess the contributions of other team members after an assignment is over. A student will be assigned to fill out a rubric form on the contributions of each teammate (LeJeune 2006). These evaluations are presented

Figure 9. Importing a CSV file of reviewer mappings

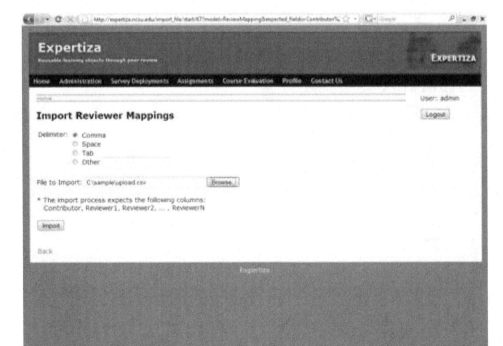

to the instructor after the assignment is complete, to factor into each student's grade. But automatic strategies for this have been devised (Pimentel et al. 2005), and could be incorporated at some future time. However, it is probably a good idea for the instructor to choose questions carefully and oversee the process to prevent a "mob mentality" from unfairly penalizing certain students (Hayes et al. 2003). Expertiza always allows an instructor to override an automatically calculated grade, recording reasons for the change (either reasons visible to the students, or reasons not visible to the student, or both).

Related Work

Egea (2002) created a Web-based system to allow tutors (TAs) and instructors to manage teams in a large (450-student) course distributed across several campuses. Students could upload a submission for their team, and instructors could view the submission, but peer review was not supported. Silva and Moreira (2003) built WebCoM, a tool to support team interaction and peer review. Their approach to team formation is similar to Expertiza's invitation mechanism, with minimum and maximum numbers of members specified for each team. Each team is assigned another group of students to review its submission, and following this, the submitters and reviewers "debate" their findings in class.

An advanced software system for supporting collaborative learning is I-MINDS (Soh et al. 2006). It uses intelligent agents to facilitate collaboration among students. One kind of agents that I-MINDS supports is group agents, which form student teams based on their profiles. It tracks participation by students in course activities and uses that information to form more effective groups. The peer-review aspect of I-MINDS consists of

Figure 10. Instructor report, main page

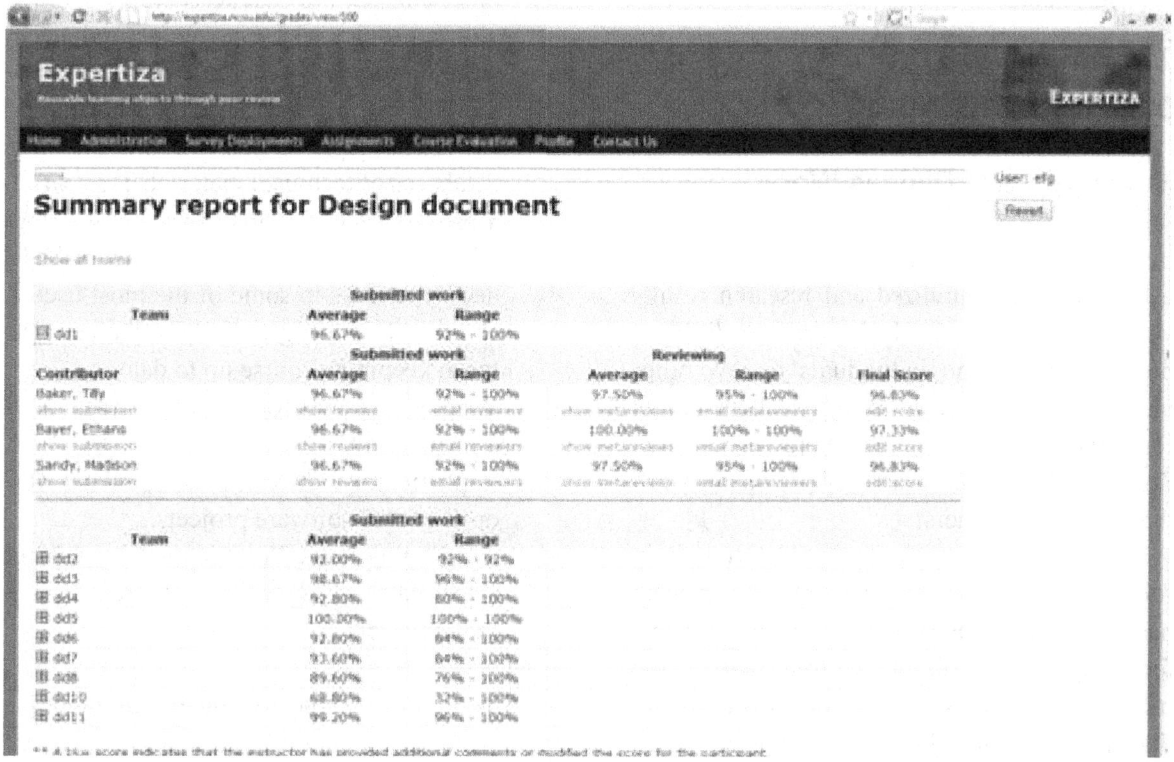

ratings by one group member of the contributions of the other group members.

Another kind of research on reviewing teams focuses on creating metrics to assess collaboration. Spada et al. (2005) identified nine dimensions of collaboration among team members, such as coordinating communication, task division, information pooling, and time management. Schümmer et al. (2005) used log files to measure collaboration and determine which users influenced others. de Pedro Puente (2007) devised a methodology for measuring experiential-reflective learning while participating in team-based wiki projects; however, the instructor did the assessment, which was quite time consuming.

Unlike other peer-review systems, Expertiza makes all of the assessment information available to the instructor in one place (Figure 10): Student submissions, peer reviews, author feedback, evaluations of teammates. The instructor actually has *more* information to use in assigning a grade to the student than in cases where all students are doing the same work and assessment is done by the course staff.

DISTRIBUTING WORK

How Expertiza Divides Work

In the academic community, peer review is how new ideas are scrutinized and research results vetted. Different individuals work on different projects, and some individuals review other individuals' work. That is an excellent model for a classroom built on collaborative learning. Students should be capable of producing work that is useful to others.

Expertiza has facilities for students to sign up for different projects (Figure 11). Each project has a limited number of "slots"; this prevents too many students (or teams) from choosing the most popular topics, and can be used to assure that all topics get chosen by someone. When the project is peer-reviewed, Expertiza tells the reviewer which choice the student or team is registered for. This prevents students who chose one topic from doing another without telling anyone. Students who do not get their selected topic may choose to be waitlisted for another. Then if another reservation is canceled (e.g., because the individual registered for the project has joined a team holding a different reservation), they may still get their first choice.

Using the signup mechanism, a large project can be broken down into parts that are manageable for a student, or a team of students. Some large projects that have been divided in this way are …

- "Annotating" online lecture notes for an entire semester with hyperlinks to relevant Web pages. A student reading the annotated notes can then click on any unfamiliar term, and be directed to a Web page describing it.
- Researching topics covered during the current semester. The instructor identifies, say, a dozen topics whose coverage may need to be modified to keep up with current research or technology. Then the students research that topic on the Web and in online databases of technical material. They write a page (typically, a wiki page) describing what they have found, including embedded hyperlinks to some of the most useful sources. This is a great help to the instructor in keeping a course up to date.
- Writing exercises for all of the chapters in a textbook for the class.
- Implementing different components for open-source software projects.
- Developing PowerPoint animations (using a template) of algorithms covered during the semester.

After the project is peer-evaluated, the highest-rated submission can be chosen for inclusion in

Figure 11. Signing up for a particular project

the assembled work. This feature has proven very useful in organizing a class to create learning objects that can be used in future classes. We believe that it could also be used to organize a class to contribute small pieces to a research project.

Related Work

While Expertiza is the only software we know of that supports parceling out pieces of a large project to students, the concept of "student-generated content" is not new. Collis (2005) reports on the advantages of having students play a role in creating class materials. Among the examples she mentions are having students work through role-play exercises, and keeping a record of the process to inform students in later classes, and designing questions that others can use to test their knowledge of the material. Hamer (2006) used Collis's approach in two courses, a CS2 data-structures course, and a course on formal methods.

His approach resembles ours, in that students were assigned different learning resources to create, and each submission underwent two rounds of peer review using the Aropā peer-review system. However, no mention is made of support for work distribution or teamwork in Aropā.

Adams and Williams (2006) developed, apparently independently, an approach very similar to Collis's. They had students in a functional-programming course create multiple-choice questions over the class material. Fewer than 10% of the questions were usable as submitted by the students, but the instructor was able to work about 80% of the remaining questions into usable shape in about half the time it would have taken to develop similar questions from scratch. Their observation that somewhat less than 10% of the questions are usable as-is matches our experience. Their observation that most of the remaining questions are salvageable is more optimistic than ours; our experience is that about 25% of the questions can be adapted with reasonable effort.

Not all student-generated content comes from computer science, of course. Good examples from other disciplines include an Online Encyclopedia of Criminal Justice (Mentor 2005), a "plant facts glossary" that includes images that were linked in by distance-education students (OSU 2007), and an Ethics in Computing site (Gehringer 2001) composed of student-generated pages on over 100 topics. Sener (2007) presents a rationale for student-generated content, and cites many examples.

RESULTS

Several experiments with Expertiza have shown its value for generating reusable course material. One of the most difficult aspects of teaching certain kinds of science, mathematics, engineering, and technology courses is coming up with enough new problems to assign to students. In the Internet age, it is risky to rely upon textbook problems, since students may have access to the solution manual (Kennedy et al. 2007). Expertiza's ability to manage creation of additional material fills the bill nicely. Students in the author's object-oriented design class have written examples and exercises

(Gehringer et al. 2006) for a new textbook on o-o design (Skrien 2008). Sixty-three percent of the students responding to a survey either agreed or strongly agreed that they learned a lot from doing the peer-reviewed exercises. What is more, 55% said they enjoyed the exercise (Figure 12). The response rate to the survey was 58%. Although students do not necessarily enjoy doing homework, in this case the sense of competition was enhanced by a "playoff round" in which the best-rated exercises from the original assignment competed for extra credit of up to 50%. This gave the authors an extra chance to revise their work. The proof of effectiveness was the fact that the publisher, McGraw-Hill, on the advice of the author, requested that 17 of the students (from a class of 74) grant copyright permission for their work, or derivative work thereof, to be included in the published textbook.

During the 2007–08 academic year, the author studied 10 classes that assigned homework to be done on wikis (Gehringer 2008b).[3] One hundred two student respondents from the 10 classes rated several statements on a 5-point Likert scale, with 1 being "strongly agree" and 5 "strongly disagree." The three classes that used peer review for the wiki assignments (60 respondents) showed stronger agreement that the wiki had helped them think

Figure 12. Student responses on learning and enjoyment of peer-reviewed exercises (Adapted from Gehringer et al. 2006)

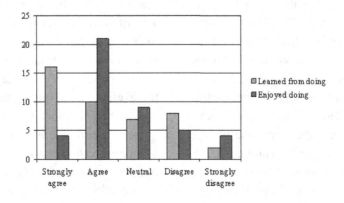

critically (2.12) than the students (42 respondents) who were reviewed by the instructor, or not reviewed at all (2.51).[4] This finding was significant at the 90% level ($p = 0.064$). They also agreed that the feedback they received helped them to improve their work (2.33 for the peer-reviewed students; 2.45 for those reviewed in other ways). This was despite the fact that they disagreed that, "I received adequate feedback on the quality of my work" (2.68 for the peer-reviewed students; 2.62 for those reviewed by other means). However, neither of the differences on feedback were significant. (see Table 1)

In spring 2008, Expertiza was used in a second-semester Java programming class for the creation of active-learning exercises (McConnell 2005). Students, after being exposed to a dozen or so active-learning exercises, were asked to create their own exercise for some topic covered in the course. They worked in teams of two or three, using a wiki as a collaborative space. When asked if they learned a lot from doing the active-learning exercises, 48% agreed or strongly agreed, compared to only 24% who disagreed or strongly disagreed (Figure 13). Students were somewhat more positive about whether they *enjoyed* doing the exercises in class; 57% agreed or strongly agreed, and only 14% disagreed or strongly disagreed. Asked whether they enjoyed devising a new active-learning exercise, 62% agreed or strongly agreed, vs. only 24% who disagreed or strongly disagreed. There were 50 students in the class, and the response rate to the survey was 42%.

Some of these student-devised exercises were then used in the course. One of the exercises was able to be used in the spring semester, because it was on a topic (mergesort) that had not yet been covered in class when the students devised the exercise. Four of the student-generated exercises were used when the same course was taught in the summer.

In the spring, the student-generated exercise ranked above the average of the instructor-generated exercises in learning (3.2 to 3.1, with a scale of 1 to 5, where 5 was high) and enjoyment (3.0 to 2.8). These differences were not significant. In the summer, the student-generated exercises ranked below the instructor-generated exercises in learning (2.9 to 3.5) but ahead of them in enjoyment (3.8 to 3.5). These differences were significant at the 99% and 90% confidence levels, respectively. The disparity can likely be explained by the fact that three of the four active-learning exercises were games—takeoffs on popular TV game shows—designed as review exercises, not intended to teach new material. The bottom line is that student-generated exercises can take their place in a course alongside instructor-generated exercises. This provides instructors with a way to incorporate many more active-learning exercises than they would have the time or creativity to design themselves, and helps circumvent the lack of published active-learning exercises on many topics that need to be covered in class. (see Table 2)

The experiment is described further by Gehringer and Miller (2009).

Table 1. Comparing peer review with other forms of wiki assessment: Student survey

	Not peer reviewed	Peer reviewed
"The experience of using a wiki helped me to think critically about the subject matter of this assignment."	2.51	2.12
"Using a wiki made it easy to collaborate with other students."	2.41	2.00
"I received adequate feedback on the quality of my work."	2.60	2.68
"The feedback I received helped me to improve my work."	2.44	2.33

All questions rated on a scale of 1 = "strongly agree" to 5 = "strongly disagree"

Figure 13. Student responses on learning and enjoyment of active-learning exercises

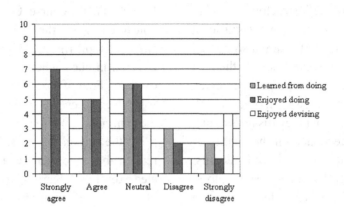

Table 2. Learning and enjoyment of active-learning exercises used in class

	Spring		Summer	
	Learning	**Enjoyment**	**Learning**	**Enjoyment**
All exercises	3.1	2.8	3.5	3.5
Instructor-generated exercises	3.1	2.8	3.7	3.3
Student-generated exercises	3.2	3.0	2.9	3.8
Student-generated games			2.9	3.9
Student-generated non-games	3.2	3.0	3.0	3.5

SUMMARY AND FUTURE WORK

The Expertiza project began as an effort to show that students could create course materials that are ready for "prime time." The evidence so far is that it has succeeded, albeit on a small scale. Efforts are underway to widen its impact. Since the project's inception, 17 instructors at 9 universities have used the system. Expertiza has evolved into a system with support for a variety of kinds of collaboration, from team formation, to feedback from authors, and evaluation of teammates.

Several enhancements to Expertiza are underway. We are working on constraint-based programming to assign students to project teams. Instructors will be able to control the demographics and relative strength of students comprising a team. To improve quality control of reviews, we are looking at automatic metareviewing. Students would submit their reviews, and the system would analyze them, to check whether there is an appropriate amount of textual feedback, and whether the feedback contains keywords from the material being reviewed. This would give the student an idea of whether a review is likely to pass muster with a human metareviewer. If the review was rated poorly by the automatic strategy, the student could improve and resubmit it.

Because it contains comments and evaluations of material by students about other students in the class, Expertiza is, in effect, a social network. This metaphor can be carried further, so students can see summary information about individuals in the class, with their permission. The system might, for example, list the top three students in several categories (best work, as reviewed by others; best reviews; best contribution to team). This would give students an incentive to try to improve their work in each of these categories.

We intend to turn Expertiza into an open-source project, and solicit contributions from software-engineering classes at other universities. This will help meet the need for open-source projects that students can develop in class. Expertiza is ideal for this role, because it requires no special hardware or peripherals, and all students are familiar with its project domain (group work in classes). Expertiza itself can be used to review code submitted by other students (Gehringer 2008c).

By providing instructors with a large amount of assessment data on project work, Expertiza makes it possible for them to place greater emphasis on projects and less on exams. This, in turn, helps to educate students for the project-based responsibilities they will encounter in their careers.

ACKNOWLEDGMENT

The Expertiza project is funded by the National Science Foundation under award 0536558. Additional support has been provided by the NCSU Faculty Center for Teaching and Learning, and the NCSU LITRE project (Learning in a Technology-Rich Environment), and the NCSU/Duke Center for Advanced Computing and Communication, through the sponsorship of the William and Ida Friday Institute for Educational Innovation.

REFERENCES

Adams, A., & Williams, S. (2006). Customer-driven development for rapid production of assessment learning objects. *The Electronic Journal of e-Learning, 4*(1), 1-6. Retrieved from http://www.ejel.org

Black, P., & Wiliam, D. (1998). Assessment and classroom learning. *Assessment in Education, 5*(1), 7–74. doi:10.1080/0969595980050102

Blackboard Academic Suite Release 8.0. (2008). *Critical thinking tools*. Retrieved September 2008, from http://www.blackboard.com/release8/

Carlson, P. A., & Berry, F. C. (2003). Calibrated peer review and assessing learning outcomes. In *Proceedings of the 33rd ASEE/IEEE Frontiers in Education Conference*. Retrieved from http://fie.engrng.pitt.edu/fie2003/papers/1066.pdf

Chapman, O. L., & Fiore, M. A. (2000). Calibrated peer review. *Journal of Interactive Instruction Development*.

Cho, K., & Schunn, C. (2007). Scaffolded writing and rewriting in the discipline: A Web-based reciprocal peer-review system. *Computers & Education, 48*, 409–426. doi:10.1016/j.compedu.2005.02.004

Cho, K., Schunn, C. D., & Wilson, R. W. (2006). Validity and reliability of scaffolded peer assessment of writing from instructor and student perspectives. *Journal of Educational Psychology, 98*(4), 891–901. doi:10.1037/0022-0663.98.4.891

Collis, B. (2005). *The contributing student: A blend of pedagogy and technology*. Australasia, Auckland, New Zealand: EDUCAUSE.

Daedalus integrated writing environment: Details. (2008). Retrieved September 2008, from http://www.daedalus.com/products_diwe_details.asp de Pedro Puente, X. (2007). New method using Wikis and forums to evaluate individual contributions in cooperative work while promoting experiential learning: Results from preliminary experience. In *Proceedings of the 2007 international Symposium on Wikis, WikiSym '07*, Montreal, Quebec, Canada (pp. 87-92). New York: ACM Press.

Denning, T., Kelly, M., Lindquist, D., Malani, R., Griswold, W. G., & Simon, B. (2007). Lightweight preliminary peer review: Does in-class peer review make sense? *SIGCSE Bulletin, 39*(1), 266–270. doi:10.1145/1227504.1227406

Dumais, S. T., & Nielsen, J. (1992). Automating the assignment of submitted manuscripts to reviewers. In N. Belkin, P. Ingwersen, & A. M. Petersen (Eds.), *Proceedings of the 15th Annual International ACM SIGIR Conference on Research and Development in Information Retrieval, SIGIR '92*, Copenhagen, Denmark (pp. 233-244). New York: ACM Press.

Edwards, S. H., & Pérez-Quiñones, M. A. (2007). Experiences using test-driven development with an automated grader. *J. Comput. Small Coll., 22*(3), 44–50.

Egea, K. (2003). Managing the managers: Collaborative virtual teams with large staff and student numbers. In T. Greeing & R. Lister (Eds.), *Proc. Australasian Computing Education Conference: Conferences in Research and Practice in Information Technology (ACE2003)*, Adelaide.

Gehringer, E. F. (2001). Building an ethics in computing Web site using peer review. In *Proc. of the 2001 Am. Society for Engineering Education Annual Conference.*

Gehringer, E. F. (2008a). Understanding and relating to your international students. In *Proceedings of the American Society for Engineering Education Annual Conference*, Pittsburgh, PA.

Gehringer, E. F. (2008b). Assessing students' Wiki contributions. In *Proceedings of the American Society for Engineering Education Annual Conference*, Pittsburgh, PA.

Gehringer, E. F. (2008c). New features for peer review of code and Wikis [faculty poster] In *Proceedings of the 39th SIGCSE Technical Symposium on Computer Science Education,* Portland, OR, USA. Retrieved from http://research.csc.ncsu.edu/efg/expertiza/presentations/Code-and-wikis-poster.ppt

Gehringer, E. F., & Cui, Y. (2002). An effective strategy for dynamic mapping of peer reviewers. In *Proc. of the 2002 Am. Society for Engineering Education Annual Conference.*

Gehringer, E. F., Ehresman, L. M., Conger, S. G., & Wagle, P. (2007). Reusable learning objects through peer review: The Expertiza approach. *Innovate: Journal of Online Education, 3*(5).

Gehringer, E. F., Ehresman, L. M., & Skrien, D. J. (2006). Expertiza: Students helping to write an OOD text. In *Companion to the 21st ACM SIGPLAN Conference on Object-Oriented Programming Systems, Languages, and Applications, OOPSLA '06*, Portland, Oregon, USA (pp. 901-906). New York: ACM Press.

Gehringer, E. F., & Miller, C. S. (2009). Student-generated active-learning exercises. In Proceedings of the *40th SIGCSE Technical Symposium on Computer Science Education, SIGCSE '09*, Chattanooga, TN, USA. New York: ACM Press. Retrieved from http://research.csc.ncsu.edu/efg/expertiza/papers/sigcse09.pdf

Griswold, W. G., & Simon, B. (2006). Ubiquitous presenter: Fast, scalable active learning for the whole classroom. In *Proceedings of the 11th Annual SIGCSE Conference on innovation and Technology in Computer Science Education, ITICSE '06*, Bologna, Italy (pp. 358-358). New York: ACM Press.

Hamer, J. (2006). Some experiences with the "contributing student approach." In *Proceedings of the 11th Annual SIGCSE Conference on innovation and Technology in Computer Science Education, ITICSE '06*, Bologna, Italy (pp. 68-72). New York: ACM Press.

Hamer, J., Ma, K. T., & Kwong, H. H. (2005). A method of automatic grade calibration in peer assessment. In A. Young & D. Tolhurst (Eds.), *Proceedings of the 7th Australasian Conference on Computing Education – Vol. 42*, Newcastle, New South Wales, Australia (pp. 67-72). Darlinghurst, Australia: Australian Computer Society.

Hayes, J. H., Lethbridge, T. C., & Port, D. (2003). Evaluating individual contribution toward group software engineering projects. In *Proceedings of the 25th international Conference on Software Engineering*, Portland, Oregon (pp. 622-627). Washington, DC: IEEE Computer Society.

Keeney-Kennicut, W., Guernsel, A. B., & Simpson, N. (2008). Overcoming student resistance to a teaching innovation. [Retrieved from http://www.georgiasouthern.edu/iostl]. *J. for the Scholarship of Teaching and Learning, 2008*(January), 1–26.

Kennedy, J., Shollenberger, K., & Widmann, J. (2007). Student use of author's textbook solution manuals: Effect on student learning of mechanics fundamentals. In *Proc. of the 2007 Am. Society for Engineering Education Annual Conference*.

Kerr, P. M., Park, K. H., & Domazlicky, B. R. (1995). Peer grading of essays in a principles of microeconomics course. *Journal of Education for Business, 70*(6), 15–25.

Lauw, H. W., Lim, E.-P., & Wang, K. (2007). Summarizing review scores of "unequal" reviewers. In *Proceedings of the 2007 SIAM International Conference on Data Mining*, Minneapolis, MN (pp. 539-544).

LeJeune, N. (2006). Assessment of individuals on CS group projects. *J. Comput. Small Coll., 22*(1), 231–237.

McConnell, J. J. (2005). Active and cooperative learning: Tips and tricks (part I). *SIGCSE Bulletin, 37*(2), 27–30. doi:10.1145/1083431.1083457

Mentor, K. (2005). *Online encyclopedia of criminal justice*. Retrieved December 2008, from http://cjencyclopedia.com

Merelo-Guervós, J., & Castillo-Valdivieso, P. (2004). Conference paper assignment using a combined greedy/evolutionary algorithm. In *Parallel problem solving from nature - PPSN VIII* (LNCS 3242, pp. 602-611). Berlin, Germany: Springer-Verlag.

Moodle. (2008). *Workshop module – MoodleDocs*. Retrieved September 2008, from http://docs.moodle.org/en/Workshop

Ohio State University. (2007). *PlantFacts glossary*. Retrieved December 2008, from http://140.254.84.203/wiki/index.php/PlantFacts_Glossary

Pesenhofer, A., Mayer, R., & Rauber, A. (2008). Automating the management of scientific conferences using information mining techniques. *J. Digital Information Management, 6*(1).

Pimentel, M., Gerosa, M. A., Fuks, H., & de Lucena, C. J. (2005). Assessment of collaboration in online courses. In *Proceedings of the 2005 Conference on Computer Support for Collaborative Learning: Learning 2005: The Next 10 Years!* Taipei, Taiwan (pp. 494-498). International Society of the Learning Sciences.

Rodriguez, M. A., & Bollen, J. (2008). An algorithm to determine peer-reviewers, In [th *ACM Conference on Information and Knowledge Management*, Napa Valley, CA.]. *Proceedings of the CIKM, 08*, 17.

Sakai Services. *Information services*. (2008). Retrieved September 2008, from http://www.nitle.org/index.php/nitle/content/view/full/1388

Schümmer, T., Strijbos, J., & Berkel, T. (2005). A new direction for log file analysis in CSCL: Experiences with a spatio-temporal metric. In *Proceedings of the 2005 Conference on Computer Support For Collaborative Learning: Learning 2005: the Next 10 Years!* Taipei, Taiwan (pp. 567-576). International Society of the Learning Sciences.

Sener, J. (2007). In search of student-generated content in online education. *e-Mentor, 4*(21). Retrieved from http://www.e-mentor.edu.pl/eng

Silva, E., & Moreira, D. (2003). WebCoM: A tool to use peer review to improve student interaction. *Journal of Educational Resources in Computing, 3*(1), 3. doi:10.1145/958795.958798

Skrien, D. (2008). *Object-oriented design using Java*. New York: McGraw-Hill.

Soh, L., Khandaker, N., Liu, X., & Jiang, H. (2006). A computer-supported cooperative learning system with multiagent intelligence. In *Proceedings of the Fifth international Joint Conference on Autonomous Agents and Multiagent Systems, AAMAS '06*, Hakodate, Japan (pp. 1556-1563). New York: ACM Press.

Spada, H., Meier, A., Rummel, N., & Hauser, S. (2005). A new method to assess the quality of collaborative process in CSCL. In *Proceedings of the 2005 Conference on Computer Support For Collaborative Learning: Learning 2005: the Next 10 Years!* Taipei, Taiwan (pp 622-631). International Society of the Learning Sciences.

Wang, F., Chen, B., & Miao, Z. (2008a). A survey on reviewer assignment problem. In *Proc. of the New Frontiers in Applied Artificial Intelligence, 21st International Conference on Industrial, Engineering and Other Applications of Applied Intelligent Systems, IEA/AIE 2008*, Wroclaw, Poland.

Wang, Y. (2002). *Dynamic assignment of peer reviewers for teams*. Unpublished master's thesis, North Carolina State University, USA. Retrieved from http://www.lib.ncsu.edu/theses/available/etd-11012002-125644/unrestricted/etd.pdf

Wang, Y., Yijun, L., Collins, M., & Liu, P. (2008b). Process improvement of peer code review and behavior analysis of its participants. In *Proceedings of the 39th SIGCSE Technical Symposium on Computer Science Education, SIGCSE '08*, Portland, OR, USA (pp. 107-111). New York: ACM Press.

Zeller, A. (2000). Making students read and review code. *SIGCSE Bulletin, 32*(3), 89–92. doi:10.1145/353519.343090

ENDNOTES

[1] There are systems to partially automate the grading of (computer) programming assignments, such as Web-CAT (Edwards & Pérez-Quiñonez 2007). But even here, style must be graded by the instructor or staff.

[2] A fourth type, Google Docs, will soon be added. Google Docs have some aspects in common with files (they are editable as files), but like URLs or wiki pages, they reside at a fixed Web address.

[3] The referenced paper only includes data from the 6 fall classes.

[4] The statement was, "The experience of using a wiki helped me to think critically about the subject matter of this assignment."

Chapter 6
Improving the Performance of Virtual Teams through Team Dynamics

Daphna Shwarts-Asher
Tel Aviv University, Israel

ABSTRACT

The aim of this chapter is to understanding how virtual teams operate in organizations. Qualitative data was collected by interviewing 20 virtual team managers and members of 20 different organizations. A semi-structured interview format was used to collect extensive information of the characteristics of the organizations, what projects virtual team participated in, how virtual teams operate and the difficulties virtual teams face. Using a comprehensive literature review and interviews summaries, a model, suggesting that team dynamics can increase the teams' output, was developed, and propositions that are raised by the model are discussed. The virtual team is a common way of working nowadays, and with the growing use of Internet applications and firms' globalization the use of virtual teams will expand in the future. Thus, this chapter provides new directions for future research in the field of virtual teams.

INTRODUCTION

Virtual teams are an integral part of many organizations today. Due to dispersion of their members in time and space, a virtual team tends to rely on electronic communication and information technologies to accomplish its work. The dispersion of members is also presenting new challenges: cultural, geographic, and time differences make it difficult for a leader to provide structure to followers, evaluate their performance, inspire and develop them, and enable them to identify with the organization. Kahai et al. (2007) suggests that we are just beginning to understand leadership in virtual teams. Tarmizi et al. (2007) stats that collaboration in distributed settings has become a reality in organizational life, yet we still have much to learn. DeRosa et al. (2004) showed that geographic distance and technological complexity are secondary to processes of adaptation, as humans remain the most complex and flexible part of the communication system.

DOI: 10.4018/978-1-60566-786-7.ch006

The aim of this investigation is to identify enabling and disenabling factors in the development and operation of virtual teams; to evaluate the importance of factors such as team structure and team dynamics as contributors to virtual team performance. This study attempts to provide a theoretical model that illustrates monitoring and assessment of activity in computer-supported collaborative projects in an e-work environment. The research question asks whether the output of virtual teams (namely teams whose members do not meet face-to-face) such as efficiency and satisfaction, is affected by the team members interaction. This question deals with the dynamics within the team: Is it social oriented? Or maybe task oriented? Is the social aspect of team work characterized by positive or negative phrases? Is the task aspect of team work characterized by question or answer phrases? Our aim is to trace the mechanism in which output is achieved in virtual settings, and the ways that these processes differ from face-to-face settings. This research contributes to a better understanding of virtual teams in hope of improving the teams work in the virtual world.

BACKGROUND

Virtual teams are becoming increasingly prevalent as businesses bring geographically dispersed members together to achieve a common goal. Majchrzak et al. (2004) stated that it isn't necessary any more to bring team members together to get their best work: In fact, they can be even more productive if they stay separated and do all their collaborating virtually; when carefully managed, the clash of perspectives led to fundamental solutions, turning distance and diversity into a competitive advantage.

Yet, virtual teams are less successful than face-to-face teams on most outcome measures (Denton, 2006; Potter & Balthazard, 2002). Despite the wide spread of virtual teams, little

is known about virtual team processes. Much of virtual team research fails to examine variations in virtual team characteristics that may affect team communication behaviors (Timmerman & Scott, 2006).

Though Potter & Balthazard (2002) argued that interaction style predicts outcomes in virtual teams in ways very similar to those seen in face-to-face teams, Branson, Clausen & Sung (2008) claimed that face-to-face teams form and function differently than computer-mediated (virtual) teams. The differences affect the ability of groups of people to successfully form a team that can function effectively. For example, Warkentin, Sayeed & Hightower (1997) found that virtual team members report lower levels of satisfaction. Lurey & Raisinghani (2001) showed that the teams' processes effecting team performance as well.

Researchers investigating virtual teams offered some explanations for the differences between virtual and face-to-face teams. One explanation refer to the different perceptions of the virtual and face-to-face team members: Webster & Wong (2008) found that local members of teams report different perceptions of local and remote members - More positive perceptions of their local than their remote members; Staples & Webster (2007) suggested that differential outcomes for traditional and technology-supported virtual teams evolve from self-efficacy differences. Another explanation refer to the different setting of the virtual teams, such as frequency and distance (Cramton & Webber, 1999), lack of feedback and information about team processes (Geister, Konradt & Hertel, 2006), the difficulty in sharing information (Thompson & Coovert, 2003) and the distance communication tools as a limiting technology (Straus & McGrath, 1994).

The time duration of a team existence also influences their output. Saunders & Ahuja (2006) claimed that ongoing distributed teams are more difficult to manage and experience greater variance in well-being outcome levels, whereas in temporary teams, members are more focused on task-related outcomes. Martell & Guzzo (1991) showed in a laboratory experiment were participants were given positive, negative, or no performance feedback that only an immediate recollections (in contrast to a delayed one) were affected from ineffective behavior. Their findings imply that temporary teams are as difficult to manage as the ongoing teams. Jarvenpaa, Knoll & Leidner (1998) suggested the presence of "swift" trust in order to built trust in teams in the short term. Shwarts-Asher, Ahituv & Etzion (2008) introduced the "swift" structure as a new tool for managing virtual teams.

Team Dynamics

Hackman (1987) suggested that team design influences the team's output through its impact on processes. Chidambaram & Tung (2005) claimed that performance is driven by social demands and task demands.

Clausen & Sung (2008) claimed that face-to-face teams form and function differently than computer-mediated (virtual) teams because different social processes in face-to-face and virtual teams. The social context of virtual teams is one of the major explanations of why virtual teams produce negative outcomes: virtual teams have weaker team identity (Bouas & Arrow, 1996), the fact that virtual team members are not familiar with one another (Gruenfeld et al., 1996), have less affection to one another (Weisband & Atwater, 1999) and a weaker social ties (Warkentin, Sayeed & Hightower, 1997). Strong social ties in virtual teams can be achieved but will take longer time than in face-to-face teams (Burke & Chidambaram, 1996).

Some social studies suggest that in order to increase the effectiveness of virtual teams, sources of conflict and ways to resolve conflict should be explored (Shin, 2005). Montoya-Weiss, Massey & Song (2001) claim that the way virtual teams manage internal conflict is a crucial factor in their success. Guerra et al. (2005) showed that relation-

ship and task conflicts decrease both workers' job satisfaction and well-being.

One possible source of the social conflict is negative emotions, which can be easily spread by the contagious effect. Ashkanasy, Hartel & Daus (2002) showed the contagious effect of employees' mood on their customers' mood, and on other team members. Hareli and Rafaeli indicated that strong emotions of one person influence not only the target of the emotion but also the observers. Barsade (2002) presented the ripple effect as an effect that can spread emotions within groups which influences both individuals and team processes. Garcia et al. (2006) showed that it doesn't matter if a negative phrase is directed to one of the team members or to the team as a whole: participants generally responded negatively to negative comments regardless of the level of identity to which the comment was directed.

The contagious effect of team members' emotions is important because the emotions within the team affect its output. Diefendorff & Gosserand (2003) stated that emotional processes at work can lead to positive or negative team output. The discussed outputs are performance, creativity, cooperation (Brief & Weiss, 2002), trust (Dunn & Schweitzer, 2005), persistence, intensiveness (Myeong-Gu, Feldman-Barrett & Bartunek, 2004), and attitude variables such as satisfaction, organizational commitment, and burnout (Thoresen, Kaplan, Barsky & de Chermont, 2003). Ashkanasy, Hartel & Daus (2002) claimed that though positive emotions lead directly to positive outputs, negative emotions have an indirect effect. They explained this partially due to the fact that negative mood is an unwanted mood that people try to get rid of. Therefore negative mood is an unstable mood, compared to a positive mood that people have a strong interest of sustaining it.

Personality and circumstances significantly contribute to emotion display (Tan, Foo, Chong & Ng, 2003; Weiss & Cropanzano, 1996) and the creation of the emotion within the team. Hillary & Sidanius (2006) found that compared to minorities, white people were less supportive of affirmative actions. From the circumstances aspect, Weiss & Cropanzano (1996) explored the internal factors of emotions at work as a team management or work team characteristics. It seems that the gender also affects emotion display: Lind (1999) explored the gender impact of virtual collaboration compared to face-to-face teams: Women in the virtual groups perceived that the team stuck together and helped each other more than men did. Also, the women were more satisfied with the virtual team than men and felt that team conflict was readily resolved. Simpson & Stroh (2004) found that woman pretends to have positive emotions while man pretends to have negative emotions.

Team members' emotions have a behavioral impact. According to the evolutionary emotion research approach, emotions are programs that were developed in order to help human beings survive. Evolutionary psychologists refer to emotions as programs that call for behavioral reactions (Weiss, 2002). Emotional driven behaviors are directly response to emotional experiment, as opposed to attitude driven behaviors. For example, retirement is a behavior which demands entire situation evaluation; therefore it is an attitude driven behavior. Absence, on the other hand, results from a spontaneous decision; therefore it is an immediate emotion level function (Weiss & Cropanzano, 1996).

Another kind of behavioral reaction is communication within the team members, their way to interact with one another and the feedback they give each other. Watts & Lee (1999) laboratory experiment concluded that participants distorted negative information less, i.e., were more accurate and honest, when they used computer-mediated communication than face-to-face or telephone communication. They concluded that delivering (and receiving) timely and accurate negative information is critical for performance improvement.

Team Structure

Division of Labor and Work Process

The division of labor does not have a direct influence on team performance, but has an indirect influence, by means of perceived efficiency and team coordination (Strijbos et al., 2004), and is a stronger predication variable than individual characteristics (Ahuja, Galletta & Carley, 2003). The use of expertise assists in reducing errors (Potter & Balthazard, 2002a) and function diversity is important in achieving team efficiency (Bunderson & Sutcliffe, 2002). A team that is structurally diverse is one that its members have different positions or tasks and are distributed in different branches, can be exposed to unique information. In this manner, sharing unique external information elevates performance (Cummings, 2004).

In large teams meeting procedures are better known and there is better technology coordination then in small groups (Bradner, Mark & Hertel, 2002). Studies show that successful teams focus: on the task (Hofner, 1996), on structured goals (Huang et al., 2003) and on the development of routine (DeSanctis, Wright & Jiang, 2001). Successful teams also take a lot of time to understand the process and contents of the work (Iacono & Weisband, 1997 ; Ocker & Fjermestad, 2000), especially in the initial stages (Hause et al., 2001). Not only does the medium limit the team's ability to coordinate information (Graetz et al., 1998), virtual teams spend a great deal of time understanding how to execute the task (Lebie, Rhoades & McGrath, 1996), and team meeting that it's members are distant physically take longer time than face-to-face meetings (Siegel et al., 1986). Coordination process are related positively to performance and satisfaction (Powell, Piccoli & Ives, 2004), and become more significant as time passes (Burke & Chidambaram, 1995).

Hierarchy and Leadership

Research on Group Decision Support Systems (GDSS) has generally focused on democratic groups whose members typically share the same objectives. In organizations, however, there are many situations where groups have a leader who has the power to override the group's recommendation, the objective of the leader may not be the same as the objective of each member, and not everyone may have the same information (Barkhi et al. 1998).

In order to explain the importance of the manager in integrative groups, Maier (1967) compares the group to a starfish and the leader of the group to the starfish's central nervous system. When individuals act as an organized unit, they become a higher type of organization - a single whole organism. Even when there is no formal division of labor, the role of the leader is divided between team members (Johnson et al., 2002). When there is a formal leader, status labels has a strong effect on team members (Weisband, Schneider & Connolly, 1995). But a series of studies has shown that more importantly, effective virtual leadership is dependent on the ability to communicate (Kayworth & Leidner, 2001/2002 ; Tyran, Tyran & Shepherd, 2003 ; Kim, Hiltz & Turoff, 2002). In practice, leaders send more messages (and longer ones) than others (Yoo & Alavi, 2004).

Employees can gain practical and highly current experiential knowledge from working in novel situations using new organizational processes and technologies. Such knowledge can provide competitive advantage (Pauleen, Corbitt & Yoong, 2007). Horwitz, Bravington, & Silvis (2006) research results indicated that cross-cultural communication improvement, managerial and leadership communication, goal and role clarification, and relationship building are most important to virtual team performance. Glückler & Schrott (2007) claims that managers of virtual knowledge networks should focus their attention not only on the qualifications of individu-

als, but also on communication structures within their work groups.

Virtual teams' leaders have to display different types of leadership style. Conducted research explores few examples: Sosik (1997) indicates that groups working under high transformational leadership generated more original solutions, supportive remarks, solution clarifications and questions about solutions and reported higher levels of perceived performance, extra effort and satisfaction with the leader than groups working under low transformational leadership (Sosik, 1997). Sivunen (2006) results show four different tactics employed in enhancing identification with the team: catering for the individual, giving positive feedback, bringing out common goals and workings and talking up the team activities and face-to-face meetings. Gil et al. (2005) stats that to make more useful change-oriented leader actions, it would be advisable to identify, modify or improve team climate, using strategies such as management by objectives, delegation and empowerment and so on. It would also be necessary to boost group potency before going ahead with change, for example, by developing the skills of team members, or by fostering the self-confidence of the team.

Virtual teams' leaders' perception of their role depends on their statues and culture: Konradt & Hoch (2007) examined the perceived importance of line managers and middle managers in virtual teams of what work roles and leadership functions are necessary to promote virtual team success and performance. They found that control-related roles were perceived to be most important. Additionally, middle managers compared to line managers perceived people oriented leadership functions and flexibility-related work roles as more important whereas line managers compared to middle managers perceived stability leadership functions as more important. Nicholson et al. (2007) stated that FTF and cross-cultural virtual team-members value different ingredients of leadership in different phases of the project. Further, within virtual teams, national culture plays a role in determining what is considered effective leadership.

In spite of the different perceptions, there are some important variables for all virtual teams' leaders and managers. Stevenson & McGrath (2004) investigated managers' perceptions of variables important to successful teams, emphasizing key differences between off-site and on-site teams. They found that key variables included reporting procedures, importance of solid work structure, team hierarchy, team leadership, and communication. Lee-Kelley (2002) identified that variables such as project objectives, team size, frequency of team changes and project duration play significant roles in the relationship between the project leader and his/her perception of project difficulties (Lee-Kelley, 2002).

In this section we presented virtual teams as a growing phenomenon and the need for further social research of them. The literature review focused on the different social processes of face-to-face and virtual teams in the light of leading virtual teams. In the next section, a summery of in-depth interviews with virtual team managers and members is presented. The purpose of the interviews was to deepen the understanding of virtual teams work in real life. Both the literature review and the interviews summery will assist in develop the research model.

IN-DEPTH INTERVIEWS WITH VIRTUAL TEAM MANAGERS AND MEMBERS

Rather than building a theoretical model based solely on the literature review, we decided to confront previous theories with the workplace environment by interviewing virtual team managers and members. The purpose of the interviews was to deepen the understanding of virtual teams work in workplace. The interviewees included employees from a wide range of organizations, who were part of a virtual team that worked

on various projects. Examples of interviewees' positions include: software engineer at a British software security company; head of a support team at an American processors manufacturing company; sales coordinator at an American semi-conductors firm and so on. The interview focused on the characteristics of the organization, the nature and activities of the virtual team, how the virtual team operates and the difficulties the virtual team faced. The aim of the interviews was to outline the difficulties virtual team members faced, by examining the development and existence of structural characteristics in virtual teams.

All interviewees defined a virtual team with five to ten members when part of its members are geographically separated, yet share the same task. The interviewees work in a wide range of organizations: organization size – a small start up companies versus a global firm; organization age- young versus well established; organizational sector- government, medication, software and so on. It seems that a virtual team is a common phenomenon in different organizations. Most of the interviewees described their team as a performance team, with simple (and not complicated) tasks, such as supplying solutions to technical problems.

The interviewees pointed out that pure virtual team (teams that never meet face to face) are not common. All virtual team conducted timely face to face meetings, even with a partial (and not complete) team member forum. Yet, most of time, team members were geographically separated.

The time duration of virtual teams projects varied: a project in the semi-conductor industry is between two to eight weeks; a software network communication system project can last more than a year; R&D of a medication product lasts two years; a support team is usually described as team with widthwise function (*"it is always needed"*), specifically, the latter exists for more than ten years. In spite of the time duration differences, there is a similarity in the (virtual and face to face) meetings patterns. During the projects, the interviewees stated that face to face meetings were scheduled periodically (for example – a monthly meetings), while virtual meetings using e-mails and phone calls were on a daily basis.

Many interviewees stated that different communication tools are served for different goals: a head of support team claimed that face to face meeting coordination is complicated; therefore face to face meetings are only conducted when a break through in the project is needed. On the other hand, e-mail communication is used for quick information transformation. A development engineer described his different communication needs:

- *The need to consult with colleagues concerning decision making*
- *Sometimes I consult others that hold information I don't have.*
- *My output code is other team member input code. We need to plan together how my code should look like.*

These types of communication are done by the development engineer using e-mails and phone calls.

There are some structural elements in teams that were described: a formal hierarchy – all teams had a team leader; an organic division of labor – marketing people, developers, and producers and so on; and a work process that outlined the team framework. For example, work process for a R&D team include: High level design, design, modules distribution, implementation, and project completion. Formal hierarchy, division of labor and work process exists in the face to face meetings, as opposed to virtual meetings. It seems that the virtual communication serves the team members for specific problems solutions.

The reason for carefully planning face to face meeting is economic. Face to face meetings are expensive: transportation cost and time spent requires the meeting to be efficient and effective.

A development engineer described the advantages and disadvantages of working with distant team members:

Our interaction with them is functional. Between ourselves, we share strong relationships. It's easier to become friends with someone you drink coffee with, rather than someone you talk to via phone. Theoretically, it's better for the company to have the team members far away from each other, because that way they share functional relationships. Yet, the absence of non official communication, that is typical for virtual teams, also has negative implementations: I think that information that is being transferred in a non official manner is very important. More than once I found mistakes I made, by looking on someone else's work above his shoulder. More than that – it is difficult to explain something via phone or e-mail; therefore you will consult with someone near you, even if the distant alternative could be better. Working in a virtual team is an opportunity to interact with new people but demands sensitivity and patience.

The summary of twenty interviews shows that virtual teams are a new phenomenon, in which managers lack the proper tools to deal with. It is obvious to virtual team members that virtual teams operate without structural characteristics. The form of communication (virtual compared to face-to-face) will determine whether the processes will be task or socially oriented: virtual communications is task oriented, while face-to-face communication will tend to include social aspects. Although the cost of virtual meetings is lower than face-to-face meetings, there is a place for improvements in order to increase productivity. Virtual communication is not inadequate, but it needs to be more organized in order to be more efficient.

Based on previous studies and paradigms shown in the literature review and in the interviews summary, a research model was developed as depicted in Figure 1. According to the model, the structure level and virtuallity level are an affecting

Figure 1. The Research Model

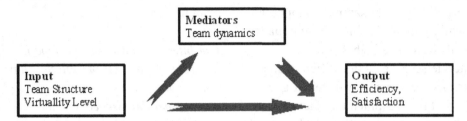

variables and it is referred to as the input of the team. The dependent variables are the outputs of the team work, such as efficiency and satisfaction. The mediators can be described as characteristics of the discussion: for example, social versus task ratio, positive versus negative ratio and questions versus answers ratio.

PROPOSITIONS AND DISCUSSION

This section briefly explains the major propositions emerged from the research model illustrated above. Planning the team's framework should enhance its outputs. Adopting different types of technologies is one way of teams to achieve this target, yet the virtual working environment complicates the team's workflow. Cramton & Webber (2005) referred to the limitation of information evolves from using different types of technologies and to the increase in hostility and aggression of the communicators toward each other. Denton (2006) and Potter & Balthazard (2002) claimed that virtual teams are less successful than face-to-face teams on most outcome measures. We argue that distant communication is a potential source of complications due to a lack of tangible information. Therefore, we assume a negative correlation between virtuallity and both the mediators and the output variables.

- **Proposition 1:** A structured team's output (with a formal Division of Labor, Hierarchy and Work Process) is superior

to an unstructured team's output (without a formal Division of Labor, Hierarchy and Work Process).
- **Proposition 2:** A virtual team's output is inferior to a face-to-face team's output.
- **Proposition 3:** A virtual-structured team's output is superior to a virtual-unstructured team's output.

Clausen & Sung (2008) claimed that computer-mediated (virtual) teams' social processes are different than face-to-face teams.

- **Proposition 4:** Virtual team's discussion orientation is different than face-to-face team's discussion orientation: the social part of the virtual team's discussion is negative oriented, while the social part of the face-to-face team's discussion is positive oriented.

Montoya-Weiss, Massey & Song (2001) suggested that managing virtual teams' conflict is the key to their success; Guerra et al. (2005) showed that the social conflict decreases satisfaction and well-being; Diefendorff & Gosserand (2003) stated that emotional processes at work can lead to positive or negative team output; Ashkanasy, Hartel & Daus (2002) claimed that positive emotions lead to positive outputs, whereas negative emotions lead to negative one. We predict that the discussion orientation will positively impact team output. The next proposition concerns with the impact of the team discussion content, namely the social characteristics of the discussion, on the teams output. It is assumes that the social context will satisfy the team members while hurting their success in achieving the task:

- **Proposition 5:** the Social orientation of the discussion influences the team's output: a positive influence on Satisfaction and Efficiency; The Positive orientation of the discussion influences the team's output: a positive influence on Satisfaction and Efficiency.

Proposition no. 5 is based on the assumption that positive discussion orientation is translated into enhanced member satisfaction and efficiency; and vice versa: Negative discussion orientation is translated into reduced member satisfaction and efficiency. As stated before, the way virtual teams manage internal conflict is a crucial factor in their success (Guerra et al., 2005; Montoya-Weiss; Massey & Song, 2001). Therefore, the positive social orientation of the team discussion is important not only as an affected variable, but as an influence variable as well.

DIRECTIONS OF FUTURE STUDIES

Timmerman & Scott (2006) claimed that much of virtual team research fails to examine variations in virtual team characteristics that may impact team communication behaviors. In this particular study we have tried to illustrate some of the challenges, and to draw some directions for future studies. An explanatory qualitative study, based on interviews, was conducted. Therefore, the theoretical model is based not only on the literature review, but also on the in-depth interviews summery.

It would be of interest to increase the sample, differentiate it by service, and to get samples from other sectors, as well as to carry out experimental and longitudinal research. It would also be interesting to further explore the conditions that implement leadership impact, environment, and external relations and so on, to examine the relationships between other variables and to study their effects on new forms of work organization and on virtual teams.

CONCLUSION

The number of virtual teams is increasing in today's workplaces. In virtual teams, the members can have different cultural backgrounds; they often work in different countries and are professionals in their own fields. In addition, as such diverse and dispersed teams communicate mainly through communication technology this raises the challenge for the team leader of how to unify the team and get the members to identify themselves with the team (Sivunen, 2006).

The research question dealt with the dynamic of the team's members: Is it socially oriented? Or maybe task oriented? Is the social part of the team work characterized by positive or by negative phrases? The findings indicate, like in previous studies, that some of the virtual teams output is inferior to face-to-face teams output. A clue for that evidence might be in the team's discussion orientation.

The main contribution of the study is that the field of team structure and dynamics needs to be adjusted to the 21st century and its communication media, specifically to the virtual environment. The motivation for this study was to examine the impact of e-infrastructure on the work place environment and to meet some of its challenges, hoping to contribute a new theoretical solution to the wide adoption of e-infrastructure across organizations. The study offers descriptions about differences concerning virtual and face-to-face teams that can assist organizations in the era of globalizations, an era in which many organizations need to employ virtual teams that are distance from one another.

REFERENCES

Ahuja, M. K., Galletta, D. F., & Carley, K. M. (2003). Individual centrality and performance in virtual R&D groups: An empirical study. *Management Science*, *49*(1), 21–38. doi:10.1287/mnsc.49.1.21.12756

Ashkanasy, N., Hartel, E., & Daus, C. (2002). Diversity and emotion: The new frontiers in organizational behavior research. *Journal of Management*, *28*, 307–338. doi:10.1177/014920630202800304

Bales, R. F. (1950). A set of factors for the analysis of small group interaction. *American Sociological Review*, *15*, 257–263. doi:10.2307/2086790

Barkhi, R., Jacob, V. S., Pipino, L., & Pirkul, H. (1998). A study of the effect of communication channel and authority on group decision processes and outcomes. *Decision Support Systems*, *23*(3), 205–227. doi:10.1016/S0167-9236(98)00048-7

Barsade, S. G. (2002). The ripple effect: Emotional contagion and its influence on group behavior. *Administrative Science Quarterly*, *47*(4), 644–675. doi:10.2307/3094912

Bouas, K. S., & Arrow, H. (1996). The development of group identity in computer and face-to-face groups with membership change. *CSCW*, *4*, 153–178.

Bradner, E., Hertel, T. D., & Mark, G. (2002). Effects of team size on participation, awareness, and technology choice in geographically distributed teams. In *Proceedings of the 36th Hawaii International Conference on System Sciences*, Hawaii, USA.

Branson, L., Clausen, T. S., & Sung, C. H. (2008). Group style differences between virtual and F2F teams. *American Journal of Business*, *23*(1), 65–71.

Brief, A. P., & Weiss, H. M. (2002). Organizational behavior: Affect in the workplace. *Annual Review of Psychology*, *53*, 279–307. doi:10.1146/annurev.psych.53.100901.135156

Bunderson, J. S., & Sutcliffe, K. M. (2002). Comparing alternative conceptualizations of functional diversity in management teams: Process and performance effects. *Academy of Management Journal*, *45*(5), 875–894. doi:10.2307/3069319

Burke, K., & Chidambaram, L. (1996). Do mediated contexts differ in information richness? A comparison of collocated and dispersed meetings. In *Proceedings of the 29th Annual Hawaii International Conference on System Sciences*, Hawaii, USA (pp. 92-101).

Chidambaram, L., & Tung, L. L. (2005). Is out of sight, out of mind? An empirical study of social loafing in technology-supported groups. *Information Systems Research*, *16*(2), 149–171. doi:10.1287/isre.1050.0051

Cramton, C. D., & Webber, S. S. (1999). *Modeling the impact of geographic dispersion on work teams* (working paper). George Mason University, Washington, DC, USA.

Cramton, C. D., & Webber, S. S. (2005). Relationships among geographic dispersion, team processes, and effectiveness in software development work teams. *Journal of Business Research*, *58*(6), 758–765. doi:10.1016/j.jbusres.2003.10.006

Cummings, J. N. (2004). Work groups, structural diversity, and knowledge sharing in a global organization. *Management Science*, *50*(3), 352–364. doi:10.1287/mnsc.1030.0134

Denton, D. K. (2006). Using intranets to make virtual teams effective. *Team Performance Management*, *12*(7/8), 253–257. doi:10.1108/13527590610711804

DeRosa, D. M., Hantula, D. A., Kock, N., & D'Arcy, J. (2004). Trust and leadership in virtual teamwork: A media naturalness perspective. *Human Resource Management, 43*(2-3), 219–233. doi:10.1002/hrm.20016

DeSanctis, G., Wright, M., & Jiang, L. (2001). Building a global learning community. *Communications of the ACM, 44*(12), 80–82. doi:10.1145/501317.501352

Diefendorff, J. M., & Gosserand, R. H. (2003). Understanding the emotional labor process: a control theory perspective. *Journal of Organizational Behavior, 24*(8), 945-959. doi:10.1002/job.230

Dunn, J. R., & Schweitzer, M. E. (2005). feeling and believing: the influence of emotion on trust. *Journal of Personality and Social Psychology, 88*(5), 736–748. doi:10.1037/0022-3514.88.5.736

Fahy, P. J. (2006). Online and Face-to-face group interaction processes compared using Bales' interaction process analysis (IPA). *European Journal of Open and Distance Learning (EURODL), 1.*

Garcia, A. L., Miller, D. A., Smith, E. R., & Mackie, D. M. (2006). Thanks for the compliment? Emotional reactions to group-level versus individual-level compliments and insults. *Group Processes & Intergroup Relations, 9*(3), 307–324. doi:10.1177/1368430206064636

Geister, S., Konradt, U., & Hertel, G. (2006). Effects of process feedback on motivation, satisfaction, and performance in virtual teams. *Small Group Research, 37*(5), 459–489. doi:10.1177/1046496406292337

Gil, F., Rico, R., Alcover, C. M., & Barrasa, Á. (2005). Change-oriented leadership, satisfaction and performance in work groups: Effects of team climate and group potency. *Journal of Managerial Psychology, 20*(3/4), 312–329. doi:10.1108/02683940510589073

Glückler, J., & Schrott, G. (2007). Leadership and performance in virtual teams: Exploring brokerage in electronic communication. *International Journal of e-Collaboration, 3*(3), 31–53.

Graetz, K., Boyle, E., Kimble, C., Thompson, P., & Garloch, J. (1998). Information sharing in face-to-face, teleconferencing, and electronic chat groups. *Small Group Research, 29*(6), 714–743. doi:10.1177/1046496498296003

Gruenfeld, D. H., Mannix, E. A., Williams, K. Y., & Neale, M. A. (1996). Group composition and decision making: How member familiarity and information distribution affect process and performance. *Organizational Behavior and Human Decision Processes, 67*(1), 1–16. doi:10.1006/obhd.1996.0061

Guerra, J. M., Martinez, I., Munduate, L., & Medina, F. J. (2005). A contingency perspective on the study of the consequences of conflict types: The role of organizational culture. *European Journal of Work and Organizational Psychology, 14*(2), 157–176. doi:10.1080/13594320444000245

Hackman, J. R. (1987). The design of work teams. In J. W. Lorsch (Ed.), *Handbook of organizational behavior* (pp. 315-342). Englewood Cliffs, NJ: Prentice-Hall.

Hareli, S., & Rafaeli, A. (in press). Emotion cycles: on the social influence of emotion in organization. *Research in Organizational Behavior, 28.*

Hause, M., Last, M., Almstrum, V., & Woodroffe, M. (2001). Interaction factors in software development performance in distributed student teams in computer science. In *Proceedings of the ACM Conference*, Boulder, CO, USA (pp. 69-72).

Haley, H., & Sidanius, J. (2006). The positive and negative framing of affirmative action: A group dominance perspective. *Personality and Social Psychology Bulletin, 32*(5), 656–668. doi:10.1177/0146167205283442

Hofner, S. D. (1996). Productive behaviours of global business teams. *International Journal of Intercultural Relations, 20*(2), 227–259. doi:10.1016/0147-1767(95)00043-7

Horwitz, F. M., Bravington, D., & Silvis, U. (2006). The promise of virtual teams: Identifying key factors in effectiveness and failure. *Journal of European Industrial Training, 30*(6), 472–494. doi:10.1108/03090590610688843

Iacono, S., & Weisband, S. (1997). Developing trust in virtual teams. In *Proceedings of the Hawaii International Conference on System Sciences*, Hawaii, USA.

Jarvenpaa, S. L., Knoll, K., & Leidner, D. E. (1998). Is anybody out there? Antecedents of trust in global virtual teams. *Journal of Management Information Systems, 14*(4), 29–65.

Johnson, S. C., Suriya, C., Yoon, S. W., Berrett, J. V., & La Fleur, J. (2002). Team development and group processes of virtual learning teams. *Computers & Education, 39*, 379–393. doi:10.1016/S0360-1315(02)00074-X

Kahai, S., Fjermestad, J., Zhang, S., & Avolio, B. (2007). Leadership in virtual teams: Past, present, and future. *International Journal of e-Collaboration, 3*(1), 1–10.

Kayworth, T., & Leidner, D. (2001/2002). Leadership effectiveness in global virtual teams. *Journal of Management Information Systems, 18*(3), 7–40.

Kim, Y., Hiltz, S. R., & Turoff, M. (2002). Coordination structures and system restrictiveness in distributed group support systems. *Group Decision and Negotiation, 11*, 379–404. doi:10.1023/A:1020492305910

Konradt, U., & Hoch, J. E. A. (2007). Work roles and leadership functions of managers in virtual teams. *International Journal of e-Collaboration, 3*(2), 16–35.

Lebie, L., Rhoades, J. A., & McGrath, J. E. (1996). Interaction process in computer-mediated and face-to-face groups. *CSCW, 4*, 127–152.

Lee-Kelley, L. (2002). Situational leadership: Managing the virtual project team. *Journal of Management Development, 21*(6), 461–477. doi:10.1108/02621710210430623

Lind, M. R. (1999). The gender impact of temporary virtual work groups. *IEEE Transactions on Professional Communication, 42*(4), 276–285. doi:10.1109/47.807966

Lurey, J. S., & Raisinghani, M. S. (2001). An empirical study of best practices in virtual teams. *Information & Management, 38*(8), 523–544. doi:10.1016/S0378-7206(01)00074-X

Maier, N. R. F. (1967). Assets & liabilities in group problem solving. *Psychological Review, 74*(4), 239–249. doi:10.1037/h0024737

Majchrzak, A., Malhotra, A., Stamps, J., & Lipnack, J. (2004). Can absence make a team grow stronger? *Harvard Business Review, 82*(5), 131–139.

Martell, R. F., & Guzzo, R. A. (1991). The dynamics of implicit theories of group performance: When and how do they operate? *Organizational Behavior and Human Decision Processes, 50*(1), 51–75. doi:10.1016/0749-5978(91)90034-Q

Montoya-Weiss, M. M., Massey, A. P., & Song, M. (2001). Getting it together: Temporal coordination and conflict management in global virtual teams. *Academy of Management Journal, 44*(6), 1251–1263. doi:10.2307/3069399

Myeong-Gu, S., Feldman-Barrett, L., & Bartunek, J. M. (2004). The role of affective experience in work motivation. *Academy of Management Review, 29*(3), 423.

Nicholson, D. B., Sarker, S., Sarker, S., & Valacich, J. S. (2007). Determinants of effective leadership in information systems development teams: An exploratory study of face-to-face and virtual contexts. *Journal of Information Technology Theory and Application, 8*(4), 39–56.

Ocker, R., & Fjermestad, J. (2000). High versus low performing virtual design teams: A preliminary analysis of communication. In *Proceedings of the 33rd Annual Hawaii Conference on System Sciences*, Maui, Hawaii, USA.

Pauleen, D. J., Corbitt, B., & Yoong, P. (2007). Discovering and articulating what is not yet known; Using action learning and grounded theory as a knowledge management strategy. *The Learning Organization, 14*(3), 222–240. doi:10.1108/09696470710739408

Potter, R. E., & Balthazard, P. A. (2002). Understanding human interactions and performance in the virtual team. *JITTA: Journal of Information Technology Theory and Application, 4*(1), 1–24.

Powell, A., Piccoli, G., & Ives, B. (2004). virtual teams: a review of current literature and directions for future research. *The Data Base for Advances in Information Systems, 35*(1), 6–37.

Saunders, C. S., & Ahuja, M. K. (2006). Are all distributed teams the same? Differentiating between temporary and ongoing distributed teams. *Small Group Research, 37*(6), 662–700. doi:10.1177/1046496406294323

Shin, Y. (2005). Conflict resolution in virtual teams. *Organizational Dynamics, 34*(4), 331–345. doi:10.1016/j.orgdyn.2005.08.002

Shwarts-Asher, D., Ahituv, N., & Etzion, D. (2008). Improving virtual teams through swift structure. In T. Torres & M. Arias (Eds.), *Encyclopedia of HRIS: Challenges in e-HRM, Vol 2(I-Z)* (pp. 510-517). Spain: Rovira i Virgili University.

Siegel, J., Dubrovsky, V., Kiesler, S., & McGuire, T. W. (1986). group processes in computer-mediated communication. *Organizational Behavior and Human Decision Processes, 37*(2), 157–188. doi:10.1016/0749-5978(86)90050-6

Simpson, P. A., & Stroh, L. K. (2004). gender differences: emotional expression and feelings of personal inauthenticity. *The Journal of Applied Psychology, 89*(4), 715. doi:10.1037/0021-9010.89.4.715

Sivunen, A. (2006). Strengthening identification with the team in virtual teams: The leaders' perspective. *Group Decision and Negotiation, 15*(4), 345–366. doi:10.1007/s10726-006-9046-6

Sosik, J. J. (1997). Effect of transformational leadership and anonymity on idea generation in computer-mediated groups. *Group & Organization Management, 22*(4), 460–488. doi:10.1177/1059601197224004

Staples, D. S., & Webster, J. (2007). Exploring traditional and virtual team members' "best practices": A social cognitive theory perspective. *Small Group Research, 38*(1), 60–97. doi:10.1177/1046496406296961

Stevenson, W., & McGrath, E. W. (2004). Differences between on-site and off-site teams: Manager perceptions. *Team Performance Management, 10*(5/6), 127–132. doi:10.1108/13527590410556854

Straus, S. G., & McGrath, J. E. (1994). Does the medium matter? The interaction of task type and technology on group performance and member reactions. *The Journal of Applied Psychology, 79*(1), 87–98. doi:10.1037/0021-9010.79.1.87

Strijbos, J. W., Martens, R. L., Jochems, W. M. G., & Broers, N. (2004). The effect of functional roles of group efficiency: Using multilevel modeling and content analysis to investigate computer-supported collaboration in small groups. *Small Group Research, 35*(2), 195–229. doi:10.1177/1046496403260843

Tan, H. H., Foo, M. D., Chong, C. L., & Ng, R. (2003). Situational and dispositional predictors of displays of positive emotions. *Journal of Organizational Behavior, 24*(8), 961. doi:10.1002/job.231

Tarmizi, H., Payne, M., Noteboom, C., & Zhang, c. (2007). collaboration engineering in distributed environments. *E-Service Journal, 6*(1), 76-98.

Thompson, L. F., & Coovert, M. D. (2003). Teamwork online: The effects of computer conferencing on perceived confusion, satisfaction, and postdiscussion accuracy. *Group Dynamics, 7*(2), 135–151. doi:10.1037/1089-2699.7.2.135

Thoresen, C. J. (2003). Affective underpinnings of job perceptions and attitudes. *Psychological Bulletin, 129*, 914–945. doi:10.1037/0033-2909.129.6.914

Timmerman, C. E., & Scott, C. R. (2006). Virtually working: Communicative and structural predictors of media use and key outcomes in virtual work teams. *Communication Monographs, 73*(1), 108–136. doi:10.1080/03637750500534396

Tyran, K. L., Tyran, C. K., & Shepherd, M. (2003). Exploring emerging leadership in virtual teams. In C. B. Gibson & S. G. Cohen (Eds.), *Virtual teams that work* (pp. 183-195). San Francisco: Jossey-Bass.

Warkentin, M. E., Sayeed, L., & Hightower, R. (1997). Virtual teams versus face-to-face teams: An exploratory study of a Web-based conference system. *Decision Sciences, 28*(4), 975–997. doi:10.1111/j.1540-5915.1997.tb01338.x

Watts, S. S., & Lee, S. (1999). Straight talk: Delivering bad news through electronic communication. *Information Systems Research, 10*(2), 150–167. doi:10.1287/isre.10.2.150

Webster, J., & Wong, W. K. P. (2008). Comparing traditional and virtual group forms: Identity, communication and trust in naturally occurring project teams. *International Journal of Human Resource Management, 19*(1), 41–62.

Weisband, S., & Atwater, L. (1999). Evaluating self and others in electronic and face-to-face groups. *The Journal of Applied Psychology, 84*(4), 632–639. doi:10.1037/0021-9010.84.4.632

Weiss, H. M. (2002). Conceptual and empirical foundations for the study of affect at work. In R. G. Lord, R. J. Klimoski, & R. Kanfer (Eds.), *Emotions in the workplace: Understanding the structure and role of emotions in organizational behavior* (pp. 20-63). San Francisco: Jossey-Bass.

Weiss, H. M., & Cropanzano, R. (1996). Affective events theory: A theoretical discussion of the structure, causes and consequences of affective experiences at work. In L. L. Cummings & B. M. Staw (Eds.), *Research in organizational behavior* (Vol. 18, pp. 1-74). Greenwich, CT: JAI Press.

Yoo, Y., & Alavi, M. (2004). Emergent leadership in virtual teams: What do emergent leaders do? *Information and Organization, 14*(1), 27–58. doi:10.1016/j.infoandorg.2003.11.001

Chapter 7
Monitoring Activity in E–Learning:
A Quantitative Model Based on Web Tracking and Social Network Analysis

E. Mazzoni
University of Bologna, Italy

P. Gaffuri
University of Bologna, Italy

ABSTRACT

In this chapter the authors will focus on the monitoring of students' activities in e-learning contexts. They will start from a socio-cultural approach to the notion of activity, which is conceived of as a context composed by actions, which, in turn, are composed by operations. Subsequently, the authors will propose a model for monitoring activities in e-learning, which is based on two principal measures. Firstly, they will take into consideration specific data collected through Web tracking, which they will elaborate further in order to obtain indicators that do not simply express frequencies, but that measure individuals' actions within a Web environment. Secondly, the authors will suggest a possible application of social network analysis (SNA) to Web interactions occurring in collective discussions within Web environments. In the model that the authors will present, Web tracking data are considered as indicators of individual actions, whereas SNA indices concern two levels: collective indices referring to the activity carried out by groups and individual indices referring to the role that members play in collective e-learning activities.

INTRODUCTION

This chapter will develop according to three principal sections. The first section will provide the theoretical background of our research. One of the main points of this section is the concept of e-

DOI: 10.4018/978-1-60566-786-7.ch007

learning. We will particularly focus on three main web artifacts, which significantly contribute to the development of e-learning: learning objects, web groups or web communities, and social networks. We will offer a brief discussion on web evolution, and then we will focus on learning objects and web groups as web artifacts 1.0, and on social networks as web artifacts 2.0. These web artifacts share one important aspect, i.e., the possibility to monitor and analyze online actions performed by students/learners. Such a possibility allows the evaluation and assessment of web activities: a further central point of this theoretical section, therefore, will be our proposal for defining web activities and, in particular, web actions that can be automatically monitored in e-learning contexts.

The second section will be focused on the monitoring of web actions and, in particular, on the indices that may be employed for analyzing or assessing individual and/or collective actions. To this purpose, we will propose two different types of indices: indices obtained from an elaboration of web tracking data for individual actions, and indices derived from Social Network Analysis (SNA) for collective actions. The first type is typically used in relation to web artifacts 1.0 (e.g., web platform), while the second type represents a proposition for integrating and constructing a model for monitoring, analyzing and assessing not only individuals, but also web groups or networks of students in e-learning environments.

The third section will finally describe our model for monitoring, analyzing and assessing individuals and groups/networks in e-learning environments. This model, based on web tracking and SNA indices, responds to three requests in e-learning processes:

- observing and analyzing e-learning processes by researchers;
- monitoring and assessing students and groups by instructors;
- self-monitoring the personal actions and the personal role in collective activity by students.

To sum up, starting from a socio-cultural approach to activity, this chapter proposes a model for monitoring students actions in e-learning environments based on web tracking and SNA.

THEORETICAL BACKGROUND

In everyday discussions, the concept of e-learning (*electronic learning*), often improperly, involves multiple aspects of distance education, which range from content selection to the organization and coordination of specific on-line courses. Nowadays, the three key aspects that could best define what we mean by "e-learning" are the so-called *learning objects*, *web groups* or *web communities*, and *social networks*. While we can conceive learning objects and web groups/communities as elements that characterize e-learning 1.0, social networks are more informal environments typical of e-learning 2.0. On the one hand, the first type of e-learning seems to be characterized principally by formal learning, i.e., a structured course, well organized and preset by an instructor, in which students have to download/upload documents, accomplish predetermined assignments/tasks and participate in controlled on-line discussions (which are normally developed through web forum). The second type of e-learning, on the other hand, is characterized by informal learning (Attwell, 2007), which enables students to manage their personal learning space (normally a blog in which access permissions are set by students themselves), construct their relational network (by inviting other students or accepting invitations), propose their discussion groups (by selecting participants) and finally choose the level of interaction to be implemented with other students or with the instructor. This may be a private, one-to-one interaction (in which messages are read only by the receiver), a personal interaction (in which the message is posted to the personal area but it is public), an interaction with the personal network (constructing specific groups) or, finally, an interaction with the whole network, which normally occurs within a web forum.

In this evolution of e-learning web artifacts, we can identify two different ways of conceiving knowledge transmission and construction in e-learning environments, which distinguish e-learning 1.0 from e-learning 2.0. e-Learning 2.0 is closer to the notion of knowledge transmission and construction that we will present in the following paragraphs.

On the one hand, e-learning is classically conceived of as pure transposition via web of educational models that are typical of face-to-face classes. According to this position, learning is considered as a mere content supply, in which the "e" component (electronic) refers only to the content in terms of design, supply and fruition. *Learning objects* represent the best example of this approach: the basic idea is "to break educational content down into small chunks that can be reused in various learning environments, in the spirit of object-oriented programming" (Wiley, 2000, p. 7). It may be argued that the very critical points of this position are content selection, construction and organization by educators and content supply by web artifacts (i.e., normally a web platform). This idea of content modularity emerges from previous approaches that remind us of Mastery Learning years, which derive from the Computer Assisted Instruction formulated within behaviorist theory, which was proposed by Block (1974) as the new promise for "teaching everything to everyone".

On the other hand, e-learning may also be conceived of as a form of collaborative learning or knowledge construction which results from interactions within a group or community of students. This second position about e-learning finds its theoretical basis in socio-constructivism (Doise & Mugny, 1984), and in the sociocultural approach to human cognitive development inspired by Vygotskij (1978). Here we may recognize various types of communities originating from real contexts, and then proposed in web environments as well: see, e.g., *Communities of Practice* (Wenger, 1998), *Knowledge Building Communities* (Scardamalia & Bereiter, 1994), *Learning Communities* (CTGV, 1993), *Communities of Learning and Thinking* (Brown & Campione, 1990), and *Communities of inquiry* (Lipman, 1991). In this case, individual development is conceived of as a result of social interactions, which are made possible by the simultaneous presence of different points of view, and by the consequent necessity to negotiate common meanings or objects (this may evoke the notion of *sociocognitive conflict*, see, e.g., Carugati & Gilly, 1993), and are developed through the support of either adult or expert peer/partner.

These two positions on e-learning presuppose a number of online actions performed by students, either individually or collectively. Examples of individual actions may be the navigation through the web contents proposed, the download and upload of files (such as works or tasks to be accomplished), and the filling in of tests or questionnaires. Collective actions are to be seen in all types of interaction (e.g., web forum discussions, private messages between students, blog posts, etc.) or collective works (e.g., writing wiki pages or composing a group blog) carried out within an e-learning environment. Constant monitoring may contribute to the support and sustain of such a complex ensemble of actions, and it may meet two essential needs: that of sustaining and supporting students during an e-learning process, and/or of assessing the online activity they have accomplished.

Thus, we believe that it is necessary to shift the focus from the question *what do students do in an e-learning environment?* to the question *how may their online activity be monitored, and, ultimately, be evaluated?*

From Individual to Collective Actions

In order to answer this last question, it is necessary to define, first of all, what we mean with "online activity", and, secondly, its fundamental elements. We adopt a socio-cultural point of view based on the initial intuitions of Leont'ev, which have recently been reinforced by the evolution of the Activity Theory contextual approach (Engeström, 1987; Kaptelinin & Nardi, 2006).

In his perspective, Leont'ev (1978) suggests that human activity may be considered as a process that is always collective and sustained by some social motive or need.

"It is understood that the motive may be either material or ideal, either present in perception or exclusively in the imagination or in thought. The main thing is that behind activity there should always be a need, that it should always answer one need or another". (Leont'ev, 1978, 63)

The processes at the basis of collective activities are goal-directed actions, which are subordinated to conscious purposes. It is important to point out here that "activity is a molar, not an additive unit" (Leont'ev, 1978, p. 50). The mere sum of actions does not constitute an activity, and, "correspondingly, actions are not special 'units' that are included in the structure of activity. Human activity does not exist except in the form of action or a chain of actions" (Leont'ev 1978, p. 64). Now, one of the most important factors that may allow the achievement of a given action goal is represented by the conditions in which such a goal is achieved, i.e., by the variable, material circumstances in which action takes place.

For this reason, in spite of its intentional aspect (what must be achieved), the action also has its operational aspect (how, by what means this can be achieved), which is determined not by the goal in itself but by the objective-object conditions of its achievement. [...] For this reason the action has a specific quality that "formulates" it specifically, and particularly methods by which it is accomplished. I call the methods for accomplishing actions, operations. (Leont'ev 1978, pp. 65-66)

In conclusion, Leont'ev suggests that human activity is sustained by a motive, which is realized by goal-directed actions, which, in turn, are accomplished by operations that are not often conscious, and that respond to situational conditions.

In light of these considerations, we can conceive "e-learning" as a collective activity that involves a group of students and one or more instructors that have a learning need/motive. This learning activity is based on the various types of actions that were briefly depicted at the end of the previous paragraph, and classified into individual and collective actions. As a matter of fact, since actions may be performed by a single person (e.g., a student that navigates and consults the resources recommended by the instructor in a web platform), but also by a group (e.g., a group of students that discuss on a web forum on a subject proposed by the instructor), we can consider actions as individual (in the case of a student that interacts with web artifacts for downloading/reading/learning contents, i.e., with a web platform or a social network) or as collective (in the case of a student that interacts with other students through web artifacts, e.g., a

Figure 1. Activity system representation (Adapted from Engeström, 1987, p. 78)

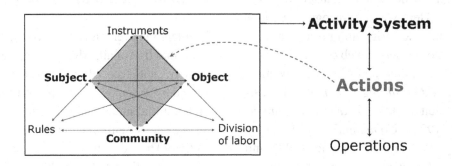

web forum, a blog, etc.). All these actions, both individual and collective, consist of operations that are carried out by actors that execute some e-learning action (e.g., moving the mouse, using the keyboard for writing, etc.).

If we observe the scheme of activity systems formulated by Engeström (1987, 1999) we may better understand the partition between individual and collective actions, and their position within an e-learning activity (fig. 1).

The *Subjects* of an e-learning activity are individuals, or groups, which use some instrument to satisfy their learning or educational needs, and whose actions constitute the focus of the analysis (Barab e al., 2002). The *object* defines the activity direction and should be considered "as a project under construction, moving from potential 'raw material' to a meaningful shape or outcome" (Hasu, 2001, p. 38). In our case the object is sustained by a motive deriving from learning or educational needs. The change and the transformation of the object into a final result (*outcome*) are operated by subjects through the use of *instruments* (e.g., in our case a web platform or a social network). As we argued previously, however, an activity is not individual, but always collective. As a matter of fact, any activity is shared within a *community*, i.e., "those individuals, groups, or both who share the same general objects, and are defined by their division of labor and shared norms and expectations" (Barab e al., 2002, pp. 78-79). The different "powers" characterizing community members are defined by *division of labor* that specifies their influence on the object of the activity (Mazzoni, 2006a). Finally, explicit and implicit *rules* represent "... regulations, norms and conventions that constrain actions and interactions within the activity system" (Hasu, 2001, p. 57). This model characterizes human activity as a real systemic whole in which all the considered elements are related to each other. "Instruments, rules and divisions of labor are artifacts (material and symbolic, external and internal) that mediate the reciprocal relationships between the three main elements of human activity: subject, object and community. Instruments mediate the subject-object relationship, rules mediate the subject-community relationship and divisions of labor mediate the object-community relationship" (Mazzoni, 2006a, 167).

Figure 1 allows a clearer view of the relations between subjects, instruments, community and object and, in our case, we can say that web artifacts are the mediators between subjects (students, instructors) and e-community (online course) that are employed for operating on the object (learning or educational need) and achieving a specific outcome (acquiring or improving knowledge on some topics). From this point of view, we can consider actions related to subjects' activity in terms of competence acquisition, because they are performed within a web artifact for knowledge acquisition/improvement (individual actions) and/or by a web artifact for interacting with others in order to share and construct collective knowledge (collective actions).

On the basis of the previous considerations, how can we monitor students' online actions in e-learning environments, both on the individual and collective level?

MONITORING ONLINE ACTIONS IN E-LEARNING

We will attempt to answer this question in the present section by proposing two principal techniques for monitoring online actions. In the first part we will present web tracking (performed by the log file data analysis or by the web platform database), as a technique for monitoring individual actions, and also some interesting indices derived from the elaboration of the raw web tracking data. In the second part, we will show that it is possible to elaborate relational data collected by web tracking for extracting the adjacency matrix and then applying the Social Network Analysis (SNA). In this part, besides presenting some of the principal indices that may be used for monitoring and evaluating individual and collective actions, we will briefly outline some critical aspects concerning relational data tracked from web forum discussions.

Monitoring Individual Online Actions

A quantitative technique for collecting data about users' actions in online environments is the *web tracking* (Calvani *et al.*, 2005; Mazzoni, 2006b; Proctor & Vu, 2005). "Through web tracking it is possible to collect a number of data about the frequency of visits and time spent on web pages during the navigation on a web artifact" (Matteucci *et al.*, in press), e.g., a web site, a web platform or a web social network. Visits or actions performed on web pages (e.g., software download, message writing, etc.) are requests that are sent by the users' browser to the web server in which the web services are located. All these requests are tracked by some specific tools, such as the web server log file or the database on which a platform or a social network is based (Romero & Ventura, 2007). Though log files and platform databases represent web tracking tools, log files are typically used by informatics for analyzing performances of web servers and the usage of web services, whereas platform databases represent a sort of register in which all the data concerning a specific e-learning environment are stored.

Before continuing with the description of web tracking tools, we would like to focus on an essential ethical issue: even if users are not aware that their navigation is being tracked (and this is an important and sensitive aspect on the experimental level), it is necessary to inform them about the presence of a web tracking engine. Actually, most web sites do not provide such information, although it would be a good practice to display it at least on the entrance page of an e-learning environment, so that information transparency and users privacy are guaranteed.

The Web Server's Log File is an ASCII text file, which is formed by sequences of strings (*hits*) that collect information about the users' visits to web services installed in the server. Each string is formed by various data that recognize information such as IP address, client machine name or user name, time and date of visit, request type, requested web page or action performed, result of the request, bytes quantity. The following string is an example of a hit in Common Log File Format:

```
62.98.76.76 username [14/
Apr/2001:14:43:14 +0200] "GET
/didattica/sviluppo_rete.htm
HTTP/1.0" 200 49164
```

There is also an extended log file format, in which further information such as users operative system, browser, desktop configuration, etc., are gathered. As may be easily understood, this information is very useful to server administrators and web providers, since it allows them to analyze the types of requests sent to the web servers, map the users profiles and adapt the web services' features, control which pages, services or actions are more often requested, and take decisions accordingly. At the same time, an appropriate elaboration of these data through specific web tools for log file analysis, or database management systems, may allow the monitoring of users' navigations in online environments. For instance, the following figure (fig. 2) shows data collected by a database and its elaborated version through SPSS statistic software.

On the left, each row is quite similar to the log file trace previously described. In fact, one can recognize the user ID, the connection, the time and the page visited (defined here by a number that is linked to a specific page-title). On the right, data have been transposed in so that each row corresponds to a user and each column to a specific page visited (defined here by the page-title). Numbers on the boxes correspond to visits made by each user.

Figure 2. Data collection of web tracking data (on the left) and their transposition in a software for statistic elaborations

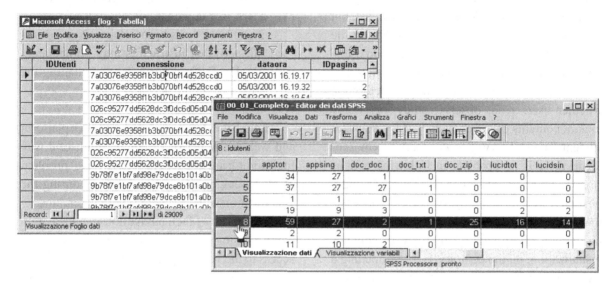

This is how tracking of raw data, and the consequent log file analysis, are normally employed for obtaining on-the-fly information about students' participative dimension in e-learning environments. Typical raw data deriving from log file elaboration are, e.g., the number and duration of sessions per participant; the number of messages sent (sorted according to participant, area/conference, date, etc.); the size of the messages sent by each participant; the number of messages read (i.e., opened) by each participant; the number of threads activated by students and instructors; the number of documents produced; the number of chats in which participants took part, etc. (Pozzi *et al.* 2007). Nurmela *et al.* (1999) go beyond this level, and consider log file analysis as the basis for elaborating perspectives on how collaboration within a web environment works. Reality, however, is not as simple as we could assume.

So far, in our description of log file data, we have used words such as users or behaviors. It is actually not so easy to interpret these data and to establish a direct relation between log file data and users' behaviors. In fact, there are many critical aspects that should be considered before trying to interpret these data as directly connected to users' behavior, particularly in the case of visit analysis. The first aspect to consider is the IP address: this address refers to a PC, and not to a user. This means that the same computers of, e.g., a faculty's informatics laboratory, which have a unique IP address, could be used by many students. Thus, it is always important to associate a specific IP address with a student's username, otherwise it would be impossible to differentiate among the multiple visits to websites that the several students do with the same computer. The same problem occurs when students access a web service from their home computer. In this case, web providers have often a flexible IP address that joins a number of users accesses. Therefore, it is important to consider both IP address and student username in this case as well. Another important critical aspect is to be seen in the usage of main memory. Before requesting a web resource to the web server, the user's browser controls whether the same resource has already been loaded in the browser memory by uploading it from this memory without any request to the web server. This procedure implies no interaction between the user's web browser and the web server and, consequently, there is no hit tracked on the log file. While these critical aspects concern the technical level, there is one last, but not least important critical aspect of the log file that refers to the relation between data and users' behaviors, and thus to the data interpretation. The question at issue here is, "how may we determine whether users read, observe, study, or simply look at contents of a web page?" If we consider students' navigation within an e-learning environment, there is no problem in following actions such as uploading/downloading files, writing a post on a web forum, blog, or wiki. In this case, the student's behavior and his/her motivation may be directly interpreted. In the case of contents visualization, on the contrary, (i.e., by opening a web page or a file on course subjects) we can only observe that a specific student visited a specific content at a given time, and, consequently, we can obtain information about the frequency of students' accesses to all the web resources of a particular e-learning environment.

Most of these critical aspects characterizing log files are resolved by the database data collected by web platforms or social networks, particularly as far as the problem of IP address is concerned, since the access to a web platform often requires the student's username for logging in. Web tracking is, in fact, a feature that characterizes almost all of today's web platforms or web social networks. In most cases, administrators can decide whether they allow instructors to view statistics about students' navigation (e.g., their access to the web resources recommended) and actions (file upload/download, posting, fill-in activities, etc.). In Italy, the legislative decree concerning Distance Universities defines the use of web tracking data as means for monitoring and evaluating students' on-line activities. The advantages of using web platform statistics instead of log file analysis are the following:

- the *tracking* system tracks all the visits of each student, it bypasses the browser

memory, and thus collects complete data about students' navigation and actions;

- there is a considerable amount of "ready-made" analysis (no elaboration is requested) that instructors may immediately employ for monitoring and evaluating the students' online activity.

Though the statistics provided by web platform and web social networks could be a useful way for monitoring students' activity, the problem of interpretation of students' actions during the visualization of web pages' contents remains.

As a matter of fact, navigation statistics often represent simple frequencies about the students' access to the various pages and resources offered by a web platform or a web social network. Therefore, information about students' actions could be further integrated by proceeding with elaborations aimed at obtaining indices that are not simply frequencies of students' navigations, but that facilitate a more adequate interpretation of students' exploitation of e-learning resources. This is the case of a study made by Calvani *et al.* (2005), in which raw data referring to the students' participation to the *Synergeia* platform were elaborated by the purposely-created Synergeia Log Miner. An important issue, which the authors of this study focus their attention on is the detail level of the tracked data, and particularly the question, what data are actually tracked by the Synergeia database, and how can such data be elaborated in order to derive indices that describe students' actions? With the purpose of establishing what was useful to their survey, Calvani *et al.* (2005) built Synergeia Log Miner and suggested a model that includes five typologies of essential data, in order to monitor interactions with the possible implications related to collaborative learning dynamics:

1. **Participation:** number of messages within a given lapse of time (considering both groups and individuals);

2. **Production:** number of documents or other products attached to messages (absolute numbers, individual differences, etc.);

3. **Reactivity:** average time of latency in the sequence of messages (average times, maximum times, standard deviation, etc.);

4. **Reading:** messages and documents read (percent values, individual index of messages/documents read);

5. **Structure (horizontal/vertical):** in depth (underlying degrees of messages with consecutive concatenate answers) vs. in width (many parallel answers at the same level). As far as this dimension is concerned, Wiley (2002) proposes the *Mean Replay Depth*, a synthetic numerical indicator that could allow the achievement of a rapid indicator of the depth of discussions in a web forum.

Other interesting similar tools are SAMOS (Juan *et al.*, 2008), proposed by the Open University of Catalonia, and especially MATEP (Zorrilla & Alvarez, 2008), i.e., Monitoring and Analysis Tool for E-learning Platforms (MATEP), which, compared with the model proposed by Calvani et al. (2005), has the advantage of being independent by the e-Learning platform used.

Of course, as we have shown, web tracking allows us to collect data on interactions among students, which may consist of, e.g., messages and replies that are sent or received. However, these data refer to individual attributes (i.e., to the number of messages that a student has sent, received, etc.) and do not provide any indication about his/her relation with the addressees. Actually, relational aspects are not taken into consideration within the log file data collected by web tracking, but this information is normally available.

"In other words, web tracking may be employed also in order to collect data about to whom a message/reply is sent, and about the identity of the receiver of a given message/reply (the so called

relational data), but these data are normally used only for summing and displaying the quantity of messages sent and received by single students". *(Matteucci et al., in press)*

Monitoring Collective Online Actions

In relation to web groups, web communities or social networks in e-learning environments, it should not be ignored, as activity theory outlines, that the final outcome of a collective activity (either a production of something, or, more simply, a discussion about something) does not derive from simple individual actions, but principally from collective actions performed by the group/community.

"In this case we consider individual actions as separated from collective actions, and we have to take into account that group performance does not derive from a sum of individual actions, but rather from indicators that allow us to map the collective actions of a group/community". *(Matteucci et al., in press)*

The possibility to collect relational data by web tracking does not only facilitate the construction of indices related to individual actions, which involve messages and replies sent and received. It also allows the elaboration of these data for their transposition in an adjacency matrix of relational data, and the application of the *Social Network Analysis* (SNA) to collective exchanges. Starting from this elaboration, that may be conducted by a database management system, SNA allows, on the one hand, to calculate indices representing concepts for describing the network's communicative structure, either on the individual or on the collective level (e.g., nodal degree, density, centrality, centralization, etc.), and, on the other hand, to graphically represent the network of relations by sociograms (fig. 3).

Levels of analysis allowed by SNA are two:

Figure 3. an example of adjacency matrix concerning a discussion between students in a web forum and the sociogram representation drawn by NetMiner (Cyram (2008). NetMiner 3.3.0.080516 Seoul: Cyram Co., Ltd)

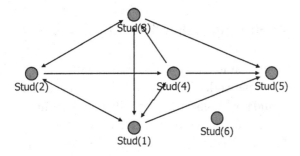

ego-centered analysis, and *whole network* or *full network analysis*. While the first focuses on individuals and their personal relations, the second is more interested in the entire network and its structural features.

"Obviously, these two aspects are related. This means that for each whole network structural indices we have also specific individual measures, e.g., the density of a network, i.e., 'the proportion of possible lines that are actually present in the graph' (Wasserman & Faust, 1994, p. 101) or more simply the percentage of aggregation of its members, derives from the degree of each member, i.e., the totality of direct contacts he/she has activated or received by others". (Matteucci et al., in press)

The same may be observed as far as centralization and centrality are concerned: the first index is collective, and represents the dependence of a network on its "most important" actors; the second index is individual, and measures the importance/prominence of each member for the communicative structure of the group, community or social network. Thanks to these related measures, we can map and analyze the actions of a collectivity both on the individual and on the collective level. In e-learning contexts, this could be very useful not only for researchers or for instructors, but also for students/participants themselves. This may be an interesting technique for researchers, because they are given the opportunity to analyze the communicative structure of a web collectivity, and the influence of the web artifacts used for interacting. Moreover, it may be positive for instructors, since SNA allows the monitoring and assessment of the role and function of each member in the community knowledge exchange (e.g., wideness and aggregation of members' neighborhood or direct contacts, their central or peripheral role in information exchange/transmission, their participation in subgroups, etc.). At the same time, instructors have the possibility to monitor the entire collectivity, to identify the network's critical zones (e.g., pendent or isolate members), to observe the aggregation, the reciprocity in discussions, the quantity and density of possible subgroups, etc.. But SNA could also be very useful to students/participants as a tool for providing them with a feedback about their participation in the collective activity, and for stimulating their self-awareness as far as the personal network of relations they are creating is concerned.

Some Interesting SNA Indices for E-Learning Environments

As could be inferred from the previous paragraph, SNA offers various types of analysis for studying and describing the relational structure of groups, community or social networks. Since we are now focusing on e-learning contexts, we will direct our attention to those analyses that we consider as most interesting and suitable for monitoring individual and collective actions in e-learning processes. Thus, we will present three main SNA analyses. i.e., neighborhood analysis, centrality analysis, and cohesion analysis.

Neighborhood Analyses as a Representation of Direct and Indirect Sustain and Exchange

The neighborhood analysis explores the solidity of relations within a definite network, and the direct ties that characterize individuals but also the entire network. Principal indicators of this analysis are *nodal degrees* and the *density index*.

"The degree of a node, [...], is the number of lines that are incident with it. Equivalently, the degree of a node is the number of nodes adjacent to it. The degree of a node is a count that ranges from a minimum of 0, if no nodes are adjacent to a given node, to a maximum of g – 1, if a given node is adjacent to all other nodes in the graph". (Wasserman & Faust, 1994, p. 100)

Two nodes that have direct ties are considered adjacent; a node with degree equal to 1 is called *pendent*; if the degree is equal to 0 it is called *isolate*. If we transpose this concept to an e-learning context, we can say that the degree of a node represents the social sustain, help and information, and knowledge exchange which a student may rely on for his/her knowledge construction process. Seen from this point of view, it is a sort of measure of the group of pairs or experts that act on the student's zone of proximal development (Vygotsky, 1978).

"While the nodal degree is an individual index, the density is related to the entire network. Degree is a concept that considers the number of lines incident with each node in a graph. We can also consider the number and proportion of lines in the graph as a whole. A graph can only have so many lines. The maximum possible number is determined by the number of nodes. [...] The density of a graph is the proportion of possible lines that are actually present in the graph. It is the ratio of the number of lines present, L, to the maximum possible". (Wasserman & Faust, 1994, p. 101)

In e-learning contexts, the density index permits to monitor, analyze and compare different collaborative networks in relation to the members' participation in the exchange.

Neighborhood analysis in e-learning contexts has numerous potentialities. Firstly, it permits to define a single index for quantifying the compactness of a network of students. Secondly, it offers the possibility to monitor ongoing network interactive dynamics, which, given the importance of feedback in web contexts, constitute a very relevant aspect in collaborative learning. The neighborhood analysis is an interesting method for analyzing the evolution of ties and exchanges that characterize an e-learning network. In particular, it is very useful for prompt revealing two important problems within collaborative knowledge construction in e-learning environments: the network reciprocity, and the isolation of some members. As far as reciprocity is concerned, the possibility to represent the ties' direction of a network allows analysts to evaluate whether there is a good feedback between members in relation to messages/requests they posted. A participant that sends messages to other four members without receiving any answer represents a possible problem to be quickly analyzed and solved. Referring to the isolation that could characterize some network members, it may be suggested that this problem derives from many possible reasons, including, e.g., the personal choice not to interact with others, or an inadequate transmission of information within the network (e.g., because there is a problem in the tools or in the communicative channel selected). In e-learning contexts, both isolation and lack in reciprocity represent important limitations to members' participation, and to the information transmission within the network. This is likely to hinder the sharing of information, and the network creativity and productivity.

Centrality and Centralization Analysis: The Peripheral and Central Participation

As we explained in the previous paragraph on nodal degree and density, also centrality and centralization are indices that refer, respectively, to individuals and to the network. The *actor centrality* is a measure of the importance/prominence of a given node for the communicative structure, whereas the *group centralization* defines the dependence of a network on its "most important" actors. Thus, the actor centrality analyzes the level of involvement of the network members, and classifies it according to a scale from 0 (completely peripheral) to 1 (completely central). The group centralization (which may range from 0 to 100%) represents instead "how variable or heterogeneous the actor centrality is. It records the extent to which a single actor has high centrality, and the others, low centrality. It also can be viewed as a measure of how unequal the individual actor values are. It is (roughly) a measure of variability, dispersion, or spread" (Wasserman & Faust, 1994, p. 176). SNA suggests various measures to indicate the importance or prominence of an actor, such as degree centrality, closeness centrality, betweenness centrality, information centrality, etc.). "All such measures attempt to describe and measure properties of "actor location" in a social network" (Wasserman & Faust, 1994, p. 169).

Following the descriptions of the important handbook of Wasserman & Faust (1994), we would like to present here three interesting centrality indices that could be very useful for analyzing group collaboration (group centralization indices) and the members' role in the collective activity (actors centrality indices) in e-learning contexts.

The first index we consider is the

"betweenness centrality. Interactions between two nonadjacent actors might depend on the other actors in the set of actors, especially the actors who lie on the paths between the two. These "other ac-

tors" potentially might have some control over the interactions between the two nonadjacent actors. [...] The important idea here is that an actor is central if it lies between other actors [...], implying that to have a large "betweenness" centrality, the actor must be between many of the actors ... ". (Wasserman & Faust, 1994, pp. 188-189)

Drawing on the definition of Scott, the betweenness actor centrality "measures the extent to which an agent can play the part of a 'broker' or 'gatekeeper' with a potential for control over others" (Scott, 1997, p. 86). Conversely, the betweenness group centralization allows "a researcher to compare different network with respect to the heterogeneity of the betweenness of the members of the networks" (Wasserman & Faust, 1994, p. 191). In e-learning contexts, the betweenness indices may be useful in order to observe and monitor the role of intermediaries that some actors play in the transmission of information and knowledge within a network.

The second index we present is the *information centrality*, which takes into account the paths' length from one node to another, and assigns a weight to each path, which is inversely proportional to its length. This index is interesting because it "focuses on the information contained in all paths originating with a specific actor. The information of an actor averages the information in these paths, which, in turn, is inversely related to the variance in the transmission of a signal from one actor to another" (Wasserman & Faust, 1994, p. 194). The Information indices might be useful in e-learning contexts for monitoring and analyzing the actors' role in the managing of information and knowledge transmission. As a matter of fact, these indices are a sort of measure of the actors' potential in content transmission.

The last index we present is the *eigenvector centrality*. This index results from the intuition of Bonacich (1972), according to which the actor centrality is not independent from the centrality of the other actors it is connected to. In other words, Bonacich explains that the more an actor is connected to actors with high centrality, the more he/she is central. In e-learning contexts, this index could be very helpful to analyze the group leadership, and the different actors' role in relation to the connections they have created within the network.

COHESION ANALYSIS: SUBGROUPS OF A COLLECTIVITY

If we observe interactions in real and virtual contexts, we may notice that participants do not often interact with all other members. They normally prefer to participate in given discussions on specific arguments, thus constituting what may be defined as sub-structures of participants that are more likely to interact among them than with other participants. In other words, although participants interact with all the members of a network, they normally show a preference for some specific "neighbors". We could define such sub-structures as "preferential neighborhoods" that involve some individuals, and normally represent the most interactive zones of a network, i.e., those in which exchange of knowledge and information is very active.

The cohesion analysis is specifically oriented towards the description of these particularly aggregate structures that characterize the principal network. The SNA suggests different typological definitions for describing the sub-structures of a network, e.g., clique, n-clique, clan, n-clan, etc. (Scott, 1991; Wasserman & Faust, 1994). One of the most interesting and frequently employed is *clique*, which represents a complete sub-group composed by at least three entirely connected actors. In other words, each actor of a clique is connected to all the other actors of the same clique.

The cohesion analysis allows verifying the presence and organization of these sub-structures, and also the involvement of the single partici-

pants to these sub-structures. Within a network of students in an e-learning context, e.g., a web group that interacts during an initial brainstorming phase or that collaborates for writing a project or a report, the presence of these sub-structures is particularly positive. As a matter of fact, they represent areas of active and rich exchange and confrontation of ideas and knowledge, which are essential prerequisites for the creativity and productivity of a group (Aviv *et al.*, 2003; Matteucci *et al.*, in press).

Constructing Adjacency Matrix from Web Forum Interactions: A Critical Issue

One of the most critical aspects to consider in creating an adjacency matrix is the correct definition of the *sender/replier* and the *receiver*. In the case of e-mail or blog it is quite easy to identify senders/receivers, as well as the connection between a reply and the message it refers to. Such identification becomes more complex in the case of web forum exchanges, since participants normally post a message in a public area, but do not send it to specific participants (it is obviously different when it comes to replying to the posts).

"Furthermore, it cannot be taken for granted that the receiver will even read, let alone reply to a message. Replies often do not refer to a single message but to a series of postings within the discussion as a whole, or are sent to different receivers referred to implicitly or explicitly in the contents of the reply". (Grion et al., 2008, p. 119)

If we consider that web forum interfaces, and particularly the interface for reading messages, influence the way actions are tracked, this issue becomes even more complex. First of all, it should be taken into account that the message that opens a discussion is not tracked, since it is not directed to a specific receiver. Web forums, in fact, are web artifacts that are aimed at encouraging collective sharing and collaboration within a network of people. Unlike e-mail or blog, which require senders to define the receiver before transmitting a message, the first message in a web forum discussion has no receiver. Thus, the question that arises is, to whom is this message directed? The only way for SNA to define the receiver of this message is to overturn the way in which the adjacency matrix is constructed, and to consider as receivers all participants that answer to the message, or read it, so that the relationship considered is *reader>sender*, and not the more usual *sender>receiver*. But there is another important problem here: not all interfaces for visualizing web forum messages allow tracking message-reading actions. We have to consider two different types of web forum interfaces:

- Sequential;
- Thread-Discussion (Hewitt, 2001).

The sequential web forum interface presents the discussion list on its main page. Users may click on a discussion, and the whole sequence of messages is displayed on the screen, with the complete contents. The user may normally read all the messages posted, and then post his/her message, or send his/her reply. In other words, it is highly probable that sequential interface users answer to solicitations coming from the previous messages, and this means that it is very difficult to know whether answers are individually or collectively directed. Furthermore, if users' actions are limited to clicking on discussions (since this enables them to view all messages), there is no way to discern which messages have actually been read and, as web tracking only tracks actions (i.e., clicks), no string appears on the log-files or on the database about messages readings. What is being registered is only readings of a discussion as a whole unit. It is therefore not possible to create an adjacency matrix *reader>sender* in a sequential web forum on the basis of automatic web tracking; it is necessary to carry out a content analysis.

The thread-discussion web forum shows the discussion list on the main page, as is the case with sequential forum. By clicking on each discussion though, users may visualize the thread of messages that compose the discussion, and that are hierarchically organized in main headings and subheadings (responses), but they may not immediately visualize message contents. Messages may be read only when the user clicks on them, and he/she can read only one message at a time. Moreover, his/her reply is a subheading directly connected to the title of the first message.

"This poses two important consequences: first, the user has to click on the message to display it, thus facilitating the creation of an adjacency matrix on the basis of messages read. The user is also well aware that the reply command refers only to that message and the answer is linked to it". (Grion et al., 2008, p. 121)

A MODEL FOR MONITORING ACTIVITY IN E-LEARNING

After having presented how to monitor individual and collective actions, and having defined the indices that we consider relevant to monitor activity in e-learning, we propose a model that takes into consideration two typologies of actions that we described in the previous paragraphs.

The model we present is a sort of "device" for representing individual and group profiles on the basis of both individual and collective actions, as previously defined. We have already described in detail the data elaborations that are necessary for both deriving interesting indicators from raw web tracking data, and for transposing relational data on an adjacency matrix. Here, therefore, we will simply summarize the model we have elaborated, and the indices it involves for representing individual and group profiles for e-learning activity. Our model (see tab. 1) is based on 5 areas of action: 3 of them are dedicated to individual actions (platform use; online loquacity; participation to online discussions) and 2 of them focus on collective actions (role in group collaboration; dealing with of group). Obviously, this is meant to be a mere suggestion that could be integrated with other indicators and indices related to web tracking and SNA; the main advantage of this model is that it may be adapted to different e-learning scenarios based on interactions, e.g. a virtual community that interacts through a web forum, a social network of students in which interactions are performed by means of blog posts or private messages, but also situations where instant messaging and chat are employed.

The three types of indicators referring to individual actions are derived from web tracking and are related to *Platform Use*, *Mean Length of Utterance in morphemes* and *Participation in online discussions*. The first is related to the use of contents and web platform tools, and it is constituted by three types of data (see tab. 1). The second derives from an elaboration of data collected through web tracking, and it particularly considers the amount of words, and the amount of utterances that participants wrote in on-line interactions. The third indicator is related to the number of messages and replies sent and received during on-line interactions, and it is composed by three web tracking data.

The two types of indicators regarding collective actions originate from SNA and are concerned with *Group Collaboration* and *Dealing with Group*. For accomplishing the SNA we have constructed the adjacency matrix by performing a content analysis to the on-line interactions drawing on the model formulated by Manca *et al.* (2007). In fact, as web tracking and SNA are principally based on numerical (quantitative) data, content analysis and qualitative data are very important for entering within the meaning and the interactions. The group collaboration is formed by three centrality indices, i.e., Information Centrality, Betweenness Centrality, and Eigenvector Centrality, whereas the dealing-with-group indicator is based on three neighborhood indices (in and out degree, and egonet density), and the cliques involvement. (see Table 1)

All web tracking indicators and SNA indexes are codified in 4 classes considering the 33% and

Table 1. Individual and collective actions hypothesized by the proposed model

Individual Actions	**Platform use**	• Sum of visits to page contents or files (with contents related to learning); • Percentage of page contents or files visited; • Sum of visits to web artifacts proposed for carrying out on-line activity (e.g., web forum, chat, blog, wiki, etc.).
	Online loquacity	Loquacity is based on the Mean Length of Utterance in morphemes index (Brown, 1973) that is calculated by the number of morphemes divided by the number of utterances. In order to automatically elaborate data coming from web tracking, and to calculate this index, we propose to replace morphemes by words. The online loquacity is thus calculated by the number of words divided by the number of utterances.
	Participation in online discussions	• Sum of on-line discussions initiated. • Sum of messages/replies sent. • Sum of messages/replies received.
Collective Actions	**Group Collaboration**	• Information Centrality; • Betweenness Centrality; • Eigenvector Centrality.
	Dealing with Group	• In-degree (ties received); • Out-degree (ties activated); • Egonet density (density of the personal network); • Cliques involvement.

66% group percentile; e.g., as far as the group collaboration and, specifically, the Information Centrality (IC) are concerned, we codified indices as follows:

- $0 \rightarrow$ IC$=0 \rightarrow$ no IC (individual completely peripheral or not-participating in on-line discussions);
- $1 \rightarrow$ from 0 to 33° percentile $\rightarrow$ low IC;
- $2 \rightarrow$ from 33° to 66° percentile $\rightarrow$ average IC;
- $3 \rightarrow$ from 66° percentile to 100% $\rightarrow$ high IC.

Thus, a participant with an IC of, e.g., 2.15 in a group ranging from 3 (33°) to 5 (66°) to 6 (100%) is codified as "low IC", whereas a participant with an IC of 3.94 is codified as "average IC". Now, summing the three codified SNA indexes for group collaboration (i.e. information centrality, betweenness centrality and eigenvector centrality), we can evaluate each participant in relation to these areas and to his/her group of reference. If, for instance, a participant features a "group collaboration" of 7 in a condition in which the maximum level achievable is 12 (i.e., the sum of the three codified indices), this means that he/she has an average role in group collaboration. If a participant's level corresponds to 11, he/she plays instead a very central role in group collaboration. We can indeed codify the group collaboration indicator (and also the other indicators) in 4 classes as follows:

- $0 \rightarrow$ no collaboration;
- $1 \rightarrow$ peripheral role in group collaboration (from 1 to 4 in the previous example);
- $2 \rightarrow$ average role in group collaboration (from 5 to 8);
- $3 \rightarrow$ important role in group collaboration (from 9 to 12)

By adopting the same procedure with the other individual and collective indicators, it is possible to represent individuals through a map of competences in relation to the potential competences achieved by the group in the 5 types of actions (fig. 4).

In summary, this model allows us to take into consideration and to monitor not only the individual actions a user performs in an e-learning environment, but also the collective actions he/she accomplishes in order to interact with his/her colleagues during on-line group collaboration. Furthermore, we can use this model for representing group performances and, thus, for comparing different groups involved in virtual learning environments characterized by collaborative activities (fig. 5).

The idea of this model is that instructors may be provided with a tool for monitoring and assessing, on the one hand, learners, and, on the other hand, groups, communities and/or social networks. The possibility to constantly monitor learners' online actions in e-learning contexts is one of the most important steps for understanding whether there are difficulties in the participation and collaboration during the online sessions and activities proposed. It is certainly not simple for instructors to learn all such indicators and indices, especially if one considers the necessity of elaborating data collected by web tracking. While waiting for a tool that may develop this model and allow its application to many web learning environments, instructors can profitably use, on the one hand, the statistics directly obtained from the web learning environments or from a web analyzer (there are a number of free web analyzers available on the web) and, on the other hand, some tools for applying SNA (free software or web applications for SNA are also available on the web). One should also consider that even though our model involves the monitoring and assessing of online actions, i.e., two activities that are based on web tracking data, the assessing may not be based simply on data related to frequencies of operations. Rather, such an assessing requires more sophisticated indices that represent specific and more complex

Figure 4. An example of comparison between two members of the same group

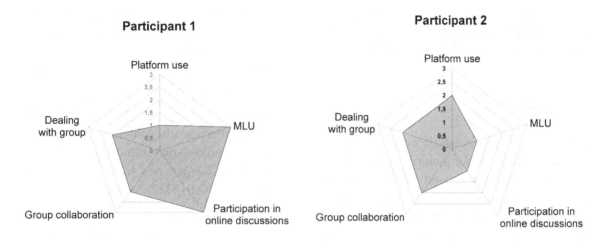

Figure 5. An example of comparison between two groups

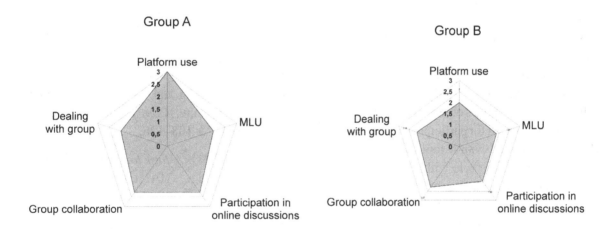

individual and collective actions. For this reason, the model proposed a specific elaboration of data tracking that permits both to monitor e-learning or blended-learning contexts and their evolution (by applying the model longitudinally) and to assess individual and/or groups during or after the course.

The originality of this model resides in the fact that by considering individuals, instructors may have a graphical and quantitative representation of single learners, of the online actions they perform, and of the roles they play for the group collaboration, and they are also given the possibility to

compare learners with each other. By considering the whole group, moreover, instructors may have a graphical and quantitative representation of the collective online activity, together with the possibility to compare different groups. However, this model is not just designed for instructors only. It is also dedicated to learners. The innovative aspect is that results of the monitoring are presented to learners so that each one of them may be aware of his/her individual actions, his/her participation in interactions and his/her collaboration and exchanges with the other learners. The idea is that looking and comparing personal actions with collective activities (performed by the group), a learner may be motivated to improve his/her participation and performance, e.g., in the actions previously described (tab.1).

CONCLUSION

In this chapter we presented an overview of two specific methods for monitoring activity in e-learning: web tracking and Social Network Analysis. Starting from a socio-cultural approach to the notion of activity, we proposed web tracking as a method for collecting data about individual actions, and SNA as a method for monitoring collective actions. Indicators derived from these two methods were integrated in the model we suggested for monitoring individual and group activity in e-learning contexts. On the one hand, this model could be very useful for instructors as a tool for monitoring online activity of individuals and groups, but also for assessing them in relation to the e-learning course's objectives. On the other hand, it is also useful for participants themselves, which are provided with a tool for monitoring their actions and their role within the collective activity, and for stimulating their self-awareness as far as their improvement potential in relation to the group performance is concerned. In light of these considerations, our model could also be seen as a tool for monitoring the competences that individuals develop and acquire in e-learning contexts, thus integrating and composing their complete e-portfolio.

REFERENCES

Attwell, G. (2007). Personal learning environments - the future of eLearning? *eLearning Papers, 2*(1). Retrieved July 20, 2008, from http://www.elearningeuropa.info/files/media/media11561.pdf

Aviv, R., Zippy, E., Ravid, G., & Geva, A. (2003). Network analysis of knowledge construction in asynchronous learning networks. [JALN]. *Journal of Asynchronous Learning Networks, 7*(3), 1–23.

Barab, S. A., Barnett, M., Yamagata-Lynch, L., Squire, K., & Keating, T. (2002). Using activity theory to understand the contradictions characterizing a technology-rich introductory astronomy course. *Mind, Culture, and Activity, 9*(2), 76–107. doi:doi:10.1207/S15327884MCA0902_02

Block, J. (1974). *Schools, society and mastery learning*. New York: Holt, Rinehart and Winston.

Bonacich, P. (1972). Factoring and weighting approaches to status scores and clique identification. *The Journal of Mathematical Sociology, 2*, 113–120.

Brown, A. L., & Campione, J. C. (1990). Communities of learning and thinking, or a context by any other name. *Contributions to Human Development, 21*, 108–126.

Brown, R. (1973). *A first language: The early stages*. Cambridge, MA: Harvard University Press.

Calvani, A., Fini, A., Bonaiuti, G., & Mazzoni, E. (2005). Monitoring interactions in collaborative learning environments (CSCL): A tool kit for Synergeia. *Journal of E-learning and Knowledge Society, 1*, 63–73.

Carugati, F., & Gilly, M. (1993). The multiple sides of the same tool: Cognitive development as a matter of social construction of meaning. *European Journal of Psychology of Education, 8*(4), 345–354.

CTGV. (1993). Anchored instruction and situated cognition revisited. *Educational Technology, 33*(3), 52–70.

Doise, W., & Mugny, G. (1984). *The social development of the intellect*. Oxford, UK: Pergamon Press.

Engeström, Y. (1987). *Learning by expanding: An activity-theoretical approach to developmental research*. Helsinki, Finland: Orienta-Konsultit.

Engeström, Y. (1999). Activity theory and individual and social transformation. In Y. Engeström, R. Miettinen, & R.-L. Punamäki (Eds.), *Perspectives on activity theory* (pp. 19-38). Cambridge, UK: Cambridge University Press.

Grion, V., Varisco, B. M., Luchi, F., Raineri, M. S., & Mazzoni, E. (2008). Building and sharing teacher professional identity in virtual communities. In B. M. Varisco (Ed.), *Psychological, pedagogical and sociological models for learning and assessment in virtual communities* (pp. 93-144). Milan, Italy: Polimetrica.

Hasu, M. (2001). *Critical transition from developers to users. Activity-theoretical studies of interaction and learning in the innovation process*. Unpublished academic dissertation, Departement of Education, Center for Activity Theory and Developmental Work Research, University of Helsinki. Retrieved June 31, 2008, from http://ethesis.helsinki.fi/julkaisut/kas/kasva/vk/hasu/

Hewitt, J. (2001). Beyond threaded discourse. *International Journal of Educational Telecommunications, 7*, 207–221.

Juan, A., Daradoumis, T., Faulin, J., & Xhafa, F. (2008). Developing an information system for monitoring student's activity in online collaborative learning. In *Proceedings of the 2nd International Conference on Complex, Intelligent and Software Intensive Systems* (pp. 270-275).

Kaptelinin, V., & Nardi, B. A. (2006). *Acting with technology. Activity theory and interaction design*. Cambridge, MA: MIT Press.

Leont'ev, A. N. (1978). *Activity, consciousness and personality*. Englewood Cliffs, NJ: Prentice-Hall. Retrieved June 15, 2008, from http://www.marxists.org/archive/leontev/works/1978/

Lipman, M. (1991). *Thinking in education*. Cambridge, MA: Cambridge University Press.

Manca, S., Delfino, M., & Mazzoni, E. (in press). Coding procedures to analyse interaction patterns in educational Web forums. [JCAL]. *Journal of Computer Assisted Learning*.

Matteucci, M. C., Carugati, F., Selleri, P., Mazzoni, E., & Tomasetto, C. (in press). Teachers' judgment from an European psychological perspective. In G. F. Ollington (Ed.), *Teachers and teaching: Strategies, innovations and problem solving*. Hauppauge, NY: Nova Science Publishers.

Mazzoni, E. (2006a). Extending Web sites' usability: From a cognitive perspective to an activity theory approach. In S. Zappala & C. Gray (Eds.), *Impact of e-commerce on consumers and small firms* (pp. 161-175). Aldershot, Hampshire, UK: Ashgate.

Mazzoni, E. (2006b). Du simple tracement des interactions à l'évaluation des rôles et des fonctions des membres d'une communauté en réseau: Une proposition dérivée de l'analyse des réseaux sociaux. *Information Sciences for Decision Making, 25*, 477-487. Retrieved March 19, 2008, from http://isdm.univ-tln.fr/

Nurmela, K., Lehtinen, E., & Palonen, T. (1999). Evaluating CSCL log files by social network analysis. In *Proceedings of the Computer Support for Collaborative Learning (CSCL) 1999 Conference* (pp. 434-442). Mahwah, NJ: Lawrence Erlbaum Associates.

Pozzi, F., Manca, S., Persico, D., & Sarti, L. (2007). A general framework for tracking and analysing learning processes in CSCL environments. *Innovations in Education and Teaching International, 44*, 169–179. doi:10.1080/14703290701240929

Proctor, R., & Vu, K. (2005). *Handbook of human factors in Web design*. Mahwah, NJ: Lawrence Erlbaum Associates, Inc.

Romero, C., & Ventura, S. (2007). Educational data mining: A survey from 1995 to 2005. *Expert Systems with Applications, 33*(1), 135–146. doi:10.1016/j.eswa.2006.04.005

Scardamalia, C., & Bereiter, M. (1994). Computer support for knowledge-building communities. *Journal of the Learning Sciences, 3*(3), 265–283. doi:10.1207/s15327809jls0303_3

Scott, J. (1991). *Social network analysis: A handbook*. London: Sage.

Vygotsky, L. S. (1978). *Mind in society: The development of higher psychological processes*. Cambridge, MA: Harvard University Press.

Wasserman, S., & Faust, K. (1994). *Social network analysis. Methods and applications*. Cambridge, UK: University Press.

Wenger, E. (1998). *Communities of practice. Learning, meaning, and identity*. Cambridge, MA: Cambridge University Press.

Wiley, D. A. (2000). Connecting learning objects to instructional design theory: A definition, a metaphor, and a taxonomy. In D. A. Wiley (Ed.). *The instructional use of learning object* (pp. 1-35). Bloomington, IN: Agency for Instructional Technology And Association For Educational Communications Of Technology. Retrieved July 23, 2008, from http://reusability.org/read/

Wiley, D. A. (2002). *A proposed measure of discussion activity in threaded discussion spaces* (working draft). Retrieved July 28, 2008, from http://wiley.ed.usu.edu/docs/discussion09.pdf

Zorrilla, M. E., & Alvarez, E. (2008). MATEP: Monitoring and analysis tool for e-learning platforms. In *Proceedings of the 2008 Eighth IEEE International Conference on Advanced Learning Technologies, volume 00* (pp. 611-613).

Chapter 8
Monitoring Students' Activity and Performance in Online Higher Education:
A European Perspective

Fernando Lera-López
Public University of Navarre, Spain

Javier Faulin
Public University of Navarre, Spain

Angel A. Juan
Open University of Catalonia, Spain

Victor Cavaller
Open University of Catalonia, Spain

ABSTRACT

In this chapter the authors first explain the recently created European Higher Education Area and its implications over instructors' and students' roles. They also analyze how e-learning management systems are contributing to modify higher education around the world, and which are the benefits and the challenges associated to their use. In this new educational scenario, the authors discuss the importance of monitoring students' and groups' activity and performance, and some of the monitoring tools already available in the most popular learning management systems are reviewed. Then, after identifying the informational necessities of online instructors and students, the authors propose a data-analysis model to assist instructors by providing them with easy-to-understand and updated visual reports. Instructors can use these reports to classify students and groups according to their activity and learning outcomes, track their evolution, and identify those who might need immediate guidance or assistance.

DOI: 10.4018/978-1-60566-786-7.ch008

INTRODUCTION

In the period 1998-2009, the development of Web-based groupware tools has involved a Copernican revolution in higher education worldwide, leading to an increasing offer of online courses (Allen & Seaman, 2008). Correspondingly, traditional procedures for measuring students' activity and performance are also evolving into more efficient ways of monitoring students' effort in learning processes. As it happens in many other processes from industry or services, monitoring e-learning processes becomes necessary if they are to be improved. Data about the learning process can be used not only to obtain summary information at the end of the semester but also to keep the learning process 'under control' during the semester, e.g., to prevent unnecessary dropouts and low academic results. When conveniently used, current technology allows instructors and students to have a better knowledge on how this learning process is being developed. Therefore, it is not surprising that some of the most popular e-learning platforms are incorporating monitoring tools to assist managers, instructors and students by providing them with critical information on the educational process. Sometimes, thought, it is not enough to provide a lot of data to these agents, either in a numerical or graphical format, since this approach can be time-consuming or not efficient if it is not well designed. On the contrary, it becomes necessary to develop standard data-analysis models that provide, just-in-time, the critical information that each different agent requires. Precisely, one of the major aims of this chapter is the proposal of such a data-analysis model for monitoring students' and groups' activity and performance in online environments. The model aims to: (a) visually identify students or groups with low online activity levels, and (b) visually identify students or groups with poor academic results. At the end, the target is to provide valuable information to online instructors who may establish just-in-time assistance for students and groups at risk.

The rest of this chapter is structured as follows: First, we introduce the recently created European Higher Education Area and explain how it is changing instructors' and students' roles in higher education. Second, we analyze how modern educational processes can benefit from the integration of e-learning management systems (LMS), and also which new challenges arise with their use. Third, we discuss why monitoring students' and groups' activity and performance are critical tasks in the higher education scenario defined by the previous sections. Fourth, we review some state-of-the-art monitoring tools that are being incorporated in three of the most popular e-learning management systems. Fifth, we identify which information should be provided to each of the online learning agents. Finally, we propose a set of graphs that aim to provide useful information that should be offered by any monitoring system.

THE EUROPEAN HIGHER EDUCATION AREA

The Bologna declaration (Van der Wende, 2000) proposes the development of the European Higher Education Area (EHEA) which, in turn, involves a drastic harmonization –both in terms of compatibility as well as comparability– of university degrees among most European countries. According to the Bologna declaration, increasing the international competitiveness and employability of European citizens are some of the main goals to be promoted by the EHEA. Also, in the EHEA framework, it is emphasized the significant relevance of life-long learning processes and the need for a curricular development more clearly oriented to the requirements of the labor markets (Mas-Colell, 2003). In this context, the establishment of an academic system of credits, the ECTS system, introduces a common process to evaluate students work and activities.

For many European countries, the new EHEA could imply a new educational paradigm which represents a shifting from a passive learning system based on the instructor lessons and the use of non-interactive learning methods –e.g. lectures and conferences– to a new and active learning system centered on the student's activity and on the use of several interactive learning methods. The instructor's role is, therefore, moving from one related to a knowledge transmission agent to another in which the instructor is in charge of assisting and supervising students' learning processes (Engelbrecht & Harding, 2005). Accordingly, for students the learning process will imply not only to acquire the fundamental knowledge of the subjects but also the development of some relevant competences. These competences, classified as generic (interdisciplinary) and specific (subject-related), should provide each student with the capacity to generate new practical knowledge by his/her own. Competences should also contribute to develop in the student some professional abilities that he/she will need to get a successful access to the labor markets. Then, there is a shift from theoretical and seat-base time to outcomes-based or employer-based competency (Howell, Williams & Lindsay, 2003). According to Gonzalez & Wagenaar (2003), some of the desired professional abilities that every student should acquire during his/her learning process are, among others: to be able to analyze and synthesize, to be able to learn by himself/herself, to be able to solve problems in a logical way, to be able to adapt to new situations and changes, to be able to apply knowledge in a practical way, to be able to conduct information, and, finally, to be able to work both in groups and autonomously.

Acquisition of these competences and abilities requires students to invest a significant amount of hours in the development of experimental and practical activities, which implies a significant modification of the learning and assessment criteria and processes currently established in some European countries. Therefore, both the incorporation of more interactive learning methods and the increase of the tutorial role performed by instructors are going to be two essential pieces in the EHEA. Likewise, new collaborative students' activities will require from new monitoring and assessment processes and systems.

USING E-LEARNING PLATFORMS IN HIGHER EDUCATION

Most universities worldwide are currently integrating e-Learning Management Systems in their higher education programs (Figure 1). These Web-based tools can be used to develop both alternative and complementary strategies to the traditional face-to-face learning systems, which allow delivering education to students who are time- or place-bound (Seufert, Lechner & Stanoevska, 2002). Also, as Howell, Williams & Lindsay (2003) point out, in some developed countries the current higher-education infrastructure cannot easily accommodate the growing educational demand due to an important increase of enrolments. Online education can be helpful to mitigate this problem in an efficient way.

Today's e-learning platforms provide fresh possibilities in the new educational scenario described before. Among other possibilities, students can use these technologies to obtain all or part of the course materials, to make self-assessment tests, to develop some individual and collaborative learning activities, to post their conceptual doubts so that instructors and other students can contribute to solve them, etc. Also, other complementary educational resources and interactive ways of communication are available for students and instructors through these online platforms. Other significant advantages for students are the following:

- **More flexibility when selecting learning timetables and schedules:** In traditional face-to-face learning processes, students

Figure 1. E-learning management system used at the Open University of Catalonia

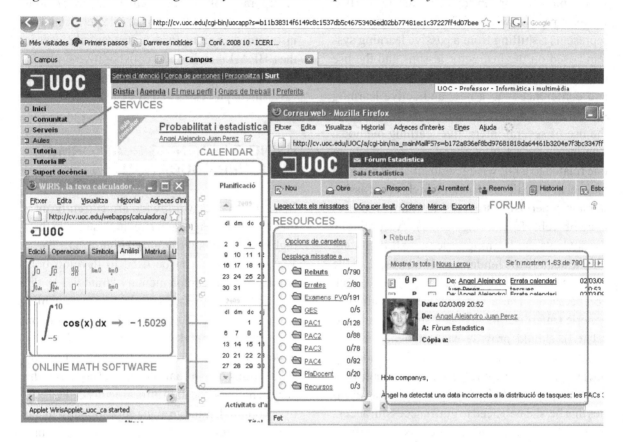

have to attend a class on campus at a scheduled time (Zirkle, 2003). In many cases, this system is only valid for full-time students. On the contrary, online learning processes tend to offer more scheduling flexibility, which is an important factor for adult students who have work or familiar duties. Moreover, students enrolled in online programs usually have the possibility of self-pacing some of the course content and activities (Seufert, Lechner, & Stanoevska, 2002). Empirical studies of online courses confirm their ability to reach students with special needs. Robinson's (2005) study found that 43% of students across 18 disciplines at 13 universities took online courses because they were convenient for work schedules, while 22% chose them due to family duties.

- **Less geographical or time bounds to communicate with other students or instructors:** This way, a more interactive communication among students and between students and instructors is promoted which, in turn, encourages the development of collaborative and working-group activities (Gómez-Laso & Benito, 2006).

- **Promotion of continuous evaluation processes:** This, in turn, allows students to receive updated feedback about their academic progression during the course. As some authors point out, interactive self-assessment might improve students' academic results and their perception of learning (Peat & Franklin, 2002; Lowry, 2005; Ibabe & Jaureguizar, 2007). Also, online platforms are very convenient tools for spreading or publishing online assessments and for sharing activities with other students. On the other hand, students are encouraged to development their autonomous work with all educational resources available in the platform (Fernandez, 2007). For example, collaborative projects make feasible an opened and flexible learning process boosting autonomous student's work and promoting the development of competences (Del Moral & Villalustre, 2008).

- **Promotion of a multimedia representation of information:** By combining text, images, voice, and video, practical knowledge transmission is facilitated. According to Zirkle (2003), e-learning technologies contribute to the development of technical skills. Howell, Williams & Lindsay (2003) emphasize that technological fluency is becoming a graduation requirement. Faulin et al. (2009) point out that these technologies can contribute to reduce the gap between theory and practice.

At the same time, there are some important challenges typically associated with e-learning:

- **Significant differences in backgrounds and technical skills:** Generally speaking, students taking online courses use to be older than typical undergraduate students (Gaytan, 2007). Consequently, and according to Simonson et al. (2003) dealing with students without too much technological background is somewhat usual. Similarly, students' physical limitations should also been accounted for, and alternative ways to access content should be provided to handicapped students (Schwartzman, 2007).
- **High dropout rates and isolation risk:** As Sweet (1986) and Truluck (2007) point

out, distance-education programs tend to present higher dropout rates than face-to-face education programs. The lack of a personal contact between the agents involved in the learning process increases the risk of a sense of isolation among students, who might feel disconnected from the instructors as well as from other students. For that reason, interactive communication needs to be facilitated and continuously encouraged by instructors. Truluck (2007) proposes interesting measures for overcoming dropouts in online courses; among others he suggests the use of informal online meetings or "coffee shops" for conversation. Additionally, also instructors can feel isolated, which can affect their satisfaction, motivation, and potential long-term involvement in online learning (Childers & Berner, 2000). Finally, online learning programs could help students to reach academic and social integration (Allen, 2006).

- **Continuous feedback and accreditation requirements:** As explained before, online learning platforms are usually associated with the use of continuous evaluation processes through different self-assessment test and through the development of individual and group activities. Consequently, it seems highly desirable that instructors could provide just-in-time guidance and assistance to students' activities as well as periodical and current feedback and assessments on these activities. This is not a trivial task. Also, related to this problem there is the necessity of developing protocols for authorship accreditation of students' academic activities (Trenholm, 2007; Juan et al., 2008b).

IMPORTANCE OF MONITORING LEARNING PROCESSES

As mentioned in the Introduction, a decisive and critical aspect of any online educational system is the possibility of monitoring students' activity and performance. On one hand, monitoring students' activities can help to anticipate students with problems such as those not participating in the proposed learning activities or even dropping out the course (Juan et al., 2009b) as well as possible internal conflicts in groups with unbalanced distribution of tasks (Juan et al., 2008a). Also, monitoring could provide instructors with significant clues to improve the online course and the communication process, to interactively modify student models, and to organize learning exercises more efficiently, thus achieving better learning outcomes (Daradoumis, Xhafa & Juan, 2006; Dillenbourg, 1999; Gaudioso, et al., 2009; Kay, 1995). On the other hand, students can also benefit from these monitoring activities, since they can have periodical feedback regarding their performance level as compared with the rest of the class. These monitoring reports could have a significant and positive influence on student motivation as well as a positive impact on the final performance (Ibabe & Jaureguizar, 2007). The monitoring impact on student motivation is very important since, according to Meyer (2002), students need motivation as a very relevant variable to learn in any online environment. Enhanced regulation facilities can also play an important instructional and social task since they lead participants to think about the activity being performed, promote collaboration through the exchange of ideas that may arise, propose new resolution mechanisms, as well as justify and refine their own contributions and thus acquire new knowledge (Stahl, 2006). Even when some important advances have been done during the last years, most instructors involved in online learning process receive, in practice, little support to monitor and assess students' activity (Jerman,

Soller & Muhlenbrock, 2001; Zumbach et al., 2002). Moreover, most current work in this area focus on instructor-oriented information, but there is a lack to offer student-oriented and institution-oriented information (Lam et al., 2006).

Directly related to our work, Rosenkrans (2000) states the necessity of using assessment tools that monitor students' progress as a way to empower instructors' role in online environments and also as a way to provide a feedback to students. This monitoring process constitutes a difficult task which demands a lot of resources and expertise from educators. As far as we know, Rada (1998) is the first author who proposed the use of statistical quality control methods and tools, which are extensively used in several industrial and services processes, to monitoring students' transactions in online learning environments. Other authors (Simoff & Maher, 2000; Gaudioso et al., 2009) discuss the lack of online data analysis and analytical processing features of Web-based educational environments and propose the use of data analysis, data mining and visualization as an integral part of these environments. Following Romero & Ventura (2007), in traditional learning environments instructors are able to obtain feedback on student learning experiences in face-to-face interactions with students, making possible a continual evaluation of their teaching activities and programs (Sheard et al., 2003). Monitoring activities in conventional teaching environments involves observing students' behavior in the classroom and estimating the effectiveness of pedagogical strategies in a continual and visual feedback. However, with online students, this informal monitoring is not possible, and teacher must look for other ways to obtain this information. Online e-learning platforms collect large volumes of data, automatically generated by web servers and collected in server access logs. In order to provide a more effective learning environment, data mining techniques can be applied (Ingram, 1999). In fact, these techniques offer a wide range of useful analysis: statistics and visualization, clustering, classification and outlier detection, association rule mining and pattern mining, and text mining. Recently, an emergent research area called Educational Data Mining is focused on the application of data mining techniques to discover information and knowledge from log files data registered in course management systems (Romero, Ventura & García, 2008; Dringus & Ellis, 2005).

MONITORING TOOLS AVAILABLE IN MAJOR E-LEARNING PLATFORMS

All modern e-learning platforms incorporate their own statistics modules and complements, which can be helpful for instructors in order to perform the monitoring and assessment processes of their students' activity. In this section, we briefly discuss the current state-of-the-art of the monitoring tools offered by some of the most popular e-learning platforms. In particular, we review the monitoring tools provided by Sakai, WebCT/Blackboard and Moodle.

The Sakai Collaboration and Learning Environment (http://www.sakaiproject.org) is an open-source courseware management system. The Sakai CLE has been a main platform for several tool deployment projects. In particular, *Site Stats* is a Sakai's tool which can be downloaded from http://bugs.sakaiproject.org/confluence/display/STAT/Home. This tool can be used for showing

Figure 2. Screenshots Site Stats: Sakai CLE (© 2008-2009 University Fernando Pessoa. Used with permission)

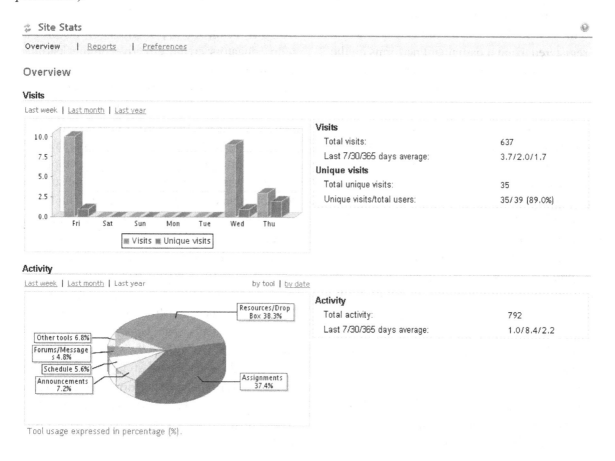

site usage statistics. Information is organized in two sections: (a) "overview", which offers summary information about site visits and activity, and (b) "reports", which are exportable reports about site visits, tools and resource activities. The Site Stats tool provides instructors with overview statistical reports for each online course and also with individual statistical reports regarding the activity of each student. Using these reports, the instructor can obtain information about how many students have accessed to the course site, the level and type of activity associated to each user and course site, etc. Figure 2 shows the main screen of this tool, which provides a basic overview of the activity developed on each online course.

A bar graph represents how many visits, unique visits, and activity events have been generated per day, month or year. In this context, total unique visits refer to how many different students have visited the online course, while total visits refer to the number of times those students have visited the course site. Activity refers to any action or registered event a participant performs on the academic worksite. The instructor can set what kinds of actions or events constitute an activity. These statistical reports are useful to monitoring the students' use of the different learning resources and spaces –such as PDF materials, wikis, blogs, forums, calendars, etc.– during the online course. The Site Stats tool also includes a report functionality which allows the instructor to follow specific actions or events developed by groups or by individual students. Beyond the Sakai Site Stats, several Sakay-related communities are currently developing promising data analysis tools, such as *Sakai Data Analysis*, which can be found at http://bugs.sakaiproject.org/confluence/display/UDAT/Home.

WebCT/Blackboard (http://www.blackboard.com) also offers monitoring tools that instructors can employ to get statistics on students' activity and on the use of different course spaces and materials. Several monitoring tools are available in this system: *Tracking Students*, *Early Warning Systems*,

Performance Dashboard, etc. For instance, the Tracking Students tool offers reports including the timestamp and frequency with which each student has accessed the course contents, specific course units and each discussion forum.

The instructor can also get a report showing the total time each student has spent working on the course contents, on specific course units and on discussion forums: average session length, average duration of sessions, average sessions per day, etc. This tool also offers instructors the possibility of configuring the system so that this tracking information will be shared with the corresponding student or group of students. The Early Warning System is an expansion of the Performance Dashboard which allows instructors to set up preventive warnings based on grade results, days since last course access, missed assignments, etc.

Finally, Moodle (http://moodle.org) is another popular open-source course management system. According to their developers, Moodle was designed using sound pedagogical principles to help educators create effective online learning communities. It also offers a monitoring tool for instructors. They can use it to obtain reports regarding the frequency of use, timestamp information and IP addresses associated to each course student. The instructor can also get a report showing the number of accesses and total time employed on each assessment for each individual student. Moodle also offers instructors the possibility of maintaining private notes about each student in a secure area. Additionally, instructors can get a summary report regarding individual student performance on assignments. Finally, instructors can set a flag on individual course components to track the frequency with which students access those components. The *Moodle Analytics* tool, designed by SITACT (http://www.sitact.net/physics), provides a dashboard-style reporting system to track the progress and performance of students. By using a graphical view, instructors have detailed assessment statistics available, making it easier to interpret students' performance.

Two other interesting initiatives based on the use of visual reports to monitoring students' activity are Moodog (Zhang et al., 2007) and CourseVis (Mazza & Dimitrova, 2004). All in all, there is a clear interest among LMS developers in providing modules for monitoring and assessment students' activity.

INFORMATION NEEDED IN MONITORING PROCESSES

In any online education system it is possible to distinguish at least three different actors, e.g., students, instructors and managers. Each of these actors might have different informational necessities and requirements. Correspondingly, we can consider the following three kinds of information (Romero & Ventura, 2007):

- **Information oriented towards instructors:** Its main purpose is to get objective feedback for evaluating the structure of the website course content and its effectiveness on the online learning process in order to achieve better learning outcomes (Daradoumis, Xhafa & Juan, 2006; Dillenbourg, 1999). Particularly, monitoring students' activities can help instructors to find the most effective tasks and the most frequently mistakes. Also, it is possible to classify students into groups based on their guidance needs and their performance. Then, instructors can personalize and customize courses and courseware, as well as establish different learning paths for different kinds of students. This information should also help the instructor to anticipate students with problems –e.g., students that are likely to drop-out or fail the course– and, in the case of collaborative e-learning scenarios, to identify groups' leaders and followers and to perceive possible group internal conflicts or malfunctions (Juan et al., 2008a).

- **Information oriented towards students:** The aim here is to be able to provide students with suggestions and recommendations regarding a set of learning activities and resources that significantly contribute to enhance their learning process. This includes general recommendations about good learning experiences and personalized suggestions based on previous activities and tasks developed by the same student or by other students with a similar profile. Also, students should have access to periodical feedback regarding their performance level as well as to the average group or class level (Juan et al., 2009a). Some empirical evidence has shown a positive influence of periodical feedback on student motivation and their final performance in the course (Ibabe & Jaureguizar, 2007; Lowry, 2005) as well as in the rate of dropouts. Consequently, students could obtain not only information in absolute terms regarding individual and group performance but they could also receive information in relative terms regarding individual and group performance as compared to the rest of students and groups in their class or course. Finally, it is important to highlight that –in contrast to what happens in a traditional face-to-face learning system, where monitoring information can only be gathered for attendant students– e-learning environments allow obtaining information regarding all registered students in a course.

- **Information oriented towards academic managers and administrators:** Its main purpose is to provide parameters that help to improve site and course efficiency and to adapt them to the behavior and specific characteristics of their users: usability, setting of e-learning environment, etc. Also, this information could help educational institutions to better organize human and material resources, and to improve the educational programs offered online.

In this chapter, we focus on information oriented to students and instructors, which can be classified according to three general criteria: background data, academic activity (access data and use of learning resources) and academic performance. Background data offer personal and academic information about each student. Some student's characteristics –such as gender, age or academic background– are usually known a priori, while other –such as technological skills, time availability for the course, etc.– must be obtained through a short survey at the beginning of the course. Academic activity collects all the information about the LMS access-data and about the use of different learning resources. Opposite to traditional face-to-face learning systems, online environments are able to offer a great quantity of data about students' actions and interactions (Romero, Ventura & Garcia, 2008). Student's usage statistics are often the starting point for evaluation and monitoring in an online e-learning environment (Zaiane, Xin & Han, 1998). During the online course, students develop different activities associated to their class or working group: they post or read notes in forums, send or read e-mails, upload or download documents, send reports, complete self-assessments, etc. Each of these activities can be considered as an event of a certain type which has been carried out by a particular student at a certain time and web space. Some of these events have only an activity dimension, while others, such as assignments, have also an academic performance dimension. Finally, academic performance is closely related to Web-based assessment. Meyen et al. (2002) suggested that assessment in online learning environments should be an integral part of instruction, that it should be continuously developed through the course and that it should provide extensive feedback to students. Also, online assessment should help students in

taking ownership of their learning by offering them immediate and effective feedback. Then, online assessment systems could have more potential than paper-based assessment systems in terms of access and flexibility for students as well as for instructors. Here, we include formative assessment –providing feedback during the e-learning process– as well as summative assessment –measuring learning at the end of the process. Also, it is important to consider the different perspectives for assessment (Kim, Smith & Maeng 2008): cognitive (acquisition of knowledge), behavioral (skill development), or humanistic (values and attitudes). Furthermore, because of the remarkable effects of collaborative learning, many online learning processes include collaborative or team-assessment tasks such as presentations, projects, case studies, reports, debates, etc. According to Freeman and McKenzie (2002) many students do not consider their team assessment to be a fair assessment method if team members are equally rewarded for unequal contributions. Consequently, improving fairness of team assessment is essential to improving students' learning from team tasks. Identifying group leaders and group followers is a necessary step to offer unequally reward for different contributions to the team assessment. Finally, for activities such as quizzes and self-assessments, not only the score and elapsed time could be necessary, but also a detailed analysis of each student's answer and the difficulty level of each assessment item.

When discussing which information should be used to generate the monitoring reports, it is important not to forget who will be the final users of the information system. If the goal is to develop a standard monitoring system that can be used by any instructor –even by those without special data-analysis or technical skills–, then the following principles must be observed:

- **Reports should contain only relevant information and they should be easy-to-**

understand for instructors and students: In this context, the use of visual graphs and figures could be strongly recommended in order to enhance an immediate and easy interpretation of the desired information. Nevertheless, some instructors could be interested in performing a deeper statistical analysis. The system should then be structured in several layers or levels of information.

- **Reports should be generated and transmitted by the system without any additional effort from instructors:** In other words, obtaining and using the monitoring reports must not represent any extra effort or duty for online instructors. We also recommend that the reports are sent directly to instructors and students directly by email or web syndication as soon as they are generated, instead of waiting for these agents to search for them in a website.

- **Reports should be generated and distributed in real time:** The monitoring information should be disseminated as soon as it has been gathered and processed. This will help instructors to prevent potential problems like unnecessary dropouts or academic low results. Also, students should receive just-in-time guidance to improve their academic activity and performance levels.

- **Reports should be personalized according to individual profiles:** Students should receive a personalized feedback regarding their academic activity and performance as compared with the rest of the class. Instructors' reports should offer the possibility of linking aggregated and individual information, and also the possibility of easily contacting an individual student or a group of students with similar characteristics.

- **Reports should be useful for instructors as well as for students:** Particularly

relevant is the fact the monitoring process should be useful for making decisions. Instructors' reports should identify those groups and students 'at risk', i.e. students with low activity levels and underperformance results, groups with unbalanced distribution of activities and tasks, etc. Thus, students and groups could receive just-in-time and personalized guidance and support to enhance and continue their individual or collaborative work. Students' reports should inform the student about his/her performance level in comparison with the average (or quartiles) class level. The goal here is that each student will be able to locate himself/herself into the course and can be strongly motivated to improve his/her academic activity and performance. In collaborative learning scenarios and team assignments, reports should include group- and individual-performance indicators.

Finally, we would like to highlight some technical requirements that, in our opinion, an efficient monitoring system should include:

- **System compatibility:** The monitoring tools should be able to interoperate with any major LMS. To this purpose, they should be able to gather data from server log-files and academic database-records provided by the most common online platforms (Moodle, WebCT, Sakai, etc.). A multi-level architecture might be necessary to ensure this compatibility (Juan et al., 2009b).

- **System universal accessibility:** The monitoring reports should be accessible from an e-mail client or a simple web navigator. No special software should be required in the client side to be able to receive and visualize the reports.

- **System usability:** The monitoring tools

should be oriented to the 'next step'. In other words, the system should offer a high level of usability for instructors. For example, the system should offer instructors the possibility of sending personalized e-mails to low-activity students through a simple click.

- **System capacity to update its data:** The monitoring system should be able to update its basic data through the course, allowing instructors to focus on some specific students. For example, if some students have decided to give up the online course, it has not sense to still including them into the monitoring reports. On the contrary, if some students or groups have been classified as 'at risk' in the past, it might be interesting to keep a focus on them for some time and check if instructors' policies have given successful results.

SOME USEFUL GRAPHS FOR A MONITORING MODEL

According with the framework described in the previous section, it is possible to design a set of descriptive graphs to be included in the monitoring reports. As already explained there, one of our goals is that these reports can be used by any instructor –even if he/she has no data-analysis or technical skills–, so the following basic principles have been considered when designing these graphs: (i) they must be easy-to-understand, (ii) they must supply the desired information about students or groups 'at risk' quickly (with a simple visualization), and (iii) they must offer the possibility of easily identifying (and contacting) an individual student or a group of students with similar characteristics.

Table 1 summarizes the most basic and significant information to be provided by monitoring reports and, at the same time, it introduces the corresponding graph that we propose to supply this information. The types of information labeled as

Table 1. Critical information contained in our model proposal

#	Type of information	Goal	Graph	Addressees	Periodicity
1	Activity: students classification	To identify those students who are likely to be "at risk" of dropping out the course	Scatterplot of Number of events per student during this week vs. Number of events per student during an average week	Instructor	Weekly
2	Activity: individual student monitoring	Monitoring activity levels of each student throughout the course	Activity control chart for each student	Instructor	Weekly
3	Activity: monitoring participation level	Monitoring the percentage of students that complete each test	Line plot	Instructor and students	After each test
4	Performance: scores distribution in each test	For each test during the course, statistical distribution of students' scores	Histogram, Bar chart or Pie chart	Instructor and students	After each test
5	Performance: students classification	To identify those students who are "at risk" of under-performance	Scatterplot of Student's score in this test vs. Average student's score	Instructor	After each test
6	Performance: individual student monitoring	Monitoring performance levels of each student throughout the course	Performance control chart for each student	Instructor and students	After each test

#1 and #2 are related to online activity, while those labeled as #3 to #6 are associated with academic performance. Some of the graphs in Table 1 can either be found already in most LMS or they can be easily implemented –since they are commonly used graphs–. For that reason, we will focus next in those other graphs that represent an original contribution of our model.

Graph #1, Students' classification according to their activity level (Figure 3), which is provided to the instructor every week throughout the course, is a scatterplot of the following two random variables: X = "Number of events generated by student i during this (current) week" ($i = 1, 2, \ldots, n$, where n is the total number of students in the class) and Y = "Number of events generated by student i during an average week". The plot also includes the vertical lines defined by the first, second and third quartiles of X, namely: $x = Q_{1X}$, $x = Q_{2X}$, and $x = Q_{3X}$. This way, x-values lower than Q_{1X} represent students who have maintained low activity levels during the last (this) week, i.e.: 25% of students with lower activity levels are on the left side of $x = Q_{1X}$. Each of these students is represented by a triangle and his/her low activity level can be interpreted as a risk factor. Special attention deserve those students (triangles) located inside the shadowed area, since they also present a low (in the first quartile) activity level during an average week. Notice that, by simply visualizing this graph, students at risk of dropping out the next learning activities or even the course are easily identified by the instructor. Furthermore, he/she can immediately contact them by e-mail (or simply demand more activity/performance information regarding any of them) with just one or two additional mouse clicks.

Similarly, we depict in Figure 4 the graph #5, a students' classification according to their performance level, which is provided to the instructor after every course test as explained in Table 1. This graph is a scatterplot of the following two random variables: X = "Score obtained by student i in this (last) test" ($i = 1, 2, \ldots, n$, where

n is the total number of students in the class) and Y = "Average score obtained by student i in the past tests (including the last one)". The plot also shows the vertical line $x = 5$ and the horizontal line $y = 5$, where it is assumed that a numerical scale from 0 to 10 is used to grade the scores, being 5 the minimum score to pass the test. This way, x-values lower than 5 (represented by a triangle or an hexagon) correspond to students who have failed to pass this (last) test, while y-values lower than 5 (represented by a triangle or a square) correspond to students who are underperforming –i.e.: they have an average score below the passing mark. Now, any student located at the shadowed area (squares and triangles) can be considered as being at risk of underperformance. Again, by simply visualizing this graph, these students are easily identified by the instructor. Furthermore, he/she can immediately contact them by e-mail (or simply to demand more activity/performance information regarding any of them) with just one or two additional mouse clicks.

Of course, other similar graphs can be designed, using the same principles, to meet the information requirements both in individual and collaborative-learning scenarios (Juan et al 2009a).

CONCLUSION

The higher education scenario worldwide is being modeled by an increasing use of e-Learning Management Systems and also by new methodological tendencies that are re-defining the traditional roles of instructors and students in our modern knowledge-based society. In the case of Europe, these tendencies are strongly associated with the creation of the European Higher Education Area, which is expected to have a great influence over how education is delivered in many countries. In this new scenario, monitoring students' and groups' activity and performance become a priority if learning processes are to be enhanced. Being acknowledged of this necessity, some learning

Figure 3. Students' classification according to their activity level

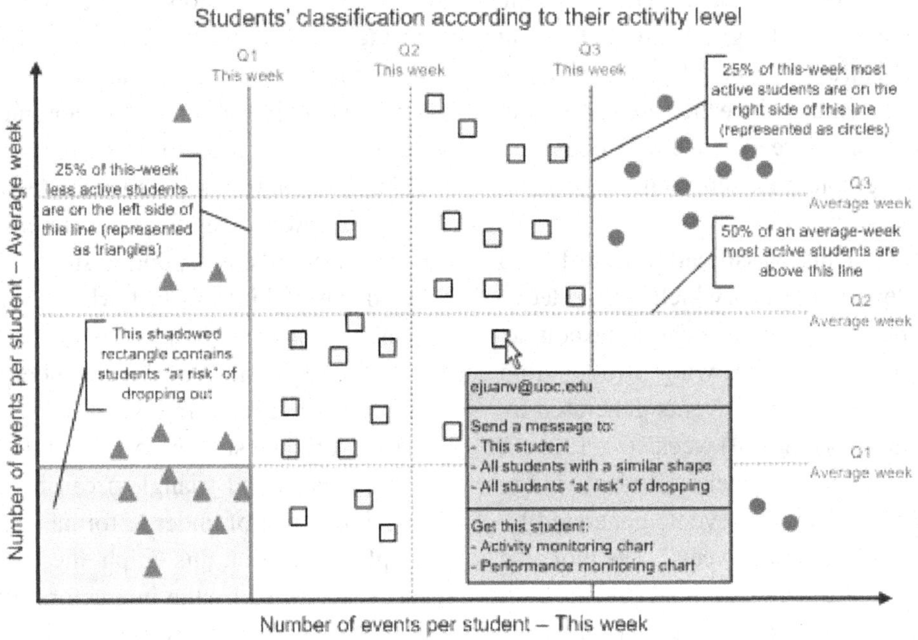

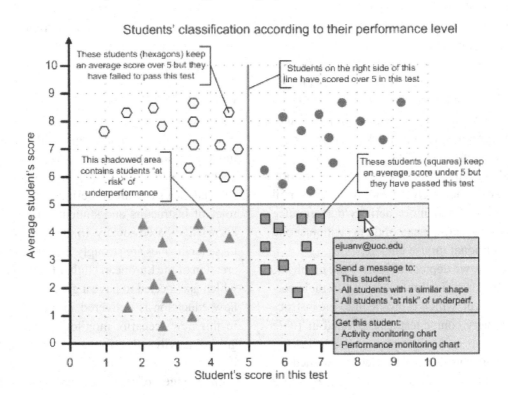

Figure 4. Students' classification according to their performance level

management systems already offer interesting data-analysis capabilities, which aim to provide support to online instructors. Yet, the most important think in any information system is not the quantity of descriptive data provided –either in a numerical or a graphical format–, but the quality of the information being generated from critical data and also the way this information is delivered to the final user. For that reason, in the years to come a lot of work is yet to be done in order to design efficient monitoring models that can be universally used by instructors and that provide useful feedback to students.

ACKNOWLEDGMENT

We would like to thank Dr. David Benito and Dr. Miguel A. Gómez-Laso, from the Department of Electric and Electronic Engineering at the Public University of Navarre (Spain), for their excellent suggestions and support in writing this chapter. This work has been partially financed by the Innovation Vicerectorate of the Open University of Catalonia under the SAMOS project (IN-PID0702).

REFERENCES

Allen, I., & Seaman, J. (2008). *Staying the course: Online education in the United States*. Newburyport, MA: The Sloan Consortium.

Allen, T. H. (2006). Raising the question #1: Is the rush to provide online instruction setting our students up for failure? *Communication Education, 55*(1), 122–126. doi:10.1080/03634520500343418

Childers, J. L., & Berner, R. T. (2000). General education issues, distance education practices: Building community and classroom interaction through the integration of curriculum, instructional design, and technology. *The Journal of General Education, 49*(1), 53–65. doi:10.1353/jge.2000.0001

Daradoumis, T., Xhafa, F., & Juan, A. (2006). A framework for assessing self, peer and group performance in e-learning. In *Self, peer, and group assessment in e-learning* (pp. 279-294). Hershey, PA: Info Sci.

Del Moral, M. E., & Villalustre, L. (2008). Wikis and collaborative education by means of Webquest in higher education. *Revista Latinoamericana de Tecnologia Educativa, 7*(1), 73–83.

Dillenbourg, P. (Ed.). (1999). *Collaborative learning. Cognitive and computational approaches*. Oxford, UK: Elsevier Science.

Dringus, L. P., & Ellis, T. (2005). Using data mining as a strategy for assessing asynchronous discussion forums. *Computers & Education, 45*, 141–160. doi:10.1016/j.compedu.2004.05.003

Engelbrecht, J., & Harding, A. (2005). Teaching undergraduate mathematics on the Internet. Part 1: Technologies and taxonomy. *Educational Studies in Mathematics, 58*(2), 235–252. doi:10.1007/s10649-005-6456-3

Faulin, J., Juan, A., Fonseca, P., Pla, L. M., & Rodriguez, S. V. (2009). Learning operations research online: Benefits, challenges, and experiences. *International Journal of Simulation and Process Modelling, 5*(1), 42–53. doi:10.1504/IJSPM.2009.025826

Fernandez, R. (2007). Experiences of collaborative e-learning in preservice teachers. *Revista Latinoamericana de Tecnologia Educativa, 6*(2), 77–90.

Freeman, M., & McKenzie, J. (2002). SPARK, a confidential Web-based template for self and peer assessment of student teamwork: Benefits of evaluation across different subjects. *British Journal of Educational Technology*, *33*(5), 551–569. doi:10.1111/1467-8535.00291

Gaudioso, E., Montero, M., Talavera, L., & Hernandez-del-Olmo, F. (2009). Supporting teachers in collaborative student modeling: A framework and an implementation. *Expert Systems with Applications*, *36*(2), 2260–2265. doi:10.1016/j. eswa.2007.12.035

Gaytan, J. (2007). Visions shaping the future of online education: understanding its historical evolution, implications, and assumptions. *Online Journal of Distance Learning Administration*, *10*(2), 1–10.

Gómez-Laso, M. A., & Benito, D. (2006). Preparing learning guides suitable for personalized learning itineraries in virtual learning scenarios. In *Proceedings of the 10th IACEE World Conference on Continuing Engineering Education (WCCEE 2006)*, Vienna, Austria.

Gonzalez, J., & Wagenaar, R. (Eds.). (2005). *Tuning project. Tuning educational structures in Europe*. European Commission. European Commission, Education and Culture DG. Retrieved from http://tuning.unideusto.org/tuningeu

Howell, S. L., Williams, P. B., & Lindsay, N. K. (2003). Thirty-two trends affecting distance education: An informed foundation for strategic planning. *Online Journal of Distance Learning Administration*, *6*(3), 1–18.

Ibabe, J., & Jaureguizar, J. (2007). Self-assessment across Internet: Metacognitive variables and academic achievement. *Revista Latinoamericana de Tecnologia Educativa*, *6*(2), 59–75.

Ingram, A. (1999). Using Web server logs in evaluating instructional Web sites. *Journal of Educational Technology Systems*, *28*(2), 137–157. doi:10.2190/R3AE-UCRY-NJVR-LY6F

Jerman, P., Soller, A., & Muhlenbrock, M. (2001). From mirroring to guiding: A review of state of the art technology for supporting collaborative learning. In P. Dillenbourg, A. Eurelings, & K. Hakkarainen (Eds.), *Proceedings of the EuroCSCL*, Maastricht, NL, (pp. 324-331).

Juan, A., Daradoumis, T., Faulin, J., & Xhafa, F. (2008a). Developing an information system for monitoring student's activity in online collaborative learning. In *Proceedings of the 2nd International Conference on Complex, Intelligent and Software Intensity Systems (CISIS)*, Barcelona, Spain (pp. 270-275).

Juan, A., Daradoumis, T., Faulin, J., & Xhafa, F. (2009a). SAMOS: A model for monitoring students' and groups' activity in collaborative e-learning. *International Journal of Learning Technology*, *4*(1/2), 53–72. doi:10.1504/IJLT.2009.024716

Juan, A., Daradoumis, T., Faulin, J., & Xhafa, F. (2009b). A data analysis model based on control charts to monitor online learning processes. *International Journal Business Intelligence and Data Mining*.

Juan, A., Huertas, M., Steegmann, C., Corcoles, C., & Serrat, C. (2008b). Mathematical e-learning: State of the art and experiences at the Open University of Catalonia. *International Journal of Mathematical Education in Science and Technology*, *39*(4), 455–471. doi:10.1080/00207390701867497

Kay, J. (1995). The um toolkit for cooperative user models. *User Modeling and User-Adapted Interaction*, *4*(3), 149–196. doi:10.1007/BF01100243

Kim, N., Smith, M. J., & Maeng, K. (2008). Assessment in online distance education: A comparison of three online programs at a university. *Online Journal of Distance Learning Administration, 11*(1), 1–16.

Lam, P., Keing, C., McNaught, C., & Cheng, K. F. (2006). Monitoring e-learning environments through analysing Web logs of institution-wide eLearning platforms. In *Proceedings of the 23rd annual ascilite conference: Who's learning? Whose technology*, Sydney, Australia.

Lowry, R. (2005). Computer-aided self assessment -an effective tool. *Chemistry Education Research and Practice, 6*(4), 198–203.

Mas-Colell, A. (2003). The European Space of Higher Education: Incentive and governance issues. *Review of Political Economy, 93*(11/12), 9–28.

Mazza, R., & Dimitrova, V. (2004). Visualising student tracking data to support instructors in Web-based distance education. In *WWW Alt. '04: Proceedings of the 13th International World Wide Web Conference on Alternate track papers & posters* (pp. 154-161). New York: ACM Press.

Meyen, E. L., Aust, R. J., Bui, Y. N., & Isaacson, R. (2002). Assessing and monitoring student progress in an e-learning personnel preparation environment. *Teacher Education and Special Education, 25*(2), 187–198.

Meyer, D. (2002). Quality in distance education. Focus on online learning. *ASHE-ERIC Higher Education Report Series, 29*(4).

Peat, M., & Franklin, S. (2002). Supporting student learning. The use of computer-based formative assessment modules. *British Journal of Educational Technology, 33*(5), 515–523. doi:10.1111/1467-8535.00288

Rada, R. (1998). Efficiency and effectiveness in computer-supported peer-peer learning. *Computers & Education, 30*(3-4), 137–146. doi:10.1016/S0360-1315(97)00042-0

Robinson, L. A. (2005). Consumers of online instruction. *Issues in Information Systems, 6*, 170–175.

Romero, C., & Ventura, S. (2007). Educational data mining: A survey from 1995 to 2005. *Expert Systems with Applications, 33*, 135–146. doi:10.1016/j.eswa.2006.04.005

Romero, C., Ventura, S., & García, E. (2008). Data mining in course management systems: Moodle case study and tutorial. *Computers & Education, 51*(1), 368–384. doi:10.1016/j.compedu.2007.05.016

Rosenkrans, G. (1999). Assessment of the adult student's progress in an online environment. *The Internet and Higher Education, 2*(2-3), 145–160. doi:10.1016/S1096-7516(00)00017-8

Schwartzman, R. (2007). Refining the question: How can online instruction maximize opportunities for all students? *Communication Education, 56*(1), 113–117. doi:10.1080/03634520601009728

Seufert, S., Lechner, U., & Stanoevska, K. (2002). A reference model for online learning communities. *International Journal on E-Learning, 1*(1), 43–54.

Sheard, J., Ceddia, J., Hurst, J., & Tuovinen, J. (2003). Inferring student learning behaviour from website interactions: A usage analysis. *Journal of Education and Information Technologies, 8*(3), 245–266. doi:10.1023/A:1026360026073

Simoff, S., & Maher, M. (2000). Analysing participation in collaborative design environments. *Design Studies, 21*(2), 119–144. doi:10.1016/S0142-694X(99)00043-5

Simonson, M., Smaldino, S., Albright, M., & Zvacek, S. (2003). *Teaching and learning at a distance*. Upper Saddle River, NJ: Merrill Prentice Hall.

Stahl, G. (2006). *Group cognition: Computer support for building collaborative knowledge*. Cambridge, MA: MIT Press.

Sweet, R. (1986). Student drop-out in distance education: An application of Tinto's model. *Distance Education, 7*(2), 201–213. doi:10.1080/0158791860070204

Trenholm, S. (2007). An investigation of assessment in fully asynchronous online math courses. *International Journal for Educational Integrity, 3*(2), 41–55.

Truluck, J. (2007). Establishing a mentoring plan for improving retention in online graduate degree programs. *Online Journal of Distance Learning Administration, 10*(1), 1–6.

Van der Wende, M. (2000). The Bologna declaration: Enhancing the transparency and competitiveness of European higher education. *Higher Education in Europe, 25*(3), 305–310. doi:10.1080/713669277

Zaiane, O., Xin, M., & Han, J. (1998). Discovering Web access patterns and trends by applying OLAP and data mining technology on Web logs. In *Proceedings of the IEEE Forum on Advances in Digital Libraries Conference* (pp. 19-29). Santa Barbara, CA: IEEE Computer Society.

Zhang, H., Almeroth, K., Knight, A., Bulger, M., & Mayer, R. (2007). Moodog: Tracking students' online learning activities. In C. Montgomerie & J. Seale (Eds.), *Proceedings of the World Conference on Educational Multimedia, Hypermedia and Telecommunications 2007* (pp. 4415-4422). Chesapeake, VA: AACE.

Zirkle, C. (2003). Distance education in career and technical education: A review of the research literature. *Journal of Vocational Education Research, 28*(2), 151–171.

Chapter 9
A Model for Monitoring and Evaluating CSCL

Donatella Persico
Istituto Tecnologie Didattiche – Consiglio Nazionale delle Ricerche, Italy

Francesca Pozzi
Istituto Tecnologie Didattiche – Consiglio Nazionale delle Ricerche, Italy

Luigi Sarti
Istituto Tecnologie Didattiche – Consiglio Nazionale delle Ricerche, Italy

ABSTRACT

This chapter tackles the issue of monitoring and evaluating CSCL (Computer Supported Collaborative Learning) processes. It starts from the awareness that most of the tasks carried out in managing, tutoring, fine tuning and evaluating online courses heavily rely on information drawn through monitoring. Information of this kind is usually needed for both the assessment of individual learning and the evaluation of a learning initiative. The development of a sound, general purpose model to organize this information serves a variety of purposes, since it makes the monitoring, assessment and evaluation processes more systematic and effective. By describing the model and providing concrete examples of its use, the goal of this chapter is to demonstrate its potential, flexibility and suitability to meet evaluators' aims in a wide range of cases. The model gathers consolidated practices in the field and is based on the most recent findings of theoretical CSCL research.

INTRODUCTION TO THE CSCL FIELD

This paper addresses the issue of monitoring and evaluating collaborative learning processes that take advantage of computer communication technology and are typically carried out at a distance. In particular, we focus on CSCL (Computer Supported Collaborative Learning) approaches based on social constructivism (Dillenbourg, 1999; Kanuka & Anderson, 1999; Vanderbilt, 1991; Scardamalia & Bereiter, 1994), where knowledge building takes place through social negotiation. In this approach, discussion with peers and teachers is the main learning method because it encourages critical thinking and, hence, understanding. Interaction is usually based on written asynchronous message exchanges in specific environments known as Computer Mediated Communication

DOI: 10.4018/978-1-60566-786-7.ch009

(CMC) systems, that allow the organization of communication along separate, topic-oriented discussion "forums" or "conferences", and provide the valuable benefit of recording most significant events for subsequent revisitation and analysis. Even in those cases where interaction occurs synchronously (e.g., through chats), the underlying communication system usually allows one to record a transcript that participants in the learning community can later retrieve.

Social constructivism promotes a shift from the traditional teacher-centred approach to a setting where students are the main actors on the learning stage and take direct responsibility for their knowledge building processes. In this kind of setting the terms "teacher / instructor", that usually indicate the actors in charge of designing, delivering and evaluating the learning event, recede in favour of two different terms: "designer", to indicate the person in charge of setting up the course, and "tutor", to identify the person in charge of orchestrating and moderating online discussions among the members of the learning community (students, experts, etc.). Accordingly, tutors are not experts who fulfil their role by dispensing domain knowledge, but rather they are in charge of setting up and maintaining collaborative processes. Of course, while orchestrating and moderating online interactions, each tutor will deploy their own personal tutoring style, but to ensure the effectiveness of their action, tutors must always have a clear picture of what is happening, who is participating and how, in order to anticipate and deal with problems, to identify different learning styles, and to help students to exploit their own individual abilities. When the learning community is large and participation is high, gathering and systematically organising these kinds of information can be quite a labour intensive task.

Currently, CMC systems provide generic statistic tools that can be used to track participant behaviours, even though most of them only provide a quantitative picture of events (EduTools,

2008). In contrast, what is needed is a complete, both quantitative and qualitative picture, able to inform the *assessment* of student individual learning (both in progress and at the end of the course) and the *evaluation* of the whole instructional initiative.

More specifically, *formative assessment* of students usually takes place during the course and is an essential condition to ensure a good degree of personalization of the learning process. As such, it relies heavily on information gathered through monitoring. *Summative assessment* of students is a frequent context requirement of formal learning institutions and generally includes not only product evaluation, that can be used as an indicator of effectiveness, but also process evaluation, based on the same data as those that inform formative assessment.

Finally, the *evaluation* of the learning event may be aimed at measuring efficiency, effectiveness, personalisation and/or other features of the whole process. Generally speaking, evaluating a learning event means carrying out a systematic study to produce a value judgment on those aspects that are the goal of the evaluation. Such a study normally encompasses the collection, analysis and interpretation of information on the event (Thorpe, 1993), such as the quality of the learning materials, the effectiveness of the tutoring, the suitability, the user-friendliness and the efficiency of the tools used. In particular, the evaluation of the *efficiency* of a learning event often includes organizational aspects or issues related to the cost-benefit ratio of the event, where costs and benefits are not considered solely from a financial standpoint. Costs can indeed also be regarded from the point of view of investments in human resources and learning materials, whilst benefits usually include educational and social outcomes. The evaluation of the cost-benefit ratio of a learning programme is therefore quite complex and involves political, social, economical and educational considerations (Phillips, 1998; Trentin, 2000).

The evaluation of the *effectiveness* implies assessing the extent to which the educational objectives have been met, in terms of modification of students' competences. However, the evaluation of a course usually goes beyond the assessment of student learning. For example, it often takes into consideration the degree of student satisfaction - which can be measured through questionnaires or interviews with the students themselves. The evaluation of a learning event produces a reliable picture of its strengths and weaknesses and is a key factor in its development since it provides information on the adequacy of the instructional design with respect to the learning objectives.

In the next section, the specificities of evaluation and assessment in the CSCL context are analyzed, with particular reference to the essential role played by monitoring (Alvino and Persico, 2008) in providing relevant information that is not available in traditional learning contexts.

Afterwards, a model is described that provides a framework for organizing the information drawn from CSCL processes, in view of the tutors' monitoring, assessment and evaluation tasks. Moreover, some real-life examples will be presented. A section on conclusions and areas that deserve further investigation concludes the paper.

BACKGROUND: MONITORING AND EVALUATION IN CSCL CONTEXTS

Research in the field of CSCL has been increasingly adopting approaches based on the analysis of interactions occurring among students and tutors during the learning process. In her seminal work, Henri (1992) proposed five dimensions for analysing online discussion:

- the participative dimension,
- the interactive dimension,
- the social dimension,
- the cognitive dimension,
- the meta-cognitive dimension.

For each dimension she proposed to identify suitable indicators, allowing one to appreciate not only the main quantitative aspects involved, as was the case in most previous studies, but also qualitative information. To do so, Henri's study focused on both *what* is said and *how* it is said. Although the proposed dimensions make up an effective structure for analysing electronic messages, the model was subsequently criticised because it does not provide researchers with operational criteria for the classification of CSCL interactions.

Henri's model was further refined and enriched by Hara et al. (2000), who examined the dynamics of an online discussion as a part of the required activities of an actual course with the aim of establishing criteria to judge the content of a computer conference from a pedagogical perspective. Several categories were added to the model, and the unit of analysis shifted from the whole message to the individual paragraph. Henri's linear model of interaction was enhanced to encompass more articulated dialogues, and a graph mapping of the messages was used to capture the interactive process.

Lally & de Laat (2002) reported on the adoption of two mutually compatible coding schemata aimed at investigating group knowledge construction and teacher presence. The first schema included cognitive, metacognitive, affective and miscellaneous categories; the second modelled teacher presence taking into account such activities as organizing the collaborative process, facilitating discourse and providing direct instruction.

Subsequent studies (Martinez et al., 2003; Lipponen et al., 2003; Aviv et al., 2003) proposed mixed evaluation methods combining traditional sources of data such as computer logs with qualitative data resulting from content analysis and social network analysis in an overall interpretative approach.

In the framework of the Communities of Inquiry Garrison & Anderson (2003) investigated the social, cognitive and teaching dimensions. Their model aimed to provide a conceptual order for investigating learning processes that occur in asynchronous-based learning environments. According to the authors, text analysis can track indicators of social, cognitive and teaching presence within students' and tutors' messages and therefore support the study of the learning dynamics taking place through computer mediated communication. Social, cognitive and teaching presence are closely interconnected dimensions, their boundaries are blurred and the related indicators often overlap. This endows the model with some flexibility, but it makes applying all three dimensions at once quite difficult. Hence, the majority of studies based on it focus on one dimension only (e.g. Lobry de Bruyn, 2004; McKlin et al., 2001; Meyer, 2003; Pawan et al., 2003; Oriogun et al., 2005; Shea et al., 2003). In order to investigate all three dimensions within the same learning experience and still obtain a clear cut classification, it is necessary to contextualize and sometimes re-define indicators.

More recently, a number of researchers have proposed other approaches; among the others, we want to remember Murphy (2004) who conceptualized collaboration as a continuum of processes that move from social presence to production of an artefact and proposed an instrument with a set of indicators for measuring collaboration in online asynchronous discussion.

Daradoumis et al. (2006) developed a framework for the analysis of group interaction that considers a variety of aspects: learning, collaboration, evaluation, and scaffolding. Learning activity indicators were identified at various levels of description and applied in a mixed interaction analysis schema relying on qualitative, quantitative and social network analyses. Subsequently, Caballé et al. (2007) described a system that produces weekly monitoring reports that provide visual information about group activities.

Schrire (2006) proposed a model for the analysis of collaborative knowledge building in asynchronous discussion, allowing an examination of the communication from the multiple perspective of interaction, cognition and discourse analysis. The model merges quantitative analysis within a qualitative methodology, thus providing "both an analytic and holistic perspective on CSCL" (Schrire, 2006).

Finally, Weinberger & Fischer (2006) proposed a multi-dimensional approach to analyze argumentative knowledge construction in CSCL from sampling the segmentation of the discourse corpora to the analysis of four process dimensions: participation, epistemic, argumentative and social mode.

Although not exhaustive, the above summary shows that researchers have been increasingly adopting approaches based on the analysis of interactions occurring among students and tutors during the learning process and that significant progress has been made in the models proposed, their effectiveness and their accuracy, especially for evaluation purposes. As we have seen, in most studies quantitative data extracted directly from the CMC system are combined with qualitative information, usually deriving from content analysis of the messages exchanged. However, qualitative approaches are eminently human based and considerably time consuming, because they call for manual analysis of a large number of messages. This has, so far, discouraged extensive real life use, especially for monitoring purposes: the idea that the tutors' job should comprehend content analysis tasks appears unacceptable to those who have experienced the pressure and tension of having to follow each and every learner without missing any situation where intervention is needed. Nonetheless, in order to pursue and sustain a high quality educational experience, a deep understanding of the learning process is required and this calls for further investigation in this field.

For these reasons, differently from the models reported in this section, the approach described in the following looks for a balance between effectiveness and efficiency, so as to become adoptable in real time and even in those contexts where there are large numbers of messages. As will be demonstrated in the following, the innovativeness of the model lies in the fact that its dimensions (both quantitative and qualitative) and the related indicators can be instantiated according to the aim of the analysis (monitoring, assessment or evaluation) and the type of learning experience, in such a way that one can choose what dimension and indicators to focus on, on the basis of the real needs and requirements of the analysis itself. This makes the model a general framework able to provide guidance for the analysis, without constraining the user to an excessive workload when this is not considered necessary.

DESCRIPTION OF THE PROPOSED MODEL

Starting from the state of the art (see previous section) and from our experience as designers, tutors and researchers in the field, we proposed a model consisting in a comprehensive framework for the analysis of CSCL processes with monitoring, assessment and evaluation purposes (Pozzi et al., 2007). The framework, mainly built on Henri's (1992) and Garrison and Anderson's (2003) models, has thereafter been extensively tested and subsequently modified according to the results obtained, thus achieving a four-dimensional approach that includes the participative, social, cognitive and teaching dimensions.

Figure 1 is an adaptation of the graphical representation of Garrison and Anderson's (2003) tri-dimensional model that illustrates the cognitive, the teaching and the social dimensions, as well as their relationship with our additional fourth dimension: the participative component. The participative dimension, in this model, is mostly based on quantitative data concerning the frequency of students' actions within the environment and underpins the other three components.

Figure 1. The four dimensions of the model

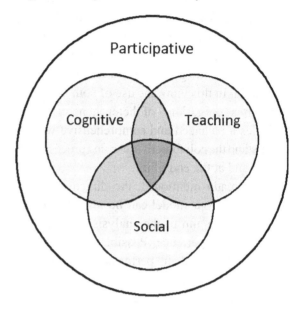

Each dimension of the model can be analyzed by looking at indicators of participants' behaviour within the records of their interactions through the CMC system, taking advantage of the fact that students' exchanges and log files are permanently recorded and can be used as sources of information to understand the learning dynamics. Thus the model makes use of data of both quantitative and qualitative nature, the former can be automatically tracked by the CMC system and are easily processed by means of statistical methods and tools (Wang, 2004); the latter can be determined by quantitatively elaborating the results of qualitative analysis of participants' interactions (Chi, 1997).

Such integration of data of different nature finds its main *raison d'être* in the fact that, although the analysis of quantitative aspects of students exchanges is easy to automate and achieve, by itself it may fail to capture in-depth understanding of learning dynamics. In contrast, qualitative analysis, which is much more complex and time-consuming, often allows a thorough investigation of specific aspects, even though its results are harder to generalize upon. Besides, qualitative analysis introduces the problem of interpretation that is usually dealt with by minimizing arbitrariness in decisions, for instance by having two raters who carry out the analysis process in parallel under the guidance of a well defined set of criteria. In this view, the use of both methods, through aggregations of heterogeneous data, provides a balanced and comprehensive way to understand the collaborative learning process both during and at the end of it.

As already mentioned, the dimensions and indicators of our model can be instantiated according to the aim of the analysis and the type of learning experience. Possible aims are: the monitoring of students performance in order to inform tutor actions during the learning process, the evaluation of the quality of the learning process or specific aspects of it (such as the way tutoring styles influence students' behaviour, the relationships between collaboration techniques employed and depth of analysis of a given topic, etc), or the assessment of individual learning processes in order to carry out formative and summative evaluation of students' performances. In other terms, in our vision the model is a *general purpose* framework, as it allows one to focus on all or some of the dimensions at a time, chosen according to the aims of the analysis. Furthermore, contrary to Henri (1992) who identified a stable set of indicators, we argue that indicators should vary or have different weights, depending on the objectives of the analysis and the context of the learning experience (including the CMC system used, which may impact on the availability of some kind of data and indicators).

In the following a brief description for each dimension is provided, together with considerations concerning the main indicators of the dimensions and reflections on how to gauge them.

The Participative Dimension

The participative dimension takes into consideration all the actions that learners perform in relation to their virtual presence in the CMC system and their involvement in the learning activities. Thus this dimension encompasses indicators of the *active participation*, the *reactive participation* and the *continuity in participation*, as illustrated in Table 1.

All the indicators of the participative dimension are based uniquely on quantitative data automatically tracked by the CMC system. Nowadays, most systems can be configured in such a way as to provide data of this kind. However, one should not underestimate the fact that the choice of the delivery system may impact on the availability of some kinds of data and indicators, as will be further argued in the "Technical considerations" section.

The Social Dimension

A definition of social presence is "the ability of participants in a community of inquiry to project themselves socially and emotionally, as 'real' people (i.e., their full personality), through the medium of communication being used" (Garrison et al., 1999, p. 94). In order to investigate social presence, it is therefore necessary to identify clues that testify, for example, to *affection* and *cohesiveness*, as illustrated in Table 2.

Investigating this dimension, as well as the cognitive and the teaching ones, entails manually carrying out content analysis of all the messages exchanged by the students. This involves a certain workload, encompassing reading each message and systematically identifying the frequency of given keywords or patterns or even expressions that are believed to reveal a feature of the communication act, and finally classifying each of them as belonging to a certain indicator category. Units of analysis can be either the message or a part of it (for example the message could be split in "units of meaning" or, as an alternative, in "syntactic units"[1]). Here it is worthwhile noting that the possibility of choosing an adequate level of granularity (i.e. the granularity of the unit) according to the aim of the analysis is another

Table 1. Main indicators of the participative dimension

dimension	category	code	indicators
Participative	*Active participation*	P1.1	sent messages
		P1.2	uploaded documents
		P1.3	attended chats
	Reactive participation	P2.1	read messages
		P2.1	downloaded documents
	Continuity	P3.1	time distribution of session duration
		P3.2	regularity in reading

Table 2. Main indicators of the social dimension

dimension	category	code	indicators
Social	*Affection*	S1.1	expressions of emotions that may be revealed either by verbal dissertation or through graphical/orthographical solutions, e.g. repetitions, use of punctuation, use of capital letters, emoticons
		S1.2	expressions of intimacy that may be revealed by the use of sarcasm, humour, irony, etc.
		S1.3	"self-disclosure" acts that may be revealed by presentations of personal anecdotes or by admission of self-vulnerability
	Cohesiveness	S2.1	occurrences of vocatives or more in general references to other people in the group
		S2.2	expressions reinforcing group cohesion that can be revealed by either expressions of group self efficacy, or use of inclusive pronouns or adjectives
		S2.3	greetings, phatics, salutations

important element of flexibility provided by the model, which allows the user to choose from time to time between a fine (unit of meaning) and a coarse grain (message).

In content analysis, the coding procedure and the assignment of the units of analysis (messages or parts of them) to the pertinent indicator, is usually carried out by a couple of coders (researchers, designers or even tutors of the course) who, after a period of training and the set up of a strict coding procedure, work separately to code the whole corpus. Furthermore, in order to estimate the level of agreement between the coders, it is quite common to calculate their inter-rater reliability (Lombard et al, 2002).

The Cognitive Dimension

Cognitive presence can be defined as "the extent to which learners are able to construct and confirm meaning through sustained reflection and discourse in a critical community of inquiry" (Garrison et al., 2001).

A collaborative activity in CSCL typically requires a first stage entailing personal re-elaborations of contents and the expression of individual points of view, and a second stage devoted to discussion and negotiation to collaboratively construct shared meanings and common interpretations of reality. In addition, the learning process and the ability of learners to control it often benefits from further reflections on the learning dynamics

Table 3. Main indicators of the cognitive dimension

dimension	category	code	indicators
Cognitive	*Individual knowledge building*	C1.1	reporting of right contents
		C1.2	recognition of a problem or expression of doubts
		C1.3	explanation or presentation of a point of view
		C1.4	provision of information or ideas sharing e.g. description of events, accounts of personal experience or real-life stories, etc.
		C1.5	contribution to brainstorming e.g. by adding an item to a list
	Group knowledge building	C2.1	expressions of disagreement that can be revealed by contradicting others
		C2.2	expressions of agreement that can be revealed by referring to others' messages or by integrating others' ideas
		C2.3	suggestions to others and/requests for confirmation e.g. through "explorative acts" such as: "Am I right?", "Is that so?"
		C2.4	offers of knowledge or competence to others
		C2.5	connections between ideas or summarizations
		C2.6	creation or contribution to the creation of new, shared meanings
	Meta-reflection	C3.1	reflections on the learning process that may be revealed by attempting to evaluate one's own knowledge, skills, limits, cognitive processes
		C3.2	intentional control of the learning process, revealed by planning, monitoring or adjusting one's own cognitive processes

Table 4. Main indicators of the teaching dimension

dimension	category	code	indicators
Teaching	*Organizational matters*	T1.1	activity planning
		T1.2	methodological proposals e.g. suggestions about the division in groups, proposals of communication rules and netiquette
		T1.3	organizational proposals e.g. proposing to open a new conference, or organizing a meeting
		T1.4	offers or requests of logistical information
	Facilitating discourse	T2.1	identification of areas of agreement/disagreement, syntheses of discussion
		T2.2	consensus seeking / achievement
		T2.3	creation of the climate for learning, encouragement, acknowledgement of participant contributions
		T2.4	solicitation of discussion and reminders of deadlines
	Provision of instruction	T3.1	presentation of contents, introduction of new knowledge
		T3.2	in depth analysis of specific topics
		T3.3	description of new activities
		T3.4	confirmation of understanding or diagnoses of misconception through assessment and explanatory feedback

taking place. Based on these considerations, in our model the cognitive dimension is revealed by indicators of *individual knowledge building*, *group knowledge building* and *meta-reflection*, as illustrated in Table 3.

The Teaching Dimension

Teaching presence is defined as "the design, facilitation, and direction of cognitive and social processes for the purpose of realizing personally meaningful and educationally worthwhile learning outcomes" (Anderson et al., 2001, p. 5). In other words, teaching presence is the binding element in cultivating a learning community: messages carry teaching presence when they address objectives like *providing guidance and instruction*, *facilitating discourse* and management of *organisational matters*. It should be mentioned that teaching presence is not necessarily reserved to tutors only: this role is sometimes covered by students as well, e.g. when they perform group leadership or reciprocal support within the learning community. (see Table 4)

Why and How to Apply the Model in Real Contexts: Examples of Use

The model described above has been extensively used in our courses to monitor the online activities, assess students and evaluate the overall process at the end of the experience (Persico et al., 2009).

In this section we will provide examples of use of the model addressing the three objectives above. The examples cited here derive from the application of the model in the "SSIS", the Italian institution which provides initial training to secondary teachers[2]. In recent years the Istituto Tecnologie Didattiche (ITD) – CNR has designed and run several blended courses for the SSIS of two Italian regions (Liguria and Veneto) on the topic "Educational Technology" (henceforth these courses will be referred to as "TD-SSIS"). Although each TD-SSIS course has its own

specificities (in terms of learning objectives, contents, activities, schedule, etc.), all of them use a CSCL approach and share a basic aim, that is promoting the development of instructional design competence, with special focus on the evaluation and selection of learning strategies, techniques and tools and on the implementation of educational technology in the school context (Delfino & Persico, 2007). These courses always envisage an alternation between face-to-face lectures and online activities. These activities, which are collaboration intensive and require students to work with peers, are considered the main part of the course, whereas the face-to-face component and the individual study of materials play a secondary role.

The cohort of students of each course edition is typically composed of about a hundred post-graduate adults with very diversified backgrounds, interests and expectations. In order to facilitate collaboration, the student cohort is usually split in groups, each group being managed by a tutor (ratio tutor/students is usually around 1/20-25). Courses may last from a minimum of 8 weeks to a maximum of 12 weeks (depending on the constraints given by the SSIS, which may vary from year to year). Anyway, the online component of the courses is always quite demanding, that is measurable in terms of number of messages exchanged by students, usually around 5000 per course edition.

The model has been applied by both the designers and the tutors at different stages (during the courses and at the end of them) and with different aims (monitoring, assessment and evaluation) thus providing a rich test-bed for its flexibility.

As far as monitoring is concerned, tutors mostly use the participative dimension in the early stages of the online activities, looking at its quantitative information to confirm or reject their first hypotheses on students' behaviour in the course. As already mentioned, quantitative data are usually automatically tracked by the CMC

Table 5. Example of data concerning the participative dimension in the Socialization phase

Course: **TD-SSIS Liguria 2007** Module: **M1 "Socialization"** - Week: **1** Total number of participants: **21** – Tutor: **1**				
PARTICIPATION				
Active participation (P1)	Sent messages			
	Total sent msgs.: **30** ([3])	Mean ([4]):**1.04**	SD: **0.74**	Range: **0-3**
	Uploaded documents			
	Total uploaded documents: **0**	Mean: /	SD: /	Range: /
Reactive Participation (P2)([5])	Mean number of messages read by participants on the total number of messages: **0.79**			
Continuity (P3)	Variance of the "mean student continuity in reading": **0.04**			

system and can be made available to the tutors through a monitor application, in such a way that tutors can easily access synthetic information regarding individual and group participation and quickly detect problems, if any. Table 5 provides an example of the way data concerning the participative dimension can be displayed.

Table 5 presents an overall view of participation of a whole class, composed of 21 students, at the end of the first week of TD-SSIS Liguria 2007. These data draw a picture of the course at its very beginning, during the Socialization activity. As one may note, even if the total number of sent messages is satisfactory (30 messages), it is also clear that some students have not yet sent their initial message (range 0-3). By looking at the same kind of data for each student, the tutor can identify those students who have not yet posted any message, and contact them to understand the reason for their lack of active participation.

At the same time, data on reactive participation show a good trend as far as read messages (students have read on average 79% of the messages present in the forum at the moment of the snapshot). Furthermore, the low value of continuity indicates stable reading behaviours of participants.

Again, by looking at the same data for each student, the tutors can confirm or reject their general idea on each student' behaviour, thus gaining a more precise image of each learner's attitudes and cognitive styles.

Quantitative data are a useful means for getting an immediate, updated picture of the situation during the whole course. However, as tasks become more complex and the level of collaboration increases, the tutor will probably need a better picture of groups' dynamics. This can be done by looking also at the qualitative dimensions of the model, considering both their evolution in time and their instantaneous values.

Figure 2 shows an example of the former: it describes the levels of social, cognitive and teaching dimensions of a class composed of 30 students over the first five weeks of one of our courses (TD-SSIS Veneto 2008).

The values in Figure 2 represent the number of messages per week belonging to a certain dimension (unit of the analysis was in this case the message and each message could be assigned to one dimension only, regarded by the coders as the prevalent one). As one may note, during the first week all the interactions (27 messages) were classified as belonging to the social dimension. This is quite reasonable, since the first activity of the course was devoted to socialization among students. After two weeks, mid-way through the learning activities, the social dimension was higher, probably denoting that the class was developing a certain sense of belonging. However, at the same time, the level of cognitive and teach-

Figure 2. Example of data concerning the social, cognitive and teaching dimensions

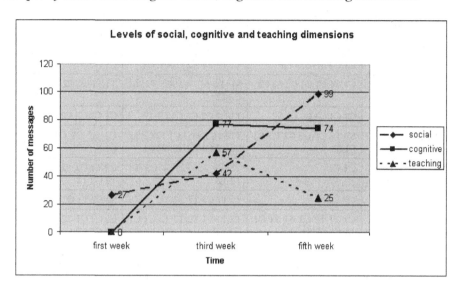

ing dimensions had also increased, testifying the fact that a learning activity was underway. At the fifth week, the social dimension was even higher, indicating a good climate, while the level of cognitive dimension was very similar to that of the previous stage. On the contrary, the teaching dimension is considerably lower here and this datum – seen in conjunction with the other two dimensions - may indicate that the group had meanwhile developed a common working method and so the need for a strong coordinating action had decreased.

As one can note, thanks to the data and indicators captured by the model, it is always possible to have an updated image of the course, seen in its multi-dimensional components, that helps the tutors in keeping the situation under control and supports them in their tasks.

All the data gathered for monitoring purposes during the learning experience may be used for learning assessment purposes as well. This means that, both during the process and at the end of it, the tutor can focus on a single student and assess his individual performance. Table 6 shows data concerning a team of seven students (within TD-SSIS Liguria 2008). In this example, each student

has been continuously monitored during the whole course and data concerning active participation and the social, cognitive and teaching dimensions were displayed in a table per module (M0, M1, M2, M3). Since each message was assigned only one indicator, each abbreviation (S1, S2, C1, C2, etc.) in the table represents a message. Besides being used by the tutor during the course to provide personalized, formative feedback to students, these data can also be used as a basis for summative assessment of individual students. Tutors were able to assign marks (last column of the table) by considering the level and kind of contribution given by each student to each module of the course. These marks can be seen as meta-indexes worked out by the tutors according to "rules" that are usually negotiated with colleagues in order to guarantee uniformity of assessment criteria. In our courses, for example, participation is an essential component, and a balanced mixture of the social, cognitive and teaching dimensions is considered to be the ideal composition of individual student contributions. Of course, such assessment can also be combined with the results obtained by students during the final exam (if any), so as to have an overall mark taking into account both the online

Table 6. Example of data per student

module	M0	M1	M2	M3	online marks[6]
duration	*1 week*	*2 weeks*	*2 weeks*	*3 weeks*	
Anna	S1	C1 C2 S1	T1 T2 C1 C2 C2 C2 C1	C1 C2	21
Francesca	S1	C1 C1 C1 C1 C2 S1 C2	S1 T2 C1 T2 T2 T2 T2 C2 T2	T1 T1 C2 T2 T2 C2 C2 S2	26
Pietro	S1 S1	C1 C1 C3 C1 C1 S2	T1 C1 C2 C2 C1 C1 T2	C1 C2 C2 C2	22
M. Teresa	S1 S2 S1	S2 T1 C1 C2 C2 C2 S2 S1 S2	T1 S1 C1 S C1 C1 T2 C2 T2 C2 T2 C1 C1 T3 C2 C1	C2 C2 C2 C2 C2 C2 C2 C2 S	28
Maura	S1	C1 C2	T1 T1 T2 T2 C2 C3 T3 T2 T2	C2 T1 C2 T2 T2 T3 T2 T2 T2 C2 T2	25
Giovanni	S1	C1	T1 T2 C1 T2 T2	S2 C2 T1 C2 C2 S1 S2	22
Marzia	S1	C1 T1 T2 C2 C1 T1 C1 T1 C2 C2 S1 T2 S2	T2 T1 T1 T2 T2 T2 C1 C1 C2 C2 C1 C1 C2 T2 C2 C2 T3 T1	C2 C1 C1 C2 C2 T1 C2 C2 C2 C2 C2 C2 C2 S1 T2 C2 S2	28

Legend: S1= Affection (Social dimension); S2=Cohesion (Social dimension), C1=Individual knowledge building (Cognitive dimension), C2= Group knowledge building (Cognitive dimension); C3=Meta-reflection (Cognitive dimension); T1=Organizational matters (Teaching dimension); T2=Facilitating discourse (Teaching dimension); T3=Provision of instruction (Teaching dimension).

process and the final learning achievements.

Such an application of the model allows an evaluation which takes into account the learning process, as opposed to an assessment focusing on the final product only.

As we have already mentioned, the model can also be used to evaluate the whole course, as the four dimensions can provide a deep insight of the interactions that occurred among students. For example, individual activities can be studied by using the model to find out how they worked and inform the design of other activities and courses.

Figure 3 shows the data concerning the cognitive dimension, during an activity carried out in TD-SSIS Veneto 2007. The group under study was composed of 24 students and 1 tutor. The activity envisaged a preliminary phase of individual study and a subsequent discussion in three sub-groups, each aimed at the co-construction of one artefact.

Since, in this case, the aim of the analysis was the evaluation, a finer grain was required and for this reason the unit of analysis adopted was the "unit of meaning". The values reported in Figure 3 stand for the number of units per indicator (each

unit could be assigned one indicator only, so the coder had to choose the prevalent one). These data indicate that, during the activity, individual reasoning (C1) was quite developed, above all through the presentation of personal points of view (C1.3), sharing personal ideas (C1.4) and brainstorming (C1.5). However, students rarely expressed doubts (C1.2) and reported contents (C1.1).

As for group knowledge building processes (C2), the expressions of agreement prevailed and were accompanied by attempts to connect ideas and make synthesis (C2.5). Nonetheless, it should be noted that disagreement (C2.1) was considerably low and this may suggest that the discussion did not enter in much detail, but rather it remained at a surface level. An alternative interpretation is that, at least in this case, this mode of interaction did not favour the manifestation of disagreement. Wegerif (1998) reports the explanation provided by one of his students for this frequent phenomenon. He said that criticizing somebody else's opinion without a full argumentation was perceived to be rude and, since providing an argumentation would have taken too long, people tended to contradict

Figure 3. Example of representation of the cognitive dimension developed during an activity

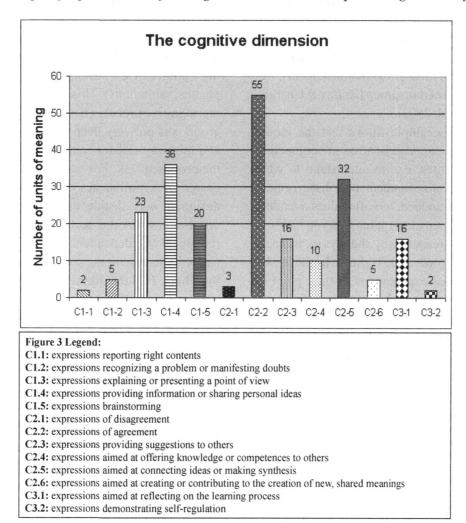

Figure 3 Legend:
C1.1: expressions reporting right contents
C1.2: expressions recognizing a problem or manifesting doubts
C1.3: expressions explaining or presenting a point of view
C1.4: expressions providing information or sharing personal ideas
C1.5: expressions brainstorming
C2.1: expressions of disagreement
C2.2: expressions of agreement
C2.3: expressions providing suggestions to others
C2.4: expressions aimed at offering knowledge or competences to others
C2.5: expressions aimed at connecting ideas or making synthesis
C2.6: expressions aimed at creating or contributing to the creation of new, shared meanings
C3.1: expressions aimed at reflecting on the learning process
C3.2: expressions demonstrating self-regulation

each other less than they would have done in a face-to-face context. As one may note, also the expressions aimed at creating new, shared meanings (C2.6), those aimed at providing knowledge or competence to others (C2.4) and even those aimed at providing suggestions (C2.3) were not so frequent. Again, these data may raise suspicions about the quality of the collaborative process, which could be considered superficial. In order to further investigate this aspect, the evaluators may decide to carry out further investigation, aimed at a deeper analysis of other indicators to better understand these aspects.

For example, the evaluators may choose to focus their attention on the extent to which each student really took into account the contribution of their peers during the discussion. This could be done for example by isolating one indicator (for example S2.1: social dimension → occurrences of vocatives or references to other people in the group) and using some kind of representation. For example, Hara et al. (2000) use graphs where the nodes are messages and the links represent reciprocal mentions. These graphs show when a student wrote a message which did not refer to any of the previous messages, when she referred to a message written by a peer, and when her message pointed to a cluster of previously written messages. Other techniques, such as the Social Network Analysis (SNA), can be used to draw a graph representation of the interactions that occurred within a certain group (Reffay & Chanier, 2003; Aviv et al, 2003).

The above example shows that the model proposed here can also be used in conjunction with other studies, e.g. to understand to what extent expressions of agreement or disagreement are motivated. Indeed, too often does a student simply say: "Great idea! I agree with you" without explaining the reasons why she says so, whereas a deeper-level processing is shown by those who provide detailed explanations of their point of view. The model can highlight these differences, by isolating messages containing the indicator C2.2 (cognitive dimension → expressions of agreement) and rating other indicators that are present in these messages. A restricted study conducted within one of the groups performing the activity carried out within TD-SSIS Veneto 2007 (the same used for the example of Figure 3), led to isolating 16 messages containing C2.2, and showed that they were very "poor"

messages, containing few indicators. In this case, the indicators were: S2.1 (which is the evidence of the reference made to the messages written by others), C1.3 (explaining or presenting a point of view), and S2.3 (initial greetings, phatics, salutations). This seems to confirm that the cognitive process arisen within the analyzed group was not very deep but rather superficial and this may call for some reconsiderations of the proposed task. For example, in view of the design of a similar activity in the future, the designers may decide to combine the group discussion with other techniques that foster the reciprocal interdependence of students and their necessity to exploit the competences developed by others, like the Jigsaw or the Peer Review (Persico et al., 2008).

One last example of the model flexibility, and of its suitability to evaluate different aspects of the learning process developed within a community, is illustrated in Figure 4, where the trend in time of all the indicators of the teaching dimension is used to shed light on the degree to which the learning community is becoming autonomous and is therefore evolving into a fully fledged community of practice.

Figure 4. The teaching dimension trend (all indicators)

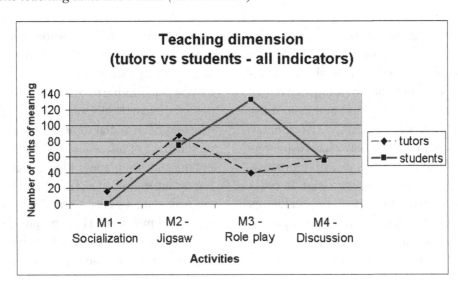

In formal learning contexts, it is generally known that the virtual community consisting of the participants in an online course strongly needs support and guidance, usually provided by the course tutors. During the course, especially when its duration is reasonably long (at least four or five weeks, but possibly more), the tutors role evolves moving from the initial duties of technical, social and methodological guidance to that of a less intrusive facilitator, who mostly intervenes when needed or requested, both on content related matters and on organisational/methodological issues.

It is only natural, therefore, to expect that the indicators of teaching presence, on the side of the tutors, show a general downward trend in time, with peaks at the beginning of each new activity that account for the need to start them up with appropriate instructions. Meanwhile, it is reasonable to expect that the same indicators in students' messages gradually increase, if only because the scaffolding and fading techniques often used by tutors actually aim to encourage students to take responsibility for their learning process, by moving from peripheral to central status in the learning community as rapidly and as smoothly as possible.

This is particularly true for courses that include, among their aims, the need to build self-regulated learning abilities and professional development competences. This is the case, for example, of our TD-SSIS courses in Educational Technology, where it is acknowledged that there is no way for the students to learn all there is to learn on the subject in two or three months, so the course objective is rather to provide them with few carefully selected basic skills and with conceptual and methodological tools that will make them able to further develop their competence in the field while practicing their profession. This entails the participation in teacher communities of practice (Lave & Wenger, 1991), which is considered a very effective method for teachers' professional development (Schlager & Fusco, 2004; Hartnell-Young, 2005; Triggs & John, 2004).

Indeed, Figure 4 allows us to compare the trend in time of the tutors' teaching presence indicators against that of students, thus revealing to what extent the community is starting to self-regulate and become autonomous, thanks to the initiative of some students who are taking up planning, monitoring and evaluation tasks. While these students move from peripheral into central participation, their tutors do the reverse. The figure also reveals that there are activities, such as role play, that seem to accentuate this process, and can therefore be adopted to trigger assumption of responsibility on the side of the students. This way, the model can be used to evaluate the effectiveness of a course with respect to the (frequent) aim of forming an independent community, able to stand on its feet as a follow up of the course.

TECHNICAL CONSIDERATIONS

Usually, online courses make use of CMC systems with a client-server architecture: participants use a client application (a web browser, or some proprietary application) to connect through the Internet to a centralized server program, which relies on a database to provide access to messages, user directories, discussion areas etc[7]. Server programs record significant events in log files, and log file analysis is the most widespread method to collect raw data. For instance, for each received http request the Apache web server appends a descriptor to a log file, with such information as the IP number of the client, a timestamp, the required web address, a success code etc. Similarly, a Centrinity FirstClass server by default records all session logins and logouts, and can be configured to record descriptors of almost any action performed by the user. Log files can be subsequently analyzed by means of specialised software[8].

Differences may exist between systems based on a proprietary protocol (for example FirstClass) that exchange a single message with any client-server transaction, as opposed to web-based systems (for example Moodle) that rely on the usual http protocol and often present a whole message thread as a single web page. Just to cite one of the differences between the two types of systems, FirstClass allows one to access the history of each message (who created the message, who modified it, who opened/read it, who replied to it, etc.) whereas Moodle does not provide such details on the single message, as it mainly deals with threads.

Log file analysis, however, can only be performed offline, and requires tutors to use separate software packages. As already mentioned, it is often useful for tutors to gain on-the-fly access to raw data, to support specific activities in their everyday role (e.g., summarizing participation to identify inactive students or lurkers, providing personalized feedback, supporting meta-cognitive reflection etc.). In all these cases the CMC system could be enriched with monitoring oriented features, which can provide up-to-date information on participation, possibly sorted by participant, group, role etc. (see the example provided in Table 5). This need is more easily met when using an open source platform such as Moodle, than with proprietary software such as FirstClass, for obvious reasons of extensibility; however, even a "closed" application like FirstClass offers the tools for a programmer to build ad hoc software able to access the server database. In addition to monitoring tools, other functions can be implemented to save tutors' time and improve the support to their work. In order to work out the indicators used in our model, we need the CMC system to track the relevant events and store them in a database. Figure 5 shows what we regard as relevant data (the database *entities*, represented by rectangular boxes) and the *relationships* between them, represented by diamonds. The whole picture makes up the conceptual model of the database we used as a foundation for the implementation of our tools.

As already mentioned, CSCL activities are

Figure 5. The database conceptual model

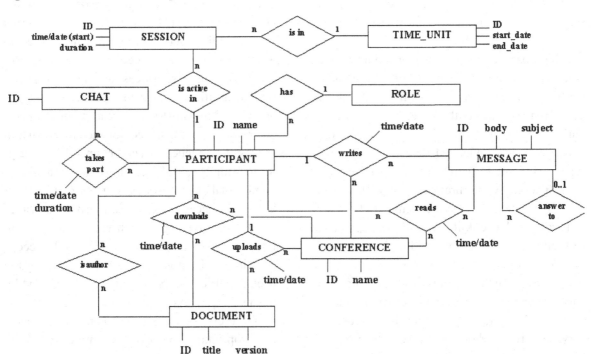

typically carried out (mostly in an asynchronous way) in discussion forums or conferences, represented in the schema by the CONFERENCE entity. PARTICIPANTs *write* and *read* MESSAGEs in a CONFERENCE, and similarly *upload* and *download* DOCUMENTS to/from a CONFERENCE[9]. MESSAGEs are linked in *answer-to* chains that represent the thread aggregation. Other relationships indicate that a PARTICIPANT *has* a ROLE, can *take-part-in* CHATs, can be the *author* of a DOCUMENT and, when logging into the system, activates (relation *is-active-in*) a SESSION that temporally falls in (*is-in*) a given calendar TIME_UNIT (e.g., week).

The conceptual schema depicted in Figure 5 provides a unified view of all the raw data that are relevant for the implementation of the proposed evaluation model. These data come from a variety of sources - mostly from the CMC system, but also from server and system logs, course design documentation, administrative enrolment lists, etc. Data might be replicated in a real database, or they could be directly accessed from their source, when these are accessible online and a suitable Application Programming Interface (API) exists. Concrete system differences can be hidden "behind" the abstract conceptual schema, which is the same regardless of the specific CMC system and therefore allows specifying the model implementation independently of the particular hosting environment.

CONCLUSIONS AND FURTHER DEVELOPMENTS

This paper proposes and exemplifies the use of a model providing a framework for monitoring and evaluating CSCL processes. In particular, the model is suitable to be adopted in online collaboration-intensive learning contexts, where the tutors per students ratio is relatively high (1/20-25).

The model takes into consideration four dimensions: the participative, the social, the cognitive and teaching dimensions. The indicators of the participative dimension are purely of a quantitative nature, and they give a preliminary view of students' involvement in the learning experience, mainly based on the actions they performed within the learning environment. The participative dimension underpins the other three dimensions, which are of a qualitative nature.

The indicators of the social, cognitive and teaching dimensions can be assessed through content analysis of the messages exchanged between students and allow the tutors and the evaluators to study different aspects of the process involved in detail. For example, the social presence, intended as the sense of belonging and the social climate within the learning community, has been studied by several authors (Lobry de Bruyn, 2004; Wegerif, 1998) and the indicators provided by our model can be used to investigate whether there are ways to favour a positive and agreeable climate within an online course. Other aspects that are often investigated are the depth of the argumentations that students have produced during a discussion and the degree to which the community members have achieved maturity and autonomy in the way they learn together.

The model, which has been used for several years in courses for trainee teachers, proved its usability, flexibility and adaptability to different aims, mostly thanks to the following features:

- the exhaustiveness and richness of dimensions and indicators, which can be used in a selective way in order to limit the workload deriving from the manual analysis of the messages,
- the possibility of changing the units of analysis used, by adopting either the message or other kinds of unit, and by choosing to consider one or more indicators per unit of analysis, possibly with different degrees of importance.

Indeed, some of the indicators reveal latent variables, i.e. aspects that are not manifest in the message texts and cannot therefore be identified with automatic tools. This is both a strength and a drawback of the approach. It is a strength because, as Rourke et al. (2001) point out, the most interesting research questions tend to require the analysis of this kind of variables. However, it is also a drawback, because the identification of latent variables cannot rely uniquely on interaction analysis. In fact, interaction records only contain the tip of the iceberg of the latent content being searched. It is therefore necessary to integrate and verify these data with other information deriving from more traditional tools, such as questionnaires and interviews.

More in general, it is often advisable to complement the data coming from interaction analysis with information of a different nature. Zorrilla & Álvarez (2008), for example, integrate the data extracted from the log files with external information such as academic and demographic data, as well as with information concerning the learning materials. In addition, visual representation of data can be very helpful (Caballé et al, 2007). Social Network Analysis, for example, offers a different key to the reading of CMC interactions, as it highlights the roles played by the various actors within the discussion and their reciprocal influence.

Further developments of this research should focus on its present limits and aim to overcome them. Perhaps one of the main criticisms raised against content analysis is that it is time consuming and labour intensive, because it has to be carried out manually. Moreover, content analysis always requires a period of training by coders (them being tutors, designers or external evaluators) before they can actually carry out the analysis. Evaluators will also need to negotiate among themselves the criteria that will inform the interpretation of the data obtained. According to the evaluation aims, there might be a need to define different meta-indexes, such as the online marks used for assessment purposes shown in Table 6.

This model partly overcomes the drawbacks of content analysis by providing a basic layer of information about the participative dimension which is automatically provided by many CMC systems. However, additional research is needed to further alleviate the burden of manual message analysis by providing useful semi-automatic tools. For example, the possibility for each coder to tag messages with indicator(s) and, possibly, a graduation of their relevance would be highly valuable, because it would allow one to carry out the analysis once and for all and exploit the results for several different purposes and possibly at different times.

In the last few months, an informal evaluation of the model accuracy has been carried out by interviewing the coders who had used it and the results of such evaluation have already informed the refinement of the model. The last version of the model (described in this paper) has been judged accurate and fit for the purpose, with the exception of the meta-reflection indicators that seem still very few and little structured. The reason for this lies in the previously mentioned considerations about latent variables: it would be useless to elaborate a detailed set of indicators for the meta-reflection component of the model, which typically belongs to the realm of latent variables.

REFERENCES

Alvino, S., & Persico, D. (2008). The relationship between assessment and evaluation in CSCL. In A. Cartelli & M. Palma (Eds.), *Encyclopaedia of information and communication technology, vol. II* (pp. 698-703). Hershey, PA: Information Science Reference.

Anderson, T., Rourke, L., Garrison, D. R., & Archer, W. (2001). Assessing teaching presence in a computer conferencing context. *Journal of Asynchronous Learning Networks, 5*(2). Retrieved from http://www.aln.org/alnweb/journal/jaln-vol5issue2v2.htm

Aviv, R., Erlich, Z., Ravid, G., & Geva, A. (2003). Network analysis of knowledge construction in asynchronous learning networks. *Journal of Asynchronous Learning Networks, 7*(3), 1–23.

Caballé, S., Daradoumis, T., & Xhafa, F. (2007). A generic platform for the systematic construction of knowledge-based collaborative learning applications. In C. Pahl (Ed.), *Architecture solutions for e-learning systems* (pp. 219-242). Hershey, PA: Idea Group Publishing.

Chi, M. T. H. (1997). Quantifying qualitative analyses of verbal data: A practical guide. *Journal of the Learning Sciences, 6*(3), 271–315. doi:10.1207/s15327809jls0603_1

Daradoumis, T., Martínez-Monés, A., & Xhafa, F. (2006). A layered framework for evaluating online collaborative learning interactions. *International Journal of Human-Computer Studies, 64*(7), 622–635. doi:10.1016/j.ijhcs.2006.02.001

de Bruyn, L. (2004). Monitoring online communication: Can the development of convergence and social presence indicate an interactive learning environment. *Distance Education, 25*(1), 67–81. doi:10.1080/0158791042000212468

Delfino, M., & Persico, D. (2007). Online or face-to-face? Experimenting with different techniques in teacher training. *Journal of Computer Assisted Learning, 23*, 351–365. doi:10.1111/j.1365-2729.2007.00220.x

Dillenbourg, P. (Ed.). (1999). *Collaborative learning: Cognitive and computational approaches*. New York: Pergamon.

EduTools. (2008). *CMS: Product list*. Retrieved December 10, 2008, from http://landonline.edutools.info/item_list.jsp?pj=4

Garrison, D. R., Anderson, T., & Archer, W. (1999). Critical inquiry in a text-based environment: Computer conferencing in higher education. *The Internet and Higher Education, 2*(2-3), 87–105. doi:10.1016/S1096-7516(00)00016-6

Garrison, R., & Anderson, T. (2003). *E-learning in the 21st century. A framework for research and practice*. New York: Routledge Falmer.

Garrison, R., Anderson, T., & Archer, W. (2001). Critical thinking, cognitive presence, and computer conferencing in distance education. *American Journal of Distance Education, 15*(1), 3–21.

Hara, N., Bonk, C. J., & Angeli, C. (2000). Content analysis of online discussion in an applied educational psychology course. *Instructional Science, 28*, 115–152. doi:10.1023/A:1003764722829

Hartnell-Young, E. (2005). *Teachers' new roles in school-based communities of practice*. Paper presented at the AARE Conference, Melbourne, Australia. Retrieved from http://www.aare.edu.au/04pap/har04257.pdf

Henri, F. (1992). Computer conferencing and content analysis. In A. R. Kaye (Ed.), *Collaborative learning through computer conferencing: The Najaden papers* (pp. 115-136). New York: Springer.

Kanuka, H., & Anderson, T. (1999). Using constructivism in technology-mediated learning: Constructing order out of the chaos in the literature. *Radical Pedagogy, 1*(2). Retrieved from http://radicalpedagogy.icaap.org/content/issue1_2/02kanuka1_2.html

Lally, V., & de Laat, M. (2002). Cracking the code: Learning to collaborate and collaborating to learn in a networked environment. In G. Stahl (Ed.), *Computer support for collaborative learning: Foundations for a CSCL community, Proceedings of the CSCL 2002*, Boulder, Colorado, USA (pp. 160-168).

Lave, J., & Wenger, E. (1991). *Situated learning: Legitimate peripheral participation*. Cambridge, UK: Cambridge University Press.

Lipponen, L., Rahikainen, M., Lallilmo, J., & Hakkarainen, K. (2003). Patterns of participation and discourse in elementary students' computer-supported collaborative learning. *Learning and Instruction, 13*, 487–509. doi:10.1016/S0959-4752(02)00042-7

Lombard, M., Snyder-Dich, J., & Bracken, C. C. (2002). Content analysis in mass communication. Assessment and reporting of intercoder reliability. *Human Communication Research, 28*(4), 587–604. doi:10.1111/j.1468-2958.2002.tb00826.x

Martinez, A., Dimitriadis, Y., Rubia, B., Gomez, E., & De La Fuente, P. (2003). Combining qualitative evaluation and social network analysis for the study of classroom social interactions. *Computers & Education, 41*(4), 353–368. doi:10.1016/j.compedu.2003.06.001

McKlin, T., Harmon, S. W., Evans, W., & Jone, M. G. (2001). Cognitive presence in Web-based learning: A content analysis of students' online discussions. *American Journal of Distance Education, 15*(1), 7–23.

Meyer, K. A. (2003). Face-to-face versus threaded discussions: The role of time and higher-order thinking. *Journal of Asynchronous Learning Networks, 7*(3), 55–65.

Murphy, E. (2004). Recognizing and promoting collaboration in an online asynchronous discussion. *British Journal of Educational Technology, 35*(4), 421–431. doi:10.1111/j.0007-1013.2004.00401.x

Oriogun, P. K., Ravenscroft, A., & Cook, J. (2005). Validating an approach to examining cognitive engagement within online groups. *American Journal of Distance Education, 19*(4), 197–214. doi:10.1207/s15389286ajde1904_2

Pawan, F., Paulus, T., Yalcin, S., & Chang, C. F. (2003). Online learning: Patterns of engagement and interaction among in-service teachers. *Language Learning & Technology, 7*(3), 119–140.

Persico, D., Pozzi, F., & Sarti, L. (2008). Fostering collaboration in CSCL. In A. Cartelli & M. Palma (Eds.), *Encyclopaedia of information communication technology* (pp. 335-340). Hershey, PA: Idea Group Reference.

Persico, D., Pozzi, F., & Sarti, L. (2009). Design patterns for monitoring and evaluating CSCL processes. *Computers in Human Behaviour.*

Phillips, J. J. (1998). The return-on-investment (ROI) process: Issues and trends. *Educational Technology, 38*(4), 7–14.

Pozzi, F., Manca, S., Persico, D., & Sarti, L. (2007). A general framework for tracking and analysing learning processes in computer-supported collaborative learning environments. *Innovations in Education and Teaching International, 44*(2), 169–179. doi:10.1080/14703290701240929

Reffay, C., & Chanier, T. (2003). How social network analysis can help to measure cohesion in collaborative distance-learning. In B. Wasson, S. Ludvigsen, & U. Hoppe (Eds.), *Designing for change in networked learning environments. Proceedings of the international conference on computer support for collaborative learning 2003* (pp. 343–352). Dordrecht, The Netherlands: Kluwer Academic Publishers.

Rourke, L., Anderson, T., Garrison, D. R., & Archer, W. (2001). Methodological issues in the content analysis of computer conference transcripts. *International Journal of Artificial Intelligence in Education, 12,* 8–22.

Scardamalia, M., & Bereiter, C. (1994). Computer support for knowledge-building communities. *Journal of the Learning Sciences, 3*(3), 265–283. doi:10.1207/s15327809jls0303_3

Schlager, M., & Fusco, J. (2004). Teacher professional development, technology, and communities of practice: Are we putting the cart before the horse? In S. Barab, R. Kling, & J. Gray (Eds.), *Designing for virtual communities in the service of learning*. Cambridge, UK: Cambridge University Press. Retrieved from http://tappedin.org/tappedin/web/papers/2004/SchlagerFuscoTPD.pdf

Schrire, S. (2006). Knowledge building in asynchronous discussion groups: Going beyond quantitative analysis. *Computers & Education, 46,* 49–70. doi:10.1016/j.compedu.2005.04.006

Shea, P., Pickett, A., & Pelt, W. (2003). A follow-up investigation of teaching presence in the SUNY learning network. *Journal of Asynchronous Learning Networks, 7*(2).

Thorpe, M. (1993). *Evaluating open and distance learning*. Harlow, UK: Longman.

Trentin, G. (2000). The quality-interactivity relationship in distance education. *Educational Technology, 40*(1), 17–27.

Triggs, P., & John, P. (2004). From transaction to transformation: Information and communication technology, professional development and the formation of communities of practice. *Journal of Computer Assisted Learning, 20*(6), 426–439. doi:10.1111/j.1365-2729.2004.00101.x

Vanderbilt (The Cognition and Technology Group at Vanderbilt). (1991). Some thoughts about constructivism and instructional design. *Educational Technology, 31*(10), 16–18.

Wang, M. (2004), Correlational analysis of student visibility and performance in online learning. *Journal of Asynchronous Learning Networks, 8*(4). Retrieved from http://www.sloan-c.org/publications/jaln/v8n4/pdf/v8n4_wang.pdf

Wegerif, R. (1998). The social dimension of asynchronous learning networks. *Journal of Asynchronous Learning Networks, 2,* 34–49.

Weinberger, A., & Fischer, F. (2006). A framework to analyze argumentative knowledge construction in computer-supported collaborative learning. *Computers & Education, 46,* 71–95. doi:10.1016/j.compedu.2005.04.003

ENDNOTES

[1]   For an exhaustive debate on the unit of analysis see (De Wever et al., 2006, p.9): "One of the issues under discussion is the choice of the unit of analysis to perform content analysis. Researchers can consider each individual sentence as a single unit of analysis (Fahy et al., 2001). A second option is to identify a consistent "theme" or "idea" (unit of meaning) in a message and to approach this as the unit of analysis (Henri, 1992). A third option is to take the complete message a student posts at a certain moment in the discussion as the unit of analysis (Gunawardena et al., 1997; Rourke et al., 2001)" [De Wever, B., Schellens, T., Valcke, M., & Van Keer, H. (2006). Content analysis schemes to analyze transcripts of

online asynchronous discussion groups: a review. Computers and Education, 46(1), 6-28].

2   SSIS is the acronym for *Scuole di Specializzazione all'Insegnamento Secondario*, that is the Specialization Schools for Secondary Teaching. The SSIS have been in charge of initial teacher training in Italy between 1999 and 2008.

3   Numbers include messages by students and tutors.

4   Mean and standard deviation do not include messages by the tutor.

5   Since Moodle, the system used in the course, does not allow one to visualize the individual message, but only the whole thread, here we consider a participant having read the messages that are present in the forum at the moment of the last visit.

6   Marks in Italy are usually given in thirties, with 18 as the lower pass mark.

7   The examples provided in this paper make reference either to Centrinity FirstClass (http://www.centrinity.com/), a commercial CMC system that the authors have adopted in a number of online courses, or to Moodle (http://www.moodle.org/), a widely used open source platform with a high level of configurability and adaptability based on the Apache web server.

8   Log analysis software include Nihuo Web Log Analyzer (http://www.loganalyzer.net/), Web Log Expert (http://www.weblogexpert.com/), Visitors (http://www.hping.org/visitors/), Web Log Explorer (http://www.exacttrend.com/WebLogExplorer/).

9   In this respect, the concept of CONFERENCE includes both asynchronous discussion forums and document sharing spaces, which in some platforms are implemented in separate and structurally different sub-environments.

Section 3
Assessment Approaches

Chapter 10
Nonverbal Communication as a Means to Support Collaborative Interaction Assessment in 3D Virtual Environments for Learning

Adriana Peña Pérez Negrón
Universidad Politécnica de Madrid, Spain

Angélica de Antonio Jiménez
Universidad Politécnica de Madrid, Spain

ABSTRACT

In the classrooms at school, when a group of students is working in a predetermined task, the teacher or the tutor identifies some problems related to collaboration by observing the students' behavior. While interacting, people interchange messages composed of speech, actions and gestures, as the wordless messages emphasize, support or even substitute speech. In 3D collaborative virtual environments (CVE), the user's graphical representation, an avatar, is the means to express this nonverbal communication (NVC). The authors' proposal is that, like in a real learning scenario, by the observation of specific NVC cues, indicators of collaborative interaction can be inferred to an extent that they can be used to foster collaboration, if necessary, in a learning task situation. The various NVC cues that have been selected for that purpose and their corresponding collaborative learning interaction indicators will be presented. An exploratory study that consisted in the analysis of a real life situation during a collaborative task accomplishment, directed to the development of an experimental 3D CVE desktop application that allows avatars' display of NVC cues, will be discussed.

DOI: 10.4018/978-1-60566-786-7.ch010

INTRODUCTION

When people interact, speech and actions are intricately related to the position and dynamics of objects, other people, and ongoing activities in the environment (Ford, 1999). Messages go through multiple channels that involve more than speech, like body movements, gestures, facial expressions or actions; these wordless messages are nonverbal communication (NVC) (DeVito & Hecht, 1990). NVC is practical for learning scenarios in a number of forms, like being a means to present information in more than one modality, usually associated with learning, or by helping to understand the words that accompany (Goldin-Meadow, Wein, & Chang, 1992).

The visual embodiment of the user in a VE, an avatar, is the means for interacting within it and for sensing the world's attributes (Guye-Vuillème, Capin, Pandzic, Thalmann, & Thalmann, 1998). In a collaborative environment the user's avatar has, in addition, relevant awareness functions, allowing: to get perception of others, knowing where they are, and visualizing what they are doing or looking at (Capin, Pandzic, Thalmann, & Thalmann, 1997). And the user's avatar is the channel to display NVC (Johnson & Leight, 2001). In computer science, research related to NVC is typically addressed to create believable human avatars; current approaches are aimed to a number of specific situations like in conversation (Padilha & Carletta, 2003), to express emotions (Fabri, Moore & Hobbs, 2004), or the more sophisticated ones to simulate a teacher or a learning partner (Ieronutti & Chittaro, 2007). But the avatar's function as a user's transmitter of NVC has not been much exploited, probably for its complexity and extension.

3D CVEs are a useful media for spatial tasks and for interaction (Park & Kenyon, 1999). Under the assumption that collaborative features and the students' behaviors related present distinctive NVC cues, our hypothesis is that the observation

of the group members' NVC should allow us to establish indicators of collaborative learning interaction. Our focus will be the collaborative interactions that take place during a task learning situation, where the task to be accomplished is the main cognitive entity, and collaborative interaction will be understood as described by Martínez (2003, p. 51): *"...an action that affects or can affect the collaborative process. The main requirement for an action to be considered a possible interaction is that the action itself or its effect can be perceived by at least a member of the group distinct of the one that performed the action"*.

Our attention, then, will be centered on those behaviors that transmit something about how the group members interact while they are collaborating to achieve a common goal. The main NVC areas related to interaction are Proxemics –the study of interpersonal distance, Kinesics –the study of communicative body motions, and Paralinguistics –the study of voice features others than meaning or content (Ladd, 1996).

An especial advantage of this proposal is that the information can be retrieved from the CVE despite of its learning domain, characteristic that makes it appropriate for generic analysis.

After a review of NVC behaviors, we believe that, through their observation in 3D CVEs, important learning indicators can be inferred such as: the members' participation rates; the extent to which the students maintain the focus on the task; the degree of the students making shared grounding; when there is division of labor; and an adequate group process for the task, including the plan, implement and evaluate phases. The NVC cues to be observed during collaborative interaction while a task is accomplished will be described and related to the aforementioned learning indicators. We are aware that probably there will be some missing learning indicators or useful NVC cues, but up to our knowledge, this is the first attempt in this direction. An empirical study to observe NVC cues in a real life collaborative task situation was applied afterwards to the development of a 3D desktop-based CVE. The study and the application will be discussed.

BACKGROUND

NVC is a wide field; it comprises all wordless message people interchange. NVC is about communication with objects like clothes or hairstyle, or how the decoration of our daily spaces are; and it is also of what is communicated through our body, like gestures, facial expressions or speech characteristics other than meaning (Argyle, 1988; Knapp & Hall, 2007; Mehrabian, 1969). During interaction, NVC main areas are Paralinguistics, Proxemics and Kinesics.

Paralinguistics comprises all non linguistic features related to speech like: the selected language, the use of simple or complex vocabulary, or the tone of voice, among others (Ladd, 1996). Paralinguistic features are challenging to be recognized by computer systems, although the study not of how people talk but of the amounts and patterns of talk can provide the means to understand the group process (Dabbs & Ruback, 1987).

Proxemics describes the subjective dimensions that surround each person –the way people handle the "bubble" or space around their body, and how persons locate themselves next to others in space –the physical distances that we try to keep from others (Hall, 1959). Proxemics analyzes the chosen distance and angle of the body during interaction (Guye-Vuillème et al., 1998). Since our body is oriented to keep a barrier of our territory that avoid or invite others to interact with us (Scheflen, 1964), following participant navigation within the scenario should help to know, for example, preferences among group members or the creation of subgroups.

Kinesics is the study of what is called "body language", all body movements except physical contact (Argyle, 1988). Kinesics includes facial expressions, gestures and postures. In computer science, facial expressions have been used mainly to give realism to avatars, and they have also been used to give emotional context in learning communications (Fabri, Moore & Hobbs, 2004). As of gesture, deictic gestures should be easy to digitize and useful for its similarity with the computer prompter. Postures have been used to determine the degree of attention or involvement, agreement, or liking or predilection for others (Scheflen, 1964). Special attention has received "the nonverbally conference table", where the table's shape, size and seating plan influences group dynamics and affects emotional tone and outcome of discussions (Givens, 2005).

NVC in CVEs

While people interact NVC involves three factors: environmental conditions, physical characteristics and behaviors of the communicators (Knapp & Hall, 2007), all of them clearly restricted to computer generated or mediated conditions in CVEs.

In a CVE for learning, environmental conditions have to do with the pedagogical strategy, which typically is the session purpose such as discussing about a proposed theme, to solve a problem or a task accomplishment. Based on the purpose of the learning session, the environment emphasis will be either on the communication media, the workspace characteristics, the surrounding objects and/or the features of the scene.

The physical characteristics are determined by the avatar's appearance that, in learning environments, usually is established by the developer, without ample possibilities of being changed by the students; and those more interesting features related to the avatar's possibilities of expressing NVC, like having or not facial expressions, navigation controls or some specific body movements (Fabri, Moore & Hobbs, 2004; Park et al., 2001; Sims & Pike, 2007). While natural human communication is based on speech, facial expressions and gestures, interaction also depends heavily on the actions, postures, movements and expressions of the talking body (Morris, Collett, Marsh, & O'Shaughnessy, 1979).

There are three different approaches to transmit NVC to a VE: directly controlled –with sensors attached to the user; user-guided –when the user guides the avatar defining tasks and movements; and semi-autonomous –where the avatar has an internal state that depends on its goals and its environment, and it is this state which is modified by the user (Capin et al., 1997). As far as NVC features are automatically digitized from the user, they should be more revealing and spontaneous. However, we believe that even if NVC is transmitted to the computer by a simple keyboard or a mouse, it can provide significance to communication and resources to understand collaborative interaction. Succinct metaphors for the visualization of NVC can enhance the users' immersion feeling (Fabri & Hobbs, 1998). As Tromp (1995) pointed out, the degree of being present in a virtual world depends more on the people's attitude than on the technology; it is the willingness to accept the stimuli offered by some medium as real what creates a state of mental absorption.

STUDYING COLLABORATIVE LEARNING INTERACTIONS VIA NVC

Current Approaches to Study Collaborative Interactions in Learning Environments

With the purpose of creating effective approaches for Computer Supported Collaborative Learning (CSCL), different techniques have been used to establish collaborative interaction (Jermann, Soller, & Muehlenbrock, 2001). But current approaches are not intended for VEs; they need that the students take part in the classification of their contributions, producing an extra job for them –via opening sentences, or structured contributions schemes (Vieira, Teixeira, Timóteo, Tedesco, & Barros, 2004; Barros & Verdejo, 2000; Soller, Lesgold Linton, & Goodman, 1999)–, or are focused just in the workspace –such as card assembling (Mühlenbrock, 2004).

Complete computer comprehension of natural language has not been accomplished yet, which is probably the main reason for trying to establish collaborative interaction through sentence openers. This approach presents a menu with expressions or sentences from which the students can choose the one that indicates their communication intention, while the rest of the message can be written in free text format, in such a way that there is no need for the system to fully understand the meaning of the communication (Soller et al., 1999). Its use in CVEs, where oral communication is more appropriate (Imai et al., 2000), presents the disadvantages of written and menu based communication that restricts communication and makes its process slower (Constantino-Gonzales & Suthers, 2001).

Approaches that present a predefined scheme for the students' contributions (Barros & Verdejo, 2000; Suthers & Hundhausen, 2001) in which classification is made either by asking the students to label or to place this contribution, the contributions are posted in a structure in which 3D environments are not required. Also, this approach is usually addressed to asynchronous communication. Thus, the display of NVC of the user's avatar is not required.

For the collaborative interaction analysis other approaches are focused on the students' contributions in the shared workspace (Mühlenbrock, 2004). Here the outside workspace interaction is not considered; still this can be solved with hybrid approaches.

Our proposal of using NVC to study collaborative learning interaction to an extent that it can be fostered, has no need of students' intervention, and it can be done automatically. Also, this approach avoids the need of understanding speakers' utterances; however, even if computers could comprehend human language to a certain extent, NVC would still be useful by providing complementary insights about interaction and communication.

NVC as a Task-Service Function

NVC varies according to social rules; the communication behaviors of the students are attached to their background. But, even if it is truth that NVC changes from one culture to another (Birdwhistell, 1970; Efron, 1941), it is also truth that it is functional, which means that different functional uses will lead to different patterns of exchange (Argyle, 1972; Ekman & Friesen, 1969). Patterson (1982) proposed what he called "nonverbal involvement behaviors" to operationally define the degree of involvement manifested between individuals; and he classified them within specific functions. These functions for NVC are: to provide information or to regulate interactions –these two are useful to understand isolated behaviors–; and to express intimacy, to exercise social control, and to facilitate service or task goals –these last three functions are useful to understand behavior over the time. The first two functions are independent of the last three in such a way that a given behavior can be either informational or regulatory and, at the same time, be part of an overall pattern serving to intimacy, social control, or service-task functions.

Of special interest to this proposal is the NVC service or task function, which is helpful to understand NVC impersonal behavior –by impersonal we mean not engaging with personality or emotions. The interpersonal involvement in these kinds of exchanges is delimited to the service or task regulations, and it is more related to the goals and outcomes of an interaction than to its intimacy or affective quality. When people are working together towards a mutual goal, individuals share common expectancies about their roles and their NVC patterns are ruled by those expectancies (Patterson, 1982). For example, if an unknown person approaches to us more than

socially accepted, it is very probable that we feel uncomfortable and try to move away, nevertheless, if this approaching person is a dentist who is going to check our teeth, this same proximity should not bother us.

Selected NVC Cues for Some Specific Collaborative Learning Indicators

In order to achieve collaboratively a task, students have to share information and create a common ground –that is, mutual knowledge, mutual beliefs, and mutual assumptions (Clark & Brennan, 1991). Group members attempt to maintain the belief that their partners have understood what they meant, at least to an extent which is sufficient to carry out the task at hand (Resnick, 1991). The *shared ground* has to be updated moment by moment, as collective actions are built on common ground and its accumulation (Clark & Brennan, 1991). Besides the discourse to construct and maintain the shared understanding, action and gestures also serve students as presentations and acceptances (Roschelle & Teasley, 1995).

During an effective collaborative learning session, dialogue is also expected among the students to express and extract ideas and knowledge from each other, and with the intention of getting agreements about the potential needed actions in order to achieve the common goal (Fischer, Bruhn, Gräsel, & Mandl, 1998). Conversation plays too an important role for social aspects related to group performance (Heldal, 2007).

On the other hand, a maintained balance between dialogue and action is desirable (Jermann, 2004); the students need to keep *focused on the task* in order to achieve the session's goals. The degree of participation between the members of the group is expected to be even, both in discussion and in implementation. In a collaborative situation, participation is expected to have symmetry (Dillenbourg, 1999).

Participation is one of the most important

conditions for a successful collaborative learning situation. Group learning possibilities grow with the participation of its members; an active participation corroborates the student interest and comprehension of group activity. Encouraging active participation increases the learning possibilities of the members of the group (Soller, 2001). As well, students' participation needs a proper structure.

If the group starts by implementing without planning or ends without evaluating, even if the task is accomplished, there are few possibilities of sharing understanding and knowledge. Group processing involves progress discussion to decide what behaviors to continue or to change (Johnson, Johnson, & Holubec, 1990). Then, during the accomplishment of a task it is desired an appropriate approach for problem solving with the *Plan-Implement-Evaluate cycle* (Jermann, 2004). In order to accomplish a task, it would be desirable first to plan how, who and when things are going to be implemented, then to make the implementation or execution, and finally to evaluate what was implemented. This is a cycle, and its phases are not always entirely separated. It is not necessary to have everything planned to make some implementation; implementation can be interrupted by new or redesigned plans, or by evaluation; and evaluation can need implementation or new plans.

When *planning*, agreements have to be reached. The discussion of the strategies to be followed helps students to construct a shared view or mental model of their goals and the required tasks to be executed. During this phase students need to discuss, look at each other to be convincing or searching for feedback.

In the *implementation* phase, activity in the shared workspace must appear. Implementation can be a joint effort where there has to be discussion and negotiation about what students are doing. If implementation is decided to be conducted by dividing activities, then activity has to be split in the shared workspace, and less discussion should

be required. The students' focus of attention has to be on the shared workspace with spare gazes at each other.

After making plans or implementing, students have to decide if some changes are needed (Johnson, Johnson, & Holubec, 1990), they have to *evaluate* what they have done. Discussion here can imply pointing, and gazes have to be directed to the shared workspace, students also have to get agreements in this phase.

The degree of expected collaboration or the kind of task to be accomplished will define if *division of labor* is or not acceptable and to what extent it is. Division of labor can be kept constant during the whole learning session or it can appear at intervals. Typically, division of labor in CSCL is used to distinguish between collaboration and cooperation (Dillenbourg, 1999; Roschelle & Teasley, 1995).

After a careful review of NVC behaviors, our hypothesis is that through them we can get indicators of the making of shared grounding, the focus on the task, of the students' participation rates, of division of labor, and of an adequate group process for the task, including the plan, implement and evaluate phases. These learning sessions' features, although as mentioned it is an open issue, we believe are good indicatives to automatically foster collaboration that can be inferred by the retrieval of NVC cues. These possibilities, as far as we know, have not been explored on their relation to CVEs for learning.

We will start our analysis with the two NVC cues most closely related to participation rates: amount of talk and implementation. Oral communication seems to be more appropriate for a VE (Imai et al., 2000), but written text can be used as a substitute to retrieve amount of talk. Other important characteristic of these two cues is that they can be retrieved from a simple desktop-based CVE with no especial hardware requirements.

The way to retrieve other NVC cues depends more on the design and configuration of the environment. We will then talk about gazes, deictic gestures and Proxemics that can be retrieved from eye, head or hand trackers, but more simply gazes can also be retrieved from the avatars' point of view, the deictic gestures can be compared to mouse pointing, and Proxemics can be obtained from the avatars' navigation, in such a way that these three NVC cues can also be transmitted to the environment through a simple keyboard or a mouse.

We will also discuss head movements and body postures, usually digitized by body trackers and that are similar because both of them present ambiguities for their interpretation in the real world. However, they could help somehow to understand collaboration combined with other NVC cues. And finally, we discuss some considerations about facial expressions.

Amount of Talk

The paralinguistic branch of NVC that studies patterns of talk has been useful for the study of interaction. Talk-silence patterns, frequency, duration and pacing of speech, have provided means for individual differentiations in social interaction, and in relation to collaborating groups, researchers have found that talkative group members seem to be more productive (Norfleet, 1948), more task dedicated (Knutson, 1960), and more likely to be task leaders (Stein & Heller, 1979). Usually based on Hidden Markovian Models, frequency and duration of speech have been used for group process analysis (Brdiczka, Maisonnasse & Reignier, 2005; McCowan et al., 2004). According to students' rates of speech we can determine whether students are participating and in some cases if that participation is or not symmetric —when for example, a student is too quiet in relation to others. Collaborative learning can then be fostered by promoting an even participation rate.

In a collaborative learning session, expectations are that the students share knowledge and ideas, and the primary means to do so is discussion. In this context, the communication process serves the learning purpose by: 1) externalization, when a student shares knowledge; 2) elicitation, when a student by externalization gets that other student contributes; and 3) getting consensus about possible actions to achieve goals (Fischer et al., 1998). Although without content comprehension no statements can be made for sure about an utterance, some patterns can be retrieved to determine if a student is an initiator –a person that initiates conversations– and the chances that this student is externalizing. By content analysis, it was found that people that communicate the most, tend to give more information and opinions than what they receive (Bales, 1970). An initial utterance followed by an answer could be understood like elicitation, and a growing speech rate with group turns could be understood as getting consensus. Periods of empty turns with no implementation could be due to the fact that the students are working on ideas too ill-formed or complicated to be introduced into the shared work, followed with intense interaction to incorporate the individual insights into the shared knowledge (Roschelle & Teasley, 1995). Also, during the planning phase high turn talking interchange is expected.

Artifact Manipulation and Implementation in the Shared Workspace

Artifacts manipulation is an object form of NVC —it can be, for instance, the form that takes an answer to a question (Clark & Brennan, 1991; Martínez, 2003). Participation is also related to the amount of manipulation in the shared workspace. Despite its quality, the amount of work a student realizes within the workspace is, by itself, a good indicator of that student's interest and participation in the task. Clearly, during the implementation phase it is expected a high intervention in the shared workspace.

Additionally, according to Jermann (2004), a combination of participation in the shared workspace with amount of talk allows establishing patterns with regards to division of labor. These patterns are: 1) symmetry in dialogue with asymmetry in implementation, when all participants discuss the plans but only some of them do the implementation; 2) asymmetry in dialogue and in implementation, when some give orders and some others follow them; and 3) symmetry in dialogue and in participation, when there is no division of labor or when division of labor is really accurate. The strategies to solve the problems can also be inferred by participation patterns: 1) alternation in dialogue and implementation reflects a plan-implement-evaluate approach; and 2) almost null dialogue and continuous implementation reflects a brut force trial. In consequence, besides participation rates, patterns composed of amount of talk and manipulation in the shared workspace would be useful for the analysis of the collaborative interaction within a learning scenario.

Gazes

In a task context, gazes, beside their function to regulate and coordinate conversation, are applied to the goals and outcomes of an interaction (Patterson, 1982). When people are working on a task, gazes serve as a means of collecting information. Through gazes people get feedback (Kleinke, 1986) about contact, perception, understanding and attitudinal reactions (Allwood, Grönqvist, Ahlsén, & Gunnarsson, 2002). The gaze is an excellent predictor of conversational attention in multiparty conversations (Argyle & Dean, 1965), and the eye direction is a high indicative of a person's focus of attention (Bailenson, Blascovich, Beall, & Loomis, 2003). Therefore, via the students' avatar gazes it can be inferred if they are paying attention to the current task and/or to which other students. Through gazes it is possible to oversee if the group maintains the focus on the task. Gazes also can be helpful to measure the degree of students' involvement in dialogue and implementation.

Deictic Gestures

Gestures within collaborative learning constitute an important resource for the coordination of interactions (Ford, 1999), and they are a central characteristic in conversation. Gestures have narrative –iconic gesture–, and grounding –deictic gesture– functions (Roth, 2002). While it can be difficult to automatically distinguish iconic gestures from the very common meaningless gestures people do when they are speaking, deictic gestures can be compared to mouse pointing. Deictic terms such as: here, there, or that, are interpreted as a result of the communication context, and when the conversation is focused on objects and their identities, they become crucial to identify the objects quickly and securely (Clark & Brennan, 1991). When a group is working with objects, communication of references is essential for getting common ground (Gergle, Kraut, & Fussell, 2004). Consequently, deictic gestures, especially those directed to the shared workspace, will be useful to determine whether students are talking about the task.

Proxemics

VEs have been used by sociologists for the research of Proxemics because results demonstrated that users keep some proxemic behaviors on them (Bailenson et al., 2003). When people are standing, they tend to form a circle in which they include or exclude other persons from the interaction (Scheflen, 1964). Then, when navigation is part of the CVE, the students' proxemic behaviors can be used to indicate peers' inclusion or exclusion of task activities, the creation of subgroups and division of labor.

Head Movements

Head position can provide a very close approximation to eye direction; head position then could be useful to replace gazes retrieval when it is not possible to follow the exact direction of a person's sight (Parkhurst, Law & Niebur, 2002), in which case they should be treated like gazes.

On the other hand, there are multitude of head movements during interaction that have to do with the nature, the purpose and the organization of it. Different patterns of head movements for conversation can be found in Heylen (2005). The automatic comprehension of head gestures becomes complex since they can carry out different functions and/or meaning that depend on the context in which they are produced. Despite this difficulty, there are some semantic head movements that can be distinguished and can be helpful for collaborative interaction analysis in context with other NVC behaviors, such as the very common nodding to show agreement or comprehension, or the side to side movement to indicate disagreement or incomprehension. Nods and jerks are typical movements involved to provide feedback (Cerrato & Skhiri, 2003).

Body Postures

Body postures are movements that spread throughout the body, visibly affecting all parts and usually involving a weight shift (Bartenieff & Davis, 1965), in contrast to gestures that are movements of only a part of the body. This type of NVC poses a more complex challenge than head movements because there is not yet a clear association between postures and their interpretation (Mota & Picard, 2003). However, for seated people there seems to be some consensus. When people are seated around a table –the most common situation for a group of students accomplishing a learning task –, the degree of orientation between the speaker's torso and the listener can show agreement, liking, and loyalty when aligning with him/her (Mehrabian, 1969) and, when not, a parallel orientation –with no inclination–, reveals neutral or passive moods (Richmond, McCroskey & Payne, 1991). In learning scenarios, correlation has been found between postures and the students' level of engagement

in the lesson (Goldin-Meadow, Wein, & Chang, 1992). There is also an association between patterns of postural behaviors and affective states, and the interest of a child working in a learning task (Mota & Picard, 2003).

Facial Expressions

Most approaches in CVEs for facial expressions use the widely accepted categorization of Ekman (1999) consistent of six universal basic emotions that can accurately be face expressed in all cultures: surprise, anger, fear, happiness, disgust/contempt and sadness. Through face, people reflect interpersonal attitudes, provide feedback to others' comments, and it is considered the primary source of information after speech (Knapp & Hall, 2007), whereas this information is mainly of emotional states (Ekman & Friesen, 1975). The ability to show emotions, empathy and understanding through facial expressions is central to ensure quality in a tutor-learner interaction (Cooper, Brna, & Martins, 2000). We believe that the most important feature of facial expressions in a task-oriented collaborative interaction is that they transmit understanding feedback to the partners. An additional difficulty is that it is very complex to transmit them precisely to the environment.

NVC Cues Related to the Collaborative Learning Indicators

Accordingly, the collaborative learning indicators to be inferred in relation to the NVC cues discussed could be as follows:

- The participation rates through A and B
- The focus on the task through A, B, C1, and D
- The making of shared grounding through A, C1 and C2, D, and F1
- Division of labor through asymmetry in A and/or B, lack of C2, and E

Where A is amount of talk; B is amount of manipulation in the shared workspace; C1 is gazes to the workspace; C2 is gazes among participants; D is deictic gestures; E is proxemic behaviors; F1 is agreement or disagreement head movements; F2 is feedback head movements; G is agreement and disagreement body postures; and H is feedback facial expressions.

And for the group process phases, –plan-implement-evaluate–, it could be useful not only to relate the NVC cues but to compare their patterns to distinguish the different phases. These patterns could be:

- Planning (Pl) = A (> Im or Ev), C1 (< Im) and C2 (> Im), D (< Ev), F2 (> Ev), G, and H
- Implementing (Im) = A (< Pl or Ev), B (> Pl or Ev), C1 (> Pl or Ev) and C2 (< Pl or Ev)
- Evaluating (Ev) = A (< Pl and A > Im), D (> Pl), F2 (< Pl), H (< Pl)

Where Pl is Planning; Im is Implementation; Ev is Evaluation; > means higher than in; and < is less than in.

The particular NVC cues to be selected will depend on the virtual environment conditions, the technology available to digitize them, and the kind of task that is expected to be accomplished. Our proposal for the data to be collected and how to interpret it requires empirical confirmation. In order to determine which NVC cues will be observed, the technology to digitize them and the task conditions will have to be considered. Hindmarsh, Fraser, Heath, Benford, and Greenhalgh, (1998) recommendations can be followed with that purpose: 1) identify all possible actions; 2) identify the target of each action; and 3) determine whether and how each action is represented on the source embodiment, target object(s) and in the surrounding environment. Also, make sure that these representations are consistent and distinguishable. In the next section we discuss how we are conducting its validation.

AN APPROACH FOR THE EMPIRICAL VALIDATION OF THE PROPOSAL

In order to get an empirical assessment of the usefulness of NVC analysis to support collaboration, and with the aim of developing a CVE application that allows the avatars to transmit useful NVC cues to foster collaborative interaction in a task accomplishment situation, we first conducted an exploratory study keeping in mind that the environment was meant to be desktop-based with no special equipment to digitize the NVC cues. Desktop collaborative virtual reality is an easy and affordable way to implement VR technology (Eastgate, 2001; Winn, 2002). The design of an application to support collaboration requires the understanding of real world collaboration in such a way that the computer tools can be explicit (Tromp, Steed & Wilsonn, 2003). The exploratory study aim was to determine the NVC indicators for a collaborative task accomplishment of use to monitor the participants' participation and the group process before taking them into a computer environment.

Exploratory Study

The exploratory study consisted in the analysis of several video-recorded sessions of a real life situation of three students seated around a table working on a simple task. The group goal was decided to be the accomplishment of a task where the implementation phase is particularly evident. The selected task consisted on placing a set of draw furniture on an apartment sketch. This task did not require any special participants' knowledge or background and there is no navigation since the group members are seated around the shared workspace on a table.

Method

One of the main factors affecting group performance is its size, a limiting condition of quantity and quality of communication that affects interpersonal relations between its members. There is no consensus about the number of members a group should have to be called small, but it has been observed that when a group is greater than five persons, group members complain of participation restrictions. On the other hand, the communication in groups of odd number tends to be more fluid, because there is no possibility of an equal division of opinions with the consequent fight for the power (Napier & Gershenfeld, 1989). Seven groups of triads were formed, in which 11 participants were male and 10 female, and each group had at least one male and one female.

Participants were voluntary computer science students, graduated students or teachers, taking care that teachers were not mixed with students because, for a collaborative situation, members of a group are expected to have symmetry of action, knowledge and status (Dillenbourg, 1999), and because homogeneity helps efficient communications. Besides, similar personal features lead to socio-emotional understandings more easily, which allows the group to liberate more energy on the task (Anzieu, 1965).

Another issue for group performance is leadership. In a collaborative learning scenario the leader's role is expected to be functional, that is, leadership functions can be performed by only one person but they also can be satisfied by different members of the group (Miles, 1959), which looks more appropriate for a real collaborative situation.

Although there is no guarantee that the expected participation rates will occur in a collaborative learning environment, the probability of getting an even participation was increased by taking into account the aforementioned conditions.

Participants were asked to put furniture as they thought it was appropriate with no special restriction like the number of persons living in the apartment or rooms designated to be a bathroom or the kitchen. Time to accomplish the task was not restricted either and the final result was not important although participants were not told. Participants were instructed not to ask for any kind of help.

The three team members can see each other and the shared workspace with no need of head movements or shift their body postures −see Figure 1. The digital video camera was located in front of the group to tape members' voices and movements.

Major actions observed for this task are: speaking, looking, pointing and grasping (Hindmarsh et al., 1998). The paralinguistic and NVC cues selected were then: the amount of talk, the shared workspace activity, gazes direction and deictic gestures. These NVC cues are consistent with the aforementioned ones when there is no navigation in the environment and they are retrieved through the keyboard and the mouse from the CVE.

Data Collection

As there was only one sound channel, each member's vocalizations were timed by watching the videos. For each person talking and silence were collected by the same person −pauses were taken as silence. Movements in the shared workspace were timed from the moment a person touched a piece of draw furniture until the moment that the person took the resting position he or she had before manipulation started. The number of times a member gazed to a group mate was also registered acquiring gaze frequency and gaze duration. Finally, the number of times each group member pointed was counted −all pointing gestures were made with the hands. Data was statistically manipulated with two points of view: 1) at individual level, to establish the NVC cues that are useful to get the degree of the participant's contribution to the task; and 2) at group level, to classify segments of the session as a plan, implement or evaluate phase

Figure 1. A group working on the task

Because methods to measure collaboration are usually applied to task outcomes (Ajiferuke, Burrell, & Tague, 1988; Egghe, 1991) and not while the task is being executed, and because human tutors base their judgments on the collaboration happening in a group of students working together on many complex and subtle factors (Soller, Jermann, Muehlenbrock, & Martínez, 2004), it was decided to use expert human tutors as the measure parameter for collaborative participation by using a post-session questionnaire. One tutor evaluator is a professor with 5 years of experience and currently a doctoral candidate in social science, and the other one is a 13 years experienced professor with a master in education.

The tutor evaluators were asked to order the participants of each group regarding their contribution to the task −all members could be at the same level. An arbitrary value of 3 points was given for the first level, 2 to the second one and only 1 point to the third level, if any. The evaluators were also asked to classify members as domineering or submissive; to domineering members an extra point was added and, on the contrary, to submissive members a point was taken. The last question they answered consisted on identifying members that needed to be encouraged to participate in a hypothetic future session; for those members an extra point was taken.

A significant 70% Pearson correlation, 2-tailed, at the level 0.01 between the two evaluators was found, which could indicate that disagreements were due to the ordinal type of the qualification. A third tutor was asked to evaluate disagreements and give a final score on them; this tutor evaluator is a 26 years experienced professor with a master in business management.

In order to find out distinctive NVC characteristics of each group process phase, videos were segmented and classified. It is difficult to establish the exact time in which the group change from one phase to other, but segments of interaction could be classified primarily as of planning, implementing or evaluating phases. After a detailed observation of the videos, it was determined that a practical segmentation to use was 20 seconds, during this time period groups usually did not change the kind of activity they were working on and phases usually last longer.

The initial categories used were the three principal group phases −planning, implementing and evaluating, but during the implementation two variants were found −division of labor or working together, and it was observed that sometimes evaluation required some implementation. Finally, the employed categories were:

1. Planning – during this phase the group decided how to accomplish the task, that is, who, when and how things were going to be done.
2. Implementation with group members' joint work.
3. Implementation with division of labor
4. Implementation due to evaluation; and
5. Evaluation – during this phase members took a look at what they had done, discussed some doubts, made comments, and sometimes decided to make changes. When changes were made the segment was classified as Implementation due to evaluation.
6. Other – for situations that could not be classified in the former categories.

Two external observers classified each twenty seconds video segment. They had no need of using the "other" category, and the agreement percentage was 90.73% with a 0.825 Kappa coefficient. These two characteristics were taken as good indicators of a proper category system. Observers were asked to get agreement on classification differences.

Results of the Individual Participation Analysis

Data was manipulated to compute group talk –when more than one participant was talking–, group activity –when more than one participant was working on the task, and floor maintenance –when only one person is speaking. Because not all sessions lasted the same, a weighted average was used to calculate time: of talk (TT), of floor maintenance (FT), of manipulation in the shared workspace (MT), of gazing a peer (GT), of being the target of a gaze (GRT); and the numbers of: utterances (UN), floor maintenance (FN), interventions in the shared workspace (IN), gazes directed to a peer (DG), gazes received from a peer (RG), mutual gazes (MG), hand pointing gestures (PN). Results are shown in Figure 2.

The model that better explains the variability found in tutors' evaluation at 80.9% is a regression model with the independent variables: time of talk (TT) and time of manipulation in the shared workspace (MT).

As shown in Figure 3, there is a positive significant correlation between the tutors' evaluation of a member (score) and the talking numbers of the member (TT, FT, FN). The tutors' evaluation of a member also has a statistically significant positive correlation –0.621– with the time a member spends working in the shared workspace (MT) and less significant correlations –at 0.05 level– with the number of times a member manipulates in the shared workspace (IN) –0.491– and the number of times that the member uses a pointing gesture (PN) –0.505.

There are also significant positive correlations between the member's talking features (TT, FT, FN) and the manipulation in the shared workspace (IN, MT) and the pointing gestures (PN). Gazes have a positive significant correlation only with pointing, probably to get feedback about the attention placed by the other members to what was being pointed.

Pointing was mainly used when making a proposition or a contra-proposition to designate the room or the furniture they were referring to –68% of the times, and in some other occasions to designate the room or the furniture involved in a question or as a reference to answer a question –27% of the times, the rest of the time they were making statements about what they were pointing at.

Despite these are laboratory groups, all participants were most of the time looking at the shared workspace and that seems to indicate that they were really interested in the task accomplishment. As anticipated, the participants gazed their partners mainly to get feedback, generally when they made a proposition that they thought could be rejected, when they were going to answer a question, or when they made a joke.

Figure 2. Weighted average participation rates

Group-Member	Score	TT	FT	MT	GT	GRT	UN	FN	IN	DG	RG	MG	PN
1-1	0	0.1694	0.1602	0.1806	0.1463	0.6856	0.1909	0.1942	0.2199	0.1463	0.5488	0.3571	0.2639
1-2	2	0.3668	0.3368	0.3316	0.2927	0.0983	0.3506	0.3512	0.3121	0.2927	0.1341	0.1429	0.2361
1-3	3	0.4637	0.5030	0.4878	0.5610	0.2162	0.4585	0.4545	0.4681	0.5610	0.3171	0.5000	0.5000
2-1	1	0.3000	0.3169	0.3090	0.2308	0.3262	0.3406	0.3391	0.3585	0.2308	0.3462	0.2143	0.3659
2-2	1	0.2211	0.1796	0.3970	0.2692	0.3047	0.2707	0.2696	0.283	0.2692	0.3077	0.4286	0.1951
2-3	3	0.4789	0.5035	0.2940	0.5000	0.3691	0.3886	0.3913	0.3585	0.5000	0.3462	0.3571	0.4390
3-1	2	0.4235	0.4431	0.3653	0.4681	0.5073	0.3553	0.3553	0.4133	0.4681	0.4167	0.4167	0.3235
3-2	0	0.1654	0.1167	0.2744	0.1277	0.0657	0.2271	0.2271	0.3333	0.1277	0.1042	0.0833	0.1176
3-3	3	0.4110	0.4402	0.3603	0.4043	0.4270	0.4176	0.4176	0.2533	0.4043	0.4792	0.5000	0.5588
4-1	2	0.3552	0.4565	0.2301	0.5110	0.2526	0.3289	0.3294	0.3406	0.5110	0.2569	0.3936	0.5303
4-2	3	0.4445	0.3744	0.4663	0.1851	0.4568	0.3574	0.3563	0.3986	0.1851	0.5083	0.3404	0.2879
4-3	1	0.2003	0.1690	0.3036	0.3039	0.2906	0.3138	0.3143	0.2609	0.3039	0.2348	0.2660	0.1818
5-1	1	0.2726	0.2548	0.2751	0.5702	0.3620	0.3018	0.3002	0.3296	0.5702	0.2936	0.4355	0.3516
5-2	2	0.2994	0.2815	0.2208	0.3021	0.2188	0.3307	0.3307	0.2235	0.3021	0.2596	0.3387	0.3736
5-3	4	0.4280	0.4638	0.5041	0.1277	0.4192	0.3676	0.3692	0.4469	0.1277	0.4468	0.2258	0.2747
6-1	2	0.3780	0.3528	0.2847	0.4016	0.4342	0.3623	0.3623	0.3282	0.4016	0.3898	0.4079	0.3556
6-2	4	0.4981	0.4606	0.4058	0.1220	0.3798	0.3784	0.3784	0.3664	0.1220	0.3386	0.1053	0.3630
6-3	0	0.1238	0.1866	0.3095	0.4764	0.1861	0.2593	0.2593	0.3053	0.4764	0.2717	0.4868	0.2815
7-1	2	0.1842	0.2027	0.3535	0.3671	0.2076	0.2591	0.2591	0.2336	0.3671	0.1899	0.3214	0.2105
7-2	2	0.2363	0.2966	0.3347	0.2911	0.3908	0.3051	0.3051	0.3659	0.2911	0.3544	0.3214	0.3509
7-3	3	0.5796	0.5008	0.3118	0.3418	0.4016	0.4358	0.4358	0.3293	0.3418	0.4557	0.3571	0.4386

Talking time (TT), floor time (FT), manipulation time (MT), gazes time (GT), received gazes time (GRT), numbers of utterances (NU), numbers of floor maintenance (FN), number of interventions in the shared workspace (IN), number of gazes directed (GD), number of received gazes (GR), number of mutual gazes (MG) and pointing gestures (PN).

Gazes and speech have a special characteristic: direction. Without knowing what group members are saying it is difficult to establish who they are talking to; it is not the same with gazes. By the observation of participants it is possible to know who they are gazing at. Figure 4 shows diagrams that indicate groups' gazes. Arrows are directed from the person that gazed to the person to whom that gaze was directed, and the percentages of gazes are annotated aside. The number in the circle is the qualification number given according to the tutors' evaluation as a contributor to task accomplishment; the numbers near the circles are the group and member identification numbers. The addition of gazes in both directions for each couple is the bigger number outside the two arrows with the % symbol. In the upright corner is the total number of gazes and the session duration. Here it can be noticed that in 6 of the 7 cases the person with the highest score for participation is part of the bi-directional channel with more gazes, and that the person with the lowest score participates in the bi-channel with the lowest number of gazes.

Given these observations, and in order to get a

Figure 3. Pearsons correlations

	PS	TT	FT	UN	FN	MT	IN	PN	GD	MG	GT
PS	-	0.855**	0.851**	0.804**	0.809**	0.621**	0.491*	0.505*			
TT	0.855**	-	0.936**	0.895**	0.900**	0.434*	0.554**	0.611**			
FT	0.851**	0.936**	-	0.889**	0.894**		0.614**	0.760**			
UN	0.804**	0.895**	0.889**	-	1.000**	0.494*	0.529*	0.697**			
FN	0.809**	0.900**	0.894**	1.000**	-	0.488**	0.525*	0.698**			
MT	0.621**	0.434*		0.494*	0.488**	-	0.664**				
IN	0.491*	0.554**	0.614**	0.529*	0.525*	0.664**	-				
PN	0.505*	0.611**	0.760**	0.697**	0.698**			-	0.539*	0.499*	0.560**

Participation score (PS), talking time (TT), floor time (FT), number of utterances (NU), number of floor maintenance (FN), manipulation time (MT), number of interventions in the shared workspace (IN), pointing times (PN), number of gazes directed (GD), number of mutual gazes (MG) and gaze time (GT).

** Correlation is significant at the 0.01 level (2-tailed).
* Correlation is significant at the 0.05 level (2-tailed).

Figure 4. Diagrams of group gazes

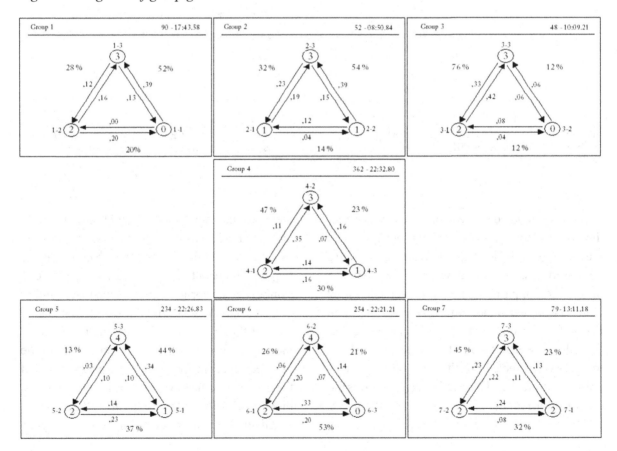

Figure 5. Boxplots of received and sent gazes

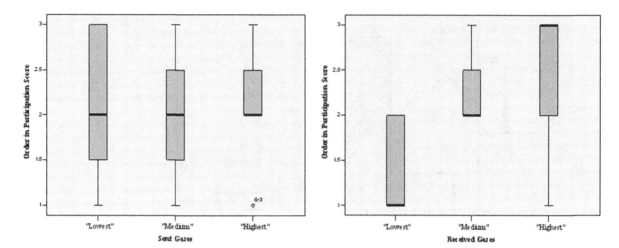

better comprehension of gazes, ordinal numbers were used to categorize participants as highest, medium or lowest regarding evaluation score —this is, the member with better evaluation, the member with lowest evaluation and the member in the middle, if any— and regarding received and sent gazes —the member that got/sent the highest number of gazes, the member who got/sent the lowest number of gazes and the member who is in the middle. Boxplots graphics were created with this data —see Figure 5— for received and sent gazes where it can be seen that the members that contributed the most to accomplish the task, according to evaluators, are also those who received more gazes, that the members with the lowest score for participation are those who received fewer gazes, and that also happens with members in the middle of both scales. Not so clear is the relation with the sent gazes, but it seems that the members with the lowest score regarding participation sent more gazes.

Results of the Group Process Phases Analysis

Since there is a statistically significant high positive correlation between frequencies and duration of talk, gazes and manipulation in the shared workspace, it was decided for simplicity to get just frequencies for these variables for each 20 seconds segment. However, for manipulation in the shared workspace, duration was also acquired because sometimes the sum of manipulation lasted more than one period. As this part of the analysis considers the group as a whole, it was the addition of the three group members' variables what was used for the data analysis.

356 segments were classified as follows: 49 as planning, 230 as implementing with joint work —referred to as Implementation, 42 as implementing with division of labor, 23 as implementing due to evaluation, and 12 as evaluation periods, Figure 6 shows these frequencies. Since the goal of the proposed task did not require a lot of strategic planning, it seems reasonable that most of the time the participants were dedicated to task execution.

Cross-tabulation tables were used to analyze information. The performed Chi-square test is statistically significant, indicating that segment classification is related to the variables —utterances, pointing, gaze, and manipulation frequencies, and manipulation duration. As not all the variables have a normal distribution for all the

Figure 6. Segments' classification frequencies

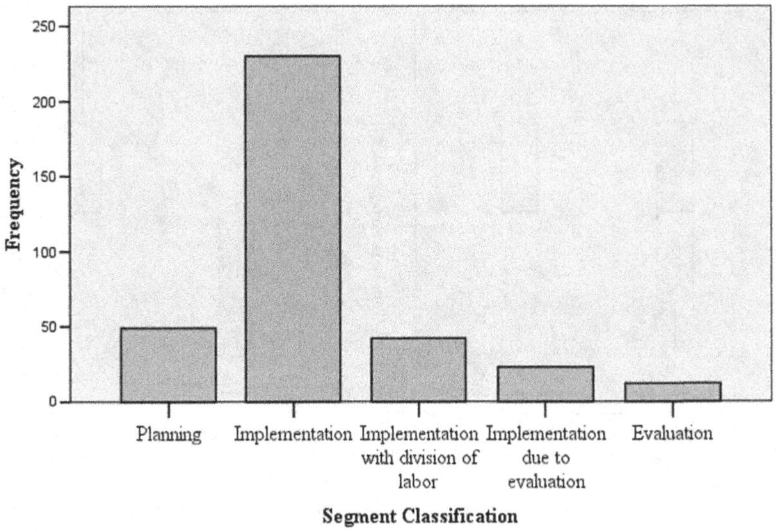

segment categories the median was selected as central tendency measure. The results are shown in Figure 7.

As expected, planning segments have the highest numbers of utterances, pointing and gaze exchange, but interventions in the shared workspace are scarce. During implementation the number of utterances is still high; pointing and gazes slow down but here the work or manipulation in the shared workspace is representatively different from planning, the difference is especially

evident in a growing time of manipulation. In division of labor there is the lowest number of utterances, no pointing or gazes, and the addition of the three members' time of manipulation on the shared workspace goes above the time of the segment, indicating that for sure more than one person was manipulating the shared workspace at the same time. During implementation due to evaluation there is a high number of utterances, there is a good number of pointing and gazes, and the number and time of manipulation in the shared

Figure 7. Variable medians by segment classification

Segment Classification	Utterances	Pointing	Gazes	Number of Manipulation	Duration of Manipulation
1 - Planning	10	3	5	1	00:02.0
2.- Implementation	9	1	1	3	00:19.0
3.- Implementation with division of labor	6	0	0	5	00:40.0
4.- Implementation due to evaluation	8	2	2	2	00:07.0
5.- Evaluation	7	1	4	0.5	00:01.0

Figure 8. Banded variable medians by segment classification

Segment Classification	Utterances	Pointing	Gazes	Number of Manipulation	Duration of Manipulation
1 - Planning	10-12	2-3	5-9	0-1	1-21 segs.
2.- Implementation	7-9	1	1-4	2-3	1-21 segs.
3.- Implementation with division of labor	7-9	1	0	3-5	36 segs. >
4.- Implementation due to evaluation	7-9	2-3	1-4	2-3	1-21 segs.
5.- Evaluation	7-9	1	1-7	0-1	0-10 segs.

workspace goes up indicating implementation. In the evaluation periods gazes are representative with a very low number of manipulations and a median of only one second of manipulation in the shared workspace.

These differences between categories are better highlighted if variables are banded as shown in Figure 8; the cut points are at the mean and one standard deviation. The planning category is the one with the highest number of utterances and gazes. When there is division of labor there are no gazes and manipulation is the highest, on the contrary, evaluation can be distinguished by very low manipulation. Implementation and implementation due to evaluation can be distinguished by the lowest number of pointing gestures while implementing.

The distinction of these group process features allows determining whether a group is having a proper distribution of them. For example, as we can see in Figure 9, it comes to our attention that Group 1 did not evaluate what they were doing at any time, or that in Group 2 members spent most of the time working on their own although they made more planning than other groups. Even if these features may depend on the kind of task goal, there is the possibility of performance comparisons among participant groups in order to generate a reference pattern for computer-based evaluation.

Experimental Application

Based on this preliminary study, the CoVETO (Collaborative Virtual Environment – Task Oriented), a desktop-based application –see Peña, de Antonio, Rodríguez, and Jacobo (2008) for details– is now under evaluation. CoVETO supports three geographically distant people to interact within a common scenario to work in a collaborative task; each user has an avatar. The same main actions to accomplish the task as in the real world exploratory study were implemented. The application permits object manipulation and pointing in the shared workspace; it allows oral communication and includes avatars' head movements that change the user's point of view from the shared workspace to one or the other two peers.

The awareness adapted representation for the NVC cues within the environment is as follows –see Figure 10: to point an object in the shared workspace, a colored arrow associated to the user is placed above it; to display when an object is grabbed, it is attached to the same arrow that is used to point it; when a user is talking, a dialogue globe appears above its avatar's head to distinguish who is currently talking; there are four possible head movements associated to a view, one directed to the shared workspace, one directed to each of

Figure 9. Segments' classification frequencies by group

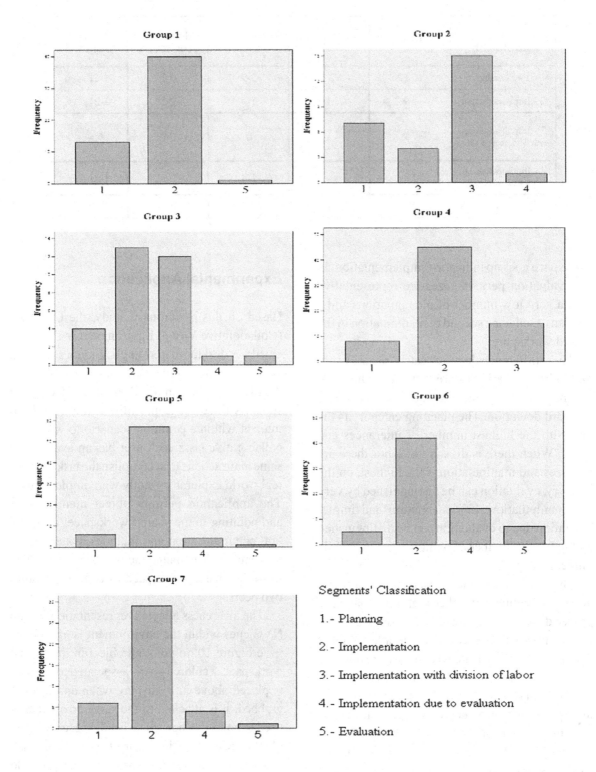

Segments' Classification

1.- Planning

2.- Implementation

3.- Implementation with division of labor

4.- Implementation due to evaluation

5.- Evaluation

Figure 10. Representation of NVC cues

the other two peers, and one directed between the other two partners that allows gazing both at the same time.

The environment is instrumented to register in text files the four NVC aforementioned cues: time of talk and number of utterances, time and the number of object manipulation in the shared workspace, the number of pointing at the shared workspace, and the number and the direction of gazes. This data can be further analyzed to infer the previously identified indicators of effective collaborative learning.

CONCLUSION

In a collaborative learning situation interaction is expected to occur, but the degree of interweaving between reasoning and interaction is difficult to define operationally. The environment then should increase the probabilities for collaborative interactions to occur (Dillenbourg, 1999). Our proposal is

to foster collaborative interaction via the analysis of NVC cues transmitted by the students' avatars in CVE learning scenarios. Avatars' NVC is currently a forefront topic for 3D CVEs, as to create more believable autonomous agent avatars as for the digitizing, across various and new devices, of the users' NVC behaviors. The researchers concern for NVC have been lately increasing (Chittaro & Ran, 2007; Schroeder, 2007).

In an effective learning task situation, we expect students to create shared plans, make the implementation and the continuous evaluation of both, plans and implementation. We propose that some NVC cues can be useful in determining if these expected conditions are taking place within the CVE. Amount of talk and manipulation in the shared workspace –two NVC cues that can be retrieved from any CVE, even desktop-based, can be used to infer participation rates, and some patterns formed by their combination can provide information about the problem solving strategy and division of labor (Jermann, 2004). Gazes are useful to follow the student's focus of attention, and deictic gestures can be a tool to infer the topic of the discourse. Observation of Proxemics can be used to determine both division of labor and subgroups formation. Some semantic head movements could be used, among other NVC cues, to establish agreement or comprehension, and disagreement or incomprehension. Body postures could also be used to study agreement or disagreement, and the students' interest on the current task. Patterns of the combination of NVC cues can be used to explain if and when the plan-implement-evaluate cycle is taking place. These are some of the effective collaborative learning features that can be inferred based on NVC behaviors.

The selected NVC cues can be retrieved without regard to the learning domain, which makes them an appropriate approach for reusability. On the other hand, NVC retrieval combined with other approaches, for example, those that interpret the users' discourse or those that interpret the movements in the shared workspace, certainly will give more accurate insights about computer mediated collaboration. Clearly, the advantages of the proposed approach should grow with the complexity and immersion of the VE. We believe this is an important and promising approximation to the possibility of automatically evaluating collaborative interaction in learning situations and fostering it in situations when the inferred effective collaborative learning indicators are taking undesirable values. However, some work is still needed in order to corroborate the potential of the proposed approach.

ACKNOWLEDGMENT

Thanks to CONACyT Scholarship Program of Mexico for funding Adriana Peña's Ph.D. and the Spanish Ministry of Education's funding through the project TIN2006-15202-C03-01.

REFERENCES

Ajiferuke, I., Burrell, Q., & Tague, J. (1988). Collaboration coefficient: A single measure of the degree of collaboration in research. *Scientometrics*, *14*(5-6), 421–433. doi:10.1007/BF02017100

Allwood, J., Grönqvist, L., Ahlsén, E., & Gunnarsson, M. (2002). Annotations and tools for an activity based spoken language corpus. In *Proceedings of the 2nd SIGdial Workshop on Discourse and Dialogue*, Aalborg, Denmark.

Anzieu, D. (1965). Les communications intragroup. In F. A. Geldard et al., (Eds.), *Communications processes*. London: Pergamon Press.

Argyle, M. (1972). Non-verbal communication in human social interaction. In R. A. Hinde (Ed.), *Non-verbal communication* (pp. 243-269). Cambridge, UK: University Press.

Argyle, M. (1988). *Bodily communication* (2nd ed.). London: Methuen & Co. Ltd.

Argyle, M., & Dean, J. (1965). Eye contact, distance, and affiliation. *Sociometry*, *28*(3), 289–304. doi:10.2307/2786027

Bailenson, J., Blascovich, J., Beall, A. C., & Loomis, J. (2003). Interpersonal distance in immersive virtual environments. *Personality and Social Psychology Bulletin*, *29*, 819–833. doi:10.1177/0146167203029007002

Bales, R. F. (1970). *Personality and interpersonal behavior*. New York: Holt.

Barros, B., & Verdejo, M. (2000). Analysing student interaction processes in order to improve collaboration. The DEGREE approach. *International Journal of Artificial Intelligence in Education*, *11*, 221–241.

Bartenieff, I., & Davis, M. A. (1965). Effort-shape analysis of movement: The unity of expression and function. In M. Davis (Ed.), *Research approaches to movement and personality*. New York: Arno Press Inc.

Birdwhistell, R. (1970). *Kinesics and context - essays on body motion communication*. Philadephia: University of Pennsylvania Press.

Brdiczka, O., Maisonnasse, J., & Reignier, P. (2005). Automatic detection of interaction groups. In *Proceedings of the 7th International Conference on Multimodal Interfaces (ICMI)*, Trento, Italy.

Capin, T. K., Pandzic, I. S., Thalmann, N. M., & Thalmann, D. (1997). Realistic avatars and autonomous virtual humans in VLNET networked virtual environments. In *Proceedings of From Desktop to Webtop: Virtual Environments on the Internet, WWW and Networks, International Conference,* Bradford, UK.

Cerrato, L., & Skhiri, M. (2003). Analysis and measurement of head movements signalling feedback in face-to-face human dialogues. In P., Paggio, K., Jokinen, & A., Jönsson (Eds.), *Proceedings of the First Nordic Symposium on Multimodal Communication, 9,* 43-52.

Chittaro, L., & Rano, R. (2007). Web3D technologies in learning, education and training. *Computers & Education, 49,* 3–18. doi:10.1016/j.compedu.2005.06.002

Clark, H. H., & Brennan, S. E. (1991). Grounding in communication. In L. B. Resnick, J. M. Levine, & S. D. Teasley (Eds.), *Perspectives on socially shared cognition* (pp. 127-149). Washington, DC: American Psychological Association.

Constantino-Gonzales, M. A., & Suthers, D. (2001). Coaching collaboration by comparing solutions and tracking participation. In P. Dillenbourg, A. Eurelings, & K. Hakkarainen (Eds.), *European Perspectives on Computer-Supported Collaborative Learning, Proceedings of the First European Conference on Computer-Supported Collaborative Learning* (pp. 173-180). Maastricht, the Netherlands: Universiteit Maastricht.

Cooper, B., Brna, P., & Martins, A. (2000). Effective affective in intelligent systems – building on evidence of empathy in teaching and learning. In A., Paiva (Ed.), *Affective interactions: Towards a new generation of computer interfaces.* London: Springer Verlag.

Dabbs, J. M., & Ruback, R. B. (1987). Dimensions of group process: Amount and structure of vocal interaction. *Advances in Experimental Social Psychology, 20,* 123–165. doi:10.1016/S0065-2601(08)60413-X

DeVito, J. A., & Hecht, M. L. (1990). *The nonverbal communication reader*. Prospect Heights, IL: Waveland.

Dillenbourg, P. (1999). What do you mean by collaborative learning? In P. Dillenbourg, (Ed.), *Collaborative-learning: Cognitive and computational approaches* (pp. 1-19). Oxford, UK: Elsevier.

Eastgate, R. (2001). *The structured development of virtual environments: Enhancing functionality and interactivity.* Unpublished doctoral dissertation, University of York. Retrieved, May 2008, from http://www.virart.nott.ac.uk/RMEPhD2001.pdf

Efron, D. (1941). *Gesture and environment.* New York: King's Crown Press.

Egghe, L. (1991). Theory of collaboration and collaborative measures. *Information Processing & Management, 27*(2-3), 177–202. doi:10.1016/0306-4573(91)90048-Q

Ekman, P. (1999). Facial expressions. In T. Dalgleish, & M. Power (Eds.), *Handbook of cognition and emotion*. New York: Wiley & Sons.

Ekman, P., & Friesen, W. (1969). The repertoire of nonverbal behavior: Categories, origins, usage, and coding. *Semiotica, 1*, 49–98.

Ekman, P., & Friesen, W. (1975). *Unmasking the face*. NJ: Prentice Hall.

Fabri, M., & Hobbs, D. (1998). What you see is what I mean: Virtual encounters in distance learning systems. In *Proceeding of the 4th EATA International Conference on Networking Entities, (NETIES98): Networking for the Millennium*, West Yorkshire, UK.

Fabri, M., Moore, D. J., & Hobbs, D. J. (2004). Mediating the expression of emotion in educational collaborative virtual environments: An experimental study. *International Journal of Virtual Reality, 7*(2), 66–81. doi:10.1007/s10055-003-0116-7

Fischer, F., Bruhn, J., Gräsel, C., & Mandl, H. (1998). *Strukturangebote für die gemeinsame wissenskonstruktion beim kooperativen lernen*. Forschungsbericht, Nr.: Universität München, Lehrstuhl f. Empirische Pädagogik und Pädagogische Psychologie.

Ford, C. E. (1999). Collaborative construction of task activity: Coordinating multiple resources in a high school physics lab. *Research on Language and Social Interaction, 32*, 369–408. doi:10.1207/S15327973rls3204_3

Gergle, D., Kraut, R. E., & Fussell, S. R. (2004). Action as language in a shared visual space. In *Proceedings of ACM Conference on Computer Supported Cooperative Work (CSCW)*, (pp. 487-496). New York: ACM Press.

Givens, D. (2005). *Nonverbal dictionary of gestures, signs & body language cues online*. Spokane, WA: Center for Nonverbal Studies Press. Retrieved April 2008, from http://members.aol.com/nonverbal2/diction1.htm

Goldin-Meadow, S., Wein, D., & Chang, C. (1992). Assessing knowledge through gesture: Using children's hands to read their minds. *Cognition and Instruction, 9*(3), 201–219. doi:10.1207/s1532690xci0903_2

Guye-Vuillème, A., Capin, T. K., Pandzic, I. S., Thalmann, N. M., & Thalmann, D. (1998). Nonverbal communication interface for collaborative virtual environments. In D. Snowdon & E. Churchill (Eds.), *Proceedings of the Collaborative Virtual Environments* (pp. 105-112). Manchester, UK: University of Manchester.

Hall, E. T. (1959). *The silent language*. Greenwich, CT: Fawcett Publications.

Heldal, I. (2007). The impact of social interaction on usability for distributed virtual environments. *International Journal of Virtual Reality, 6*(3), 45–54.

Heylen, D. (2005). *Challenges ahead: Head movements and other social acts in conversations*. AISB - Social Presence Cues Symposium.

Hindmarsh, J., Fraser, M., Heath, C., Benford, S., & Greenhalgh, C. (1998). Fragmented interaction: Establishing mutual orientation in virtual environments. In *Proceedings of the ACM conference on Computer supported cooperative work (CSCW '98)* (pp. 217-226). New York: ACM Press.

Ieronutti, L., & Chittaro, L. (2007). Employing virtual humans for education and training in X3D/VRML worlds. *Computers & Education, 49*(1), 93–109. doi:10.1016/j.compedu.2005.06.007

Imai, T., Qui, Z., Behara, S., Tachi, S., Aoyama, T., Johnson, A., & Leigh, J. (2000). Overcoming time-zone differences and time management problem with tele-immersion. In *Proceedings of INET*, Yokohama, Japan.

Jermann, P. (2004). *Computer support for interaction regulation in collaborative problem-solving.* Unpublished doctoral dissertation, University of Genéva, Genéva, Switzerland. Retrieved, November 2005, from http://craftsrv1.epfl.ch/~colin/thesis-jermann.pdf

Jermann, P., Soller, A., & Muehlenbrock, M. (2001). From mirroring to guiding: A review of state of the art technology for supporting collaborative learning. In *Proceedings of the European Conference on Computer Supported Collaborative Learning,* Maastricht, The Netherlands.

Johnson, A., & Leigh, J. (2001). Tele-immersive collaboration in the CAVE research network. In E. F. Churchill, D. N. Snowdon, & A. J. Munro (Eds.), *Collaborative virtual environments: Digital places and spaces for interaction* (pp. 225-243). Berlin, Germany: Springer.

Johnson, D., Johnson, R., & Holubec, E. J. (1990). *Circles of learning: Cooperation in the classroom* (3rd ed.). Edina, MN: Interaction Book Company.

Kleinke, C. (1986). Gaze and eye contact: A research review. *Psychological Bulletin, 100,* 78–100. doi:10.1037/0033-2909.100.1.78

Knapp, M. L., & Hall, J. A. (2007). *Nonverbal communication in human interaction* (5th ed.). Florence, KY: Thomas Learning.

Knutson, A. L. (1960). Quiet and vocal groups. *Sociometry, 23,* 36–49. doi:10.2307/2786136

Ladd, R. D. (1996). *Intonational phonology.* Cambridge, UK: Cambridge University Press.

Martínez, A. (2003). *A model and a method for computational support for CSCL evaluation* (in Spanish). Unpublished doctoral dissertation, University of Valladolid, Valladolid. Retrieved, November 2005, from http://www.infor.uva.es/~amartine/research/phd/tesis_amartine.pdf

McCowan, I., Gatica-Perez, D., Bengio, S., Lathoud, G., Barnard, M., & Zhang, D. (2005). Automatic analysis of multimodal group actions in meetings. *IEEE Transactions on Pattern Analysis and Machine Intelligence, 27*(3), 305–317. doi:10.1109/TPAMI.2005.49

Mehrabian, A. (1969). Significance of posture and position in the communication of attitude and status relationships. *Psychological Bulletin, 71*(5), 359–372. doi:10.1037/h0027349

Miles, M. (1959). *Learning to work in groups.* New York: Columbia University Press.

Morris, D., Collett, P., Marsh, P., & O'Shaughnessy, M. (1979). *Gestures, their origin and distribution.* London: Jonathan Cape Ltd.

Mota, S., & Picard, R. W. (2003). Automated posture analysis for detecting learner's interest level. In *Proceedings of the Workshop on Computer Vision and Pattern Recognition for Human-Computer Interaction, (CVPR, HCI).* Madison, WI: IEEE Computer Society.

Mühlenbrock, M. (2004). Shared workspaces: Analyzing user activity and group interaction. In H. U. Hoppe, M. Ikeda, H. Ogata, & F. Hesse (Eds.), *New technologies for collaborative learning, computer-supported collaborative learning series.* Amsterdam: Kluwer.

Napier, R. W., & Gershenfeld, M. K. (1989). *Groups: Theory and experience* (4th ed.). Boston: Houghton Mifflin.

Nortfleet, B. (1948). Interpresonal relations and group productivity. *The Journal of Social Issues, 2,* 66–69.

Padilha, E., & Carletta, J. (2003). Nonverbal behaviours improving a simulation of small group discussion. In *Proceedings of the 1st Nordic Symposium on Multimodal Communications*, Copenhagen, Denmark (pp. 93-105)

Park, K., & Kenyon, R. (1999). Effects of network characteristics on human performance in a collaborative virtual environment. In *Proceedings of the IEEE VR*, Houston, TX.

Park, K., Leigh, J., Johnson, A., Carter, B., Brody, J., & Sosnoski, J. (2001). Distance learning classroom using virtual Harlem. In *Proceedings of the VSMM*, Berkeley, CA.

Parkhurst, D., Law, K., & Niebur, E. (2002). Modeling the role of salience in the allocation of overt visual attention. *Vision Research, 42*, 107–123. doi:10.1016/S0042-6989(01)00250-4

Patterson, M. L. (1982). A sequential functional model of nonverbal exchange. *Psychological Review, 89*, 231–249. doi:10.1037/0033-295X.89.3.231

Peña, A., de Antonio, A., Rodríguez, F. I., & Jacobo, J. O. (2008). CoVETO: Collaborative virtual environment with interaction indicators based on nonverbal communication cues. In *Proceedings of the Workshop of Intelligent Virtual Environments (WIVE) of the Iberamia*, Lisbon, Portugal.

Resnick, L. B. (1991). Shared cognition: Thinking as social practice. In. L. Resnick, J. Levine, & S. Teasley (Eds.), *Perspectives on socially shared cognition* (pp. 1-22). Hyattsville, MD: American Psychological Association.

Richmond, V. P., McCroskey, J. C., & Payne, S. K. (1991). *Nonverbal behavior in interpersonal relations* (2nd ed.). Englewood Cliffs, NJ: Prentice Hall.

Roschelle, J., & Teasley, S. D. (1995). Construction of shared knowledge in collaborative problem solving. In C. O'Malley (Ed.), *Computer-supported collaborative learning*. New York: Springer-Verlag.

Roth, W. M. (2001). Gestures: Their role in teaching and learning. *Review of Educational Research, 71*, 365–392. doi:10.3102/00346543071003365

Scheflen, A. E. (1964). The significance of posture in communication systems. *Psychiatry, 27*, 316–331.

Schroeder, R. (2007). An overview of ethical and social issues in shared virtual environments. *Futures, 39*(6), 704–717. doi:10.1016/j.futures.2006.11.009

Sims, E. M., & Pike, W. Y. (2007). Reusable, lifelike virtual humans for mentoring and role-playing. *Computers & Education, 49*(1), 75–92. doi:10.1016/j.compedu.2005.06.006

Soller, A. (2001). Supporting social interaction in an intelligent collaborative learning system. *International Journal of Artificial Intelligence in Education, 12*, 40–62.

Soller, A., Jermann, P., Muehlenbrock, M., & Martínez, M. (2004). Designing computational models of collaborative learning interaction: Introduction to the workshop proceedings. In *Proceedings of the 2nd International Workshop on Designing Computational Models of Collaborative Learning Interaction at ITS*, Maceió, Brazil.

Soller, A., Lesgold, A., Linton, F., & Goodman, B. (1999). What makes peer interaction effective? Modeling effective communication in an intelligent CSCL. In *Proceedings of the AAAI Fall Symposium on Psychological Models of Communication in Collaborative Systems*, Cape Cod, MA.

Stein, R. T., & Heller, T. (1979). An empirical analysis of the correlations between leadership status and participation rates reported in the literature. *Journal of Personality and Social Psychology, 37*, 1993–2002. doi:10.1037/0022-3514.37.11.1993

Suthers, D. D., & Hundhausen, C. D. (2001). Learning by constructing collaborative representations: An empirical comparison of three alternatives. In P. Dillenbourg, A. Eurelings, & K. Hakkarainen (Eds.), *European Perspectives on Computer-Supported Collaborative Learning, Proceedings of the First European Conference on Computer-Supported Collaborative Learning* (pp. 577-584). Maastrict, The Netherlands: Universiteit Maastricht.

Tromp, J., Steed, A., & Wilsonn, J. (2003). Systematic usability evaluation and design issues for collaborative virtual environments. *Presence (Cambridge, Mass.), 12*(3), 241–267. doi:10.1162/105474603765879512

Tromp, J. G. (1995). Presence, tele-presence and immersion: The cognitive factors of embodiment and interaction in virtual environments. In *Proceedings of Conference of the FIVE Group, Framework for Immersive Virtual Environments*, London, UK.

Vieira, A. C., Teixeira, L., Timóteo, A., Tedesco, P., & Barros, F. A. (2004). Analyzing on-line collaborative dialogues: The OXEnTCHÊ-Chat. In J. C. Lester, R. M. Vicari, & F. Paraguaçu (Eds.), *Proceedings of the 7th International Conference on Intelligent Tutoring Systems*, Maceiò, Alagoas, Brazil (pp. 315-324).

Winn, W. D. (2002). Current trends in educational technology research: The study of learning environments. *Educational Psychology Review, 14*(3), 331–351. doi:10.1023/A:1016068530070

Chapter 11
Improvement of Self-Assessment Effectiveness by Activity Monitoring and Analysis

Dumitru Dan Burdescu
University of Craiova, Romania

Marian Cristian Mihăescu
University of Craiova, Romania

ABSTRACT

Self-assessment is one of the crucial activities within e-learning environments that provide learners with feedback regarding their level of accumulated knowledge. From this point of view, the authors think that guidance of learners in self-assessment activity must be an important goal of e-learning environment developers. The scope of the chapter is to present a recommender software system that runs along the e-learning platform. The recommender software system improves the effectiveness of self-assessment activities. The activities performed by learners represent the input data and the machine learning algorithms are used within the business logic of the recommender software system that runs along the e-learning platform. The output of the recommender software system is represented by advice given to learners in order to improve the effectiveness of self-assessment process. The methodology for obtaining improvement of self-assessment is based on embedding knowledge management into the business logic of the e-learning platform. Naive Bayes Classifier is used as machine learning algorithm for obtaining the resources (e.g., questions, chapters, and concepts) that need to be further accessed by learners. The analysis is accomplished for disciplines that are well structured according to a concept map. The input data set for the recommender software system is represented by student activities that are monitored within Tesys e-learning platform. This platform has been designed and implemented within Multimedia Applications Development Research Center at Software Engineering Department, University of Craiova. Monitoring student activities is accomplished through various techniques like creating log files or adding records into a table from a database. The logging facilities are embedded in the business logic of the e-learning platform. The e-learning platform is based on a software development framework that uses only open source software. The software architecture of the e-learning platform is based on MVC (model-view-controller) model that ensures the independence between the model (represented by MySQL

DOI: 10.4018/978-1-60566-786-7.ch011

database), the controller (represented by the business logic of the platform implemented in Java) and the view (represented by WebMacro which is a 100% Java open-source template language).

INTRODUCTION

At international scale there is a tremendous pre-occupation regarding e-Learning domain due to huge interest in e-Learning activities (Blackboard, WebCT, ATutor, Moodle, 2008). Generally, existing platforms have as main goal the efficient management of activities performed by all involved parties: management, secretaries, professors and learners. In this light, existing platforms implement for involved parties complex functionalities that provide a good activity flow. Any e-Learning may be regarded as a collaborating system that integrates specific implemented functionalities for involved parties. Regardless the collaborating system, for each of the four main actors there exist some common implemented functionality. In general, for secretaries there are implemented functionalities regarding the general setup of environment, like sections, professors, disciplines, students and other settings like year's structure. For professors there are implemented functionalities regarding the management of assigned disciplines. Students are the main beneficiaries of the environment. They may follow courses, communicate, self –assess and take final exams.

The Tesys e-Learning platform (Burdescu, Mihaescu, 2006) represents a collaborative environment in which all involved parties (e.g. secretaries, professors, students and administrators) accomplish their duties. The administrator, with the help of secretaries and professors are responsible for managing the environment in which the students will be through-out the e-Learning process. The platform has built in capability of monitoring and recording user's activity. The activity represents valuable data since it is the raw data for the machine learning and modeling process. The activity of each learner is seen as a

sequence of sessions. A session starts when the student logs in and finishes when the student logs out. Under these circumstances, a sequence of actions makes up a session.

User's activity is monitored and recoded through a dedicated module implemented within the business logic of the platform. This facility was taken into consideration since the design phase of the platform. In was one of the requirements that the platform to be able to record user's performed actions with fine granularity.

The paper presents a recommender software system that selects the resource(s) that need further attention of learner. Guiding the learning may have important benefits regarding the improvement of self-assessment effectiveness. The scope of the recommender system is making the learner obtain the maximum knowledge from the self-assessment activity. This is accomplished by the classifier according with all previous learners's performed activity. The activity is represented by the number of answers to questions regarding that concept, the average result of answered questions and the final result at the discipline. Each filtered resource is to be recommended or not. There will be defined the values each feature may have.

Following the structure of the discipline (chapters, concepts, and concepts maps) the professor creates a set of quizzes that may be accessed by the learner. Self-assessment activity is represented by taking a certain number of on-line quizzes. The scope of the recommender system is to guide the student to the resource he/she needs to access in order to make learning progress to be an effective one. The objective measure of accumulated knowledge is obtained from self-assessment activity. We think that this activity must be coordinated along with other learning activities. This coordination represents the means by which the recommender system makes the self-assessment as effective as possible.

The whole process is represented by an analysis procedure that has as input data representing the performed activities by learners. As learning algorithm it was employed Naive Bayes classifier (Mitchell, 1997). The classifier will predict the resources that the learner needs to access and study for improving his proficiency regarding the studied subject.

Regarding the design of software architecture of Tesys e-Learning platform many issues appear because it contains a mixture of data access code, business logic code, and presentation code. Such applications are difficult to maintain, because interdependencies between all of the components cause strong ripple effects whenever a change is made anywhere. The Model-View-Controller (Krasner, Pope, 1998) (MVC for short) design pattern solves these problems by decoupling data access, business logic, and data presentation and user interaction.

RELATED WORK

A method of enhancing the quality of services offered by e-Learning platforms is the transformation of the environment into an adaptive one (Brusilovsky, 1996, 2001). An example of such system is AHA! (deBra, 2003). AHA! system implements a default adaptation technique by hiding less relevant hyper lines. Another research direction courses web-usage-based mining (Srivastava, 2000). In this direction there are major contributions regarding preprocessing and preparing of data (Cooley, 1999), recommendation of actions in e-Learning according performed actions (Zaiane, 2001, 2002).

There were proposed models for assisting evaluation of learner's in e-Learning systems (Guo, 2004). Implementing many of these research directions has been done using data mining algorithms (Abramovicz, 2004). There were employed

clustering algorithms (Han and Camber, 2001), algorithms for obtaining sequential models (Srikant, Agrawal, 1996), and algorithms for association rule creation (Tan, et. al. 2004; Agrawal, and Srikant, 1994). These research directions concretized into non invasive recommendation systems for learners (Lin, Alvarez, 2002; Spertus, Stein, 1998; Burdescu, Mihaescu, 2007). Such system is also employed for obtaining recommendations regarding the materials that need to be studied by learners (Tang, Mccalla, 2003). Implementation of such facilities has been accomplished by usage of dedicated pre-processing software fools that offer the possibility of automatization of performed operations (Marquardt, 2004).

Ausubel et. al. (1978) made the very important distinction between rote learning and meaningful learning. Meaningful learning requires three conditions: 1. The material to be learned must be conceptually clear and presented with language and examples relatable to the learner's prior knowledge. Concept maps can be helpful to meet this condition, both by identifying large general concepts held by the leaner prior to instruction of more specific concepts, and by assisting in the sequencing of learning tasks though progressively more explicit knowledge that can be anchored into developing conceptual frameworks; 2. The learner must possess relevant prior knowledge. This condition can be met after age 3 for virtually any domain of subject matter, but it is necessary to be careful and explicit in building concept frameworks if one hopes to present detailed specific knowledge in any field in subsequent lessons. We see, therefore, that conditions (1) and (2) are interrelated and both are important; 3. The learner must choose to learn meaningfully. The one condition over which the teacher or mentor has only indirect control is the motivation of students to choose to learn by attempting to incorporate new meanings into their prior knowledge, rather than simply memorizing concept definitions or propositional statements or computational procedures. The indirect control over this choice is primarily in instructional strategies used and the evaluation strategies used. Instructional strategies that emphasize relating new knowledge to the learner's existing knowledge foster meaningful learning. Evaluation strategies that encourage learners to relate ideas they possess with new ideas also encourage meaningful learning. Typical objective tests seldom require more than rote learning (Holden, 1992).

CONCEPT MAPS

The need for having well structured disciplines led to usage of concept maps. Concept maps are a result of Novak and Gowin's (Novak, Gowin, 1984) research into human learning and knowledge construction. Novak (Novak, 1977) proposed that the primary elements of knowledge are concepts and relationships between concepts are propositions. Novak (Novak, 1998) defined concepts as "perceived regularities in events or objects, or records of events or objects, designated by a label". Propositions consist of two or more concept labels connected by a linking relationship that forms a semantic unit. Concept maps are a graphical two-dimensional display of concepts (usually represented within boxes or circles), connected by directed arcs encoding brief relationships (linking phrases) between pairs of concepts forming propositions. The simplest concept map consists of two nodes connected by an arc representing a simple sentence such as 'flower is red,' but they can also become quite intricate.

One of the powerful uses of concept maps is not only as a learning tool but also as an evaluation tool, thus encouraging students to use meaningful-mode learning patterns (Mintzes, 2000; Novak, 1990; Novak, Gowin, 1984). Concept maps are also effective in identifying both valid and invalid ideas held by students, and this will be discussed further in another section. They can be as effective as more time-consuming clinical interviews for identifying the relevant knowledge a learner

possesses before or after instruction (Edwards, Fraser, 1983).

Concept mapping may be used as a tool for understanding, collaborating, validating, and integrating curriculum content that is designed to develop specific competencies. Concept mapping, a tool originally developed to facilitate student learning by organizing key and supporting concepts into visual frameworks, can also facilitate communication among faculty and administrators about curricular structures, complex cognitive frameworks, and competency-based learning outcomes. To validate the relationships among the competencies articulated by specialized accrediting agencies, certification boards, and professional associations, faculty may find the concept mapping tool beneficial in illustrating relationships among, approaches to, and compliance with competencies (McDaniel, et. al. 1988).

Researchers suggest that learning can be enhanced by hands-on activities in which learners actively identify the attributes of concepts. For example, Harpaz, Balik, and Ehrenfeld (2004) recently demonstrated the efficacy of concept mapping in encouraging students to think independently and to find connections among concepts. Concept maps are powerful tools for helping learners identify general concepts prior to instruction focused on more specific content, as well as an evaluation tool of the knowledge that is formed afterward (Mintzes, et. al., 2000; Novak, Gowin, 1984).

In much the same way concept mapping has moved from being a knowledge representation to becoming a tool actively used by students during learning, curriculum developers have deployed concept maps during the initial curricular planning process. For example, Edmondson (1995) used concept mapping to develop a problem-based veterinary curriculum. He found that using concept mapping principles in the curricular planning process resulted in course content being more accessible and easily integrated by students. Concept mapping also provides educators a more comprehensive understanding of what students need to learn and helps eliminate sequencing errors in the development of lesson plans (Martin, 1994).

Recent decades have seen an increasing awareness that the adoption of refined procedures of evaluation contributes to the enhancement of the teaching/learning process. In the past, the teacher's evaluation of the pupil was expressed in the form of a final mark given on the basis of a scale of values determined both by the culture of the institution and by the subjective opinion of the examiner. This practice was rationalized by the idea that the principal function of school was selection - i.e. only the most fully equipped (outstanding) pupils were worthy of continuing their studies and going on to occupy the most important positions in society.

According to this approach, the responsibility for failure at school was to be attributed exclusively to the innate (and, therefore, unalterable) intellectual capacities of the pupil. The learning/teaching process was, then, looked upon in a simplistic, linear way: the teacher transmits (and is the repository of) knowledge, while the learner is required to comply with the teacher and store the ideas being imparted (Vecchia, Pedroni, 2007). Usage of concept maps may be very useful for students when starting to learn about a subject. The concept map may bring valuable general overlook of the subject for the whole period of study. It may be advisable that at the very first meeting of students with the subject to include a concept map of the subject.

NAÏVE BAYES CLASSIFIER

Naive Bayes is one of the most effective and efficient classification algorithms. In classification learning problems, a learner attempts to construct a classifier from a given set of training examples with class labels. Assume that A1, A2,...,An are n attributes. An instance E is represented by a vector (a1; a2; … ; an),where ai is the value of Ai. Let C represent the class variable, which takes two values: P (the positive class) or N (the negative class). We use c to represent the value that C takes. A naive Bayesian classifier, or simply naive Bayes, is defined as:

$$CNB(E) = \arg\max p(c)\prod_{i=1}^{n} p(ai|c)$$

Because the values of p(ai|c) can be estimated from the training examples, naive Bayes is easy to construct. It is also, however, surprisingly effective (Kononenko, 1990). Naive Bayes is based on the conditional independence assumption that all attributes are independent given the value of the class variable. It is obvious that the conditional independence assumption is rarely true in reality. Indeed, naive Bayes is found to work poorly for regression problems (Frank et. al., 2000), and produces poor probability estimates (Bennett, 2000).

Bayes theorem provide a method to calculate the probability of a hypothesis based on its prior probability, the probability of observing various data given the hypothesis, and the observed data itself (Mitchell, 1997). Then, considering a set of instances D belonging a set of known classes C, the most probable classification of a new instance is obtained combining the predictions of all hypothesis (the prior probabilities of each one of them) weighted by their posterior probabilities. The naive part in this approach is the assumption of word independence: the conditional probability of a word given a category is assumed to be independent from the conditional probabilities of other words given that category. This assumption makes the computation more efficient than considering word combinations as predictors and so,

$$P(c_j \mid d) = \frac{P(c_j) \times P(d \mid c_j)}{P(d)} = \frac{P(c_j) \times \Pi_i P(t_i \mid c_j)}{P(d)}$$

where $P(c_j | d)$ is the probability of a instance $d \in D$ belongs to $c_j \in C$ and $P(t_i | c_j)$ is the probability of a term $t_i \in V$ belongs a class c_j. The vocabulary V is created from the union of all terms that appear in D. Thus, if does not exit a prior knowledge about the prior probabilities of all the classes and pages, they can be assigned as equals and then the most probable class, given a new instance, will be $c_j = \arg\max_{c_j} \Pi_i P(t_i | c_j)$. Rather than maximizing this expression, its logarithmic transformation is chosen due to the logarithm of f is a non-decreasing function of f. Therefore, maximizing the logarithm of f also implies the maximization the function f. Finally, $c_j = \arg\max_{c_j} \Sigma_i \ln P(t_i | c_j)$

In this point, we must search expressions to estimate the prior probabilities $P(t_i | c_j)$ that optimize the classification task.

SOFTWARE ARCHITECTURE OF TESYS E-LEARNING PLATFORM

This architecture of the platform allows development of the e-learning application using MVC architecture. This three-tier model makes the software development process a little more complicated but the advantages of having a web application that produces web pages in a dynamic manner is a worthy accomplishment. The model is represented by DBMS (Data Base Management System) that in our case is represented by MySQL. The controller, which represents the business logic of the platform is Java based, being build around Java Servlet Technology. As servlet container Apache Tomcat 5.0 is used.

As for as we know there has not been yet solved the problem of development and integration of a software toolkit that uses data mining algorithms for analyzing actions performed by learners and which contributes to enhancement of quality of offered services by the e-Learning platform in which it has been integrated. This work presents a

novel solution as well as generic for enhancement of quality of services implemented by e-Learning platforms. Researches within the project will be finalized by a software product that may be integrated into e-Learning platforms. The effort and resources involved in this research work of designing a toolkit that may be integrated into e-Learning platforms are continuous, efficient and adaptive to user's needs.

In the figure 1 there are presented the main software components from the MVC point of view.

MainServlet, Action, Manager, Bean, Helper and all Java classes represent the Controller. The Model is represented by the DBMS itself while the Webmacro templates represent the View. The model is built without any knowledge about views and controllers. We present platform from developer point of view.

The business logic of the application uses Java classes. As it can be seen in figure 1, there are four levels of dependency between classes. The levels are: servlets, actions, managers and beans.

The MainServlet can be seen as the main gate of the application. Its main purpose is to check whether the request may be fulfilled or not from user's role point of view. By default, a user is a visitor and may execute only non-critical actions. The MainServlet redirects visitor users to welcome page where they are supposed to provide a username and a password in order to login. All other requests are divided into three categories: login, logout and actions. When running a login or logout request the MainServlet delegates control to Login or Logout action classes. If the user is logged (i.e. he has provided a valid username and password) the MainServlet identifies his role within the application and for each requested it will check if he may run that action. If it can, MainServlet will delegate control to appropriate action class that will effectively fulfill the request.

The second level of classes in the dependency tree has the action classes that effectively take care of the requests. The main action classes are Login,

Figure 1. Software components of the application from MVC point of view

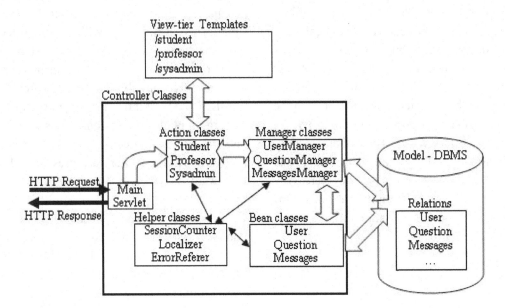

Logout, Sysadmin, Secretary, Student and User.

The third level of classes in dependency tree has the manager classes that are extensively used by action classes. Manager classes are in close relationship with the database relations. We have implemented twelve manager classes for the most important relations. A manager class implements all needed operations on a specific relation. For example, QuestionsManager class has methods for insertion, deletion and updates a question. There are also methods that check whether a question exists or not, compute and save the result of a test or exam, save the questions that were part of the test or exam in database for later use. Finally, there are methods used to take a question from the database and prepare it for display or vice versa. The same type of methods may be found in manager classes for sections, disciplines, users, results, year structure, messages, and logs or blocked IPs.

The last level of classes consists of bean classes. These classes are used mainly in manager classes and are in one to one correspondence with the relations from the database. In fact, for each

relation there was defined a bean class. We may say that an instance of a bean class represents a record from the correspondent relation from the database.

MONITORING ACTIVITY IN TESYS E-LEARNING PLATFORM

Tracking of actions is required to facilitate the data collection for the needed performed actions. The design of actions tracking module needs to select proper features that describe the performed actions of the learned. Among these features (or attributes) there are: user id, the date and time the action has been performed, details about the performed action, and so on. From the design phase of the platform, there were adopted two methodologies for monitoring actions.

Since the business logic of the platform is Java based, *log4j* utility package was employed as a logging facility and is called whenever needed within the logic of the application. The utility package is easy to use; *log4j.properties* properties file manages the logging process. The setup process states the logs are saved in *idd.log* file. The main drawback of this technique is that the data from the file is in a semi-structured form. This makes the information retrieval to be not so easy task to accomplish. On the advantages, logging activity may be very helpful in auditing the platform or even finding security breaches. This logging facility is also very helpful when debugging during development or when analyzing peculiar behavior during deployment.

To overcome the semi-structured shape of logged activity a structured way of gathering activity information was enforced. The activity table was added in the database and all actions were recorded in the manner of one record per action. In the table 1 it is presented the structure of activity table.

In Table 1 the action field is represented by a tag. The detailed explanation of what the tag means is set in a properties file. For each language a separate properties file is created, each file containing the same tags but with description in a different language.

The details field stores specific information regarding the action that was executed. For example, if a secretary modifies the profile of a student in the details field there will be stored information about what fields were updated. The level field specifies the importance of the executed action. There are defined three level of importance: 0, 1 and 2 where level 0 specifies the critical actions. After five months of deployment, the activity

Table 1. Structure of activity table

Field	Description
id	primary key
userid	identifies the user who performed the action
date	stores the date when the action was performed
action	stores a tag that identifies the action
details	stores details about performed action
level	specifies the importance of the action

table contains more than 50,000 records and we suppose that until the end of the learning cycle there will be close to 100,000 records. All this logged activity may also be very helpful in an audit process of the platform. The records from the activity table represent the raw data of our analyzing process.

DATA FILTERING AND OBTAINING RECOMMENDATIONS

The decision model helps to determine whether a given concept is appropriate to be displayed to the learner as a recommendation for study. The obtained Bayes classifier and its behavior is quite similar to a content-based recommender system. A recommender system tries to present to the user the information items he/she is interested in. To do this the user's profile is compared to some reference characteristics. These characteristics may be from the information item (the content-based approach) or the user's social environment (the collaborative filtering approach). Our approach is close to the latter approach.

The information about the concept and the user's activity are presented to the classifier as input, having as output a probability that represents the appropriateness of the concept for this student (or how interesting the item is for this user). Building the initial model needs the authors to specify that match the learner's activity with the concept and overall result in order to determine if more study of the concept in discussion is necessary.

The training and testing data that are used for building the model is represented by instances. Each instance represents the activity of a learner regarding a concept. The structure of an instance is:

```
instance(conceptId, noOfTests,
avgTests, finalResult, recommend)
```

The *conceptId* feature represents the concept

for which the other features are valid. This is a numeric field. The *noOfTests* feature represents the number of tests that were submitted by the learner regarding the *conceptId* concept. The *avgTests* feature represents the average grade of tests that were submitted by the learner from the *conceptId* concept. The *finalResult* feature represents the grade obtained by the learner at the discipline to which *conceptId* belongs. The recommend feature represents the recommendation made by course manager. The result set of available concepts will be partitioned into these two classes. For Naïve Bayes algorithm these are the values of the target function.

This is one of the setups used for experiments. Many other setups were used, using different sets of features (Mihaescu, Burdescu, 2006, 2007). In these work there were studied intensely how attribute selection influences results. Since in many practical situations there are far too many attributes for learning schemes to handle, and some of them – perhaps the overwhelming majority – are clearly irrelevant or redundant. Consequently, the data must be preprocessed to select a subset of attributes to use in learning. Of course, learning schemes themselves try to select attributes appropriately and ignore irrelevant and redundant ones, but in practice their performance can frequently be improved by preselection. For example, experiments show that adding useless attributes causes the performance of learning schemes such as decision trees and rules, linear regression, instance-based learners, and clustering methods to deteriorate (Witten, Eibe, 2000).

Obtaining recommendations is the last step of the analysis process. Once the model has been obtained and its quality has been acknowledged the effective process of obtaining recommendations may run. The acknowledgement of the quality of model is done by specifying thresholds regarding the percentage of correctly classified instances. These values are set up in a configuration file of the analysis module. In our setup, the model system stared making recommendations after the percentage of correctly classified instances raised above 80%.

Obtaining recommendations for students is accomplished by finding the concepts that obtain "yes" as estimation of target function. The current status of the student is evaluated at the moment he logs in the LMS. Then, the model selects the concepts that have as estimated target value "yes" and display those concepts. Each time the learner accesses the LMS the current performed activity is matched against the current model and the corresponding concepts that end up as "recommended" are displayed. After each week of running, the new data is considered for being included in training and testing data. This new data is added and new data and a challenger model is obtained. If the challenger model has better accuracy regarding the percentage of correct classified instance, it will replace the old model.

Sometimes it happens that during the usage of the system, the student could change his/her type of interaction with LMS. The problem of changes of the users' preferences is known as concept drift and has been discussed in several works about the use of machine learning for user modeling (Koychev, Schwab, 2000; Webb et. al., 2001). Concept drift can occur either because the acquired learning information needs to be adjusted or because the student simply changes his/her habits. In these scenarios, adaptive decision models, capable of better fitting the current student's preferences, are desirable.

If a concept drift is observed, the model is adapted accordingly. The proposal of improvement of the approach is proposed in (Castillo et. al., 2005), where the learning style once acquired was no more refined and the decision model was modeled using an adaptive Naïve Bayes classifier. In this approach it was used a Dynamic Bayesian Network for modeling learning styles and a 2-DBC (Dependence Bayesian Classifier) (Sahami, 1996) classifier to initialize the decision model.

ANALYSIS PROCESS AND EXPERIMENTAL RESULTS

The experimental results were obtained on Tesys e-Learning platform (Burdescu, Mihaescu, 2006). On this platform there was set Algorithms and Data Structures discipline. The tests were performed for five chapters: Simply/Double Linked Lists, Binary Search Trees, Height Balanced Trees, B Trees and Graphs. The first step was to build the General Concept Map by joining the concept maps from all chapters.

The concept map for Binary Search Trees is presented in figure 2. It contains 16 concepts, 11 linking phrases and 14 propositions.

The concepts are presented in table 2.

The list of propositions with two concepts and one linking phrase is presented in table 3. The list of propositions with three concepts and two linking phrases is presented in table 4.

Once the concept map has been built the general graph of the each chapter may be created. In this

graph, each proposition will become an edge that links the first concept and the last concept. The domain knowledge expert will assign a weight for each edge. While the students answers questions the number of correct and wrong answers will determine the knowledge weight of that edge.

There is one proposition with five concepts and four linking phrases: "BST" may be "Traversed" in "Preorder" determines "Key" in "Ascending Order". The concepts are bolded and put between quotation marks, while linking phrases are italic and underlined.

Knowledge evaluation is closely related with cognitive processes performed by an individual. After an initial step of goal setting a student has at first to identify task-relevant knowledge and to evaluate it with respect to his own knowledge regarding that goal. Self-evaluation of individual knowledge is a step that should be performed before any learning process. For example, if the task is to acquire expert knowledge, the structure of an individuals' knowledge as represented in an

Figure 2. Binary search tree concept map

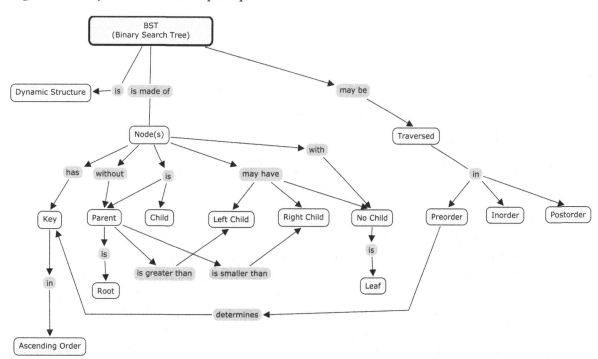

Table 2. List of concepts

ID	Concept	ID	Concept
C1	BST	C9	Right child
C2	Dynamic Structure	C10	No child
C3	Node(s)	C11	Root
C4	Traversed	C12	Leaf
C5	Key	C13	Preorder
C6	Parent	C14	Inorder
C7	Child	C15	Postorder
C8	Left child	C16	Ascending rder

Table 3. List of propositions with two concepts and one linking phrase

Id	Concept	Linking phrase	Concept
P1	BST	is	Dynamic Structure
P2	BST	is made of	Node(s)
P3	Node	has	key
P4	Node	is	Parent
P5	Node	is	Child
P6	Parent	is greater than	Left child
P7	Parent	is smaller than	Right child
P8	Node	may have	Left child
P9	Node	may have	Right child
P10	Node	may have	No child

Table 4. List of propositions with three concepts and two linking phrase

Id	C	LP	C	LP	C
P11	Node	without	parent	is	Root
P12	BST	may be	traversed	in	Preorder
P13	BST	may be	traversed	in	Inorder
P14	BST	may be	traverse	in	Postorder

individual knowledge map may be compared with the knowledge structure of an expert as represented in an expert map. The potential of knowledge maps as means for diagnosing individual structures of knowledge has been shown in a variety of empirical studies (Jonassen et. al., 1997). In self-regulated learning scenarios the particular contribution of computer-based concept maps is

that they may support self-assessment (Kommers, Lanzing, 1997; Shavelson et. al., 1994).

A concept map may be seen as an oriented graph where vertexes are represented by concepts and edges are represented by verbs. Within e-Learning platform for each proposition from the concept map may will be represented by a weighted edge and will have associated a number of quiz ques-

Figure 3. Functionality of decision support system

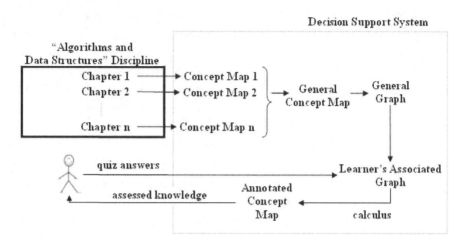

tions. Under these circumstances we have created an algorithm for building the associated graph of a concept map. The parameters of edges are continuously updated as the student answers quizzes. In the experimental part of the paper there will be presented the obtained graph. Each edge in the graph will have four parameters: the weight, the total number of questions, the correctly answered questions and the wrong answered questions.

Knowledge evaluation procedure takes into account the parameters of edges from the associated graph of concept map. The weight of an edge is set by the domain knowledge expert from a scale from 1 to 10 where 1 means very simple proposition and 10 means very hard proposition. All other parameters take different values according with learner's experience. In the experimental part there will be presented the formulas that synthesize the knowledge level of the learner.

The analysis of concept's map associated graph represents the core part of decision support system that runs along the e-Learning platform. The architecture of the decision support system is presented in figure 3.

Each chapter has associated a concept map build by the domain expert. From the concept map a transformation procedure creates the general graph of the chapter. In this graph, each sentence becomes an edge, weighted by the domain expert. Besides the associated weight, each proposition has associated a set of quiz questions that are to be answered by learners.

When the learner starts answering questions, the Decision Support System starts building learner's associated graph. This graph represents the input data for the calculus procedure that assesses the knowledge of the students regarding each chapter and the discipline as a whole. Whenever a student logs in the Decision Support System builds the learner's associated graph such that at request the knowledge status will be delivered in the form of an annotated concept map. The query of the annotated map returns information regarding the concept coverage at chapter and at discipline level. It is the option of the domain expert to specify different weights to chapters. This situation occurs when the domain expert considers that concepts from one chapter are more important than concepts covered by other chapter. Under these circumstances for each chapter there will be assigned a certain percentage such that the sum of percentages for all chapters is 100.

If:

W: the weight of the edge
CA: the number of correct answers

WA: the number of wrong answers
N: the number of questions

Than

KW: the knowledge weight of the edge

and

$$KW = \frac{CA - WA}{N} \frac{1}{W} * 100$$

Under these circumstances the knowledge weight may also be negative. At any time there may be estimated the overall knowledge level of the learner as the ratio between overall knowledge weight and overall weight. Figure 4 presents the general graph associated with the concept map.

The algorithm transforming the Concept Map into General Graph is strait forward. Each proposition becomes an edge with a weight assigned by domain knowledge expert. In this way it was obtained the Binary Search Tree General Graph.

Once the General Graph has been set up the professor has to set up the quiz questions for the chapter. For each edge in the graph it will correspond a certain number of quiz questions. There is no specification regarding the number of quiz questions but a minimum (e.g. five) number is still required. Once the quiz questions have been set up, for each student there may be constructed the learner's associated graph. This graph will have associated with the edges the history of correct and wrong answered questions. The Calculus engine will reconstruct an Annotated Concept Map which will present to the learner the current status of his knowledge level at Concept level. In this way, the learner will have an exact overview of his knowledge level regarding that chapter.

The Annotated Concept Map may represent the important information for learner in having a decision regarding which part of the chapter needs more study.

Table 5 presents a sample of the setup of the Binary Search Trees chapter.

Figure 4. Binary search tree general graph

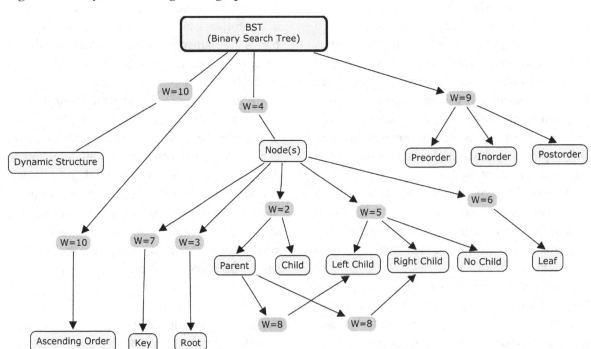

Table 5. Sample setup of BST chapter

Proposition	Weight	No. of questions
P1	10	8
P2	4	7
P3	7	6
P4	3	5
P5	2	7

Table 7. Sample weights assigned to chapters

Chapter	Weight
Simply/Double Linked Lists	15
Binary Search Trees	15
Height Balanced Trees	25
B Trees	25
Graphs	20

Table 6 presents sample values of the Learner's Associated Graph corresponding to BST chapter.

The values from table 5 are marked in an Annotated Concept Map that is finally presented to the learner. The Annotated Concept Map is the final outcome of the Decision Support System and is supposed to guide the learner regarding the necessary future efforts.

Table 7 presents the weights of chapters as they were assigned by the domain expert.

The analysis process for building the model is presented in figure 5.

Firstly, it is solved the cold-start problem. This means the data is collected such that the decision model is created. All performed activities are filtered such that training and testing data is obtained. Because we use Weka the data is extracted and translated into a standard format called ARFF, for Attribute Relation File Format (Garner et. al. 1995; Holmes et. al., 1994). This involves taking the physical log files and database relations and processing them through a series of steps to generate an ARFF dataset.

The values of attributes are computed for each instance through a custom developed off-line Java application. The outcome of running the application is in the form of a file called *activity. arff* that will later be used as source file for Weka workbench (Weka, 2008).

The *activity.arff* file has a standard format which is composed of two sections. In the first one there is defined the name of the relation and the attributes. For each attribute there is defined the set of nominal values it may have. In the next lines it is presented the first section of the file.

```
@relation activity
@attribute resourcetId {1, 2, 3, 4}
@attribute noOfTests {1, 2, 3, 4, 5}
@attribute avgTests {1, 2, 3, 4, 5}
@attribute finalResult {1, 2, 3, 4, 5}
@attribute recommend {yes,no}
```

In this section of the file are defined all attributes. An important decision that is needed is to establish the granularity for each attribute which is represented by the number of nominal

Table 6. Sample values for learner's associated graph

Proposition (Weight)	No. of questions	CA	WA	KW (%)
P1 (10)	8	3	2	1.25
P2 (4)	7	4	2	7.14
P3 (7)	6	1	3	-4.76
P4 (3)	5	3	1	13.3
P5 (2)	7	2	4	-14.2

Figure 5. The selection of recommended resources

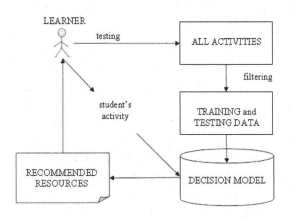

values it may take. As it can be seen from the above presented lines we consider five possible values for *noOfTests* feature. In the same there are defined the set of possible values for each of the features.

The second section of the *activity.arff* file is represented by the data itself. Here are all the instances that will enter the classification process. In the next lines there are presented few instances that may be found in this section.

```
@data
1, 1, 2, 3, no
1, 2, 3, 2, no
2, 3, 4, 3, yes
```

Each row represents an instance. For example, the first row represents an instance (a learner) which used resource 1 very many tests, obtained high grades for tests regarding this resource and obtained an average result at final examination. For this student the decision is not to show resource one in the set of recommended resources. In the same way there can be interpreted all other instances. At this point we may say we have obtained useful data that may be used for experimentation with machine learning schemes.

The Naïve Bayes algorithm was run in Weka. The original dataset was divided into a training of 90% of instances and a test set of 10% of instances. The model was constructed using four attributes: *resourceId, noOfTests, avgTests, finalResult* and *recommend* as the value of the target function.

More detailed results regarding the obtained model are presented in Box 1.

The performance of the model was evaluated by using 10-fold cross validation technique. The results are presented as percentage of correctly classified instances (81.17%) and incorrectly classified instances (18.82%) and confusion matrix.

DISCUSSON AND CONCLUSION

In this chapter we have presented an analysis process that creates a user model aimed at discovering the student's needs regarding the resources that need more study. This model has been used in Tesys e-Learning system for filtering the resources of a discipline the learner needs to study. To discover the user's needs there is used information about all previous learner's performed activities. The advantages of using these information is that this allows refining the initial beliefs acquired by the system by observing the student's performed actions over time thus computing up-to-date learning activity for each student. For classification of resources there was used Naïve Bayes classifier as the machine learning algorithm for determining whether a resource is appropriate to be recommended for a specific learner or not. The experiments carried out to obtain an initial model are described in detail.

Tesys e-Learning platform has been designed such that on-line testing activities may me performed as they were set up by course managers. It has been created a Concept Map for a Binary Search Trees chapter as well as for each chapter of Algorithms and Data Structures course. The Concept maps have been the staring point in creating the sets of quiz questions. Each quiz question refers to a certain proposition from the concept map.

Box 1.

```
=== Run information ===
Scheme: weka.classifiers.bayes.NaiveBayes
Relation: activity
Instances: 850
Attributes: 5
resourceId, noOfTests, avgTests, finalResult, recommend
Test mode: evaluate on training data
=== Classifier model (full training set) ===
Naive Bayes Classifier
Class yes: Prior probability = 0.45resourceId: Counts = 85 122 152 135 (Total = 530)
noOfTests: Counts= 100 118 134 95 60(Total= 512)
avgTests: Counts= 110 105 130 124 93(Total= 565)
finalResult:Counts=90 122 132 130 86 (Total = 560)
Class no: Prior probability = 0.55
resourceId:Counts=75 159 106 80 110 (Total = 520)
noOfTests: Counts=70 161 101 105 108(Total= 545)
avgTests:Counts = 72 152 110 99 114 (Total = 547)
finalResult:Counts=72 122 120 109 124(Total= 547)
=== Evaluation on training set ===
=== Summary ===
Correctly Classified Instances 690 81.1764%
Incorrectly Classified Instances 160 18.8235%
Kappa statistic 0.6271
Mean absolute error 0.3153
Root mean squared error 0.1951
Relative absolute error 41.4597%
Root relative squared error 75.8637%
Total Number of Instances 850
=== Confusion Matrix ===
a b <-- classified as
150 110 | a = yes
50 540 | b = no
```

For the designed Concept Maps it has been derived a General Graph in which edges are represented by the propositions from the General Concept Map. For each edge the domain knowledge expert (i.e. course manager) assigned a specific weight. A weight has been assigned for each chapter such that the sum of all weights is 100.

After the setup has been put in place, the learners started using the platform. At request, from the general graph there was derived the learner's associated graph and on this one there may be performed calculus such that the level of knowledge regarding the chapter may be estimated at proposition level. Using the general formula with weights for the chapters it was estimated the knowledge level at discipline level. These calculus represent the annotations in the original concept. The annotated concept map represents what the learner finally receives upon his request.

The business logic computes the knowledge of the student about a certain resource as a knowledge weight and regarding the discipline as a percentage of covered resources. Resources may be questions, concepts or even chapters. This weight is computed as a function of resource's weight, number of questions assigned to that resource, the number of correct answered questions and number of wrong answered questions.

After the setup has been put in place, the learners started using the platform. At request, from the general graph there was derived the learner's associated graph and on this one there may be performed calculus such that the level of knowledge regarding the resource may be estimated. These calculus represent the annotations in the original concept. The annotated concept map represents what the learner finally receives upon his request.

This whole mechanism represents the functionality of a decision support system that runs along the Tesys e-Learning platform. For each learner there is initialized a decision model from data obtained from all previous learner's performed activities. The outcome of the Decision Support System is represented by a set of recommended resources that are presented to the learner.

Each learner's individual decision model is then adapted from the observations of the learner's performed activities. Moreover, the model is also able to adapt itself to changes in the learner's performed activities. Knowledge was obtained by employing an automated discovery process of iterative manner. A dataset was taken and analyzed using the facilities provided by Weka workbench for manipulating datasets, configuring learning schemes and handling output.

For learners, it was observed that students that followed the recommendations had better results in shorter time due to optimization of their learning scenarios. After new more data is collected a challenger decision model may be created and replace the old one if its accuracy is higher.

Within Tesys e-Learning platform set up there were registered 375 students. After six month of running the platform there were over 40.000 recorded actions that represent the raw data. Filtering this data had as output an arff file with 850 instances.

To summarize, the results from our experiments show the feasibility of machine learning in improving self-assessment effectiveness by activity monitoring and analysis. The machine learning approach gives a wide field of action in the area of adaptive e-Learning platforms due to the wide variety of models that may be used for description or prediction. For learners, the main benefit regards improvement in their meta-cognitive skills to observe, analyze and improve their learning process. For course managers, this approach helps understanding and interpreting the ongoing course at individual learner level and also at group level.

In future there may be tested different setups, with more test questions and adjusted weights. The weights may be adjusted by comparing the end results with the estimated results. In this way, there may be discovered resources that need increase or decrease in weight.

As future works there are two directions that may be discussed. One regards the used features and the other regards the employed algorithms. Since the range of activities is much wider than the one used in this chapter, there may be performed new experiments with different sets of features. For example, features like the number of sent messages to course manager may be added to the feature set. Regarding the employed algorithms we plan using other flavors of Naïve Bayes like Bayes Net or Multinominal Naïve Bayes.

REFERENCES

Abramovicz, W., Kaczmarek, T., & Kowalkiewicz, M. (2004). Supporting topic map creation using data mining techniques. *Australian Journal of Information Systems*.

Agrawal, R., & Srikant, R. (1994). Fast algorithms for mining association rules. In *Proc. of the 20th Int. Conf. on Very Large Databases*, Santiago, Chile.

ATutor. (2008). Retrieved from http://atutor.com

Ausubel, D. P., Novak, J. D., & Hanesian, H. (1978). *Educational psychology: A cognitive view* (2nd ed.). New York: Holt, Rinehart and Winston.

Bennett, P. N. (2000). *Assessing the calibration of Naive Bayes' posterior estimates* (Tech. Rep. No. CMU-CS00-155).

Blackboard. (2008). Retrieved from http://www.blackboard.com

Brusilovsky, P. (1996). Methods and techniques of adaptive hypermedia. *User Modeling and User-Adapted Interaction, 6*(2-3), 87–129. doi:10.1007/BF00143964

Brusilovsky, P. (2001). Adaptive hypermedia. *User Modeling and User-Adapted Interaction, 11*(1/2), 87–110. doi:10.1023/A:1011143116306

Burdescu, D. D., & Mihăescu, M. C. (2006). Tesys: E-learning application built on a Web platform. In *Proceedings of International Joint Conference on e-Business and Telecommunications*, Setubal, Portugal (pp. 315-318).

Burdescu, D. D., & Mihăescu, M. C. (2007). Enhancing the assessment environment within a learning management systems. In *Proceedings of the EUROCON 2007 – The International Conference on "Computer as a Tool,"* Warsaw, Poland (pp. 2438-2443).

Castillo, G., Gama, J., & Breda, A. M. (2005). An adaptive predictive model for student modeling. In *Advances in Web-based education: Personalized learning environments* (pp. 70-92). Hershey, PA: Information Science Publishing.

Cooley, R., Mobasher, B., & Srivastava, J. (1999). Data preparation for mining World Wide Web browsing patterns. *Knowledge and Information Systems, 1*(1), 5–32.

de Bra, P., Berden, B., de Lange, B., Rousseau, B., Santic, T., Smits, D., & Stash, N. (2003). AHA! The adaptive hypermedia architecture. In *Proceedings of the ACM Conference on Hypertext and Hypermedia*, Nottingham, UK.

Edmondson, K. M. (1995). Concept mapping for the development of medical curricula. *Journal of Research in Science Teaching, 32*(7), 777–793. doi:10.1002/tea.3660320709

Edwards, J., & Fraser, K. (1983). Concept maps as reflections of conceptual understanding. *Research in Science Education, 13*, 19–26. doi:10.1007/BF02356689

Frank, E., Trigg, L., Holmes, G., & Witten, I. H. (2000). Naive Bayes for regression. *Machine Learning, 41*(1), 5–15. doi:10.1023/A:1007670802811

Garner, S. R., Cunningham, S. J., Holmes, G., Nevill-Manning, C. G., & Witten, I. H. (1995). Applying a machine learning workbench: Experience with agricultural databases. In *Proceedings of the Machine Learning in Practice Workshop, Machine Learning Conference*, Tahoe City, CA, USA, (pp. 14-21).

Guo, L., Xiang, X., & Shi, Y. (2004). Use Web usage mining to assist background online e-learning assessment. In *Proceedings of the 4th IEEE ICALT*.

Han, J., & Camber, M. (2001). *Data mining concepts and techniques*. San Francisco: Morgan Kaufman.

Harpaz, I., Balik, C., & Ehrenfeld, M. (2004). Concept mapping: An educational strategy for advancing nursing education. *Nursing Forum, 39*(2), 27–30. doi:10.1111/j.0029-6473.2004.00027.x

Holden, C. (1992). Study flunks science and math tests. *Science Education, 26*, 541.

Holmes, G., Donkin, A., & Witten, I. H. (1994). Weka: A machine learning workbench. In *Proceedings of the 1994 Second Australian and New Zealand Conference on Intelligent Information Systems*, Brisbane, Australia, (pp. 357-361).

Jonassen, D. H., Reeves, T. C., Hong, N., Harvey, D., & Peters, K. (1997). Concept mapping as cognitive learning and assessment tools. *Journal of Interactive Learning Research, 8*(3/4), 289–308.

Kommers, P., & Lanzing, J. (1997). Student's concept mapping for hypermedia design. Navigation through the World Wide Web (WWW) space and self-assessment. *Journal of Interactive Learning Research, 8*(3/4), 421–455.

Kononenko, I. (1990). Comparison of inductive and Naive Bayesian learning approaches to automatic knowledge acquisition. In *Current trends in knowledge acquisition*. Amsterdam: IOS Press.

Koychev, I., & Schwab, I. (2000). Adaptation to drifting user's interests. In *Proceedings of ECML2000 Workshop: Machine Learning in New Information Age*.

Krasner, G. E., & Pope, S. T. (1998). A cookbook for using the model-view-controller user interface paradigm in smalltalk-80. *Journal of Object Oriented Programming, 1*(3), 26–49.

Lin, W., & Alvarez, S. (2002). Efficient adaptive-support association rule mining for recommender systems. *Data Mining and Knowledge Discovery, 6*(1), 83–105. doi:10.1023/A:1013284820704

Marquardt, C. G. (2004). A preprocessing tool for web usage mining in distance education domain. In *IDEAS: Proc. of the 8th Int. Database Engineering and Applications Symposium*.

Martin, D. J. (1994). Concept mapping as an aid to lesson planning: A longitudinal study. *Journal of Elementary Science Education, 6*(2), 11–30.

McDaniel, E., Roth, B., & Miller, M. (1988). Concept mapping as a tool for curriculum design. *Issues in Informing Science and Information Technology, 2*, 505–513.

Mihaescu, M. C., & Burdescu, D. D. (2006). Testing attribute selection algorithms for classification performance on real data. In *Proceedings of the 3rd IEEE International Conference on Intelligent Systems (IS)* (pp. 581-586). Washington, DC: IEEE Press.

Mihaescu, M. C., & Burdescu, D. D. (2007). Classification of students using their data traffic within an e-learning platform. In *Proceedings of the International Joint Conference on e-Business and Telecommunications -International Conference on e-Business (ICE-B)* (pp. 315-321). INSTICC Press.

Mintzes, J. J., Wandersee, J. H., & Novak, J. D. (2000). *Assessing science understanding: A human constructivist view*. San Diego, CA: Academic Press.

Mitchell, T. (1997). *Machine learning*. New York: McGraw Hill.

Moodle. (2008). Retrieved from http://www.moodle.com

Novak, J. D. (1977). *A theory of education*. Ithaca, NY: Cornell University Press.

Novak, J. D. (1990). Concept maps and vee diagrams: Two metacognitive tools for science and mathematics education. *Instructional Science, 19*, 29–52. doi:10.1007/BF00377984

Novak, J. D. (1998). *Learning, creating, and using knowledge: Concept maps as facilitative tools in schools and corporations*. Mahwah, NJ: Lawrence Erlbaum Associates.

Novak, J. D., & Gowin, D. B. (1984). *Learning how to learn*. New York: Cambridge University Press.

Sahami, M. (1996). Learning limited dependence Bayesian classifiers. In *Proceedings of the Second International Conference on Knowledge Discovery and Data Mining, KDD-96* (pp. 335-338). Menlo Park, CA: AAAI Press

Shavelson, R. J., Lang, H., & Lewin, B. (1994). *On concept maps as potential "authentic" assessments in science* (Technical Report 388). Los Angeles, CA: UCLA, Center for the Study of Evaluation (CSE/CRESST).

Spertus, E., & Stein, L. A. (1998). A hyperlink-based recommender system written in squeal. In *Proc. of the ACM CIKM'98 Workshop on Web Information and Data Management.*

Srikant, R., & Agrawal, R. (1996). Mining sequential patterns: Generalizations and performance improvements. In *EDBT: Proc. of the 5ᵗʰ Int. Conf. On Extending Database Technologies.*

Srivastava, J., Cooley, R., Deshpande, M., & Tan, P. N. (2000). Web usage mining: Discovery and applications of usage patterns from Web data. *SIGKDD Explorations, 1*(2), 12–23. doi:10.1145/846183.846188

Tan, P. N., Kumar, V., & Srivastava, J. (2004). Selecting the right objective measure for association analysis. *Information Systems, 29*(4), 293–313. doi:10.1016/S0306-4379(03)00072-3

Tang, T., & Mccalla, G. (2003). Smart recommendation for evolving e-learning system. In *Proc. of the Workshop on Technologies for Electronic Documents for Supporting Learning, Int. Conf. on Artificial Intelligence in Education*, Sydney, Australia.

Vecchia, L., & Pedroni, M. (2007). Concept maps as a learning assessment tool. *Issues in Informing Science and Information Technology, 4*, 307–312.

Web, C. T. (2008). Retrieved from http://www.webct.com

Webb, G., Pazzani, M., & Billsus, D. (2001). Machine learning for user modeling. *User Modeling and User-Adapted Interaction, 11*(1/2), 19–29. doi:10.1023/A:1011117102175

Weka. (2008). Removed from http://www.cs.waikato.ac.nz/ml/weka

Witten, I. H., & Eibe, F. (2000). *Data mining – practical machine learning tools and techniques with java implementations.* San Francisco: Morgan Kaufmann Publishers.

Zaiane, O. R. (2001). Web usage mining for a better Web-based learning environment. In *Proc. Of. The Conf. On Advanced Technology for Education*, Banff, Alberta.

Zaiane, O. R. (2002). Building a recommender agent for e-learning systems. In *Proc. of the 7ᵗʰ Int. Conf. On Computers in Education*, Auckland, New Zeeland.

Chapter 12
Computer–Supported Collaboration in Language Learning

Bin Zou
Xi'an Jiaotong-Liverpool University, China

ABSTRACT

Studies suggest that the computer can support collaborative learning between learners. This chapter discusses collaboration between language learners while using computer-based tasks. The researcher aims to look at in what ways students collaborate when completing tasks using computers during language learning, particularly in developing their listening and speaking skills. This chapter also explores the possibilities of monitoring and assessment for this collaborative language learning. The analysis is based on interview, observation and questionnaire data from both teachers and students at two UK university language centers. The findings indicate that collaboration in computer-based environments organized by teachers is useful for students to develop their language skills. Computer-supported collaboration increases students' confidence and encourages them to maintain active learning, thus reduces the passive reliance on teachers' feedback.

INTRODUCTION

Computers have been applied in many subjects in education. Studies have found that computers have large potential impact on education and can enhance students' learning (e.g. Sutherland et al., 2004). Computers allow students to carry out tasks and self-assessment with the function of instant feedback. The computer user can use feedback from the computer as the monitor to "reshape their actions in response to the feedback" (Facer et al., 2003, p. 191). Therefore, students can assess themselves with the use of the computer.

In language learning, current studies in the computer-assisted language learning (CALL) field suggest that the computer provides material and feedback for learners to practise the target language in and outside the classroom and has been seen as a positive tool for language learners in their individual study. As Chapelle (2003) suggests, CALL programs

DOI: 10.4018/978-1-60566-786-7.ch012

offer the potential for interaction between the computer and the language learner which refers to the learner's responding questions and receiving correct answers. Hence, the computer is also seen as a potential language tutor by providing assessment for students' responses (Levy, 1997). In addition, students' autonomous language learning and self-assessment can be widely available through the web rather than being tied to a particular class (Chapelle, 2001).

Regarding practising listening skills, students can monitor their exercises on the computer at their own pace. They can complete tasks and click buttons to receive assessment from the computer. Computers combine listening materials and various tasks with immediate assessment together through easy control. All these characteristics are much more convenient than using other media (Slater & Varney-Burch, 2001). In terms of speaking, computer programs are also designed for second language students to specifically practise pronunciation skills. For example, learners can record their speaking activities, and then these are evaluated by comparing them with a pre-recorded model version by listening or looking at a graphical representation of the two recordings. This helps learners monitor their language production. This monitoring strategy is helpful to assess and improve learners' speaking skills and the teacher can use the recordings to assess learners' performance and give feedback (Slater & Varney-Burch, 2001; Hegelheimer, & Tower, 2004).

Nonetheless, does the computer provide sufficient monitoring and assessment for learners' individual learning? According to Prain and Lyons (2000), learners will not be the lead players in their learning on computers. Although computers can provide feedback and assessment, computers may not be able to explain why students' answers are wrong or how to correct their errors. Hence, language learners still need to have collaboration with other learners and to receive support from peers and tutors. Furthermore, the above literature

primarily presents the monitoring and assessment for individual learning on the computer; it does not provide approaches of monitoring and assessment for collaborative learning.

BACKGROUND

Collaboration in Learning

In the classroom, students often work together to communicate, solve problems or share information. Dillenbourg (1999) identifies that collaboration involves pairs or groups interacting to learn something together. Collaboration may benefit students' learning. As Phipps (1999) describes: "Working with a partner is less intimidating than being singled out to answer in front of the class and it brings a realistic element into the classroom by simulating the natural conversation setting" (p. 1). Further, researchers have found that teachers can enhance students' motivation by setting up activities including pair or group work (e.g. Pintrich & Schunk 1996). Collaboration between learners in an organized classroom provides powerful motivation for learning which can produce "learning gains and student achievement" (Dörnyei, 2001, p. 40). This demonstrates that collaboration seems to enhance students' motivation which in turn improves their learning achievement.

In language field, studies have found that second language learners need to use the language to have interactions to learn the target language because interactions between students can reinforce their language learning (Chapelle, 1998; Pica, 1994). Pair work can promote communication and autonomous learning (Phipps, 1999). This is particularly true in second language classrooms because learners need to use the target language to talk to other people to improve their language skills. When they talk to peers, they are less inhibited to express their meaning to each other. In these natural conversations, they can talk to learn the target language and increase their communicative skills (Phipps, 1999). As Nunan (1992) suggests, collaboration encourages language students to develop communicative skills and enhances their language learning. Hence, collaboration helps students become more confidence and encourages them to create active learning rather than have a passive reliance on teachers' feedback (Mendoca & Johnson, 1994; Pica, 1987).

With the development of computer technology, computers provide students with opportunities to learn collaboratively. Many researchers have found that computers support collaboration, such as Dillenbourg (1999); Egbert (2005); Veerman (2003). Learners learn collaboratively through synchronous or asynchronous communication in computer-mediated environment (Dillenbourg, 1999). With the increasing use of computers in second language teaching and learning, students are provided with more opportunities for collaboration experiences on computers (Benson, 2001; Butler-Pascoe & Wiburg, 2003; Warschauer & Healey, 1998). As Benson (2001) and Warschauer & Healey (1998) note, a key feature of computers is to provide similar opportunities to the classroom environment for collaboration and interactions among learners, and between learners and native speakers or teachers. Computer-based tasks engage students in tasks with the target language and spoken communication with other students. This suggests that students collaborate in using computers as is the case in face-to-face pair work, such as pair work for discussions and role play. Computer programs which provide learners with opportunities to engage in interactions in the target language may assist learners in using the language efficiently and provide understanding of how to use the language in real situations (Harless et al., 1999). Collaboration is particularly achieved when learners have a discussion, share information and share problem solution in CALL context (Veerman, 2003). Similarly, Egbert (2005) addresses that although individual practice can help language learners to improve their language learning on the computer, they will learn more effectively with

peer interaction to listen and respond. Moreover, students can interact with learners from all over of world, and they can communicate with each other for language learning (Chapelle, 2001).

Thus, collaboration between learners is considered as key to learn a second language because they work together and help each other in learning process (Chapelle, 2001). Despite it, collaborative learning may have some disadvantages and is still a new challenge in CALL research context. Students may feel difficult to communicate with each other on computers and may rely on others to complete tasks. In addition, work and time schedule is also a problem with online collaboration (Curtis & Lawson, 2001). However, the above studies do not discuss monitoring and assessment of learners' collaborative learning in CALL context. Moreover, the literature above does not provide examples of what contents learners discuss or have role play for language learning with the use of computers. Thus, more samples of collaboration between learners and how to enhance, monitor and assess this collaboration need to be further explored. The author intends to look at examples and contents of students' collaboration and the possibilities to monitor and assess this collaboration in the current study, based on developing listening and speaking skills in CALL context.

Collaboration in Listening and Speaking Activities

During listening and speaking activities in language learning, researchers suggest that listening and speaking are linked together. For example, fluent speaking also includes listening, that is, understanding what other people said. Listening links with speaking in the discussion on listening materials between peers (e.g. Hedge, 2000; Murphy, 1991). In order to speak the target language fluently, various speaking tasks/activities as a sort of collaboration need to be integrated into language learning process for students to practise and use the target language (Ellis, 2003).

A few researchers provide examples of speaking activities in second language classrooms. Speaking activities can be "rehearsing dialogues, completing information-gap activities, playing interactive games, discussing topic issues, problem solving, role playing and completing speaking task" (Murphy, 1991, p. 55).

Similarly, Hedge (2000) suggests three basic sorts of speaking activities: free discussion, role play and information gap activities. Hedge states that discussion encourages students to use the target language to carry on the conversation and practise the strategies in communication. Discussion offers crucial opportunities for developing fluency in talking a range of topics. Role play includes different activities, ranging from a simple conversation based on particular information on role cards, to more complex situations through various stages. Oxford (1997) also describes role play as acting out particular roles within a social setting, for example, a conversation between a doctor and a patient. Information gap "involves each learner in pairs or a group possessing information which the other learners do not have. The learners' information must be shared in order to achieve an outcome" (Hedge, 2000, p. 281). Learners exchange information and negotiate to find solutions for a particular problem through this collaboration. Hedge contends that all three activities are useful to help students to speak English fluently. In fact, these activities are collaboration between students which enables students to work together to help each other improve their communicative skills, including listening and speaking.

With regard to discussions between learners for developing speaking skills, Butler-Pascoe & Wiburg (2003) address the benefits of this type of collaboration with computer-based activities:

The primary benefit of a technology-enhanced environment for development of speaking skills is the speech that occurs as students talk to each other while working on collaborative tasks and projects or while just chatting around the com-

puter. It is while engaged in these activities that students call on their oral skills to negotiate with each other and take risks to use new language in order to get across their meaning. (p. 96)

This suggests that students talk to each other to negotiate meaning with the use of computers in the collaboration. In this way, students practise their speaking skills together. Hence, computers offer language learners not only activities focusing on oral skills but also opportunities to use these skills in communication (Butler-Pascoe & Wiburg, 2003). For example, teachers use web sources to set up activities for students to have discussions to develop their speaking skills (Dudeney, 2000; Teeler & Gray, 2000). Chen et al. (2004) also found in their study that students gave positive comments on collaboration between learners during the web-based environment in their language learning. Students were able to talk with peers and they gained help from peers on the Internet.

Thus, collaboration is considered key to learning a second language with the use of computers (Chapelle, 2001). Collaborative learning around the computer is also an active process during listening and speaking activities in students' language learning. However, few CALL studies focus on monitoring and assessment of learners' collaboration in the context of developing listening and speaking skills.

METHODOLOGY

This study adopted three types of data collection including semi-structured interview, questionnaire and observation at two university language centers in the UK. The two language centers provide computer programs for students to practise their listening and speaking skills such as *eLanguages, SKY, EASE, Streaming Speech* and *TASK*. Students also use web cameras to develop listening and speaking skills. The aim of the interviews used in this study was to investigate interviewees' opin-

Table 1. Various types of collaboration between learners during CALL activities

Types of collaboration	Collaboration format	Collaboration focus
Discussion	In pairs or in groups	Discussing what they understood and what they found on the websites or software programs
Role play	In pairs	Practising speaking with different roles in the conversations or interviews
Recording voice and assessing for each other	In pairs	Identifying each other's errors in recording and correcting for each other

ions, experiences and feelings in using computers for collaboration between learners in depth. 21 students and 15 tutors were interviewed at the two centers. Two groups of students (3-5 in each university) involved a focus-group interview. Students came from different countries, such as China, Italy, Cyprus, Spain, Korea, Japan, Philippine, Brazil, and so forth, covering undergraduate to PhD levels. All interviews lasted for about thirty minutes to one hour and were recorded by a digital recorder after permission. Notes were also taken during interviews to help the transcriptions later. Additionally, 121 questionnaires were collected from students and 4 classroom observations were conducted in the computer rooms in the two centers. As Chapelle (2001) suggests, learner's opinions on the value of the CALL task can be collected by using questionnaire data. Further, observation in this study was to use researcher's own eyes to see direct evidence and to provide detailed information on collaboration between learners in the computer room. Finally, all the analysis of questionnaires, interviews and observations were synthesized and the relevant information from the three types of data were identified and put into same categories for the analysis. These methods allow me to develop this study as broadly and completely as possible.

FINDINGS AND DISCUSSION

In this study, various types of collaboration between students occurred through speaking tasks in the computer room. Students reported from interviews and questionnaires that they practised their listening and speaking skills on computers with peers. Table 1 summarizes the three types of collaboration that took place during CALL activities (as reported by interviewees in the two centers). It can be seen that collaboration between students include discussions, role play and recording their speech on computers and assessing each other's speech.

The questionnaire data shows that 83% of the students reported that they have frequently received feedback for their speaking activities from their peers. More than half of students (51%) reported liking to use computer technologies to search for information and topic online or on the computer packages and talk to each other offline in the class. In terms of online chatting, 67% of students reported liking to talk on line by audio very much or somewhat with others; 52% of students like to talk by video (e.g. web cameras) very much or somewhat with others. In addition, the questionnaire data demonstrates that only 27% of the students prefer assessment from the computer for listening tasks and 13% expect computers' assessment for speaking tasks. In contrast, 35% of the students like receiving feedback from peers, but more than 60% of the students reported valuing feedback from teachers in class both for listening and speaking tasks. The findings indicate that students seemed to prefer teachers' assessment. The interview data illustrates more details in the next section.

Discussions with Peers

Students from interviews reported that they discussed information from computers with peers in class to develop their comprehension of listening materials and speaking skills. For example, students in the group interview in University One reported that after working at the computer individually, the teacher asked them to discuss their results with each other. In these discussions, they developed their speaking skills as well as listening skills. As John noted:

The teacher sends us homework to access the Internet to find material of learning style. And we discuss the next following day, in a group, to find the advantages and disadvantages, and how we compare each other, how to manage our time effectively.

Students commented that it was interesting to use the information they found on the computer as a basis for discussion, and this type of task motivated them to practise their speaking skills; they said that they liked discussions with peers and it was crucial for their language learning. Cynthia said that the discussion concerning the online information they had found helped them to improve their speaking skills, because:

usually you got new information and different idea; you need to explain to your partner why. Let him or her understand. So it helps your speaking and thinking, express yourself clearly. We would like to share together. Usually new information and different ideas, you would like to show to other people, so it helps you express yourself. It helps your speaking.

Adam, Amanda, Alan and Hans also said that because they had similar interesting topics, they liked talking with peers after obtaining the information on computers. Adam noted: "I like discussion with friends after searching interesting information on the web... because I think with people, I can improve my speaking skills to communicate." Actually, the discussions developed their listening skills while they talked to each other. In addition, Amanda asserted: "To communicate with friends is also important, not only from (the) teacher."

The comments above suggest that students found discussions useful for language learning and they liked discussing with peers, indicating that students were motivated in this collaboration. As Dörnyei (2001) supports, when students feel valuable and interested in an activity, they are motivated in their learning processes. Further, students developed their communicative skills through discussions, which means they might enhance their language learning, which supports Dörnyei's (2001) suggestion that collaboration promotes students' learning.

Teachers also thought that the discussion was a useful way for the students to share the information they had found on computers. Therefore, they liked to ask students to work in pairs to complete computer-based tasks. Ms. Ellis gave an example of using online sources to make students discuss 'humor'. They looked at the web, and found a speech by George Bush. She gave students a task to discuss and analyze his linguistic mistakes to see why people laughed. She said her students felt it interesting and enjoyed this task. This task was able to develop students' speaking skills as well as understanding of these kinds of humor. This suggests that the teacher believed that discussing the topic of humor motivated students to practise their speaking skills because students were interested in it, which supports Dörnyei (2001), who suggests that the teacher can use interesting sources, such as humor to increase students' motivation.

Ms. Mitchell said that she usually liked students to work in pairs on computers when they conducted research, so that they worked in a team, speaking to one another, to decide which web site and what materials to use. Mr. Cater provided an example of using *Web Quest*, a web site for teachers to set up activities with online information and create tasks. He asked his students to work in groups of three to design a travel plan to spend 500 pounds. In this way, students developed their speaking skills in the discussion. As he said:

We have a task, for example, looking at a few web sites to try to get travel information to buy air ticket, organize a holiday. What they need to do is to discuss in pairs, in groups, to negotiate each other, where to go, how much they are going to spend, what they are going to do.

Mr. Carter pointed out that students' working on the computer individually might reduce the time for interaction with peers. Therefore, he liked asking students to work in pairs or groups, so that speaking practice and team working carried on. He remarked: "Speaking often does not come from the interaction with the computer, but from the interactions with other students, discussing the task." As he said, teachers needed to set up a task that included a context and a web page for searching for information for language practice which was credible or of interest. Mr. Cater emphasized: "The interaction is between students. You must make sure they make collaboration, negotiation and discussion to complete the task."

Actually, this task is authentic because students may encounter similar collaboration in discussing online information in their real academic study in future. This task is related to people's real life, which can motivate students in language learning (Dörnyei, 2001). These perspectives above support Pica (1994) and Chapelle's (1998) claims that interactions between students in using the target language can enhance their language learning and hence develop their communicative skills.

During the observation of the student use of online sources in *TASK* package, students had several opportunities to discuss the information that they found on the Internet in pairs or groups. Students were keen to discuss what they found on the web within their groups and observation

data indicates that they were laughing and discussing actively, which suggests that they were engaged with the material. In these discussions, students developed their skills in listening, speaking, communication and team working, and so forth. During this observation, it was found that the teacher used a worksheet with 10 questions for students to answer using online information. After students answered these questions in pairs and assessed for each other, the teacher asked them to answer the questions to the whole class and checked if their answers were correct. This suggests that the teacher monitor and assess their discussion in the final stage.

Ms. Kelly very often used web-based sources to stimulate discussion between the students; they discussed various topics and assessed what they found on the web. She stated that students liked these activities very much. It was quite helpful to students to share experiences with the web-based extension material. She said: "The extension material is always web-based. It's written by language experts. It looks at language skills. I think students like to use it." She also asserted that one of the useful aspects in *TASK* was creating an information gap and sending students to search for information on the Internet and then asking them to exchange information. But the most important factor, she noted, was to make students realize that the Internet was a great source of information. Then, students practised their speaking skills on the topics to gain critical ideas, which was a very integrated activity. Ms. Kelly added that the purpose of the discussion in using online resources in *TASK* was to enhance students' understanding of academic culture for study.

The above results show that teachers set up activities for students to work with peers to discuss a range of topics on the Internet. Both students and teachers considered that it was useful for students to carry out collaboration with peers with the use of web-based materials to develop their communication skills. Students felt it interesting and they liked discussing with peers, supporting questionnaire data above. This suggests that the discussions with information on computers motivated them to develop their listening and speaking skills. As Dörnyei (2001) and Pintrich & Schunk (1996) suggest, collaboration organized by the teacher can motivate students to achieve better learning, and can improve their communicative skills, and this is supported by the findings above. The results also suggest that the discussions about online information help learners to develop spoken English. This supports Dudeney (2000) and Butler-Pascoe & Wiburg's (2003) suggestions that teachers can ask students to use online sources to have discussions to practise their speaking skills.

This collaboration also links authenticity because students may encounter similar situation in their academic study in future (see also Chapelle, 2001; MacDonald et al., 2000). Therefore, these findings suggest that discussing information on computers in class, with peers, appears to be a useful way for students to develop their listening and speaking skills.

It should be noticed that during this learning process, the computer programs are unable to monitor and assess students' language production. Students rely on peers' assessment in their collaborative activities. Meanwhile, teachers play the key role of monitoring and assessing students' discussion.

Role Play

Teachers reported using role play for students to collaborate with peers in their development of speaking skills using web-based information. Ms. Kelly liked using *Web Quest* to set up collaborative activities among students. She asked students to act in various roles with sources they found on the Internet. She offered an example:

One of my favorite Web Quest involves group of students, one is historic in the group, one is social science in the group, and one is medical person

in the group. They set up tasks. They have got different information in relationship with their special area. They have problems to solve. They bring back the information they got from the web. They are given to the website to check. They can do their own research. They come back together. They solve the problems, but use different sources. Some of them are to evaluate the information from the web site.

Ms. Kelly commented that students improved their speaking skills when they were "being someone else" while speaking because it helped them to "establish a new identity with the use of the new language." It was a very useful way to apply the Internet in teaching. As she said: "I really love it (role play)". This means Ms. Kelly believed that role play provided good practice for students to develop their speaking skills.

Similarly, Ms. Mitchell based role play activities on news or stories on the Internet, asking students to produce interviews after they found information on the Internet. For instance, she used famous people quite often, so that students chose a famous person whom they would like to interview; students searched for information on famous people on the web. For example, one interview was about Madonna, and they had a stage interview in pairs in class. One student was the journalist, and the other was Madonna. Another famous person her students liked was Tony Blair. She thought role play was quite good for students to practise their speaking skills, and students "like to do acting role play." This suggests that students may be interested in this activity, which may enhance their motivation in working with peers using computer resources. As Dörnyei (2001) supports, using pop stars or famous people can motivate students in their language learning.

The findings in this section suggest that teachers believed that role play was one of good collaboration for students to practise their communicative skills, supporting Hedge (2000); Murphy (1991)'s suggestions that role play is a good type of speaking activity for students to develop speaking skills. It also develops their listening skills in conversations. Furthermore, the finding suggests that the success of the role play depends on the information the students get from the Internet, which is up to date and authentic. In this computer-supported collaboration, teachers acted as the key monitors and assessors for students' role play. At the same time, students can also offer comments to each other. Similarly, the computer programs used in the two centers cannot monitor and assess students' role play.

Recording Voice Together and Assessing Each Other's Recording

The third collaboration that interviewees reported was recording voice, comparing and assessing their speech with the original pronunciation or presentations. Despite the fact that some of the computer programs in the two centers offer the recording function and assume students can monitor and assess their recording themselves, participants commented that students preferred monitoring and assessing by their partners or teachers. Interviewees reported that the teachers asked them to record their speech in pairs and assess for each other. John commented that recording their voices together with peers enabled them to identify stress, and to talk in pairs or groups to explain "why you decide the full stress, how (to) stress words." In this collaboration, they helped each other to improve their speaking skills. Amanda and Mike agreed that this collaborative activity was helpful for speaking. They were able to listen to their speech for each other and gave positive feedback. As Mike noted: "My classmates also hear my record file. We listen to each other. I think it's good. I think this kind of education is very useful."

Teachers held similar views. Ms. Millar said she asked students to work in pairs to record together on computers. She asked students to focus on the intonation and word stress. She thought it was helpful when students worked in pairs to record their speech because they were able to compare their speech together, so that they learned from each other and helped each other to identify their problems. Ms. Taylor liked students to record speech together and explained: "The whole purpose of having them working together and recording themselves is, they have more control over what they are learning. I act as a guide to make sure they are able to notice and able to pay attention." This suggests that students control their own learning to assess for each other through this collaboration and the teacher can stay back as a monitor in this learning process.

Ms. Jones also liked her students to work in pairs or groups to record voices. She commented:

That's nice because they prepare activities together, and they aren't just on their own in front of the computer. I think in the classroom, there is a way making interaction. You know, the students can talk to each other as well as purely with the computer.

This means that this type of collaboration helped them solve their own problems in pronunciation and speaking, indicating that the collaboration improved their autonomous learning. Students help each other to monitor and assess their production of speaking. The awareness of the value of it indicates that this collaboration also motivates students in their language learning processes.

The discussion above demonstrates positive attitudes to using computers in pronunciation exercises, but this was not always the case. Three students did not seem to like assessment from peers on their recordings. Simon explained that because sometimes peers gave him the wrong idea and he had to complete the task again, which occurred many times. Two students who come from China argued that they did not like to receive feedback from their Chinese colleagues for their recordings because they often gave wrong suggestions on pronunciation. This might be because students from the same culture background find it hard to hear the pronunciation errors. As Tom remarked:

I think it's not good for Chinese students to give feedback to each other, because we Chinese people come from the same culture. We can't jump out of same culture circle.

Amy also noted that there were many Chinese students in her class, and she did not think they were able to receive valuable assessment from each other, because she thought Chinese people always said it was good rather than pointing out mistakes. Their comments suggest that the students would prefer to receive feedback from students from other cultures.

Similarly, Ms. Collins did not quite like the interaction between students themselves when they worked on computer programs because when students helped each other, they sometimes offered wrong information related to each other's recording. It was fine only when students were able to give correct assessment to each other. As she described:

Sometimes students and students have interaction, but not often. I don't think it is very helpful, because it's all right if you are sure if they can help each other correctly, but they often help each other, but it's not right. (Laughing) Two of them get wrong.

The comments above suggest that some students might not identify their mistakes in their recordings and might not give appropriate assessment when they worked together. This suggests that if students talks about pronunciation, some students have difficulties with it and cannot provide positive assessment for each other. This indicates that the collaboration for pronunciation issue may not be as very useful as other types of collaboration: discussion and role play. Despite

this, Adam and Amanda pointed out that although it was a better way for the teacher to assess their recordings, the problem was that the teacher was unable to listen to all students' recordings in class. In relationship to this point, Amanda stated it was helpful for them to exchange their recorded work with each other and to check the recording for each other. This suggests that when teachers are not available to assess students' recordings, it is useful for students to work together and check for each other.

Another interesting finding concerns using the web camera during collaboration. Each computer in the computer room in University Two Language Center is connected to a web camera. Ms. Taylor and Ms. Millar reported asking students to use the web camera in the computer room in pairs or groups when they used computer programs. They walked around to monitor students' collaboration. Ms. Taylor offered an example of students using web cameras with *Melissi Lab*, the software with telephoning function, where they were able to talk in pairs on the local network in the classroom. She said:

I think it (the web camera) is extremely useful. The students have used the web camera in the computer room here. There are four people, two were in one side of room, two people were in other side of the room. They decided they were going to work together recording their voices. They may like actually recording themselves, speaking together, so their dialogue was not just recorded for sounds. They did take film themselves basically. They filmed them having a dialogue. And it was quite funny because they are shy. They did enjoy it after a while.

This suggests that students used web cameras to record their voices including sounds and conversations. They were motivated in working with peers in using web cameras.

Ms. Millar also encouraged students to use the web camera to practise their speaking skills.

She asked students to talk to each other to make performances, just like on television. Additionally, she asked students to use the web camera in pairs to record their pronunciation. She commented that the web camera was useful for students, because they "either talk to each other to the web camera, so they can observe each other…, or they record themselves and look at back themselves afterwards and assess their own pronunciations developments." She said students found it valuable and they tried harder in their pronunciation practice with this type of interaction, indicating that students were motivated in this interaction. She pointed out that the main reason for the problem in pronunciation might be the mouth shape. Therefore, using the web camera was really helpful. They played back in order to monitor and assess the shapes of their mouths between each other. She added:

If I just record with the audio, they can hear between their sounds, but it didn't tell them how to change the shapes of their mouth. So using a web camera, I mean I can take the sound of myself into the class, and they can practise with them, and they can evaluate each other to the web camera. For online learning, it's very useful as well. Usually I ask students to use the web camera in pairs, because they can look at each other.

This is an example of combining various software in face-to-face language teaching and learning. Students can use web cameras to monitor and assess their pronunciation in collaborative learning. It shows that it is possible to combine different programs when using the new technology. This is also the advantage of using the new technology to develop pronunciation and speaking skills.

During students' individual interviews, 15 out of 21 students said it was useful and interesting to use the web camera to practise their listening and speaking skills with peers. In group interviews, five out of eight students agreed that the web camera helped them to develop their listening and speak-

ing skills. For example, Jim stated that it was very helpful to use the web camera to see people when talking in English because they were able to see the facial expression, such as lip movement, which was very important for learning pronunciation. His view supports Ms. Millar's point above, in the respect of seeing mouth shape. Susan agreed that the web camera was very useful to talk to others because they were able to see their own face and it offered more information for understanding. Susan noted that it was a useful way to improve her speaking and it was interesting, indicating that she was motivated to work through the web camera, so that she could spend a long time on it. As Susan highlighted:

With the web camera talking with others, I can take a long time. You can learn from others. Only voice, it's absent. With the web camera, you can catch more information. It's more attractive.

The above comments suggest that the web camera provides students with another opportunity to have interaction through computers, apart from having face-to-face interaction in class. They can monitor and assess their production of language on computers. Students felt it useful and interesting, indicating that students were motivated to practise their communicative skills in using web cameras. This supports findings from questionnaire data.

The results have shown that the computer programs used in the two language centers cannot provide monitoring and assessment for this collaboration. The findings suggest that, generally speaking, it is helpful for students to record their speech with peers and help each other to identify mistakes to improve their speaking together, but teachers need to monitor whether students give correct comments or not. It is particularly useful when teachers cannot give feedback on students' recordings. The results suggest that when students can recognize their errors and give correct feedback to each other, then this collaboration in recording tasks is useful. However, the findings reveal that when students are not able to identify their errors or give advice correctly, the teacher's feedback on students' record work and advice on how to correct their mistakes are significant. This suggests that teachers' monitoring and assessing students' recorded work is more helpful than students' assessing themselves.

The findings also show that the web camera is a useful tool to help students talk to each other to practise their listening and speaking skills. The web camera provides an opportunity for students to monitor and assess their speech with peers on computers via the network. Students were motivated to use this new tool.

Recommendations

According to the results above, the author suggests that teachers should organize various types of collaborative activities between students when using CALL programs. Teachers can ask students to discuss particular topics or information on the computer programs. This is also a good way to help students develop their comprehension for listening materials as well as speaking skills. More importantly, this authentic activity will help students become used to discussions as the basis for their future academic study. From the findings on role play, the researcher suggests that teachers can ask students to search for information on the Internet about famous people or pop stars (e.g. George Bush and Madonna) for speaking practice, and then to have role play with peers. Students can be motivated to participate in different roles. Speaking practice can come through from this activity in peers.

Regarding recording activity, the author suggests that teachers ask students to record their speech in computers together and monitor and assess each other's recordings, particularly when the teacher cannot check all students' recordings. For example, students might not be able to recognize the differences between their own voices and the original ones. It might be easy for their peers to

monitor and assess their recorded speech. Then, they can help each other to recognize their own strengths and weaknesses. Although the technology can provide function for students to obtain an analysis of their speech from the computer focusing on articulatory descriptions and charts of phonetic alphabet and vowel and students can learn what the difference is between their own pronunciation and the originals on computers, they still need peers and teachers' monitoring and assessment. As Celce-Murcia et al. (1996) point out, students require explicit instructions on how to use them effectively. This point indicates that students may still need assistance from the teacher to understand the task. Furthermore, the teacher needs to monitor students whether they can receive correct assessment from peers or not. The teacher can adopt 'analytical-linguistic' approach (Celce-Murcia et al., 1996), that is, the teacher takes a more scientific approach to analyze students' pronunciation from the articulator. Teachers normally give models either by themselves or from the computer for students to listen and imitate, and then give students feedback on their pronunciation. For instance, teachers can monitor and assess students' recordings and tell students whether their pronunciation is correct or incorrect, and analyze their errors. Teachers can write the common errors that students made in their recordings on the white board, and then tell students how to correct their mistakes. As Hedge (2000: 286) suggests, normally teachers have the responsibility to "decide when to focus on pronunciation, and on which aspects." The teacher has a role in assisting students to develop pronunciation, such as providing suggestions, feedback, support and encouragement (Morely, 1991). This indicates the main role of the teacher in teaching pronunciation.

From the result concerning the web camera, the author suggests that if the language centers provide a web camera on each computer, students will take more advantage of technology to practise their listening and speaking skills. Teachers may ask students to record their speech together, watch their mouth shapes and assess for each other on the recordings from the web camera. Although face-to-face interactions may be better than using the web camera in class, students feel interested, thus suggesting that students can be motivated to accomplish more work on it. Teachers can use web cameras to encourage students to talk with peers in class or in different campuses (this can be useful in cases where universities have different campuses located in different places in the city, such as is the case with University Two). Several English teachers mentioned that they would try to use web cameras to let students talk to each other from the different campuses in the university. Students can have group discussions with web cameras in their own places, such as their flats, but it depends on if all students have web cameras. Moreover, teachers may ask students to find peers in another city or around the world to develop speaking skills via web cameras. Students are likely to be interested in using this new way to speak with peers around the world, particularly for distance learning, where students do not have opportunities to have face-to-face talk. However, the effect of using the web camera also depends on the quality of the web camera and the stability and speed of the network. Further, how to monitor and assess this type of collaboration is under researched. In the current study, the findings solely showed that the teacher walked around and monitor students when they used web camera for collaboration.

With the respect to feedback, the results suggest that students can provide significant assessment for each other during their collaboration. However, teachers still need to monitor and assess students' collaborative activities because students sometimes cannot give correct feedback and students prefer teachers' evaluation.

FUTURE TRENDS

With the appearance of new tools, such as web cameras which enable online 'face-to-face' communication and more advanced and user-friendly software and online programs for language learning, language learners potentially have more opportunities to use computer-based technology to enhance their development in listening and speaking skills. For instance, with a web camera, via online chat rooms such as MSN or Yahoo Messenger for one-to-one talk, or Skype for discussion among a group of people (three or more than three), learners are able to have online chat to practise their speaking skills. Language teachers can organize a group of students within campus or around the world to have an online oral discussion. This type of online face-to-face communication may increase the learners' communicative skills, confidence and motivation.

In addition, the increasing interest in mobile learning has heightened the need of research in the use of mobile technologies such as mobile phones and PDAs (a handheld computer) in teaching and learning. CALL tasks with audio and video files can be downloaded into the mobile device. It may be more convenient for learners to develop listening and speaking skills in any location using a handheld device rather than working in front of a computer. It would be possible for students to practise their listening skills by listening to lectures and practise their speaking skills by completing tasks, recording and checking their voices, or having a video chat with other learners around the world. Being able to communicate in any location at any time with a variety of people may engage learners to be more interested in using these new advanced technologies as a way to develop their language skills.

Moreover, with the increasing use of artificial intelligence in monitoring and assessing individual language learner's speaking production on the computer, it has potential possibility to use computer technology to monitor and assess students' collaborative speaking activities discussed in this study. Students can use computers to record their discussion, role play and talking to each other, and then use the artificial intelligence to provide assessment for them. For instance, the computer program can indentify pronunciation and speech errors in students' discussions, role play and recording activities between peers and then offer suggestions to correct their mistakes. Students therefore are able to reinforce their communicative skills according to this feedback, reducing the reliance on teachers' monitoring and assessment in the CALL environment.

Hence, further research is needed in these contexts, with these devices, to develop recommendations to teachers and policy makers about how to integrate technologies into language teaching, how to guide students to use computers collaboratively to develop listening and speaking skills and how to monitor and assess students' collaboration in CALL context. This research could explore in detail the way they are used, and could investigate problem areas, in particular the ways of developing speaking skills with new technology, perhaps developing and testing solutions to these problems. The potential for these types of tools need full investigation, but my suggestion is that it provides exciting opportunities for learners to develop their language skills collaboratively with the new and advanced computer technology.

CONCLUSION

The results in this paper have shown how teachers organized various collaborative activities for students to work with peers to develop their speaking as well as listening skills during CALL environment. The findings have illustrated that students were invited to have discussions in pairs with information on the computer programs. Role play was another way for students to have collaboration to improve their language skills. The third type of collaboration between students was

that they worked in pairs to record their speech and helped each other to assess their recording work. These speaking activities are also basic tasks in traditional language classrooms, which give students opportunities to use and practise spoken English. Participants in this study commented that these types of collaboration in computer-based environments organized by teachers were useful for students to develop their language skills and they felt interested in working this way. Further, collaboration improves students' confidence and encourages them to have active learning, thus reduces the passive dependence on teachers' feedback. Students can monitor and assess for each other. However, the findings also have demonstrated that the computer programs used in the two centers cannot provide monitoring and assessment for students' collaboration when they develop listening and speaking skills in their second language learning. The teacher, thus, seems to be still key role of evaluating students' work, apart from students' assessing themselves. Despite this, the function of recording that the computer program provides and the use of the web camera seem to offer a sort of opportunity for students to monitor and assess their production of language collaboratively.

Therefore, this study indicates that collaboration is also a key to successfully using computers to learn a second language, supporting Chapelle (2001) and Harless et al.'s (1999) claims that collaboration between learners in using CALL programs helps them learn to use the target language effectively. The collaboration between students not only enables students to share their opinions with peers and assess their language production for each other, but also motivates students to work on CALL tasks together to foster their learning. This encourages students to practise their communication skills together through using computers. Meanwhile, the findings suggest that collaboration may also promote students autonomous learning. The findings support Phipps's (1999) claims that collaboration can improve students' communication and autonomous learning. The results also support Chen et al.'s (2004) study that peer interaction is helpful to students to use CALL programs in language learning and motivates students' work on computers. In addition, the discussion between peers is nature communication, which resonates with authenticity supported by several studies. This authentic communication practice is likely to help students become used to discussions with peers in academic situations. More importantly, this paper shows the important role of teachers in organizing activities, monitoring and assessing for collaboration between students in computer-based environments. It is hoped that the findings in this research can help institutions and teachers to gain some sense of how to integrate CALL programs into assisting students in collaborative language learning and enhance their language teaching. Institutions should encourage teachers to provide support and organize a variety of collaborative activities to assist students to successfully improve their language learning on computers. Moreover, the positive findings on collaborative learning between students can be recommended to students who prefer to work on computers individually to work with peers in order to achieve a better learning outcome in CALL environment. Students are likely to have more responsibility in their learning than that in the past due to the characteristics of autonomous learning with peers on computers.

Although the current CALL programs are unable to offer effective monitoring and assessment for students' collaboration during their listening and speaking activities on computers, with the development of technology, the computer may be able to provide reliable functions to monitor and assess language learners' collaborative learning in the future. These functions need to be further researched in CALL field in order to increase the reliability of using computers to support language learners' collaborative learning.

ACKNOWLEDGEMENT

I wish to thank Dr. Sally Barnes and Professor Pauline Rea-Dickins, from the Graduate School of Education at the University of Bristol (UK), for their terrific support through this study. I am also grateful for referees' suggestions and comments on this paper.

REFERENCES

Benson, P. (2001). *Teaching and researching autonomy in language learning*. Harlow, UK: Longman.

Butler-Pascoe, E. M., & Wiburg, M. K. (2003). *Technology and teaching English language learners*. Boston: Allyn and Bacon / Pearson.

Chapelle, A. C. (1998). Multimedia CALL: Lessons to be learned from research on instructed SLA. *Language Learning & Technology*, 2(1), 22–34.

Chapelle, A. C. (2001). *Computer applications in second language acquisition: Foundations for teaching, testing and research*. Cambridge, UK: Cambridge University Press.

Chapelle, A. C. (2003) *English language learning and technology*. Amsterdam: John Benjamins Publishing Company.

Chen, J., Belkada, S., & Okamoto, T. (2004). How a Web-based course facilities acquisition of English for academic purposes. *Language Learning & Technology*, 8(2), 33–49.

Curtis, D. D., & Lawson, M. J. (2001). Exploring collaborative online learning. *Journal of Asynchronous Learning Networks*, 5(1), 21–34.

Dillenbourg, P. (1999). What do you mean by collaborative learning? In P. Dillenbourg (Ed.), *Collaborative-learning: Cognitive and computational approaches* (pp. 1-19). Oxford, UK: Elsevier.

Dörnyei, Z. (2001). *Teaching and researching motivation*. Harlow, UK: Longman.

Dörnyei, Z. (2001). *Motivational strategies in the language classroom*. Cambridge, UK: Cambridge University Press.

Dudeney, G. (2000). *The Internet and the language classroom*. Cambridge, UK: Cambridge University Press.

Egbert, J. (2005). *CALL essentials: Principles and practice in call classrooms*. Alexandria, VA: TESOL.

Ellis, R. (2003). *Task-based language learning and teaching*. Oxford, UK: Oxford University Press.

Facer, K., Fulong, J., Furlong, R., & Sutherland, R. (2003) *ScreenPlay: Children and computing in the home*. London: RoutledgeFalmer.

Hanson-Smith, E. (1997). *Technology in the classroom: Practice and promise in the 21st century* (TESOL Professional Papers 2). Alexandria, VA: Teachers of English to Speakers of Other Languages.

Harless, W., Zier, A., & Duncan, R. (1999). Virtual dialogs with native speakers: The evaluation of an interactive multimedia method. *CALICO Journal*, *16*(3), 313–336.

Hedge, T. (2000). *Teaching and learning in the language classroom*. Oxford, UK: Oxford University Press.

Hegelheimer, V., & Tower, D. (2004). Using CALL in the classroom: Analyzing student interactions in an authentic classroom. *System*, *32*(2), 185–205. doi:10.1016/j.system.2003.11.007

Levy, M. (1997). *Computer-assisted language learning: Context and conceptualization*. Oxford, UK: Clarendon Press.

MacDonald, M., Badger, R., & White, G. (2000). The real thing?: Authenticity and academic listening. *English for Specific Purposes*, *19*(3), 253–267. doi:10.1016/S0889-4906(98)00028-3

Mendonça, C., & Johnson, K. (1994). Peer review negotiations: Revision activities in ESL writing instruction. *TESOL Quarterly*, *28*(4), 745–768. doi:10.2307/3587558

Murphy, M. J. (1991). Oral communication in TESOL: Integrating speaking, listening and pronunciation. *TESOL Quarterly*, *25*(1), 51–75. doi:10.2307/3587028

Nunan, D. (Ed.). (1992). *Collaborative language learning and teaching*. Cambridge, UK: Cambridge University Press.

Phipps, W. (1999). *Pairwork: Interaction in the modern language classroom*. London: CiLT.

Pica, T. (1987). Second language acquisition, interaction and the classroom. *Applied Linguistics*, *8*, 3–21. doi:10.1093/applin/8.1.3

Pica, T. (1994). Research on negotiation: What does it reveal about second-language learning conditions, processes and outcomes? *Language Learning*, *44*(3), 493–527. doi:10.1111/j.1467-1770.1994.tb01115.x

Pintrich, R. P., & Schunk, H. D. (1996). *Motivation in education: Theory, research, and applications*. Upper Saddle River, NJ: Prentice Hall.

Slater, P., & Varney-Burch, S. (2001). *Multimedia in language learning*. London: CiLT.

Sutherland, R., Armstrong, V., Barnes, S., Brawn, R., Gall, M., & Matthewman, S. (2004). Transforming teaching and learning: Embedding ICT into every-day classroom practices. *Journal of Computer Assisted Learning Special Issue*, *20*(6), 413–425. doi:10.1111/j.1365-2729.2004.00104.x

Teeler, D., & Gray, P. (2000). *How to use the Internet in ELT*. Edinburgh, UK: Pearson Education Limited.

Veerman, A. (2003). Constructive discussions through electronic dialogue. In J. Andriessen, M. Baker, & D. Suthers (Eds.), *Arguing to learn: Confronting cognitions in computer-supported collaborative learning environments* (pp. 117-143). Dordrecht, The Netherlands: Kluwer Academic Publishers.

Warschauer, M., & Healey, D. (1998). Computers and language learning: An overview. *Language Teaching*, *31*, 57–71. doi:10.1017/S0261444800012970

Chapter 13

Proposal of a Set of Reports for Students' Tracking and Assessing in E-Learning Platforms

Marta E. Zorrilla Pantaleón
University of Cantabria, Spain

Elena E. Álvarez Sáiz
University of Cantabria, Spain

ABSTRACT

The teaching-learning process has undergone a deep change with the appearance of new technologies. E-learning environments and, in particular, learning content management systems have provided capacities and tools which have contributed notably to this change. Their use has spread rapidly in the educational environments due to the advantages that they offer: freedom of timetable, ubiquity, tools for the communication and collaboration, etc. However, they still lack a suitable tool for the monitoring and follow-up of the students that allows the instructors, in an easy and intuitive way, to know what is happening with their distance students. This lack of knowledge is, to a great extent, the cause of a higher number of dropouts and a lower students' performance in comparison to traditional education. Consequently, in this chapter, the authors propose a set of reports, designed from an educational point of view, which help instructors to carry out this task and an architecture software for their implementation.

INTRODUCTION

Information and Communication Technologies (ICTs) are the tools and the support for the advancement in the building of the Knowledge Society. These have been and continue being the engine of social, economic, labour and formative change of the 21st century to respond to a productive sector that needs highly qualified professionals, technologically prepared and requiring constant recycling - "lifelong learning". Among all available technologies, the World Wide Web is the one that has made the sharing of information and resources possible and effective and, in this respect, it has allowed the democratization of knowledge to advance more rapidly.

DOI: 10.4018/978-1-60566-786-7.ch013

In the education field, the use of ICTs has meant a revolutionary change in the teaching and learning process: new ways of communication, new methods of work, new education techniques have appeared and, as a result, a new educational paradigm has emerged. In this new model, students become active subjects and both students and the activities they do are the centre of the learning process. Moreover, instructors help students to learn and they are no longer mere transmitters of knowledge but designers of courses who supervise and assist in the pupils' learning process (Gonzalez & Wagener, 2003).

There is a wide range of technologies that give support to this new educational paradigm as will be seen in Section 2. One of them is the Learning Content Management Systems (LCMS) which, nowadays, are extensively used in different environments such as educational institutions (universities, high schools, etc), research institutes as well as global enterprises.

These systems provide instructors with different tools with which they design their online courses. These virtual course design tools can be classified in the following groups according to (Edutools, 2008):

- **Communication tools:** Discussion Forum, Discussion Management, File Exchange, Internal Email, Online Journal/Notes, Real-time Chat, Whiteboard.
- **Productivity tools:** Bookmarks, Calendar/ Progress Review, Searching within Course, Work Offline/Synchronize, Orientation/ Help.
- **Student Involvement Tools:** Groupwork, Community Networking, Student Portfolios.
- **Course Delivery Tools:** Test Types, Automated Testing Management, Automated Testing Support, Online Marking Tools, Online Gradebook, Course Management, Student Tracking.

With regard to the last area mentioned, it must be said that whereas the tools such as quizzes, assessments, etc. generally offered by e-learning platforms in order to assess the student's performance are appropriate, the student tracking tools still present certain shortcomings (Avouris, Komis, Fiotakis, Margaritis & Voyiatzaki, 2005; Juan, Daradournis, Faulin & Xhafa, 2008; Mostow, Beck, Cen, Cuneo, Gouvea & Heiner, 2005; Pozzi, 2006; Romero & Ventura, 2006; Zaïane, 2001; Zorrilla, Menasalvas, Marín, Mora & Segovia, 2005). They do not allow instructors to thoroughly track and assess all the activities performed by all learners, nor to evaluate the structure of the course content or its effectiveness in the learning process in an easy and simple way.

In fact, these systems provide the instructor with certain information but this is limited and not very significant to make the teaching-learning process assessment. In general, they offer a report with summarised access information such as the dates of the first and the last connection, the number of visited pages, the number of read/ sent mails and so on by each student; and another report, about the use of resources (announcements, discussions, etc.) with parameters such as number of accesses and spent time on each one. But, as can be deduced, it is difficult to extract from their analysis the answers to questions like the following: In what topics are our learners working each day? Do they follow the sequence of the course properly? What is the best day of the week in order to propose an activity? Consequently, reports with more information of interest must be defined and developed in order to help instructors in the tracking and assessment of their students and their virtual courses.

Furthermore, it is important not only to define the parameters to be shown but also the way to present them since the reports must be intuitive and graphical so that the instructor, with just a glimpse, can get to know the students' situation in the course. On the other hand, it is essential that these reports can be generated in real time so that the instructor can act the very moment the problems and the fearsome dropouts are detected in the course.

In this chapter, we attempt to offer a set of reports that fulfil the characteristics previously mentioned and that allows instructors to do their task in a more assisted way, providing them with useful information by means of simple and intuitive reports. The definition of these reports relies on the experience acquired in the imparting of virtual courses (Álvarez & Zorrilla, 2008), in the use of different e-learning platforms (WebCT 4.0, Blackboard 6.0 and Moodle 1.8) and in the development and use of the Matep tool (Zorrilla & Álvarez, 2008). Moreover, the necessity and the content of these reports are justified by the results of a survey that was sent to the instructors involved in virtual teaching in some Spanish Universities.

The chapter is organized as follows. First, we make a brief summary about Web-Based Distance Education, advantages of its use and problems not solved. Next, we discuss a survey sent to instructors of different virtual courses in Spanish Universities with the aim of knowing what information the reports must gather in order to meet instructors' tracking needs. After that, we analyse tracking and assessment tools which the most known and used e-learning platforms, both commercial and open source, provides according to the needs specified by instructors in our survey. Then, we describe in detail both the set of reports which we propose and an architecture for their development. Finally, we draw the main conclusions.

WEB-BASED DISTANCE EDUCATION

Up to the 80´s, the teaching-learning process basically took place in a classroom and with no more resources than some chalk and a blackboard, although pen-and-paper correspondence courses were also available. The appearance of the PC at a reasonable price made it possible to use it in the classroom, mainly in labs. At the same time the advancement of communication technologies (IP protocol, operating systems, networks, etc.) made both electronic communication (chat, mail) and information exchange (ftp, etc.) possible between students and the instructor and also among students. But it was in 1992 when new opportunities for distance education appeared thanks to the WWW which has made it possible to create a virtual course to bring together a community of learners using different teaching strategies, activities and technologies.

According to (Kahiigi, Ekenberg, Hansson, Tusubira & Danielson, 2008) these technologies can be classified in:

- **Learning Management Systems (LMS)** are Web-based software applications used to plan, implement, and assess a specific learning process. Typically, an LMS provides an instructor with a way to create and deliver content, monitor student participation, and assess student performance. It may also provide students with the ability to use interactive features such as threaded discussions, video conferencing, and discussion forums. Examples of LMS include WebCT 4.0 (WebCT, 2003) and JoomlaLMS (JoomlaLMS, 2008).
- **Content Management Systems (CMS)** are Web-based applications developed to facilitate the collaborative creation of content and to organise, control and manage the publication of documents in a centralized environment. This category mainly includes Cooperative Working Tools such as BSCW (BSCW, 2005) and software to create and maintain Blogs and Wikis.
- **Learning Content Management Systems (LCMS)** are mostly web-based systems that combine the management and administrative functionalities of LMS and CMS to authorize, approve, publish, and manage learning content. Blackboard (Blackboard,

2006), Moodle (Moodle, 2007) and Claroline (Claroline, 2005) are some examples of LCMS.

- **Multimedia Communities and Virtual Worlds** provide a learning environment that stimulates learners' high order thinking and knowledge development and creates social groups according to (Cross, O'Driscoll & Trondsen, 2007).

- **Learning objects** are digital resources created to provide useable content in various disciplines and context, resulting in a reduction of production time and cost, enhancing productivity and improving the quality of learning (Koohang, 2004).

- **Authoring technologies** aim at enhancing and facilitating the students' learning process through built-in simulations and interactions (Gee, 2004; Tai & Ting, 2007).

Of all of these, LCMSs are those most used to both deliver training material through the net and facilitate the interaction among students and tutors. There are many reasons to justify their successful use (Britain & Liber, 1999), which can be summarized in:

- They support many of the activities that occur in the classroom and allow the use of different multimedia resources, generally, interactive ones.

- They facilitate communication and feedback - key to effective online learning.

- They support different styles of learning: collaborative learning, discussion-led learning, student-centred learning, and resource-based learning.

- They allow flexibility of time and place. Just-in-time training.

- They cope with large numbers of students.

- They facilitate sharing and re-use of resources.

But not all are advantages. Their use poses some shortcomings for both students and instructors. There is a list of problems encountered by students studying on-line courses, including the students' feeling of isolation due to lack of contact with the instructor, disorientation in the course hyperspace, loss of student motivation and lack of institutional support (help with technical problems, inflexible administrative bureaucracy, etc.) (Conrad, 2002; Mazza & Dimitrova, 2007). On the other hand, instructors lack the appropriate tools in order to supervise the students´ work in the current LCMSs (Hijon & Velazquez, 2006). Secondly, they are sometimes overwhelmed by the great quantity of queries that they receive by mail and not addressed though the forum (the students do not work in a very collaborative way). In addition, generally the number of drop-outs in this type of learning is higher (Xenos, Pierrakeas & Pintelas, 2002; Jusung, 2005; Levy, 2007) and students get worse marks (Zinn & Scheuer, 2006) than in traditional learning.

In our opinion and that of many other authors (Juan, Daradournis, Faulin & Xhafa, 2008; Mazza & Milani, 2005; Mazza & Dimitrova, 2007; Zhang, Almeroth, Knight, Bulger & Mayer, 2007) these problems could be reduced, and to some extent avoided, if the instructors had a better understanding of what is happening with their students in their virtual course: are they reading materials according to how the instructor has designed the course? Are they participating in discussions? Are they doing the proposed exercise, tests, and so on? Is the course designed according to the students' profile? How much effort do the students need to make in order to pass the course? Is the workload of the course balanced? etc. If instructors knew this information, they could act as soon as they detected the problem as teachers in a traditional classroom would when they observe that a student is making a strange face or seems to be bored. In the first case, they can explain the concepts in a different way and, in the second case, they can change the activity so that the student can get motivated and not dropout of the course. The problem is that the lack of physical contact does not allow instructors to assess these aspects through the web or mail, and thus some parameters must be defined in order to measure the effort and the work made by the student in the virtual course as well as to be able to evaluate the course itself and its effectiveness in the teaching process.

Although, as has been said before, e-learning platforms offer reports with parameters about the activity of the students in the course, these do not show all the information the instructors are interested in. For instance, they cannot know the progress of their students with regard to the learning goals of the course or if their students visit all the pages that the instructor considers to be important or to know what the profile of their students is. LCMSs lack the needed contextual information to answer these questions. On the other hand, the organization of the information in the reports as well as the format that they use, generally in tabular format, does not help instructors to diagnose the problems in a simple and understandable way. In addition, none of the known LCMSs offers reports that allow instructors to evaluate the design of their courses. Therefore, it is necessary to design tools for the monitoring and evaluation of both students and virtual courses to be used according to the educational perspective.

INSTRUCTORS' SURVEY

In this section, we present the survey that we prepared in order to know the needs that instructors who use e-learning platforms have in relation to the students' tracking and assessment.

Although we designed Matep, its use during an academic year allowed us to detect some needs uncovered by the tool and, before developing them, we considered it appropriate to know the information which other experts in virtual teaching considered essential to track the distance students.

The survey consisted of two parts. The first part aimed at profiling those who participated in filling-out the survey; this profile included, for instance, the university in where they teach, knowledge area, experience as an instructor, experience as an e-learning instructor, educational category, gender and e-learning platforms used.

The second part included questions organised in four sections: students' identification, students' course follow-up, students' behaviour patterns and design and structure of the course (see Table 1). Instructors were asked to evaluate the questions with regard to interest on a scale from 1 "None/I find it uninteresting" to 5 "Essential/Very necessary". Instructors were also asked to give any feedback with regard to the appropriateness of our proposals.

The survey was sent to 130 instructors who are responsible for at least one virtual course in the largest virtual campus in Spain, called G9. This offered 86 subjects in the academic year 2007-08 and had 4744 registered students (Sevilla, 2008). We use the term virtual course to refer to courses offered via the web, with no required face-to-face contact with the instructor.

At the time of writing, 52 instructors had participated in the study. 76.2% of the participants were assistant professors, 4.8% were professors and the rest occupied other educational university posts. Two thirds (68%) of the participants were male. In general they were instructors with great educational experience (18.5 years in average) and they had been working in virtual teaching for 4 years on average. Mainly, the learning systems used were Blackboard/WebCT (61%) and Moodle (57.1%) and, in minor proportion, RedCampus (4.7%), Ekasi (9%) and Sakai (4.7%). It must be outlined most of them (90.0% as opposed to 9%) were willing to incorporate additional information about their courses (context) in order to obtain further information about their students.

Regarding the results of the survey, as can be observed in Figure 1, all questions have received

Table 1. Survey

About the students: Identification
Q1. Students' profile: gender, age, degree.
Q2. Experience in the use of computers/Internet.
Q3. Previous knowledge related to the subject topic.
Q4. Motivation to study the subject.
Q5. Foreseen time to work on the subject.
About the students: Course follow-up
Q6. Learn about the distribution of visits to the material per day, time-slot, week, month, etc. carried out by students in comparison with the group average.
Q7. Learn about the distribution of accesses to collaborative and communication tools per day of the week and time-slot, per week, per month, etc. carried out by students in comparison with the group average.
Q8. Learn about the course periods of more or less intensity considering the number of sessions, the time spent on them, the number of pages visited and so on.
Q9. Detect when a course drop-out is about to occur.
Q10. Learn about the student's session assessment according to the instructor's learning goals.
Q11. Learn about the most appropriate way to establish an effective student-instructor communication through the number of accesses per tool, number of mail messages read.
About the students: Behaviour patterns
Q12. Know how much work students do during the course by means of the time spent on each session and the number of pages visited according to their age, gender and degree.
Q13. Know what resources students use according to their age, gender and degree.
Q14. Know statistics of the students' assessable activities available in the e-learning platform (tasks, tests, etc.) according to their age, gender and degree.
Q15. Know how often students read the information facilitated through the communication tools available in the e-learning platform (mail, forum, etc.) according to their age, gender and degree.
About the course structure and design
Q16. Learn about how students surf analysing the sequence of pages visited per session and the time spent on each of them.
Q17. Learn about how interesting the instructor's material is for students: percentage of accesses and which pages are the most and the least visited in a certain period of time.
Q18. Learn about the suitability of the task distribution during the course and detect the moments of relaxation and overwork.

an average valuation higher than 3. This means that all of them are considered sufficiently necessary and as a consequence, the existence of a specific report for each one is justified. The highest scored questions for each section were Q3, Q9, Q15 and Q18 and the lowest were Q2, Q7, Q13 and Q16. Once again, it is clearly shown that instructors are mainly worried about detecting the dropouts before they happen, knowing if the information that they send students is read and if the distribution of tasks is balanced during the course.

TRACKING AND ASSESSMENT TOOLS ANALYSIS

There is a wide range of student tracking approaches and implementations. The features and limitations of student tracking tool depend on the characteristics of the e-learning systems. Next we will carry out an analysis of the tools which are provided by the most known and used LCMSs, according to (Álvarez, 2008) and our survey, such as Blackboard (Blackboard, 2006) and Moodle (Moodle, 2007) as well as those that have been developed in the research environment and that offer a general and sufficiently suitable solution, such as CourseVis (Mazza & Dimitrova, 2007), Gismo (Milani & Mazza, 2007), Moodog (Zhang, Almeroth, Knight, Bulger & Mayer, 2007) and Matep (Zorrilla & Álvarez, 2008) indicating to what extent they respond to the questions raised in the survey.

As can be observed in the previous section, questions Q1 to Q5 and Q12 to Q15 aim at knowing the profile of the learners and their behaviour pattern in virtual courses. Given that student demographic data is generally not gathered in the LCMSs, these do not provide us with reports to answer these questions. Matep is an exception. It offers two reports with which questions Q12 and Q14 are answered, thanks to the information provided by the academic information system to which it is connected.

Focusing on the questions about the course follow-up, it has to be said that questions Q10 and Q11 are not answered by any tool either, with the exception of Matep that answers Q10 using the information that the instructor provides previously to the tool for each resource category (communication, productivity, learning, etc.).

We now discuss to what extent the tools under analysis answer the rest of inquiries.

Moodle answer questions Q6 to Q9 but not directly. The instructor, using the "*Moodle activity report*", can obtain all the entries carried out by the learner or the group in a period of time and/ or about a certain activity. Later, exporting this information to a tool such as Excel, the instructor can filter and do the pertinent calculations in order to give response to the questions.

Blackboard provides 7 reports for tracking student progress although 6 of them show the data aggregated by course. It offers more information than Moodle about the use of the course, for instance, the most and least visited pages, average user session length, most active day and so on. Its "*student tracking report*" allow instructors to get the answer to questions Q6 to Q9 but only for an individual student. Instructors must export the data of each student and process them together in order to do a global study. They can also use the *course item usage report* and the *tool usage report* to partially answer Q6 and Q7. As with Moodle, it allows instructors to filter the information that the report shows, though only for a range of dates.

On the other hand, Moodog (information extracted from Zhang, Almeroth, Knight, Bulger & Mayer, 2007) is an application which reads Moodle logs and makes a multidimensional analysis of their content: Who is connected? What resources do they use? When do they connect? And where do they spend their time? The information that

Figure 1. Results of the survey

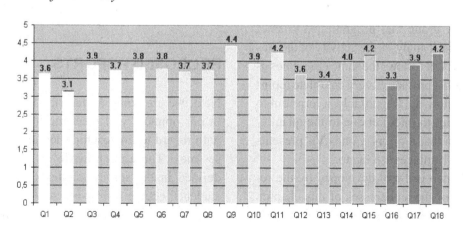

the tool handles and the way in which it does it, would allow the tool to give response to questions Q6 to Q9, but not thoroughly. In Zhang, Almeroth, Knight, Bulger & Mayer's (2007) study, it is not indicated whether the instructor can select the period of analysis or if the information can be exported. Both characteristics are considered of great interest to instructors. It must be highlighted that it allows students to easily compare their own progress with others in the class.

Alternatively, Gismo is an open-source graphical interactive student monitoring and tracking tool that extracts tracking data from Moodle. It offers graphical information of accesses carried out by students to the different resources of the course in the period of dates specified by instructors; and information about the different activities submitted to be evaluated and the grade obtained. The design of these reports, exclusively graphical, makes their analysis simple. With just a glimpse, instructors have a clear image of what is happening in the course. However, they lack statistical information with which they can measure and compare students' behaviour, as well as observe the same information in an aggregated way (analysis per learner and per course, per day, week or month, per topic, etc). Furthermore, the reports do not show the number and duration of accesses or the period of the day when these take place and, in our opinion, these are essential in order to evaluate the design of the course and the behaviour of the students and their progress.

CourseVis is another tool developed by the same research group that programmed Gismo, but, in this case, it analyses the activity of the students in WebCT. It follows the same guidelines as Gismo, though it provides a very complete report for student follow-up. Regrettably, it turns out to be a bit difficult to interpret due to the quantity of information that it offers. CourseVis presents the same disadvantages as Gismo.

Lastly, Matep is a tool developed by the research group of the authoresses of this chapter. At present, it is in test phase. Matep offers reports

that answer most of the questions of the survey, with the exception of the questions in the student identification section, though not in such a graphical and visual format as we propose in this chapter. There are some differences with respect to what we propose here. On the one hand, the content pages are not organizing by topics together with their activities, but rather are classified in two levels (class and subclass) to be defined by the instructor. On the other hand, the learner's profile is studied globally, and not by the use of resources and content pages independently. Moreover in this proposal, we have added some new and interesting reports such as *discussion graph report, instructors-learners communication report, course usage comparative report, performance pattern report* and *communication tool usage pattern report.*

Regarding the questions about the design and structure of the course, we can say that Moodle and Blackboard can answer these questions although the instructor must export the activity entries and post-process them. On the other hand, Moodog, Gismo and CourseVis do not offer any report that allows instructors to carry out this analysis. In contrast, Matep offers 4 reports with which these questions can be answered: *sequence of visited pages, top 5 pages, non-visited pages and activity per week* (in our current proposal named *student dropout*). However, in the current proposal, this last report is more graphical and easy to analyse and the study of the most and least visited pages is not limited to a certain number.

PROPOSED REPORTS

Next, we are going to describe the reports that, in our opinion, will meet the instructors' needs with regard to the teaching-learning process assessment. These are shown following the sections defined in the survey: students' identification, students' course follow-up, students' behaviour patterns and design and structure of the course.

For each report we indicate its name, questions that it can answer, the parameters that it shows and the dimensions under which these measures are observed. Likewise, we say if the report allows instructors to filter the information that they want to observe and if the report requires contextual information, which means information provided by instructors about the organization and learning goals of their virtual courses. Lastly we include an example of each report.

Regarding the student-tracking tool, we consider it should have the following general characteristics:

- Independent but easy to integrate with different LCMSs.
- Usable interface, preferably web-based.
- Data exportation in different formats (csv, xls,...).
- Daily updated information.
  And, the reports would be
- Parameter-driven.
- Easy to interpret, which means, expressive and intuitive reports and graphs.
- Easy to handle.

Before describing the reports, we define some of the terms that are used in this section:

- **Click stream:** the record of what a computer user clicks on while Web browsing.
- **User:** person who connects to the virtual course such as student or instructor.
- **User session:** a series of requests by the same identified student (user) from the moment he or she connects to the course until he or she disconnects or leaves it. This data can be difficult to calculate exactly, generally a timeout is defined.
- **Course access:** each time a student or instructor connects to the course.
- **Page view:** each time a web page or file is requested by a user. Content pages, urls,

assessments, tests, etc. are included in this group.

- **Resource access:** each time a user accesses a communication tool (mail, chat, etc.) or a productivity tool (bookmark, calendar, etc.).
- **Session length:** amount of time that learner spends on the course each time he or she visits it. This data may not be exact due to the fact that the length of the final page view is difficult to obtain (timeout).
- **Total time:** amount of time that user has spent on the resources of the course.

Student Identification Report

In this section, a report which answers questions Q1 to Q5 is defined. This report allows instructors to have an initial overview of profile of their students very useful at the beginning of the course.

As can be observed in Figure 2, the report includes the following parameters: previous knowledge level in topics related to the course contents, experience in the use of Internet and computer tools, motivation level with which learners enrol in the course and, the number of hours per week that they plan to dedicate to the course. All these parameters are considered with regard to gender, age, and the degree which students are studying.

For each parameter and the value of each dimension, the report shows the number of students and, graphically, the number of different answers given at each score, as well as the average value. The valuation of each question is from 1 to 5 as shown in the legend in the upper part of the report. In addition, the total number of students who answered each question and the average value for each parameter are shown in the last row of the table.

For example, instructors analysing Figure 2 can draw the conclusion that, in general, their students have some knowledge about the topics of the course and they plan to dedicate few hours per week to the subject. Furthermore, they can appreciate that the age group "24 to 27" is the most numerous and heterogeneous with respect to any of the report parameters; and that the groups with older students are smaller in percentage but their members are more motivated and have more experience in the use of Internet.

Consequently, with this report instructors will be able to determine if they must include additional material for learners with little knowledge on the subject, or propose activities which encourage students to participate and work in the course, or dissuade learners from following the course if their profile is not the appropriate one, etc.

The information that this report provides must be obtained by means of a survey carried out, preferably, at the beginning of the course.

The reporting tool which generates this report must allow instructors to choose the virtual course and the dimensions under which they want to observe these parameters, degree and gender, degree and age or age and gender. The report will recalculate the value of the parameters according

to the items selected in the upper-left box (remaining dimension).

Students Tracking Reports

This section describes 10 reports with which instructors can track their students.

The first, *course activity report* aims at showing a summary of the activity made by all the students involved in the virtual course for each educational unit or topic defined by the instructor in a certain range of dates.

As can be observed in Figure 3, the report shows the educational unit chosen in the upper-left box with the different resources (assessments, tests, etc.) that the instructor has selected and indicates the total number of page views or resource accesses, the number of distinct students who have visited the pages, and the total time spent by all of them. Likewise, it informs us about both the average time spent per student and the average number of page views or accesses per student (indicated by white circles). It also shows, for each

Figure 2. Student identification report

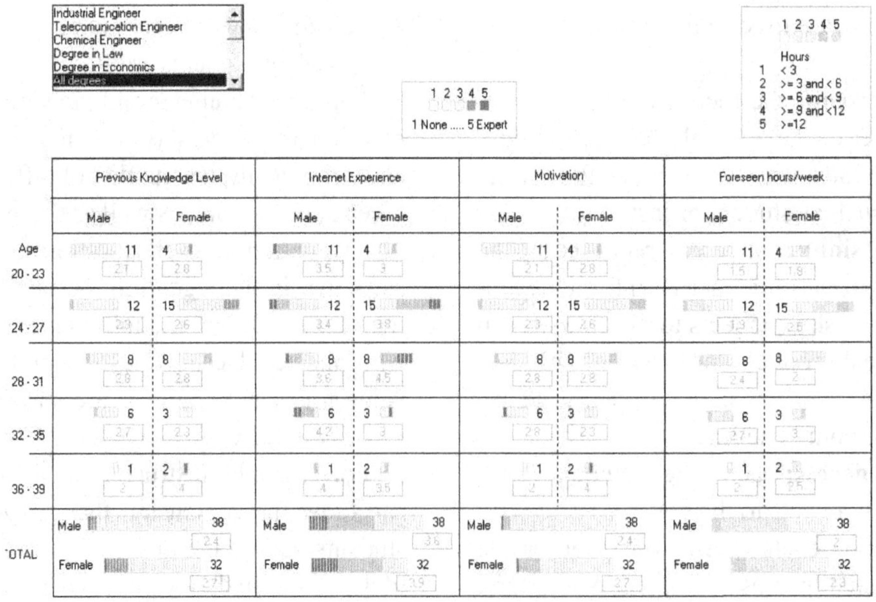

unit, the 25th and 75th percentile of both measures (shown in grey double line boxes) in order to see if the average is affected by the existence of extreme values.

The percentages that the report shows in the row which sums up the activity of each unit are with respect to the rest of units, and the percentages in each resource summary row (contents, assessment, etc.) are in relation to the unit.

For example, instructors observing Figure 3 can discover that only 45 students of 70 enrolled in the course have visited some resource of unit 1 in the chosen dates; and, in particular, the content section has only been visited by 30 students, who, on average, have acceded 17 times to each page. Page 1 has been the page visited by most students with an average time of 20 minutes. With regard to the rest of tools, instructors can appreciate that students have scarcely used the forum and the glossary, and in contrast, assessable tasks and tests pages have been visited by more students.

Consequently, with this report instructors can know the pace of work of their students, if they study the units according to the order proposed by the instructor (we consider that the units are organised in time order), if there are learners who have never connected, if there are resources that have never been used, etc.

It must be mentioned that few LCMSs allow instructors to define the educational unit, as for example, Moodle. Consequently, instructors must insert this information (context) in a database so that the reporting tool can use it.

The *student activity report* (see Figure 4) has the same format and shows the same information as the previous one, but in this case, both the number of page views and the total time are per student and the average values are regarding the group so that instructors can compare them.

Thanks to this report, instructors can know how individual learners progress in the course, the units in which they have spent more time, and the resources which they use most frequently, if their effort is higher or lower than the group average and so on.

In this case, we consider appropriate that instructors can get the report querying by student,

Figure 3. Course activity report

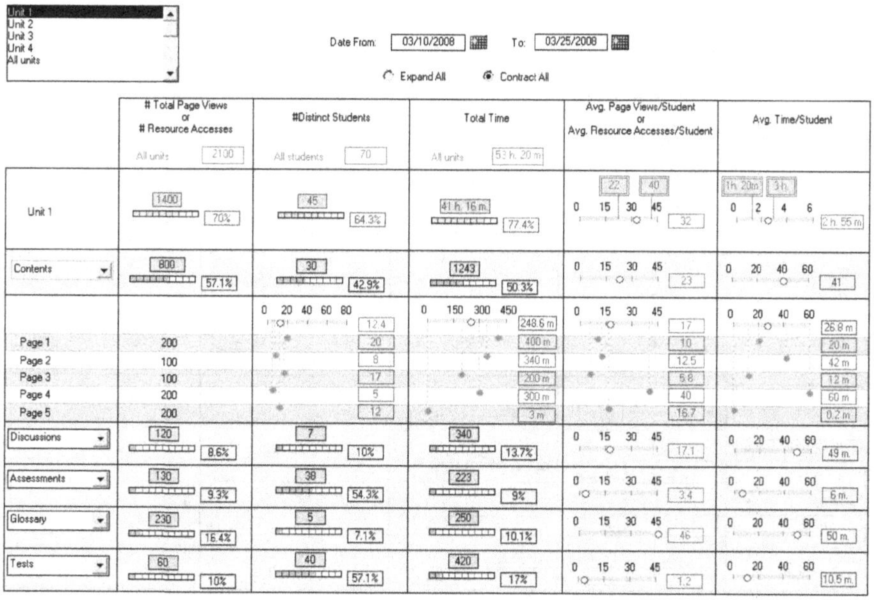

unit and range of dates. In this way, instructors can focus on their study in certain periods of the course, for instance, days prior to submitting a task or do an exam.

The *student session report* (see Figure 5) aims at knowing the order in which the student has visited the pages of the course. So, instructors can detect if students follow the learning paths defined by them or there are some undesirable jumps from one unit to another which can be due to a bad design of the course or student learning style (Graf, Kindhuk & Liu, 2008). In any case, instructors can already take actions to solve the problem, for example, checking if other learners do the same things or contacting the student to clarify his or her doubts.

This report presents the user sessions which have taken place in a certain period of time. These can be filtered for a specific student selected in the upper-left box. For each session, the report shows the number of distinct pages viewed and resources accessed and illustrates graphically with a coloured bar, the pages visited in each unit. In this way, instructors can observe easily if a session contains pages from different units or not. In addition, the report shows the total number of requests, the session length, the date and the day of the week, and lastly, the session value.

The session value is a number between 0 and 10 which indicates the extent to which the student has achieved the learning goals established by the instructor. To this aim, the instructor must classify every activity (context) that a learner can perform in the course into a category according to its predominant characteristic (communication, evaluation, learning, additional information, etc.) and assign a weight to every category. Hereby, the valuation of a session is carried out "weighing" the activities performed by the student in the session. In this way,

Figure 4. Student activity report

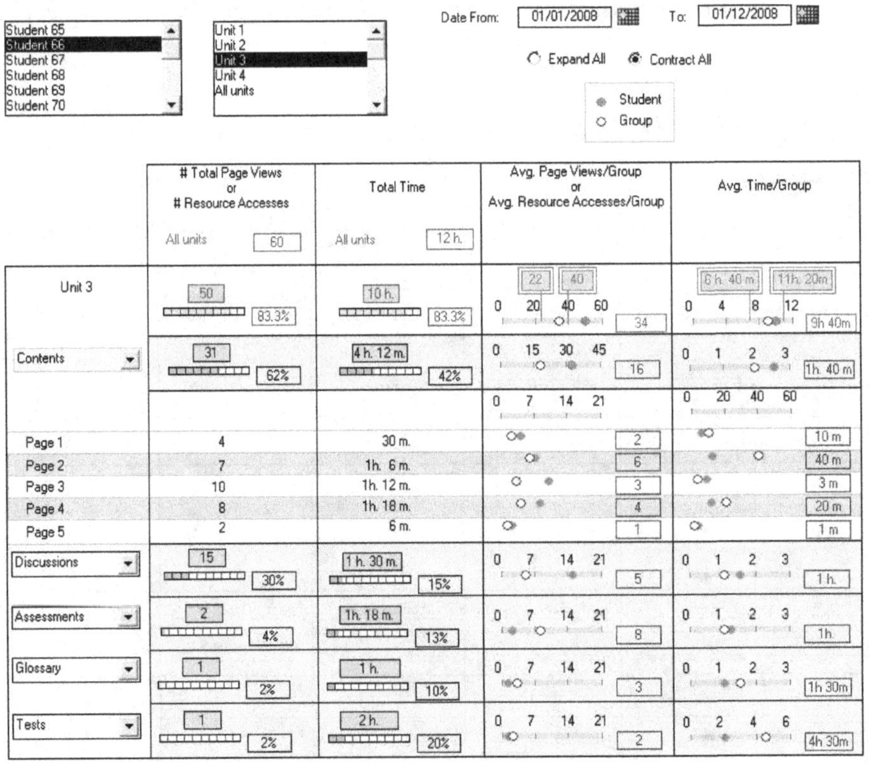

if the course has n categories established, the value of the session will be obtained as:

$$SessionValue = \sum_{i=1}^{n} Weight_i * SessionCategoryValue_i \quad where \quad \sum_{i=1}^{n} Weight_i = 1$$
$$and \quad 0 \leq SessionCategoryValue_i \leq 1$$

In addition, the report also allows instructors to unfold a session and see the pages viewed in the order in which the student requested them for the first time. Likewise, it shows the number of times that the student requested the page (this data can be difficult to obtain because of proxies, caches, etc) and the total time spent on it.

Finally, it can be said that the time shown in the first row of the report corresponds with the average session length of the sessions which are visualised and the diagram which represents the day of week indicates the first and the second most frequent day of visit.

It is also interesting for the instructor to be able to compare their learners by the content pages and the resources which they have accessed in a certain period. With this aim, we have designed the *course usage comparative report* (see Figure 6).

This report shows for each student, the number of accesses to each page or resource, the total time spent and the average time spent. The histogram, at the bottom, represents the number of distinct students who have visited each page or resource (ordered by units) in the period selected, and the scatter plot above it shows whether the students selected in the upper-left box have visited the pages. In this way, instructors can, on one hand, know the different styles of learning of their students and on the other hand, evaluate the design of their courses. If students do not visit certain pages which are considered necessary to do a certain activity, perhaps students do not realise the relevance of these pages or they are difficult to reach.

The *content page activity distribution report* allows instructors to know, for a range of dates, which day of week and in which range of hours the course has had more activity. With this infor-mation, instructors can organise collaborative activities, propose online tutorship or plan exams in accordance with the preferences of the students.

As can be observed in Figure 7, this report shows, for each day of week, the total and average number of distinct users who connected, the total and average number of page views and the total and average time spent. It must be outlined that these parameters only take into account students' activity in content pages.

In addition, in the first row of the report, the percentage of distinct users with respect to the total number of students and, the 25th, 50th and 75th percentile of each average parameter are shown. At the bottom, the report represents graphically the number of accesses in each period of the day (morning, afternoon, evening and night). The range of hours of each period must be defined in the application (context).

The *tool usage report* aims to show how often students use the resources which the instructor selects for his course. As can be observed in Figure 8, this report shows the total and average number of accesses to each tool (in this case mail and forum) by the group and the total number of accesses that each student selected in the upper-left box done in the period of dates selected. The "Graphic" button shows the graph with the number of accesses for each day of week and range of hours.

With this report, instructors can know which resources are more frequently used, what prefer-ences individual learners have, if there are students who are more active than others and so on.

For the particular case of forums, the *discussion graph* proposed by (Mazza & Dimitrova, 2007) is considered to be very suitable. This graph (see Figure 9) represents the number of threads started by each student and the number of follow-ups received for each thread. So, the instructor can gain insights about the feedback received from other students on threads generated by a student, learners with low or null activity, discussions which have ensued from major interest, etc.

Another question that instructors need to know

Figure 5. Student session report

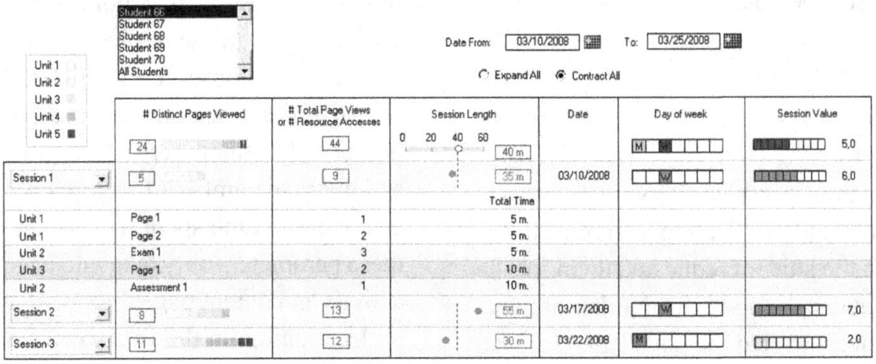

Figure 6. Course usage comparative report

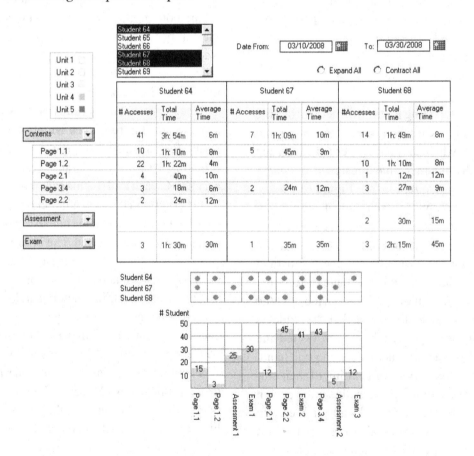

is whether the students regularly follow the information facilitated by means of the available tools of communication in the e-learning platforms (mail, forum, announcements). Consequently,

instructors-learners communication report (see Figure 10) has been designed.

It must be highlighted that this report only takes into account the messages sent by instructors. It

Figure 7. Content page activity distribution report

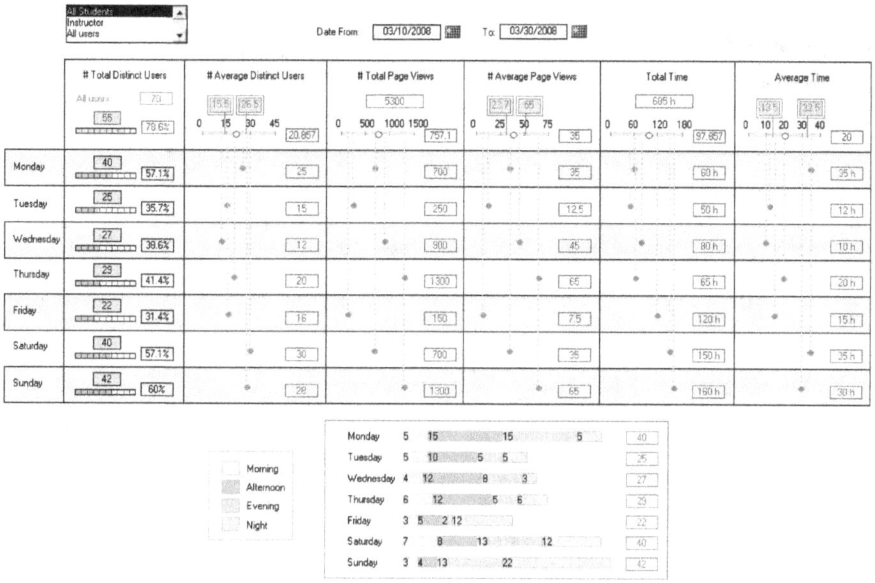

shows, for a certain period of dates, the number of the distinct students who have accessed each message, the total sum of the time it took students to read the message for the first time (necessary to calculate the average) and the average time per student. As can be observed, the messages are organised by the date sent in ascendant order. As in preceding reports, the information can be filtered for a specific forum, announcement or mail or a combination of these using the upper-left box.

This report allows instructors to estimate the time to ensure that their messages, announcements, etc. are read by all their students in good time.

The objective of the *global course usage report* is to know the periods of more and less activity in the course per student or per group of students. This report includes the following parameters: the number of sessions, the number of distinct students, the average time per session and the average number of page views or resource accesses per session according to the option selected (radial button above the column). As Figure 11 illustrates, it allows instructors to choose the period of analysis and the student or group of students and shows the information organised per months and

weeks. At the bottom, a graphical representation of these parameters is shown.

The last report in this subsection is the *student dropout report*. This report (see Figure 12) is very interesting for instructors since they can detect, with just a glimpse, if a learner does not follow the course regularly and whether there is much chance of him or her dropping out or, perhaps if he or she has already done so. The report which we propose is based on the one that CourseVis provides (Mazza & Dimitrova, 2007). In our opinion, it is graphical enough and clear. Furthermore, in our proposal, the information can be filtered by a specific range of dates and a set of users.

The scatter plot represents bivariate data of students and dates, where a bullet represents at least one access to the course made by the student on the date. The histogram represents the number of course accesses carried out by all students on each date included in the selected period.

Behaviour Patterns Reports

The reports that are described in this section allow instructors to obtain their students' behaviour

Figure 8. Tool usage report

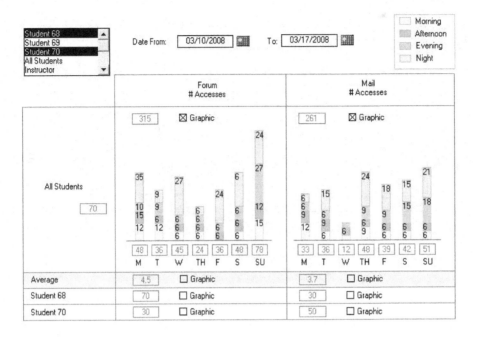

Figure 9. Discussion graph

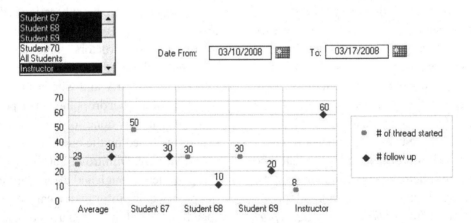

patterns according to their age, gender and degree. All of them show the information for the range of dates that instructors choose; in this way, they can check if the patterns change during the course.

The reporting tool which generates these reports must allow instructors to manipulate them in the same way as the *student identification report*.

The *dedication pattern report* (see Figure 13)

shows the average time connected and the average number of page views (only content pages). In addition, it presents two reference values, one for each parameter. The reference value with which the time connected is compared is calculated as the hours that the instructor estimates that students must dedicate to the course per week multiplied by the number of weeks of the period of query; and, the reference value for page views is the

Figure 10. Instructors-learners communication report

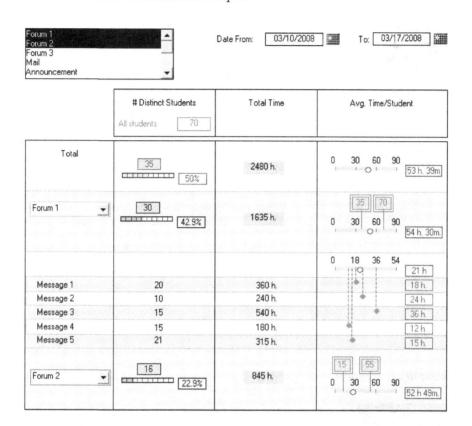

average number of page views by the students of the course in that period.

The *resource usage pattern report* (see Figure 14) shows the same information but in this case, the average number of page views is substituted by the average number of resource accesses. The reference parameters are calculated the same way.

Figure 15 illustrates the *performance pattern report* which shows the number of learners, the average number of assessable tasks carried out and the percentage that these suppose with regard to the whole of activities, and the average mark. This report requires that the instructor indicates previously the activities that will be evaluated (context).

Finally, the *communication tool usage pattern report* (see Figure 16), shows the number of students and the average time which elapses between

the instructor sending the message and this being read by the students for first time.

All these reports help instructors to prepare future editions of the course, in which they can propose new itineraries and recommendations as well as decide what the most effective way of announcing the information is.

Course Structure and Design Reports

In this subsection, we describe some reports with which instructors can evaluate whether the design and the structure of their courses are suitable for learning.

In order to assess how students surf in the course, instructors can use the *student session report* (see Figure 5) described in previous subsection. Analysing the paths, instructors will be able

Figure 11. Global course usage report

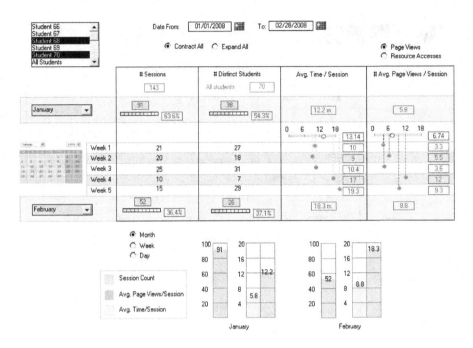

Figure 12. Student dropout report

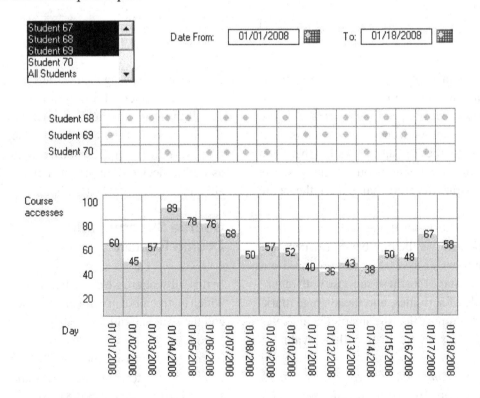

Figure 13. Dedication pattern report

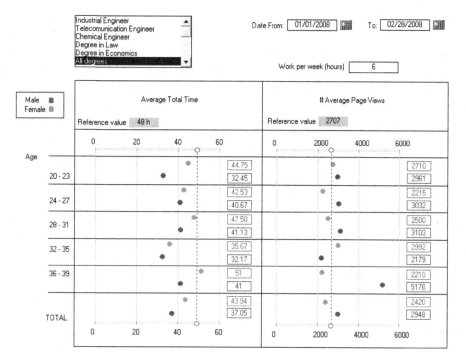

Figure 14. Resource usage pattern report

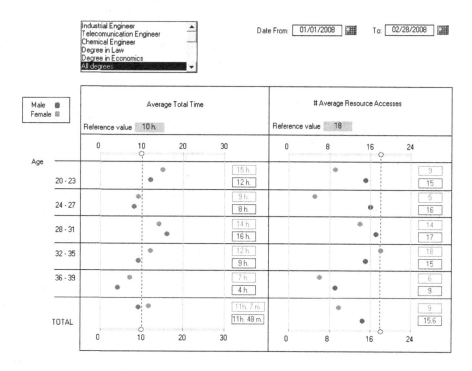

to observe if there are undesirable jumps among units, the pages in which students spend more time, the last page they visit and so on.

It is interesting for instructors to know which pages are the most visited and those which have never been requested in the specified range of dates. Therefore, we have designed the *page access distribution report* (see Figure 17).

The most visited pages allow instructors to know if they present some special difficulty, or if, on the contrary, they include some characteristics which make them interesting, and thus it is recommended to extend their use. On the other hand, the non-visited pages allow instructors to know if there is a failure in the design (link not attainable, many clicks to get to the page, etc) or if their content is not essential and hence their low number of requests.

As can be observed in Figure 17, pages which instructor considers interesting (context) are marked with a white point in order to make the report's analysis easier. As in previous reports, instructors can filter the information by unit and range of dates.

Finally, in order to know if the distribution of the tasks programmed by the instructor is balanced adequately over the period of the course and detect possible moments of overload or relaxation, instructors can use the *global course usage report* (Figure 11), choosing the item "All students" in the upper-left box.

Survey Questions vs. Proposed Reports

As summary, the relationship between the survey questions and the reports which answer them is gathered in Table 2.

SYSTEM ARCHITECTURE

In this subsection, we describe the general software architecture that we propose to develop the students' monitoring and assessment tool. Our proposal relies on developing this tool following the general guidelines of design of Business Intelligence (BI) applications (Mundy, Thorthwaite & Kimball, 2005) which enable the handling, consolidating and analyzing of large volumes of data, transforming these into valuable information for decision-making. This is the architecture used by our Matep tool (Zorrilla, Marín & Álvarez, 2007).

As can be observed in Figure 18, the reporting tool reads the data from a data warehouse which gathers the students' activity data from the e-learning platform previously transformed and integrated with the context information and academic data (if this is available).

The information highlighted as context in this chapter (demographic data, course organization, assessable tasks, etc) must be defined by instructors inside the e-learning platform, if it is possible, or gathered by means of a specific software application developed for it (context database). This information turns out to be indispensable in order to observe tracking data from a more pedagogical point of view. This necessity of adding context is used in other applications such as CourseVis, Gismo or Matep.

The tasks of extraction, transformation and load will be carried out by a specific module for each e-learning platform. These tasks will vary depending on whether the students' tracking data (n° of sessions, pages visited per student, time in each page, etc) can be read directly from a database (for example, Moodle), or if this information must be extracted from web log files or from files with a dependent-platform format. An explanation of how to pre-process web log files is found in (Srivastava, Cooley, Deshpande & Tan, 2000; Zorrilla, 2009). Likewise, this module is responsible for integrating and transforming the

Figure 15. Performance pattern report

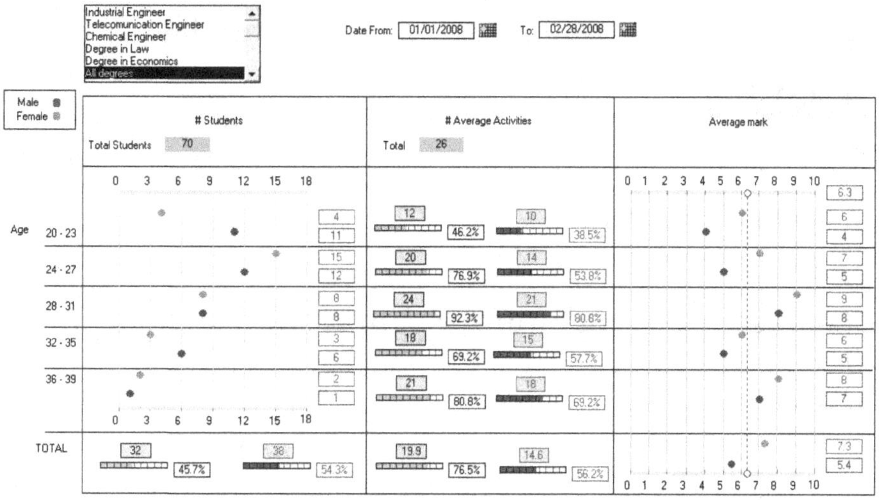

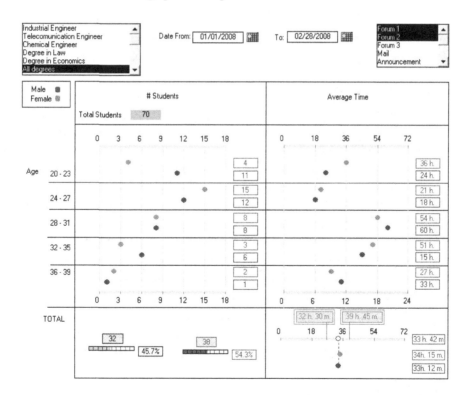

Figure 16. Communication tool usage pattern report

information of student activity and context of the course, and loading them into the data warehouse, for which it will use the staging area. A suitable schema for the e-learning dimensional database is described in (Zorrilla, 2009).

The student tracking tool, as we have already described, must include a broad spectrum of reports, both static and parameter-driven. In

Figure 17. Page access distribution report

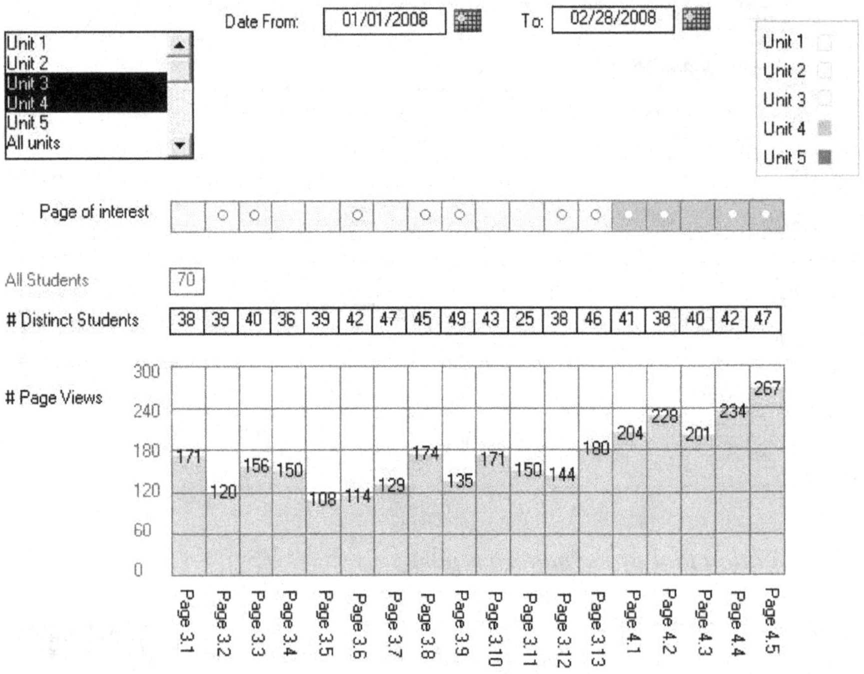

Table 2. Survey questions vs reports

Question	Report
Q1	Student identification report
Q2	Student identification report
Q3	Student identification report
Q4	Student identification report
Q5	Student identification report
Q6	Content page activity distribution report, course activity report, student activity report, course usage comparative report
Q7	Tool usage report, discussion graph, course activity report, student activity report, course usage comparative report
Q8	Global course usage report
Q9	Student dropout report
Q10	Student session report
Q11	Instructors-learners communication report
Q12	Dedication pattern report
Q13	Resource usage pattern report
Q14	Performance pattern report
Q15	Communication tool usage pattern report
Q16	Student session report
Q17	Page accessdistribution report
Q18	Global course usagereport

Figure 18. The system architecture

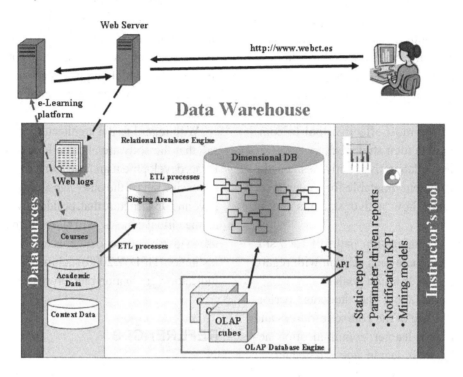

order to generate the reports quickly, regardless of data volume in the dimensional database, we strongly recommend the use of OLAP technology (Thomsen, 2002). This technology builds multi-dimensional structures called cubes that contain pre-calculated summary data (aggregations). Consequently, querying existing aggregated data is close to instantaneous compared to doing cold queries (SQL queries) with non pre-calculated summaries in place.

CONCLUSION

In this chapter, we describe the current situation of web-based distance learning and the use of Learning Content Management Systems in the teaching-learning process. Although the advantages that these technologies provide are many and well-known, they still present some shortcomings. One of these is the lack of tracking tools designed to

monitor and assess the daily activity of individual learners from an educational point of view. This means a tool which allows instructors, with just a glimpse, to know what is happening with their students in the virtual course.

Our goal, in short, is to provide instructors with enough suitable information which allow them to find out the difficulties that students have in the course and act as soon as they are detected. This information is shown by means of reports as this is the simplest and most used tool to analyze information, not only in the educational context but also in the field of the engineering and the business (Juan, Daradoumis, Faullin & Xhafa, 2009). Therefore, we propose both a set of 16 reports, useful and easy to interpret by instructors, and a software architecture independent from the e-learning platforms for their implementation.

In summary, this information system will allow instructors to:

- Learn about the profile of their students.
- Track the frequency and time spent per student and group in each course component.
- Learn about the course periods of more or less intensity per student and group.
- Detect when a course drop-out is about to occur.
- Ascertain the most effective tool to communicate with their students.
- Organise collaborative activities in the most convenient timetable for students.
- Learn about how active students are in forums.
- Analyse the navigation paths of each student and evaluate each session with regard to instructor's learning goals.
- Get patterns about the students' performance, the use of the course resources and the instructor-learner communication according to their degree, age and gender.
- Assess the course design and structure with regard to how students have used the resources and how these are organised.

In conclusion, the proposed reports will provide instructors with valuable information with respect to the online activity of students, both numerically and graphically, which allows them to offer timely guidance and assistance to students and groups. The positive results obtained when we used our tool Matep (which offers less information and has a poorer format) to analyse a virtual course with 22 students (read conclusions in Álvarez & Zorrilla 2008) make us confident that these reports will successfully satisfy instructors' needs. Furthermore, in this proposal more reports are offered, so that the system will give response to questions of a greater number of instructors. The existence of such a high number of reports does not mean that instructors should use all, but they will choose in each moment those which allow them to analyse concrete situations that worry them (the progress of students with low marks, the participation in forums, the period in which more dropouts take place, etc.).

The only inconvenience of this system is that in order for instructors to obtain more accurate information they must specify the course context information, which supposes an extra effort for instructors. However, it must be said that it is not indispensable.

With regard to the architecture it is possible to say that the software and the hardware necessary for its development and use can turn out to be a bit expensive but on the other hand, organizations will have an infrastructure that, besides giving support to all the virtual courses, will allow them to extend its use to give response to other academic needs of the institution (HEDW, 2008) such as to obtain academic indicators (graduation rate, dropout rate, etc.).

REFERENCES

Álvarez, E., & Zorrilla, M. E. (2008). Orientaciones en el diseño y evaluación de un curso virtual para la enseñanza de aplicaciones informáticas. *Revista Iberoamericana de Tecnologías del Aprendizaje, 3*(2), 1–10.

Álvarez, V. (2008). *E-learning survey*. Retrieved from http://www.di.uniovi.es/~victoralvarez/survey/

Avouris, N., Komis, V., Fiotakis, G., Margaritis, M., & Voyiatzaki, G. (2005). Logging of fingertip actions is not enough for analysis of learning activities. In *Proceedings of Workshop Usage Analysis in learning systems (AIED'05)*, Amsterdam (pp. 1-8).

Blackboard. (2006). Retrieved from http://www.blackboard.com

Britain, S., & Liber, O. (1999). A framework for the pedagogical evaluation of virtual learning environments. In *JISC Technology Applications Programme: Report 041*. University of Wales, UK. Retrieved from http://www.jisc.ac.uk/uploaded_documents/jtap-041.doc

BSCW. (2005). *Be smart cooperate worldwide.* Retrieved from http://public.bscw.de/

Claroline. (2005). Retrieved from http://www.claroline.net/

Conrad, D. L. (2002). Engagement, excitement, anxiety and fear: Learners' experiences of starting an online course. *American Journal of Distance Education, 16*(4), 205–226. doi:10.1207/S15389286AJDE1604_2

Cross, J., O'Driscoll, T., & Trondsen, E. (2007). *Another life: Virtual worlds as tools for learning.* Retrieved from http://www.scribd.com/doc/2245570/Another-Life-Virtual-Worlds-for-Learning

EduTools homepage. (2008). Retrieved from http://www.edutools.info/static.jsp?pj=4&page=HOME

Gee, J. P. (2004). *Learning by design: Good video games as learning machines.* Retrieved from http://www.academiccolab.org/resources/documents/Game%20Paper.pdf

Gonzalez, J., & Wagener, R. (2003). *Tuning educational structures in Europe* (Final report [phase one]). Universidad de Deusto. Retrieved from http://www.relint.deusto.es/TUNINGProject/documentos/Tuning_phase1/Tuning_phase1_full_document.pdf

Graf, S. Kinshuk, & Liu, T. (2008). Identifying learning styles in learning management systems by using indications from students' behaviour. In *Proceedings of the 8th IEEE International Conference on Advanced Learning Technologies,* Santander, Spain (pp. 482-486).

HEDW. (2008). *Higher education data warehousing forum.* Retrieved from http://ws.cc.sunysb.edu/offires/hedw/index.html

Hijon, R., & Velazquez, A. (2006). E-learning platforms analysis and development of students tracking functionality. In E. Pearson & P. Bohman (Eds.), *Proceedings of World Conference on Educational Multimedia, Hypermedia and Telecommunications* (pp. 2823–2828). Chesapeake, VA: AACE.

Joomla, L. M. S. (2008). Retrieved http://www.joomlalms.com/

Juan, A., Daradoumis, T., Faulin, J., & Xhafa, F. (2008). A data analysis model based on control charts to monitor online learning processes. *International Journal of Business Intelligence and Data Mining.*

Juan, A., Daradournis, T., Faulin, J., & Xhafa, F. (2008). Developing an information system for monitoring student's activity in online collaborative learning. In *Proceedings of the 2nd International Conference on Complex, Intelligent and software intensive systems,* Barcelona, Spain (pp. 270-275).

Jusung, J. (2005). Understanding e-dropout? *International Journal on E-Learning, 4*(2), 229–240.

Kahiigi, E. K., Ekenberg, L., Hansson, H., Tusubira, F. F., & Danielson, M. (2008). Exploring the e-learning state of art. In *Electronic Journal of e-Learning, 6*(2), 77-88.

Koohang, A. (2004). Creating learning objects in collaborative e-learning settings. *Issues in Information Systems, 4*(2), 584–590.

Levy, Y. (2007). Comparing dropouts and persistence in e-learning courses. *Computers & Education, 48,* 185–204. doi:10.1016/j.compedu.2004.12.004

Mazza, R., & Dimitrova, V. (2007). CourseVis: A graphical student monitoring tool for supporting instructors in Web-based distance courses. *International Journal of Human-Computer Studies, 65*(2), 125–139. doi:10.1016/j.ijhcs.2006.08.008

Mazza, R., & Milani, C. (2005). Exploring usage analysis in learning systems: Gaining insights from visualisations. In *Proceedings of the Workshop on usage analysis in learning systems, 12th International Conference on Artificial Intelligence in Education (AEID 2005)*, Amsterdam, The Netherlands (pp. 65-72).

Milani, C., & Mazza, R. (2007). *GISMO: A graphical interactive student monitoring system for Moodle*. Retrieved from http://gismo.source-forge.net

Moodle. (2007). Retrieved from http://moodle.org/

Mostow, J., Beck, J., Cen, H., Cuneo, A., Gouvea, E., & Heiner, C. (2005). An educational data mining tool to browse tutor-student interactions: Time will tell! In *Proc. of the Workshop on educational data mining* (pp. 15-22).

Mundy, J., Thorthwaite, W., & Kimball, R. (2006). *The Microsoft data warehouse toolkit: With SQL Server 2005 and the Microsoft Business Intelligence toolset*. New York: John Wiley & Sons.

Pozzi, F. (2006). Assessment, evaluation and monitoring in e-learning systems: A survey from the DPULS project. *Information Science for Decision Making, 25*, 354.

Romero, C., & Ventura, S. (2006). Data mining in e-learning. *Advances in Management Information, 4.*

Sevilla, J. (2008). The virtual campus of the Spanish Group 9 of Universities (G9). In *Proceedings of the LMAIA Final Conference*, Rome, Italy. Retrieved from http://www.lemaia.eu/PagDefault.asp?idPag=90

Srivastava, J., Cooley, R., Deshpande, M., & Tan, P. (2000). Web usage mining: Discovery and applications of usage patterns from Web data. *SIGKDD Explorations, 1*(2), 12–23. doi:10.1145/846183.846188

Tai, Y., & Ting, R. Y. (2007). Authoring tools in e-learning: A case study. In *Proceedings of the Seventh IEEE International Conference on Advanced Learning Technologies (ICALT 2007)*, Niigata, Japan (pp. 271-273).

Thomsen, E. (2002). *OLAP solutions: Building multidimensional information systems* (2nd ed.). New York: John Wiley & Sons.

Web, C. T. 4.0. (2003). Retrieved from http://www.webct.com/ce4

Xenos, M., Pierrakeas, C., & Pintelas, P. (2002). A survey on student dropout rates and dropout causes concerning the students in the course of informatics of the Hellenic Open University. *Computers & Education, 39*(4), 361–377. doi:10.1016/S0360-1315(02)00072-6

Zaïane, O. (2001). Web usage mining for a better Web-based learning environment. In *Proceedings of Conference on Advantage Technology for Education*, Alberta, Canada (pp. 60-64).

Zhang, H., Almeroth, K., Knight, A., Bulger, M., & Mayer, R. (2007). Moodog: Tracking students' online learning activities. In *Proceedings of the World Conference on Educational Multimedia, Hypermedia & Telecommunications (ED MEDIA)*, Vancouver, Canada.

Zinn, C., & Scheuer, O. (2006). Getting to know your student in distance learning context. In *Innovative approaches for learning and knowledge sharing* (LNCS 4227, pp. 437-451). Berlin, Germany: Springer.

Zorrilla, M. (2009). Data warehouse technology for e-learning. In. D. Zakrzewska, E. Menasalvas, & L. Byczkowska-Lipińska (Eds.), *Methods and Tools for Data Analysis*. Berlin, Germany: Springer-Verlag.

Zorrilla, M. E., & Álvarez, E. (2008). MATEP: Monitoring and analysis tool for e-learning platforms. In *Proceedings of the 8th IEEE International Conference on Advanced Learning Technologies*, Santander, Spain (pp. 611-613).

Zorrilla, M. E., Marín, D., & Álvarez, E. (2007). Towards virtual course evaluation using Web intelligence. In *Proceedings of the Computer aided systems theory: EUROCAST 2007* (LNCS 4739, pp. 392-399). Berlin, Germany: Springer.

Zorrilla, M. E., Menasalvas, E., Marín, D., Mora, E., & Segovia, J. (2005). Web usage mining project for improving Web-based learning sites. In *Proceedings of the Computer aided systems theory: EUROCAST 2005* (LNCS 3643, pp. 205-210). Berlin, Germany: Springer.

Compilation of References

A.D.L. (2006). *SCORM 2004 3rd edition, sharable content object reference model*. Alexandria, VA: Advanced Distributed Learning.

Abramovicz, W., Kaczmarek, T., & Kowalkiewicz, M. (2004). Supporting topic map creation using data mining techniques. *Australian Journal of Information Systems*.

Adams, A., & Williams, S. (2006). Customer-driven development for rapid production of assessment learning objects. *The Electronic Journal of e-Learning, 4*(1), 1-6. Retrieved from http://www.ejel.org

Agius, H. W., & Angelides, M. C. (1999). Developing knowledge-based intelligent multimedia tutoring systems using semantic content-based modelling. *Artificial Intelligence Review, 13*(1), 55–83. doi:10.1023/A:1006569626086

Agrawal, R., & Srikant, R. (1994). Fast algorithms for mining association rules. In *Proc. of the 20th Int. Conf. on Very Large Databases*, Santiago, Chile.

Ahuja, M. K., Galletta, D. F., & Carley, K. M. (2003). Individual centrality and performance in virtual R&D groups: An empirical study. *Management Science, 49*(1), 21–38. doi:10.1287/mnsc.49.1.21.12756

Ajiferuke, I., Burrell, Q., & Tague, J. (1988). Collaboration coefficient: A single measure of the degree of collaboration in research. *Scientometrics, 14*(5-6), 421–433. doi:10.1007/BF02017100

Alavi, M. (1994). Computer-mediated collaborative learning: An empirical evaluation. *MIS Quarterly, 18*(2), 159–174. doi:10.2307/249763

Allen, I., & Seaman, J. (2008). *Staying the course: Online education in the United States*. Newburyport, MA: The Sloan Consortium.

Allen, T. H. (2006). Raising the question #1: Is the rush to provide online instruction setting our students up for failure? *Communication Education, 55*(1), 122–126. doi:10.1080/03634520500343418

Allwood, J., Grönqvist, L., Ahlsén, E., & Gunnarsson, M. (2002). Annotations and tools for an activity based spoken language corpus. In *Proceedings of the 2nd SIGdial Workshop on Discourse and Dialogue*, Aalborg, Denmark.

Álvarez, E., & Zorrilla, M. E. (2008). Orientaciones en el diseño y evaluación de un curso virtual para la enseñanza de aplicaciones informáticas. *Revista Iberoamericana de Tecnologías del Aprendizaje, 3*(2), 1–10.

Álvarez, V. (2008). *E-learning survey*. Retrieved from http://www.di.uniovi.es/~victoralvarez/survey/

Alvino, S., & Persico, D. (2008). The relationship between assessment and evaluation in CSCL. In A. Cartelli & M. Palma (Eds.), *Encyclopaedia of information and communication technology, vol. II* (pp. 698-703). Hershey, PA: Information Science Reference.

Anderson, J. R. (1988). The expert module. In M. Polson & J. J. Richardson (Eds.), *Foundations of intelligent tutoring systems*. Hillsdale, NJ: Lawrence Erlbaum Associates.

Anderson, T., Rourke, L., Garrison, D. R., & Archer, W. (2001). Assessing teaching presence in a computer conferencing context. *Journal of Asynchronous Learning Networks, 5*(2). Retrieved from http://www.aln.org/alnweb/journal/jaln-vol5issue2v2.htm

Antonietti, A., & Giorgetti, M. (1997). The verbalizer-visualizer questionnaire: A review 1. *Perceptual and Motor Skills, 86*(1), 227–239.

Anzieu, D. (1965). Les communications intra-group. In F. A. Geldard et al., (Eds.), *Communications processes.* London: Pergamon Press.

Argyle, M. (1972). Non-verbal communication in human social interaction. In R. A. Hinde (Ed.), *Non-verbal communication* (pp. 243-269). Cambridge, UK: University Press.

Argyle, M. (1988). *Bodily communication* (2nd ed.). London: Methuen & Co. Ltd.

Argyle, M., & Dean, J. (1965). Eye contact, distance, and affiliation. *Sociometry, 28*(3), 289–304. doi:10.2307/2786027

Ashkanasy, N., Hartel, E., & Daus, C. (2002). Diversity and emotion: The new frontiers in organizational behavior research. *Journal of Management, 28*, 307–338. doi:10.1177/014920630202800304

Attwell, G. (2007). Personal learning environments - the future of eLearning? *eLearning Papers, 2*(1). Retrieved July 20, 2008, from http://www.elearningeuropa.info/files/media/media11561.pdf

ATutor. (2008). Retrieved from http://atutor.com

Ausubel, D. P., Novak, J. D., & Hanesian, H. (1978). *Educational psychology: A cognitive view* (2nd ed.). New York: Holt, Rinehart and Winston.

Aviv, R., Erlich, Z., Ravid, G., & Geva, A. (2003). Network analysis of knowledge construction in asynchronous learning networks. *Journal of Asynchronous Learning Networks, 7*(3), 1–23.

Avouris, N., Komis, V., Fiotakis, G., Margaritis, M., & Voyiatzaki, G. (2005). Logging of fingertip actions is not enough for analysis of learning activities. In *Proceedings of Workshop Usage Analysis in learning systems (AIED'05)*, Amsterdam (pp. 1-8).

Bailenson, J., Blascovich, J., Beall, A. C., & Loomis, J. (2003). Interpersonal distance in immersive virtual environments. *Personality and Social Psychology Bulletin, 29*, 819–833. doi:10.1177/0146167203029007002

Bajraktarevic, N., Hall, W., & Fullick, P. (2003). *ILASH: Incorporating learning strategies in hypermedia.* Paper presented at the Fourteenth Conference on Hypertext and Hypermedia.

Baldoni, M., Baroglio, C., Patti, V., & Torasso, L. (2004). *Reasoning about learning object metadata for adapting SCORM courseware.* Paper presented at the EAW'04.

Bales, R. F. (1950). A set of factors for the analysis of small group interaction. *American Sociological Review, 15*, 257–263. doi:10.2307/2086790

Bales, R. F. (1970). *Personality and interpersonal behavior.* New York: Holt.

Barab, S. A., Barnett, M., Yamagata-Lynch, L., Squire, K., & Keating, T. (2002). Using activity theory to understand the contradictions characterizing a technology-rich introductory astronomy course. *Mind, Culture, and Activity, 9*(2), 76–107. doi:doi:10.1207/S15327884MCA0902_02

Barkhi, R., Jacob, V. S., Pipino, L., & Pirkul, H. (1998). A study of the effect of communication channel and authority on group decision processes and outcomes. *Decision Support Systems, 23*(3), 205–227. doi:10.1016/S0167-9236(98)00048-7

Barros, B., & Verdejo, M. (2000). Analysing student interaction processes in order to improve collaboration. The DEGREE approach. *International Journal of Artificial Intelligence in Education, 11*, 221–241.

Barsade, S. G. (2002). The ripple effect: Emotional contagion and its influence on group behavior. *Administrative Science Quarterly, 47*(4), 644–675. doi:10.2307/3094912

Bartenieff, I., & Davis, M. A. (1965). Effort-shape analysis of movement: The unity of expression and function. In M. Davis (Ed.), *Research approaches to movement and personality*. New York: Arno Press Inc.

Bejar, I., & Mislevy, R. (2006). Automated scoring of complex tasks in computer-based testing: An introduction. In D. Williamson, R. Mislevy, & I. Bejar (Eds.), *Automated scoring of complex tasks in computer-based testing*. Mahwah, NJ: Erlbaum.

Bell, J. T. (1996). On the use of anonymous quizzes as an effective feedback mechanism in engineering education. *Chemical Engineering Education, 31*(1).

Bellas, F., & Alonso, A. (2007). Metodología de trabajo y experiencias de aprendizaje colaborativo y evaluación continua en la disciplina de sistemas multiagente. In *Proceedings of the Actas JENUI 2007*.

Benfer, R., Brent, E., & Furbee, L. (1991). *Expert systems*. Newbury Park, CA: Sage.

Bennett, P. N. (2000). *Assessing the calibration of Naive Bayes' posterior estimates* (Tech. Rep. No. CMU-CS00-155).

Benson, P. (2001). *Teaching and researching autonomy in language learning*. Harlow, UK: Longman.

Birdwhistell, R. (1970). *Kinesics and context - essays on body motion communication*. Philadephia: University of Pennsylvania Press.

Black, P., & Wiliam, D. (1998). Assessment and classroom learning. *Assessment in Education, 5*(1), 7–74. doi:10.1080/0969595980050102

Blackboard Academic Suite Release 8.0. (2008). *Critical thinking tools*. Retrieved September 2008, from http://www.blackboard.com/release8/

Blackboard. (2008). Retrieved from http://www.blackboard.com

Blanchard, E., & Frasson, C. (2004). An autonomy-oriented system design for enhancement of learner's motivation in e-learning. In *Intelligent tutoring systems* (LNCS 3220, pp. 34-44). Berlin, Germany: Springer.

Block, J. (1974). *Schools, society and mastery learning*. New York: Holt, Rinehart and Winston.

Bloom, B. (1956). *Taxonomy of educational objectives: The classification of educational goals*. Susan Fauer Company, Inc.

Bonacich, P. (1972). Factoring and weighting approaches to status scores and clique identification. *The Journal of Mathematical Sociology, 2*, 113–120.

Botsios, S., & Georgiou, D. (2008). Recent adaptive e-learning contributions towards a standard ready architecture. In *Proceedings of the 5th International Conference on Adaptive Hypermedia and Adaptive Web-Based Systems*, Hannover, Germany

Botsios, S., Georgiou, D., & Safouris, N. (2007). Learning style estimation via Bayesian networks. In *Proceedings of the WEBIST 2007*, Barcelona, Spain.

Botsios, S., Georgiou, D., & Safouris, N. (2008). Contributions to adaptive educational hypermedia systems via on-line learning style estimation. [IEEE]. *Journal of Educational Technology & Society, 11*(3), 322–339.

Botsios, S., Mitropoulou, V., Georgiou, D., & Panapakidis, I. (2006). *Design of virtual co-learner for asynchronous collaborative e-learning*. Paper presented at the Sixth International Conference on Advanced Learning Technologies, ICALT 2006.

Bouas, K. S., & Arrow, H. (1996). The development of group identity in computer and face-to-face groups with membership change. *CSCW, 4*, 153–178.

Bowker, N., & Tuffin, K. (2004). Using the online medium for discursive research about people with disabilities. *Social Science Computer Review, 22*(2), 228–241. doi:10.1177/0894439303262561

Bradner, E., Hertel, T. D., & Mark, G. (2002). Effects of team size on participation, awareness, and technology choice in geographically distributed teams. In *Proceedings of the 36th Hawaii International Conference on System Sciences*, Hawaii, USA.

Branson, L., Clausen, T. S., & Sung, C. H. (2008). Group style differences between virtual and F2F teams. *American Journal of Business, 23*(1), 65–71.

Braun, H., Bejar, I., & Williamson, D. (2006). Rule based methods for automated scoring: Application in a licensing context. In D. Williamson, R. Mislevy, & I. Bejar (Eds.), *Automated scoring of complex tasks in computer based testing.* Mahwah, NJ: Erlbaum.

Brdiczka, O., Maisonnasse, J., & Reignier, P. (2005). Automatic detection of interaction groups. In *Proceedings of the 7th International Conference on Multimodal Interfaces (ICMI)*, Trento, Italy.

Brent, E., & Townsend, M. (2007). Automated essay grading in the sociology classroom: Finding common ground. In P. Frietag Ericsoon & R. Haswell (Eds.), *Machine scoring of student essays: Truth or consequences?* Logan, UT: Utah State University Press.

Brent, E., Carnahan, T., & McCully, J. (2006). *Students improve learning by 20 percentage points with essay grading program, SAGrader™.* Columbia. MO: Idea Works, Inc.

Brent, E., Carnahan, T., McCully, J., & Green, N. (2006). *SAGrader™: A computerized essay grading program, version 2.* Columbia, MO: Idea Works, Inc.

Brief, A. P., & Weiss, H. M. (2002). Organizational behavior: Affect in the workplace. *Annual Review of Psychology, 53,* 279–307. doi:10.1146/annurev. psych.53.100901.135156

Britain, S., & Liber, O. (1999). A framework for the pedagogical evaluation of virtual learning environments. In *JISC Technology Applications Programme: Report 041.* University of Wales, UK. Retrieved from http://www.jisc.ac.uk/uploaded_documents/jtap-041.doc

Brown, A. L., & Campione, J. C. (1990). Communities of learning and thinking, or a context by any other name. *Contributions to Human Development, 21,* 108–126.

Brown, E. J., & Brailsford, T. (2004). *Integration of learning style theory in an adaptive educational hypermedia (AEH) system.* Paper presented at the ALT-C Conference.

Brown, E., Cristea, A., Stewart, C., & Brailsford, T. (2005). Patterns in authoring of adaptive educational hypermedia: A taxonomy of learning styles. *Educational Technology and Society, 8*(3), 77–90.

Brown, R. (1973). *A first language: The early stages.* Cambridge, MA: Harvard University Press.

Brusilovsky, P. (1996). Methods and techniques of adaptive hypermedia. *User Modeling and User-Adapted Interaction, 6*(2-3), 87–129. doi:10.1007/BF00143964

Brusilovsky, P. (2001). Adaptive hypermedia. *User Modeling and User-Adapted Interaction, 11*(1/2), 87–110. doi:10.1023/A:1011143116306

Brusilovsky, P. (2003). Adaptive navigation support in educational hypermedia: The role of student knowledge level and the case for meta-adaptation. *British Journal of Educational Technology, 34*(4), 487–497. doi:10.1111/1467-8535.00345

Brusilovsky, P. (2003). Developing adaptive educational hypermedia systems: From design models to authoring tools. In T. Murray, S. Blessing, & S. Ainworth (Eds.), *Authoring tools for advancing technology learning environment* (pp. 377-409). Dordrecht, The Netherlands: Kluwer Academic Publishers.

Brusilovsky, P., & Miller, P. (2001). Course delivery systems for the virtual universities. In T. Tschang & T. Della Senta (Eds.), *Access to knowledge: New information technologies and the emergence of virtual university* (pp. 167-206). Amsterdam: Elsevier Science.

Brusilovsky, P., & Pyelo, C. (2003). Adaptive and intelligent Web-based educational systems. *International Journal of Artificial Intelligence in Education, 13*(2-4), 159–172.

Brusilovsky, P., & Rizzo, R. (2002). Map-based horizontal navigation in educational hypertext. *Journal of Digital Information, 3*(1).

Brusilovsky, P., & Sosnovsky, S. (2005). Individualized exercises for self-asssesment of programming knowledge: An evaluation of QuizPACK. *ACM Journal of Educational Resources in Computing, 5*(3).

BSCW. (2005). *Be smart cooperate worldwide.* Retrieved from http://public.bscw.de/

Bunderson, J. S., & Sutcliffe, K. M. (2002). Comparing alternative conceptualizations of functional diversity in management teams: Process and performance effects. *Academy of Management Journal, 45*(5), 875–894. doi:10.2307/3069319

Burdescu, D. D., & Mihăescu, M. C. (2006). Tesys: E-learning application built on a Web platform. In *Proceedings of International Joint Conference on e-Business and Telecommunications*, Setubal, Portugal (pp. 315-318).

Burdescu, D. D., & Mihăescu, M. C. (2007). Enhancing the assessment environment within a learning management systems. In *Proceedings of the EUROCON 2007 – The International Conference on "Computer as a Tool,"* Warsaw, Poland (pp. 2438-2443).

Burke, K., & Chidambaram, L. (1996). Do mediated contexts differ in information richness? A comparison of collocated and dispersed meetings. In *Proceedings of the 29th Annual Hawaii International Conference on System Sciences*, Hawaii, USA (pp. 92-101).

Burstein, J. (2003). The e-rater® scoring engine: Automated essay scoring with natural language processing. In M. Shermis & J. Burstein (Eds.), *Automated essay scoring: A cross-disciplinary perspective*. Mahwah, NJ: Erlbaum.

Butler-Pascoe, E. M., & Wiburg, M. K. (2003). *Technology and teaching English language learners*. Boston: Allyn and Bacon / Pearson.

Caballé, S., Daradoumis, T., & Xhafa, F. (2007). A generic platform for the systematic construction of knowledge-based collaborative learning applications. In C. Pahl (Ed.), *Architecture solutions for e-learning systems* (pp. 219-242). Hershey, PA: Idea Group Publishing.

Calvani, A., Fini, A., Bonaiuti, G., & Mazzoni, E. (2005). Monitoring interactions in collaborative learning environments (CSCL): A tool kit for Synergeia. *Journal of E-learning and Knowledge Society, 1*, 63–73.

Capin, T. K., Pandzic, I. S., Thalmann, N. M., & Thalmann, D. (1997). Realistic avatars and autonomous virtual humans in VLNET networked virtual environments. In *Proceedings of From Desktop to Webtop: Virtual Environments on the Internet, WWW and Networks, International Conference*, Bradford, UK.

Carlson, P. A., & Berry, F. C. (2003). Calibrated peer review and assessing learning outcomes. In *Proceedings of the 33rd ASEE/IEEE Frontiers in Education Conference*. Retrieved from http://fie.engrng.pitt.edu/fie2003/papers/1066.pdf

Carugati, F., & Gilly, M. (1993). The multiple sides of the same tool: Cognitive development as a matter of social construction of meaning. *European Journal of Psychology of Education, 8*(4), 345–354.

Carver, C. A. Jr, Howard, R. A., & Lane, W. D. (1999). Enhancing student learning through hypermedia courseware and incorporation of student learning styles. *IEEE Transactions on Education, 42*(1), 33–38. doi:10.1109/13.746332

Castillo, G., Gama, J., & Breda, A. M. (2005). An adaptive predictive model for student modeling. In *Advances in Web-based education: Personalized learning environments* (pp. 70-92). Hershey, PA: Information Science Publishing.

Cerrato, L., & Skhiri, M. (2003). Analysis and measurement of head movements signalling feedback in face-to-face human dialogues. In P., Paggio, K., Jokinen, & A., Jönsson (Eds.), *Proceedings of the First Nordic Symposium on Multimodal Communication, 9*, 43-52.

Chan, T. W., & Baskin, A. B. (1990). Learning companion system. In C. Frasson & G. Gauthier (Eds.), *Intelligent tutoring systems: At the crossroad of artificial intelligence and education* (pp. 6-33). Norwood, NJ: Ablex.

Chapelle, A. C. (1998). Multimedia CALL: Lessons to be learned from research on instructed SLA. *Language Learning & Technology, 2*(1), 22–34.

Chapelle, A. C. (2001). *Computer applications in second language acquisition: Foundations for teaching, testing and research*. Cambridge, UK: Cambridge University Press.

Chapelle, A. C. (2003) *English language learning and technology*. Amsterdam: John Benjamins Publishing Company.

Chapman, O. L., & Fiore, M. A. (2000). Calibrated peer review. *Journal of Interactive Instruction Development*.

Chen, C. M., Lee, H. M., & Chen, Y. H. (2005). Personalized e-learning system using item response theory. *Computers & Education, 44*(3), 237–255. doi:10.1016/j.compedu.2004.01.006

Chen, C. M., Liu, C. Y., & Chang, M. H. (2006). Personalized curriculum sequencing utilizing modified item response theory for Web-based instruction. *Expert Systems with Applications, 30*(2), 378–396. doi:10.1016/j.eswa.2005.07.029

Chen, J. N., Huang, Y. M., & Chu, W. C. C. (2005). Applying dynamic fuzzy petri net to Web learning system. *Interactive Learning Environments, 13*(3), 159-178. doi:10.1080/10494820500382810

Chen, J., Belkada, S., & Okamoto, T. (2004). How a Web-based course facilities acquisition of English for academic purposes. *Language Learning & Technology, 8*(2), 33–49.

Chi, M. T. H. (1997). Quantifying qualitative analyses of verbal data: A practical guide. *Journal of the Learning Sciences, 6*(3), 271–315. doi:10.1207/s15327809jls0603_1

Chidambaram, L., & Tung, L. L. (2005). Is out of sight, out of mind? An empirical study of social loafing in technology-supported groups. *Information Systems Research, 16*(2), 149–171. doi:10.1287/isre.1050.0051

Childers, J. L., & Berner, R. T. (2000). General education issues, distance education practices: Building community and classroom interaction through the integration of curriculum, instructional design, and technology. *The Journal of General Education, 49*(1), 53–65. doi:10.1353/jge.2000.0001

Chittaro, L., & Rano, R. (2007). Web3D technologies in learning, education and training. *Computers & Education, 49*, 3–18. doi:10.1016/j.compedu.2005.06.002

Cho, K., & Schunn, C. (2007). Scaffolded writing and rewriting in the discipline: A Web-based reciprocal peer-review system. *Computers & Education, 48*, 409–426. doi:10.1016/j.compedu.2005.02.004

Cho, K., Schunn, C. D., & Wilson, R. W. (2006). Validity and reliability of scaffolded peer assessment of writing from instructor and student perspectives. *Journal of Educational Psychology, 98*(4), 891–901. doi:10.1037/0022-0663.98.4.891

Chou, C. Y., Chan, T. W., & Lin, C. J. (2003). Redefining the learning companion: The past, present, and future of educational agents. *Computers & Education, 40*(3), 255–269. doi:10.1016/S0360-1315(02)00130-6

Chung, G., & Baker, E. (2003). Issues in the reliability and validity of automated scoring of constructed responses. In M. Shermis & J. Burstein (Eds.), *Automated essay scoring: A cross-disciplinary approach*. Mahwah, NJ: Erlbaum.

Clark, H. H., & Brennan, S. E. (1991). Grounding in communication. In L. B. Resnick, J. M. Levine, & S. D. Teasley (Eds.), *Perspectives on socially shared cognition* (pp. 127-149). Washington, DC: American Psychological Association.

Claroline. (2005). Retrieved from http://www.claroline.net/

Clinton, B. D., & Kohlmeyer, J. M. III. (2005). The effects of group quizzes on performance and motivation to learn: Two experiments in cooperative learning. *Journal of Accounting Education, 23*, 96–116. doi:10.1016/j.jaccedu.2005.06.001

Coffield, F., Moseley, D., Hall, E., & Ecclestone, K. (2004). *Should we be using learning styles? What research has to say to practice*. London: Learning and Skills Research Centre (LSRC).

Cohen, J. (1969). *Statistical power analysis for the behavioral sciences*. New York: Academic Press.

Cole, R. (1997). *Survey of the state of the art in human language technology*. Cambridge, UK: Cambridge University Press and Giardini.

Collis, B. (2005). *The contributing student: A blend of pedagogy and technology*. Australasia, Auckland, New Zealand: EDUCAUSE.

Conati, C. (2002). Probabilistic assessment of user's emotions in educational games. *Applied Artificial Intelligence*, *16*(7-8), 555–575. doi:10.1080/08839510290030390

Connolly, T., & Stansfield, M. (2006). Using games-based elearning technologies in overcoming difficulties. *Teaching Information Systems . Journal of Information Technology Education*, *5*, 459–476.

Conrad, D. L. (2002). Engagement, excitement, anxiety and fear: Learners' experiences of starting an online course. *American Journal of Distance Education*, *16*(4), 205–226. doi:10.1207/S15389286AJDE1604_2

Constantino-Gonzales, M. A., & Suthers, D. (2001). Coaching collaboration by comparing solutions and tracking participation. In P. Dillenbourg, A. Eurelings, & K. Hakkarainen (Eds.), *European Perspectives on Computer-Supported Collaborative Learning, Proceedings of the First European Conference on Computer-Supported Collaborative Learning* (pp. 173-180). Maastricht, the Netherlands: Universiteit Maastricht.

Cooley, R., Mobasher, B., & Srivastava, J. (1999). Data preparation for mining World Wide Web browsing patterns. *Knowledge and Information Systems*, *1*(1), 5–32.

Cooper, B., Brna, P., & Martins, A. (2000). Effective affective in intelligent systems – building on evidence of empathy in teaching and learning. In A., Paiva (Ed.), *Affective interactions: Towards a new generation of computer interfaces*. London: Springer Verlag.

Cramton, C. D., & Webber, S. S. (1999). *Modeling the impact of geographic dispersion on work teams* (working paper). George Mason University, Washington, DC, USA.

Cramton, C. D., & Webber, S. S. (2005). Relationships among geographic dispersion, team processes, and effectiveness in software development work teams. *Journal of Business Research*, *58*(6), 758–765. doi:10.1016/j.jbusres.2003.10.006

Cross, J., O'Driscoll, T., & Trondsen, E. (2007). *Another life: Virtual worlds as tools for learning*. Retrieved from http://www.scribd.com/doc/2245570/Another-Life-Virtual-Worlds-for-Learning

CTGV. (1993). Anchored instruction and situated cognition revisited. *Educational Technology*, *33*(3), 52–70.

Cummings, J. N. (2004). Work groups, structural diversity, and knowledge sharing in a global organization. *Management Science*, *50*(3), 352–364. doi:10.1287/mnsc.1030.0134

Curtis, D. D., & Lawson, M. J. (2001). Exploring collaborative online learning. *Journal of Asynchronous Learning Networks*, *5*(1), 21–34.

Dabbs, J. M., & Ruback, R. B. (1987). Dimensions of group process: Amount and structure of vocal interaction. *Advances in Experimental Social Psychology*, *20*, 123–165. doi:10.1016/S0065-2601(08)60413-X

Daedalus integrated writing environment: Details. (2008). Retrieved September 2008, from http://www.daedalus.com/products_diwe_details.asp

Daradoumis, T., Martínez-Monés, A., & Xhafa, F. (2006). A layered framework for evaluating on-line collaborative learning interactions. *International Journal of Human-Computer Studies*, *64*(7), 622–635. doi:10.1016/j.ijhcs.2006.02.001

Daradoumis, T., Xhafa, F., & Juan, A. (2006). A framework for assessing self, peer and group performance in e-learning. In *Self, peer, and group assessment in e-learning* (pp. 279-294). Hershey, PA: Info Sci.

de Bra, P., Berden, B., de Lange, B., Rousseau, B., Santic, T., Smits, D., & Stash, N. (2003). AHA! The adaptive hypermedia architecture. In *Proceedings of the ACM Conference on Hypertext and Hypermedia*, Nottingham, UK.

de Bruyn, L. (2004). Monitoring online communication: Can the development of convergence and social presence indicate an interactive learning environment. *Distance Education, 25*(1), 67–81. doi:10.1080/0158791042000212468

De Freitas, S. (2009). *Learning in immersive worlds: A review of game based learning report*. Retrieved from http://www.jisc.ac.uk/media/documents/programmes/elearninginnovation/gamingreport_v3.pdf

de Pedro Puente, X. (2007). New method using Wikis and forums to evaluate individual contributions in cooperative work while promoting experiential learning: Results from preliminary experience. In *Proceedings of the 2007 international Symposium on Wikis, WikiSym '07,* Montreal, Quebec, Canada (pp. 87-92). New York: ACM Press.

Deane, P. (2006). Strategies for evidence identification through linguistic assessment of textual responses. In D. Williamson, R. Mislevy, & I. Bejar (Eds.), *Automated scoring of complex tasks in computer-based testing*. Mahwah, NJ: Erlbaum.

Del Moral, M. E., & Villalustre, L. (2008). Wikis and collaborative education by means of Webquest in higher education. *Revista Latinoamericana de Tecnologia Educativa, 7*(1), 73–83.

Delfino, M., & Persico, D. (2007). Online or face-to-face? Experimenting with different techniques in teacher training. *Journal of Computer Assisted Learning, 23,* 351–365. doi:10.1111/j.1365-2729.2007.00220.x

Denning, T., Kelly, M., Lindquist, D., Malani, R., Griswold, W. G., & Simon, B. (2007). Lightweight preliminary peer review: Does in-class peer review make sense? *SIGCSE Bulletin, 39*(1), 266–270. doi:10.1145/1227504.1227406

Denton, D. K. (2006). Using intranets to make virtual teams effective. *Team Performance Management, 12*(7/8), 253–257. doi:10.1108/13527590610711804

DeRosa, D. M., Hantula, D. A., Kock, N., & D'Arcy, J. (2004). Trust and leadership in virtual teamwork: A media naturalness perspective. *Human Resource Management, 43*(2-3), 219–233. doi:10.1002/hrm.20016

DeSanctis, G., Wright, M., & Jiang, L. (2001). Building a global learning community. *Communications of the ACM, 44*(12), 80–82. doi:10.1145/501317.501352

DeVito, J. A., & Hecht, M. L. (1990). *The nonverbal communication reader*. Prospect Heights, IL: Waveland.

Diefendorff, J. M., & Gosserand, R. H. (2003). Understanding the emotional labor process: a control theory perspective. *Journal of Organizational Behavior, 24*(8), 945-959. doi:10.1002/job.230

Dillenbourg, P. (Ed.). (1999). *Collaborative learning: Cognitive and computational approaches*. New York: Pergamon.

Dillenbourg, P., & Self, J. (1992). A framework for learner modeling. *Interactive Learning Environments, 2*(2), 111–137. doi:10.1080/1049482920020202

Dillenbourg, P., & Self, J. (1992). People power: A human-computer collaborative learning system. In *Proceedings of the Second Int'l Conf. Intelligent Tutoring Systems* (pp. 651-660). Berlin, Germany: Springer Verlag.

Dillon, A., & Gabbard, R. B. (1999). Prepared to be shocked: Hypermedia does not improve learning! In *Proceedings of the Fifth Americas Conference on Information Systems*, Milwaukee, WI (pp. 369-371).

Doak, E. D., & Keith, M. (1986). Simulation in teacher education: The knowledge base and the process. *Tennessee Education, 16*(2), 14–17.

Doise, W., & Mugny, G. (1984). *The social development of the intellect*. Oxford, UK: Pergamon Press.

Dörnyei, Z. (2001). *Motivational strategies in the language classroom*. Cambridge, UK: Cambridge University Press.

Dörnyei, Z. (2001). *Teaching and researching motivation.* Harlow, UK: Longman.

Dringus, L. P., & Ellis, T. (2005). Using data mining as a strategy for assessing asynchronous discussion forums. *Computers & Education, 45,* 141–160. doi:10.1016/j.compedu.2004.05.003

Dudeney, G. (2000). *The Internet and the language classroom.* Cambridge, UK: Cambridge University Press.

Duffy, P. (2008). Engaging the YouTube Google-eyed generation: Strategies for using Web 2.0 in teaching and learning. *The Electronic Journal of e-Learning, 6*(2), 119-130.

Dumais, S. T., & Nielsen, J. (1992). Automating the assignment of submitted manuscripts to reviewers. In N. Belkin, P. Ingwersen, & A. M. Petersen (Eds.), *Proceedings of the 15ᵗʰ Annual International ACM SIGIR Conference on Research and Development in Information Retrieval, SIGIR '92,* Copenhagen, Denmark (pp. 233-244). New York: ACM Press.

Dunn, J. R., & Schweitzer, M. E. (2005). feeling and believing: the influence of emotion on trust. *Journal of Personality and Social Psychology, 88*(5), 736–748. doi:10.1037/0022-3514.88.5.736

Dunn, R., & Dunn, K. (1992). *Teaching elementary students through their individual learning styles.* Boston: Allyn and Bacon.

Eastgate, R. (2001). *The structured development of virtual environments: Enhancing functionality and interactivity.* Unpublished doctoral dissertation, University of York. Retrieved, May 2008, from http://www.virart.nott.ac.uk/RMEPhD2001.pdf

e-Class. (2008). *Open eClass portal.* Retrieved December 10, 2008, from http://www.openeclass.org/

Edmondson, K. M. (1995). Concept mapping for the development of medical curricula. *Journal of Research in Science Teaching, 32*(7), 777–793. doi:10.1002/tea.3660320709

EduTools homepage. (2008). Retrieved from http://www.edutools.info/static.jsp?pj=4&page=HOME

EduTools. (2008). *CMS: Product list.* Retrieved December 10, 2008, from http://landonline.edutools.info/item_list.jsp?pj=4

Edwards, J., & Fraser, K. (1983). Concept maps as reflections of conceptual understanding. *Research in Science Education, 13,* 19–26. doi:10.1007/BF02356689

Edwards, S. H., & Pérez-Quiñones, M. A. (2007). Experiences using test-driven development with an automated grader. *J. Comput. Small Coll., 22*(3), 44–50.

Efron, D. (1941). *Gesture and environment.* New York: King's Crown Press.

Egbert, J. (2005). *CALL essentials: Principles and practice in call classrooms.* Alexandria, VA: TESOL.

Egea, K. (2003). Managing the managers: Collaborative virtual teams with large staff and student numbers. In T. Greeing & R. Lister (Eds.), *Proc. Australasian Computing Education Conference: Conferences in Research and Practice in Information Technology (ACE2003),* Adelaide.

Egghe, L. (1991). Theory of collaboration and collaborative measures. *Information Processing & Management, 27*(2-3), 177–202. doi:10.1016/0306-4573(91)90048-Q

Ekman, P. (1999). Facial expressions. In T. Dalgleish, & M. Power (Eds.), *Handbook of cognition and emotion.* New York: Wiley & Sons.

Ekman, P., & Friesen, W. (1969). The repertoire of nonverbal behavior: Categories, origins, usage, and coding. *Semiotica, 1,* 49–98.

Ekman, P., & Friesen, W. (1975). *Unmasking the face.* NJ: Prentice Hall.

Elliot, S. (2003). Intellimetric™: From here to validity. In M. Shermis & J. Burstein (Eds.), *Automated essay scoring: A cross-disciplinary perspective.* Mawah, NJ: Lawrence Erlbaum Associates, Inc.

Ellis, R. (2003). *Task-based language learning and teaching.* Oxford, UK: Oxford University Press.

Engelbrecht, J., & Harding, A. (2005). Teaching undergraduate mathematics on the Internet. Part 1: Technologies and taxonomy. *Educational Studies in Mathematics, 58*(2), 235–252. doi:10.1007/s10649-005-6456-3

Engeström, Y. (1987). *Learning by expanding: An activity-theoretical approach to developmental research.* Helsinki, Finland: Orienta-Konsultit.

Engeström, Y. (1999). Activity theory and individual and social transformation. In Y. Engeström, R. Miettinen, & R.-L. Punamäki (Eds.), *Perspectives on activity theory* (pp. 19-38). Cambridge, UK: Cambridge University Press.

Fabri, M., & Hobbs, D. (1998). What you see is what I mean: Virtual encounters in distance learning systems. In *Proceeding of the 4th EATA International Conference on Networking Entities, (NETIES98): Networking for the Millennium*, West Yorkshire, UK.

Fabri, M., Moore, D. J., & Hobbs, D. J. (2004). Mediating the expression of emotion in educational collaborative virtual environments: An experimental study. *International Journal of Virtual Reality, 7*(2), 66–81. doi:10.1007/s10055-003-0116-7

Facer, K., Fulong, J., Furlong, R., & Sutherland, R. (2003) *ScreenPlay: Children and computing in the home.* London: RoutledgeFalmer.

Fahy, P. J. (2006). Online and Face-to-face group interaction processes compared using Bales' interaction process analysis (IPA). *European Journal of Open and Distance Learning (EURODL), 1.*

Faulin, J., Juan, A., Fonseca, P., Pla, L. M., & Rodriguez, S. V. (2009). Learning operations research online: Benefits, challenges, and experiences. *International Journal of Simulation and Process Modelling, 5*(1), 42–53. doi:10.1504/IJSPM.2009.025826

Felder, R. M., & Silverman, L. K. (1988). Learning and teaching styles in engineering education. *English Education, 78*(7), 674–681.

Fernandez, R. (2007). Experiences of collaborative e-learning in preservice teachers. *Revista Latinoamericana de Tecnologia Educativa, 6*(2), 77–90.

Findley, C. (1988). *Collaborative networked learning: On-line facilitation and software support.* Burlington, MA: Digital Equipment Corporation.

Fischer, F., Bruhn, J., Gräsel, C., & Mandl, H. (1998). *Strukturangebote für die gemeinsame wissenskonstruktion beim kooperativen lernen.* Forschungsbericht, Nr.: Universität München, Lehrstuhl f. Empirische Pädagogik und Pädagogische Psychologie.

Ford, C. E. (1999). Collaborative construction of task activity: Coordinating multiple resources in a high school physics lab. *Research on Language and Social Interaction, 32*, 369–408. doi:10.1207/S15327973rls3204_3

Frank, E., Trigg, L., Holmes, G., & Witten, I. H. (2000). Naive Bayes for regression. *Machine Learning, 41*(1), 5–15. doi:10.1023/A:1007670802811

Frasson, C., & Aimeur, E. (1997). Lessons learned from a university-industry cooperative project in tutoring systems. *Int. J. Failures and Lessons learned in Information Technology Management, 1*(2) 149-157.

Frasson, C., Mengelle, T., Aimeur, E., et al. (1996). An Actor-based architecture for intelligent tutoring systems. In C. Frasson, G. Gauthier, & A. Legold (Eds.), *Proceedings of the ITS'96 Conference, Third International Conference on Intelligent Tutoring Systems* (LNCS 1086, pp. 57-65). Berlin, Germany: Springer.

Freeman, M., & McKenzie, J. (2002). SPARK, a confidential Web-based template for self and peer assessment of student teamwork: Benefits of evaluation across different subjects. *British Journal of Educational Technology, 33*(5), 551–569. doi:10.1111/1467-8535.00291

Galotti, K. M., Clinchy, B. M., Ainsworth, K., Lavin, B., & Mansfield, A. F. (1999). A new way of assessing ways of knowing: The attitudes towards thinking and learning survey (ATTLS). *Sex Roles, 40*(9/10), 745–766. doi:10.1023/A:1018860702422

Garcia, A. L., Miller, D. A., Smith, E. R., & Mackie, D. M. (2006). Thanks for the compliment? Emotional reactions to group-level versus individual-level compliments and insults. *Group Processes & Intergroup Relations, 9*(3), 307–324. doi:10.1177/1368430206064636

Garner, S. R., Cunningham, S. J., Holmes, G., Nevill-Manning, C. G., & Witten, I. H. (1995). Applying a machine learning workbench: Experience with agricultural databases. In *Proceedings of the Machine Learning in Practice Workshop, Machine Learning Conference,* Tahoe City, CA, USA, (pp. 14-21).

Garris, R., Ahlers, R., & Driskell, J. E. (2002). Games, motivation, and learning: A research and practice model. *Simulation & Gaming, 33*(4), 441–467. doi:10.1177/1046878102238607

Garrison, D. R., Anderson, T., & Archer, W. (1999). Critical inquiry in a text-based environment: Computer conferencing in higher education. *The Internet and Higher Education, 2*(2-3), 87–105. doi:10.1016/S1096-7516(00)00016-6

Garrison, R., & Anderson, T. (2003). *E-learning in the 21st century. A framework for research and practice.* New York: Routledge Falmer.

Garrison, R., Anderson, T., & Archer, W. (2001). Critical thinking, cognitive presence, and computer conferencing in distance education. *American Journal of Distance Education, 15*(1), 3–21.

Gaudioso, E., Montero, M., Talavera, L., & Hernandez-del-Olmo, F. (2009). Supporting teachers in collaborative student modeling: A framework and an implementation. *Expert Systems with Applications, 36*(2), 2260–2265. doi:10.1016/j.eswa.2007.12.035

Gaytan, J. (2007). Visions shaping the future of online education: understanding its historical evolution, implications, and assumptions. *Online Journal of Distance Learning Administration, 10*(2), 1–10.

Gee, J. P. (2004). *Learning by design: Good video games as learning machines.* Retrieved from http://www.academic-colab.org/resources/documents/Game%20Paper.pdf

Gehringer, E. F. (2001). Building an ethics in computing Web site using peer review. In *Proc. of the 2001 Am. Society for Engineering Education Annual Conference.*

Gehringer, E. F. (2008). Assessing students' Wiki contributions. In *Proceedings of the American Society for Engineering Education Annual Conference,* Pittsburgh, PA.

Gehringer, E. F. (2008). New features for peer review of code and Wikis [faculty poster] In *Proceedings of the 39th SIGCSE Technical Symposium on Computer Science Education,* Portland, OR, USA. Retrieved from http://research.csc.ncsu.edu/efg/expertiza/presentations/Code-and-wikis-poster.ppt

Gehringer, E. F. (2008). Understanding and relating to your international students. In *Proceedings of the American Society for Engineering Education Annual Conference,* Pittsburgh, PA.

Gehringer, E. F., & Cui, Y. (2002). An effective strategy for dynamic mapping of peer reviewers. In *Proc. of the 2002 Am. Society for Engineering Education Annual Conference.*

Gehringer, E. F., & Miller, C. S. (2009). Student-generated active-learning exercises. In Proceedings of the *40th SIGCSE Technical Symposium on Computer Science Education, SIGCSE '09,* Chattanooga, TN, USA. New York: ACM Press. Retrieved from http://research.csc.ncsu.edu/efg/expertiza/papers/sigcse09.pdf

Gehringer, E. F., Ehresman, L. M., & Skrien, D. J. (2006). Expertiza: Students helping to write an OOD text. In *Companion to the 21st ACM SIGPLAN Conference on Object-Oriented Programming Systems, Languages, and Applications, OOPSLA '06,* Portland, Oregon, USA (pp. 901-906). New York: ACM Press.

Gehringer, E. F., Ehresman, L. M., Conger, S. G., & Wagle, P. (2007). Reusable learning objects through peer review: The Expertiza approach. *Innovate: Journal of Online Education, 3*(5).

Geister, S., Konradt, U., & Hertel, G. (2006). Effects of process feedback on motivation, satisfaction, and performance in virtual teams. *Small Group Research*, *37*(5), 459–489. doi:10.1177/1046496406292337

Georgiou, D. A., & Makry, D. (2004). *A learner's style and profile recognition via fuzzy cognitive map.* Paper presented at the IEEE International Conference on Advanced Learning Technologies.

Gergle, D., Kraut, R. E., & Fussell, S. R. (2004). Action as language in a shared visual space. In *Proceedings of ACM Conference on Computer Supported Cooperative Work (CSCW)*, (pp. 487-496). New York: ACM Press.

Gil, F., Rico, R., Alcover, C. M., & Barrasa, Á. (2005). Change-oriented leadership, satisfaction and performance in work groups: Effects of team climate and group potency. *Journal of Managerial Psychology*, *20*(3/4), 312–329. doi:10.1108/02683940510589073

Givens, D. (2005). *Nonverbal dictionary of gestures, signs & body language cues online*. Spokane, WA: Center for Nonverbal Studies Press. Retrieved April 2008, from http://members.aol.com/nonverbal2/diction1.htm

Glass, G., McGaw, B., & Smith, M. (1981). *Analysis in social research*. London: Sage Publications.

Glückler, J., & Schrott, G. (2007). Leadership and performance in virtual teams: Exploring brokerage in electronic communication. *International Journal of e-Collaboration*, *3*(3), 31–53.

Goldin-Meadow, S., Wein, D., & Chang, C. (1992). Assessing knowledge through gesture: Using children's hands to read their minds. *Cognition and Instruction*, *9*(3), 201–219. doi:10.1207/s1532690xci0903_2

Gómez-Laso, M. A., & Benito, D. (2006). Preparing learning guides suitable for personalized learning itineraries in virtual learning scenarios. In *Proceedings of the 10th IACEE World Conference on Continuing Engineering Education (WCCEE 2006)*, Vienna, Austria.

Gonzalez, J., & Wagenaar, R. (Eds.). (2005). *Tuning project. Tuning educational structures in Europe*. European Commission. European Commission, Education and Culture DG. Retrieved from http://tuning.unideusto.org/tuningeu

Gonzalez, J., & Wagener, R. (2003). *Tuning educational structures in Europe* (Final report [phase one]). Universidad de Deusto. Retrieved from http://www.relint.deusto.es/TUNINGProject/documentos/Tuning_phase1/Tuning_phase1_full_document.pdf

Goodman, B., Soller, A., Linton, F., & Gaimari, R. (1998). Encouraging student reflection and articulation using a learning companion. *International Journal of Artificial Intelligence in Education*, *9*(3-4).

Graetz, K., Boyle, E., Kimble, C., Thompson, P., & Garloch, J. (1998). Information sharing in face-to-face, teleconferencing, and electronic chat groups. *Small Group Research*, *29*(6), 714–743. doi:10.1177/1046496498296003

Graf, S. Kinshuk, & Liu, T. (2008). Identifying learning styles in learning management systems by using indications from students' behaviour. In *Proceedings of the 8th IEEE International Conference on Advanced Learning Technologies*, Santander, Spain (pp. 482-486).

Graf, S., & Kinshuk. (2007). *Considering cognitive traits and learning styles to open Web-based learning to a larger student community.* Paper presented at the International Conference on Information and Communication Technology and Accessibility.

Graven, O. G., & MacKinnon, D. (2005). A survey of current state of the art support for lifelong learning. In *Proceedings of the ITHET 6th Annual International Conference.*

Griffin, F. (2005). The MacQTeX quiz project. In *Proceedings of the 7th International Conference on Technology in Mathematics Teaching (ICTMT7)*, Bristol, UK (pp. 242–249).

Grion, V., Varisco, B. M., Luchi, F., Raineri, M. S., & Mazzoni, E. (2008). Building and sharing teacher professional identity in virtual communities. In B. M. Varisco (Ed.), *Psychological, pedagogical and sociological models for learning and assessment in virtual communities* (pp. 93-144). Milan, Italy: Polimetrica.

Griswold, W. G., & Simon, B. (2006). Ubiquitous presenter: Fast, scalable active learning for the whole classroom. In *Proceedings of the 11th Annual SIGCSE Conference on innovation and Technology in Computer Science Education, ITICSE '06*, Bologna, Italy (pp. 358-358). New York: ACM Press.

Gritz, E., Fingeret, M. C., Vidrine, D. J., Lazev, A. B., Mehta, N. V., & Reece, G. P. (2006). Successes and failures of the teachable moment: Smoking cessation in cancer patients. *Cancer, 106*(1), 17–27. doi:10.1002/cncr.21598

Gruenfeld, D. H., Mannix, E. A., Williams, K. Y., & Neale, M. A. (1996). Group composition and decision making: How member familiarity and information distribution affect process and performance. *Organizational Behavior and Human Decision Processes, 67*(1), 1–16. doi:10.1006/obhd.1996.0061

Guerra, J. M., Martinez, I., Munduate, L., & Medina, F. J. (2005). A contingency perspective on the study of the consequences of conflict types: The role of organizational culture. *European Journal of Work and Organizational Psychology, 14*(2), 157–176. doi:10.1080/13594320444000245

Guo, L., Xiang, X., & Shi, Y. (2004). Use Web usage mining to assist background online e-learning assessment. In *Proceedings of the 4th IEEE ICALT*.

Gutl, C., Pivec, M., Trummer, C., Garcia-Barrios, V. M., Modritscher, F., Pripfl, J., et al. (2005). AdeLE (adaptive e-learning with eyetracking): Theoretical background, system architecture and application scenarios. *European Journal of Open, Distance and E-Learning (EURODL)*.

Guye-Vuillème, A., Capin, T. K., Pandzic, I. S., Thalmann, N. M., & Thalmann, D. (1998). Nonverbal communication interface for collaborative virtual environments. In D. Snowdon & E. Churchill (Eds.), *Proceedings of the Collaborative Virtual Environments* (pp. 105-112). Manchester, UK: University of Manchester.

Hackman, J. R. (1987). The design of work teams. In J. W. Lorsch (Ed.), *Handbook of organizational behavior* (pp. 315-342). Englewood Cliffs, NJ: Prentice-Hall.

Hadiana, A., & Kaijiri, K. (2002). The construction of asynchronous Q&A support system. In *Information Technology Letters Forum on Information Technology* (pp. 249-250).

Hadiana, A., Zhang, T., Ampornaramveth, V., & Ueno, H. (2006). WEB e-learning based on concept of online whiteboard. *WEBIST,* (2). 387-391.

Haley, H., & Sidanius, J. (2006). The positive and negative framing of affirmative action: A group dominance perspective. *Personality and Social Psychology Bulletin, 32*(5), 656–668. doi:10.1177/0146167205283442

Hall, E. T. (1959). *The silent language.* Greenwich, CT: Fawcett Publications.

Hamer, J. (2006). Some experiences with the "contributing student approach." In *Proceedings of the 11th Annual SIGCSE Conference on innovation and Technology in Computer Science Education, ITICSE '06*, Bologna, Italy (pp. 68-72). New York: ACM Press.

Hamer, J., Ma, K. T., & Kwong, H. H. (2005). A method of automatic grade calibration in peer assessment. In A. Young & D. Tolhurst (Eds.), *Proceedings of the 7th Australasian Conference on Computing Education – Vol. 42*, Newcastle, New South Wales, Australia (pp. 67-72). Darlinghurst, Australia: Australian Computer Society.

Han, J., & Camber, M. (2001). *Data mining concepts and techniques.* San Francisco: Morgan Kaufman.

Hanson-Smith, E. (1997). *Technology in the classroom: Practice and promise in the 21st century* (TESOL Professional Papers 2). Alexandria, VA: Teachers of English to Speakers of Other Languages.

Hara, N., Bonk, C. J., & Angeli, C. (2000). Content analysis of online discussion in an applied educational psychology course. *Instructional Science, 28*, 115–152. doi:10.1023/A:1003764722829

Hareli, S., & Rafaeli, A. (in press). Emotion cycles: on the social influence of emotion in organization. *Research in Organizational Behavior, 28.*

Harless, W., Zier, A., & Duncan, R. (1999). Virtual dialogs with native speakers: The evaluation of an interactive multimedia method. *CALICO Journal, 16*(3), 313–336.

Harpaz, I., Balik, C., & Ehrenfeld, M. (2004). Concept mapping: An educational strategy for advancing nursing education. *Nursing Forum, 39*(2), 27–30. doi:10.1111/j.0029-6473.2004.00027.x

Hartnell-Young, E. (2005). *Teachers' new roles in school-based communities of practice.* Paper presented at the AARE Conference, Melbourne, Australia. Retrieved from http://www.aare.edu.au/04pap/har04257.pdf

Hasu, M. (2001). *Critical transition from developers to users. Activity-theoretical studies of interaction and learning in the innovation process.* Unpublished academic dissertation, Departement of Education, Center for Activity Theory and Developmental Work Research, University of Helsinki. Retrieved June 31, 2008, from http://ethesis.helsinki.fi/julkaisut/kas/kasva/vk/hasu/

Hause, M., Last, M., Almstrum, V., & Woodroffe, M. (2001). Interaction factors in software development performance in distributed student teams in computer science. In *Proceedings of the ACM Conference*, Boulder, CO, USA (pp. 69-72).

Hayes, J. H., Lethbridge, T. C., & Port, D. (2003). Evaluating individual contribution toward group software engineering projects. In *Proceedings of the 25th international Conference on Software Engineering*, Portland, Oregon (pp. 622-627). Washington, DC: IEEE Computer Society.

Hedge, T. (2000). *Teaching and learning in the language classroom.* Oxford, UK: Oxford University Press.

HEDW. (2008). *Higher education data warehousing forum.* Retrieved from http://ws.cc.sunysb.edu/offires/hedw/index.html

Hegelheimer, V., & Tower, D. (2004). Using CALL in the classroom: Analyzing student interactions in an authentic classroom. *System, 32*(2), 185–205. doi:10.1016/j.system.2003.11.007

Heldal, I. (2007). The impact of social interaction on usability for distributed virtual environments. *International Journal of Virtual Reality, 6*(3), 45–54.

Henri, F. (1992). Computer conferencing and content analysis. In A. R. Kaye (Ed.), *Collaborative learning through computer conferencing: The Najaden papers* (pp. 115-136). New York: Springer.

Hewitt, J. (2001). Beyond threaded discourse. *International Journal of Educational Telecommunications, 7*, 207–221.

Hewson, C., & Laurent, D. (2008). Research design and tools for Internet research. In N. Fielding, R. M. Lee, & G. Blank (Eds.), *Online research methods.* London: Sage Publications.

Heylen, D. (2005). *Challenges ahead: Head movements and other social acts in conversations.* AISB - Social Presence Cues Symposium.

Hietala, P., & Niemirepo, T. (1998). The competence of learning companion agents. *International Journal of Artificial Intelligence in Education, 9*, 178–192.

Hijon, R., & Velazquez, A. (2006). E-learning platforms analysis and development of students tracking functionality. In E. Pearson & P. Bohman (Eds.), *Proceedings of World Conference on Educational Multimedia, Hypermedia and Telecommunications* (pp. 2823–2828). Chesapeake, VA: AACE.

Hindmarsh, J., Fraser, M., Heath, C., Benford, S., & Greenhalgh, C. (1998). Fragmented interaction: Establishing mutual orientation in virtual environments. In *Proceedings of the ACM conference on Computer supported cooperative work (CSCW '98)* (pp. 217-226). New York: ACM Press.

Hofner, S. D. (1996). Productive behaviours of global business teams. *International Journal of Intercultural Relations, 20*(2), 227–259. doi:10.1016/0147-1767(95)00043-7

Holden, C. (1992). Study flunks science and math tests. *Science Education, 26*, 541.

Holmes, G., Donkin, A., & Witten, I. H. (1994). Weka: A machine learning workbench. In *Proceedings of the 1994 Second Australian and New Zealand Conference on Intelligent Information Systems*, Brisbane, Australia, (pp. 357-361).

Honey, P., & Mumford, A. (2000). *The learning styles helper's guide*. Maidenhead, UK: Peter Honey Publications.

Horwitz, F. M., Bravington, D., & Silvis, U. (2006). The promise of virtual teams: Identifying key factors in effectiveness and failure. *Journal of European Industrial Training, 30*(6), 472–494. doi:10.1108/03090590610688843

Howell, S. L., Williams, P. B., & Lindsay, N. K. (2003). Thirty-two trends affecting distance education: An informed foundation for strategic planning. *Online Journal of Distance Learning Administration, 6*(3), 1–18.

Hürst, W., Jung, S., & Welte, M. (2007). Effective learn-quiz generation for handled devices. In *Proceedings of the 9ᵗʰ International Conference on Human Computer Interaction with Mobile Devices and Services (Mobile HCI'07)*.

I.M.S. (2001). *IMS learner information packaging information model specification*. Instructional Management Systems.

Iacono, S., & Weisband, S. (1997). Developing trust in virtual teams. In *Proceedings of the Hawaii International Conference on System Sciences*, Hawaii, USA.

Ibabe, J., & Jaureguizar, J. (2007). Self-assessment across Internet: Metacognitive variables and academic achievement. *Revista Latinoamericana de Tecnologia Educativa, 6*(2), 59–75.

Ieronutti, L., & Chittaro, L. (2007). Employing virtual humans for education and training in X3D/VRML worlds. *Computers & Education, 49*(1), 93–109. doi:10.1016/j.compedu.2005.06.007

Imai, T., Qui, Z., Behara, S., Tachi, S., Aoyama, T., Johnson, A., & Leigh, J. (2000). Overcoming time-zone differences and time management problem with tele-immersion. In *Proceedings of INET*, Yokohama, Japan.

Ingram, A. (1999). Using Web server logs in evaluating instructional Web sites. *Journal of Educational Technology Systems, 28*(2), 137–157. doi:10.2190/R3AE-UCRY-NJVR-LY6F

Jarvenpaa, S. L., Knoll, K., & Leidner, D. E. (1998). Is anybody out there? Antecedents of trust in global virtual teams. *Journal of Management Information Systems, 14*(4), 29–65.

Jerman, P., Soller, A., & Muhlenbrock, M. (2001). From mirroring to guiding: A review of state of the art technology for supporting collaborative learning. In P. Dillenbourg, A. Eurelings, & K. Hakkarainen (Eds.), *Proceedings of the EuroCSCL*, Maastricht, NL, (pp. 324-331).

Jermann, P. (2004). *Computer support for interaction regulation in collaborative problem-solving*. Unpublished doctoral dissertation, University of Genéva, Genéva, Switzerland. Retrieved, November 2005, from http://craftsrv1.epfl.ch/~colin/thesis-jermann.pdf

Jermann, P., Soller, A., & Muehlenbrock, M. (2001). From mirroring to guiding: A review of state of the art technology for supporting collaborative learning. In *Proceedings of the European Conference on Computer Supported Collaborative Learning*, Maastricht, The Netherlands.

Johnson, A., & Leigh, J. (2001). Tele-immersive collaboration in the CAVE research network. In E. F. Churchill, D. N. Snowdon, & A. J. Munro (Eds.), *Collaborative virtual environments: Digital places and spaces for interaction* (pp. 225-243). Berlin, Germany: Springer.

Johnson, D., Johnson, R., & Holubec, E. J. (1990). *Circles of learning: Cooperation in the classroom* (3rd ed.). Edina, MN: Interaction Book Company.

Johnson, S. C., Suriya, C., Yoon, S. W., Berrett, J. V., & La Fleur, J. (2002). Team development and group processes of virtual learning teams. *Computers & Education, 39*, 379–393. doi:10.1016/S0360-1315(02)00074-X

Jonassen, D. (1995). Supporting communities of learners with technology: A vision for integrating technology with learning in schools. *Educational Technology*, (July/August): 60–63.

Jonassen, D. H., & Grabowski, B. L. (1993). *Handbook of individual differences: Learning and instruction.* Hillsdale, NJ: Lawrence Erlbaum Associates.

Jonassen, D. H., & Wang, S. (1993). Acquiring structural knowledge from semantically structured hypertext. *Journal of Computer-Based Instruction, 20*(1), 1–8.

Jonassen, D. H., Peck, K., & Wilson, B. (1999). *Learning with technology: A constructivist perspective.* Upper Saddle River, NJ: Merrill.

Jonassen, D. H., Reeves, T. C., Hong, N., Harvey, D., & Peters, K. (1997). Concept mapping as cognitive learning and assessment tools. *Journal of Interactive Learning Research, 8*(3/4), 289–308.

Joomla, L. M. S. (2008). Retrieved http://www.joomlalms.com/

Juan, A., Daradoumis, T., Faulin, J., & Xhafa, F. (2008). A data analysis model based on control charts to monitor online learning processes. *International Journal of Business Intelligence and Data Mining.*

Juan, A., Daradoumis, T., Faulin, J., & Xhafa, F. (2008). Developing an information system for monitoring student's activity in online collaborative learning. In *Proceedings of the 2nd International Conference on Complex, Intelligent and Software Intensive Systems* (pp. 270-275).

Juan, A., Daradoumis, T., Faulin, J., & Xhafa, F. (2008). Developing an information system for monitoring student's activity in online collaborative learning. In *Proceedings of the 2nd International Conference on Complex, Intelligent and Software Intensity Systems (CISIS)*, Barcelona, Spain (pp. 270-275).

Juan, A., Daradoumis, T., Faulin, J., & Xhafa, F. (2009). A data analysis model based on control charts to monitor online learning processes. *International Journal Business Intelligence and Data Mining.*

Juan, A., Daradoumis, T., Faulin, J., & Xhafa, F. (2009). SAMOS: A model for monitoring students' and groups' activity in collaborative e-learning. *International Journal of Learning Technology, 4*(1/2), 53–72. doi:10.1504/IJLT.2009.024716

Juan, A., Daradournis, T., Faulin, J., & Xhafa, F. (2008). Developing an information system for monitoring student's activity in online collaborative learning. In *Proceedings of the 2nd International Conference on Complex, Intelligent and software intensive systems,* Barcelona, Spain (pp. 270-275).

Juan, A., Huertas, M., Steegmann, C., Corcoles, C., & Serrat, C. (2008b). Mathematical e-learning: State of the art and experiences at the Open University of Catalonia. *International Journal of Mathematical Education in Science and Technology, 39*(4), 455–471. doi:10.1080/00207390701867497

Jusung, J. (2005). Understanding e-dropout? *International Journal on E-Learning, 4*(2), 229–240.

Kahai, S., Fjermestad, J., Zhang, S., & Avolio, B. (2007). Leadership in virtual teams: Past, present, and future. *International Journal of e-Collaboration, 3*(1), 1–10.

Kahiigi, E. K., Ekenberg, L., Hansson, H., Tusubira, F. F., & Danielson, M. (2008). Exploring the e-learning state of art. In *Electronic Journal of e-Learning, 6*(2), 77-88.

Kanuka, H., & Anderson, T. (1999). Using constructivism in technology-mediated learning: Constructing order out of the chaos in the literature. *Radical Pedagogy, 1*(2). Retrieved from http://radicalpedagogy.icaap.org/content/issue1_2/02kanuka1_2.html

Kaptelinin, V., & Nardi, B. A. (2006). *Acting with technology. Activity theory and interaction design.* Cambridge, MA: MIT Press.

Karampiperis, P., & Sampson, D. (2005). Adaptive learning resources sequencing in educational hypermedia systems. *Educational Technology and Society, 8*(4), 128–147.

Karampiperis, P., Lin, T., Sampson, D. G., & Kinshuk, . (2006). Adaptive cognitive-based selection of learning objects. *Innovations in Education and Teaching International, 43*(2), 121–135. doi:10.1080/14703290600650392

Katzeff, C. (2000). The design of interactive media for learners in an organisational setting – the state of the art. In *Proceedings of the NordiCHI 2000.*

Kay, J. (1995). The um toolkit for cooperative user models. *User Modeling and User-Adapted Interaction, 4*(3), 149–196. doi:10.1007/BF01100243

Kayworth, T., & Leidner, D. (2001/2002). Leadership effectiveness in global virtual teams. *Journal of Management Information Systems, 18*(3), 7–40.

Kearsley, G. (1995). *The nature and value of interaction in distance learning.* Paper presented at the Third Distance Education Research Symposium.

Keeney-Kennicut, W., Guernsel, A. B., & Simpson, N. (2008). Overcoming student resistance to a teaching innovation. [Retrieved from http://www.georgiasouthern. edu/iostl]. *J. for the Scholarship of Teaching and Learning, 2008*(January), 1–26.

Kennedy, J., Shollenberger, K., & Widmann, J. (2007). Student use of author's textbook solution manuals: Effect on student learning of mechanics fundamentals. In *Proc. of the 2007 Am. Society for Engineering Education Annual Conference.*

Kerr, P. M., Park, K. H., & Domazlicky, B. R. (1995). Peer grading of essays in a principles of microeconomics course. *Journal of Education for Business, 70*(6), 15–25.

Kim, N., Smith, M. J., & Maeng, K. (2008). Assessment in online distance education: A comparison of three online programs at a university. *Online Journal of Distance Learning Administration, 11*(1), 1–16.

Kim, Y., Hiltz, S. R., & Turoff, M. (2002). Coordination structures and system restrictiveness in distributed group support systems. *Group Decision and Negotiation, 11,* 379–404. doi:10.1023/A:1020492305910

Kleinke, C. (1986). Gaze and eye contact: A research review. *Psychological Bulletin, 100,* 78–100. doi:10.1037/0033-2909.100.1.78

Knapp, M. L., & Hall, J. A. (2007). *Nonverbal communication in human interaction* (5th ed.). Florence, KY: Thomas Learning.

Knutson, A. L. (1960). Quiet and vocal groups. *Sociometry, 23,* 36–49. doi:10.2307/2786136

Kolb, D. A. (1999). *Learning style inventory - version 3: Technical specifications.* TRG Hay/McBer, Training Resources Group.

Kommers, P., & Lanzing, J. (1997). Student's concept mapping for hypermedia design. Navigation through the World Wide Web (WWW) space and self-assessment. *Journal of Interactive Learning Research, 8*(3/4), 421–455.

Kononenko, I. (1990). Comparison of inductive and Naive Bayesian learning approaches to automatic knowledge acquisition. In *Current trends in knowledge acquisition.* Amsterdam: IOS Press.

Konradt, U., & Hoch, J. E. A. (2007). Work roles and leadership functions of managers in virtual teams. *International Journal of e-Collaboration, 3*(2), 16–35.

Koohang, A. (2004). Creating learning objects in collaborative e-learning settings. *Issues in Information Systems, 4*(2), 584–590.

Koychev, I., & Schwab, I. (2000). Adaptation to drifting user's interests. In *Proceedings of ECML2000 Workshop: Machine Learning in New Information Age.*

Krasner, G. E., & Pope, S. T. (1998). A cookbook for using the model-view-controller user interface paradigm in smalltalk-80. *Journal of Object Oriented Programming, 1*(3), 26–49.

Krause, U. M., Stark, R., & Madl, H. (2009). The effects of cooperative learning and feedback on e-learning in statistics. *Learning and Instruction, 19*(2), 158–170. doi:10.1016/j.learninstruc.2008.03.003

Ladd, R. D. (1996). *Intonational phonology.* Cambridge, UK: Cambridge University Press.

Lagoze, C., & Davis, J. R. (1995). Dienst: An architecture for distributed document libraries. *Communications of the ACM, 38*(4), 47. doi:10.1145/205323.205331

Lagoze, C., Shaw, E., Davis, J. R., & Krafft, D. B. (1995). *Dienst: Implementation reference manual* (TR95-1514). Cornell University, USA.

Lally, V., & de Laat, M. (2002). Cracking the code: Learning to collaborate and collaborating to learn in a networked environment. In G. Stahl (Ed.), *Computer support for collaborative learning: Foundations for a CSCL community, Proceedings of the CSCL 2002,* Boulder, Colorado, USA (pp. 160-168).

Lam, P., Keing, C., McNaught, C., & Cheng, K. F. (2006). Monitoring e-learning environments through analysing Web logs of institution-wide eLearning platforms. In *Proceedings of the 23rd annual ascilite conference: Who's learning? Whose technology,* Sydney, Australia.

Landauer, T., Foltz, P., & Laham, D. (1998). Introduction to latent semantic analysis. *Discourse Processes, 25,* 259–284.

Landauer, T., Laham, D., & Foltz, P. (2000). The intelligent essay assessor. *IEEE Intelligent Systems, 15,* 27–31.

Landauer, T., Laham, D., Rehder, B., & Schreiner, M. (1997). *How well can passage meaning be derived without word order? A comparison of latent semantic analysis and humans.* Paper presented at the Cognitive Science Society, Mahwah, NJ.

Lauw, H. W., Lim, E.-P., & Wang, K. (2007). Summarizing review scores of "unequal" reviewers. In *Proceedings of the 2007 SIAM International Conference on Data Mining,* Minneapolis, MN (pp. 539-544).

Lave, J., & Wegner, E. (1991). *Situated learning: Legitimate peripheral participation.* Cambridge, UK: Cambridge University Press.

Lebie, L., Rhoades, J. A., & McGrath, J. E. (1996). Interaction process in computer-mediated and face-to-face groups. *CSCW, 4,* 127–152.

Lee-Kelley, L. (2002). Situational leadership: Managing the virtual project team. *Journal of Management Development, 21*(6), 461–477. doi:10.1108/02621710210430623

LeJeune, N. (2006). Assessment of individuals on CS group projects. *J. Comput. Small Coll., 22*(1), 231–237.

Lemaire, P. (1999). *Psychologie cognitive.* Bruxelles, Belgium: De Boeck Universite.

Leont'ev, A. N. (1978). *Activity, consciousness and personality.* Englewood Cliffs, NJ: Prentice-Hall. Retrieved June 15, 2008, from http://www.marxists.org/archive/leontev/works/1978/

Levy, M. (1997). *Computer-assisted language learning: Context and conceptualization.* Oxford, UK: Clarendon Press.

Levy, Y. (2007). Comparing dropouts and persistence in e-learning courses. *Computers & Education, 48,* 185–204. doi:10.1016/j.compedu.2004.12.004

Liaw, S. S., Huang, H. M., & Chen, G. D. (2007). Surveying instructor and learner attitudes toward e-learning. *Computers & Education, 49*(4), 1066–1080. doi:10.1016/j.compedu.2006.01.001

Lin, W., & Alvarez, S. (2002). Efficient adaptive-support association rule mining for recommender systems. *Data Mining and Knowledge Discovery, 6*(1), 83–105. doi:10.1023/A:1013284820704

Lind, M. R. (1999). The gender impact of temporary virtual work groups. *IEEE Transactions on Professional Communication, 42*(4), 276–285. doi:10.1109/47.807966

Lipman, M. (1991). *Thinking in education*. Cambridge, MA: Cambridge University Press.

Lipponen, L., Rahikainen, M., Lallilmo, J., & Hakkarainen, K. (2003). Patterns of participation and discourse in elementary students' computer-supported collaborative learning. *Learning and Instruction, 13*, 487–509. doi:10.1016/S0959-4752(02)00042-7

Lombard, M., Snyder-Dich, J., & Bracken, C. C. (2002). Content analysis in mass communication. Assessment and reporting of intercoder reliability. *Human Communication Research, 28*(4), 587–604. doi:10.1111/j.1468-2958.2002.tb00826.x

Lowry, R. (2005). Computer-aided self assessment -an effective tool. *Chemistry Education Research and Practice, 6*(4), 198–203.

Lurey, J. S., & Raisinghani, M. S. (2001). An empirical study of best practices in virtual teams. *Information & Management, 38*(8), 523–544. doi:10.1016/S0378-7206(01)00074-X

MacDonald, M., Badger, R., & White, G. (2000). The real thing?: Authenticity and academic listening. *English for Specific Purposes, 19*(3), 253–267. doi:10.1016/S0889-4906(98)00028-3

Maier, N. R. F. (1967). Assets & liabilities in group problem solving. *Psychological Review, 74*(4), 239–249. doi:10.1037/h0024737

Majchrzak, A., Malhotra, A., Stamps, J., & Lipnack, J. (2004). Can absence make a team grow stronger? *Harvard Business Review, 82*(5), 131–139.

Major, H., & Levenburg, N. (1999). Learner success in distance environments: A shared responsibility. *The Technology Source*.

Malone, T. W., & Lepper, M. R. (1987). Making learning fun: A taxonomy of intrinsic motivations for learning. In *Aptitude, learning and instruction. Volume 3: Cognitive and affective process análisis* (pp. 223-253).

Manca, S., Delfino, M., & Mazzoni, E. (in press). Coding procedures to analyse interaction patterns in educational Web forums. [JCAL]. *Journal of Computer Assisted Learning*.

Manochehr, N. N. (2006). The influence of learning styles on learners in e-learning environments: An empirical study. *CHEER, 18*, 10–14.

Marquardt, C. G. (2004). A preprocessing tool for web usage mining in distance education domain. In *IDEAS: Proc. of the 8th Int. Database Engineering and Applications Symposium*.

Martell, R. F., & Guzzo, R. A. (1991). The dynamics of implicit theories of group performance: When and how do they operate? *Organizational Behavior and Human Decision Processes, 50*(1), 51–75. doi:10.1016/0749-5978(91)90034-Q

Martin, D. J. (1994). Concept mapping as an aid to lesson planning: A longitudinal study. *Journal of Elementary Science Education, 6*(2), 11–30.

Martínez, A. (2003). *A model and a method for computational support for CSCL evaluation* (in Spanish). Unpublished doctoral dissertation, University of Valladolid, Valladolid. Retrieved, November 2005, from http://www.infor.uva.es/~amartine/research/phd/tesis_amartine.pdf

Martinez, A., Dimitriadis, Y., Rubia, B., Gomez, E., & De La Fuente, P. (2003). Combining qualitative evaluation and social network analysis for the study of classroom social interactions. *Computers & Education, 41*(4), 353–368. doi:10.1016/j.compedu.2003.06.001

Mas-Colell, A. (2003). The European Space of Higher Education: Incentive and governance issues. *Review of Political Economy, 93*(11/12), 9–28.

Matteucci, M. C., Carugati, F., Selleri, P., Mazzoni, E., & Tomasetto, C. (in press). Teachers' judgment from an European psychological perspective. In G. F. Ollington (Ed.), *Teachers and teaching: Strategies, innovations and problem solving*. Hauppauge, NY: Nova Science Publishers.

Mazza, R., & Dimitrova, V. (2004). Visualising student tracking data to support instructors in Web-based distance education. In *WWW Alt. '04: Proceedings of the 13ᵗʰ International World Wide Web Conference on Alternate track papers & posters* (pp. 154-161). New York: ACM Press.

Mazza, R., & Dimitrova, V. (2007). CourseVis: A graphical student monitoring tool for supporting instructors in Web-based distance courses. *International Journal of Human-Computer Studies, 65*(2), 125–139. doi:10.1016/j.ijhcs.2006.08.008

Mazza, R., & Milani, C. (2005). Exploring usage analysis in learning systems: Gaining insights from visualisations. In *Proceedings of the Workshop on usage analysis in learning systems, 12th International Conference on Artificial Intelligence in Education (AEID 2005)*, Amsterdam, The Netherlands (pp. 65-72).

Mazzoni, E. (2006). Du simple tracement des interactions à l'évaluation des rôles et des fonctions des membres d'une communauté en réseau: Une proposition dérivée de l'analyse des réseaux sociaux. *Information Sciences for Decision Making, 25,* 477-487. Retrieved March 19, 2008, from http://isdm.univ-tln.fr/

Mazzoni, E. (2006). Extending Web sites' usability: From a cognitive perspective to an activity theory approach. In S. Zappala & C. Gray (Eds.), *Impact of e-commerce on consumers and small firms* (pp. 161-175). Aldershot, Hampshire, UK: Ashgate.

Mbarika, V. W., Sankar, C. S., Raju, P. K., & Raymond, J. (2001). Importance of learning-driven constructs on perceived skill development when using multimedia instructional materials. *Journal of Educational Technology Systems, 29*(1), 67–87.

McConnell, J. J. (2005). Active and cooperative learning: Tips and tricks (part I). *SIGCSE Bulletin, 37*(2), 27–30. doi:10.1145/1083431.1083457

McCowan, I., Gatica-Perez, D., Bengio, S., Lathoud, G., Barnard, M., & Zhang, D. (2005). Automatic analysis of multimodal group actions in meetings. *IEEE Transactions on Pattern Analysis and Machine Intelligence, 27*(3), 305–317. doi:10.1109/TPAMI.2005.49

McDaniel, E., Roth, B., & Miller, M. (1988). Concept mapping as a tool for curriculum design. *Issues in Informing Science and Information Technology, 2*, 505–513.

McKlin, T., Harmon, S. W., Evans, W., & Jone, M. G. (2001). Cognitive presence in Web-based learning: A content analysis of students' online discussions. *American Journal of Distance Education, 15*(1), 7–23.

Mehrabian, A. (1969). Significance of posture and position in the communication of attitude and status relationships. *Psychological Bulletin, 71*(5), 359–372. doi:10.1037/h0027349

Mendonça, C., & Johnson, K. (1994). Peer review negotiations: Revision activities in ESL writing instruction. *TESOL Quarterly, 28*(4), 745–768. doi:10.2307/3587558

Mentor, K. (2005). *Online encyclopedia of criminal justice.* Retrieved December 2008, from http://cjencyclopedia.com

Merelo-Guervós, J., & Castillo-Valdivieso, P. (2004). Conference paper assignment using a combined greedy/evolutionary algorithm. In *Parallel problem solving from nature - PPSN VIII* (LNCS 3242, pp. 602-611). Berlin, Germany: Springer-Verlag.

Meyen, E. L., Aust, R. J., Bui, Y. N., & Isaacson, R. (2002). Assessing and monitoring student progress in an e-learning personnel preparation environment. *Teacher Education and Special Education, 25*(2), 187–198.

Meyer, D. (2002). Quality in distance education. Focus on online learning. *ASHE-ERIC Higher Education Report Series, 29*(4).

Meyer, K. A. (2003). Face-to-face versus threaded discussions: The role of time and higher-order thinking. *Journal of Asynchronous Learning Networks, 7*(3), 55–65.

Mihaescu, M. C., & Burdescu, D. D. (2006). Testing attribute selection algorithms for classification performance on real data. In *Proceedings of the 3ʳᵈ IEEE International Conference on Intelligent Systems (IS)* (pp. 581-586). Washington, DC: IEEE Press.

Mihaescu, M. C., & Burdescu, D. D. (2007). Classification of students using their data traffic within an e-learning platform. In *Proceedings of the International Joint Conference on e-Business and Telecommunications -International Conference on e-Business (ICE-B)* (pp. 315-321). INSTICC Press.

Milani, C., & Mazza, R. (2007). *GISMO: A graphical interactive student monitoring system for Moodle.* Retrieved from http://gismo.sourceforge.net

Miles, M. (1959). *Learning to work in groups.* New York: Columbia University Press.

Milosevic, D. (2006). Designing lesson content in adaptive learning environments. *International Journal of Emerging Technologies in Learning, 1*(2).

Milosevic, D., Brkovic, M., Debevc, M., & Krneta, R. (2007). Adaptive learning by using SCOs metadata. *Interdisciplinary Journal of Knowledge and Learning Objects, 3,* 163–174.

Mintzes, J. J., Wandersee, J. H., & Novak, J. D. (2000). *Assessing science understanding: A human constructivist view.* San Diego, CA: Academic Press.

Mitchell, T. (1997). *Machine learning.* New York: McGraw Hill.

Montoya-Weiss, M. M., Massey, A. P., & Song, M. (2001). Getting it together: Temporal coordination and conflict management in global virtual teams. *Academy of Management Journal, 44*(6), 1251–1263. doi:10.2307/3069399

Moodle. (2007). Retrieved from http://moodle.org/

Moodle. (2008). *Workshop module – MoodleDocs.* Retrieved September 2008, from http://docs.moodle.org/en/Workshop

Moore, A., Brailsford, T. J., & Stewart, C. D. (2001). *Personally tailored teaching in WHURLE using conditional transclusion.* Paper presented at the ACM Conference on Hypertext.

Morris, D., Collett, P., Marsh, P., & O'Shaughnessy, M. (1979). *Gestures, their origin and distribution.* London: Jonathan Cape Ltd.

Mostow, J., Beck, J., Cen, H., Cuneo, A., Gouvea, E., & Heiner, C. (2005). An educational data mining tool to browse tutor-student interactions: Time will tell! In *Proc. of the Workshop on educational data mining* (pp. 15-22).

Mota, S., & Picard, R. W. (2003). Automated posture analysis for detecting learner's interest level. In *Proceedings of the Workshop on Computer Vision and Pattern Recognition for Human-Computer Interaction, (CVPR, HCI).* Madison, WI: IEEE Computer Society.

Mühlenbrock, M. (2004). Shared workspaces: Analyzing user activity and group interaction. In H. U. Hoppe, M. Ikeda, H. Ogata, & F. Hesse (Eds.), *New technologies for collaborative learning, computer-supported collaborative learning series.* Amsterdam: Kluwer.

Mundy, J., Thorthwaite, W., & Kimball, R. (2006). *The Microsoft data warehouse toolkit: With SQL Server 2005 and the Microsoft Business Intelligence toolset.* New York: John Wiley & Sons.

Murphy, E. (2004). Recognizing and promoting collaboration in an online asynchronous discussion. *British Journal of Educational Technology, 35*(4), 421–431. doi:10.1111/j.0007-1013.2004.00401.x

Murphy, M. J. (1991). Oral communication in TESOL: Integrating speaking, listening and pronunciation. *TESOL Quarterly, 25*(1), 51–75. doi:10.2307/3587028

Murray, C., & Sixsmith, J. (1998). Mail: A qualitative research medium for interviewing? *International Journal of Social Research Methodology: Theory and Practice, 48*(12), 103–121.

Myeong-Gu, S., Feldman-Barrett, L., & Bartunek, J. M. (2004). The role of affective experience in work motivation. *Academy of Management Review, 29*(3), 423.

Napier, R. W., & Gershenfeld, M. K. (1989). *Groups: Theory and experience* (4th ed.). Boston: Houghton Mifflin.

Nash, S. S. (2005). Learning objects, learning object repositories, and learning theory: Preliminary best practices for online courses. *Interdisciplinary Journal of Knowledge and Learning Objects, 1,* 217–228.

Nicholson, D. B., Sarker, S., Sarker, S., & Valacich, J. S. (2007). Determinants of effective leadership in information systems development teams: An exploratory study of face-to-face and virtual contexts. *Journal of Information Technology Theory and Application, 8*(4), 39–56.

Nortfleet, B. (1948). Interpersonal relations and group productivity. *The Journal of Social Issues, 2,* 66–69.

Novak, J. D. (1977). *A theory of education.* Ithaca, NY: Cornell University Press.

Novak, J. D. (1990). Concept maps and vee diagrams: Two metacognitive tools for science and mathematics education. *Instructional Science, 19,* 29–52. doi:10.1007/BF00377984

Novak, J. D. (1998). *Learning, creating, and using knowledge: Concept maps as facilitative tools in schools and corporations.* Mahwah, NJ: Lawrence Erlbaum Associates.

Novak, J. D., & Gowin, D. B. (1984). *Learning how to learn.* New York: Cambridge University Press.

Nunan, D. (Ed.). (1992). *Collaborative language learning and teaching.* Cambridge, UK: Cambridge University Press.

Nurmela, K., Lehtinen, E., & Palonen, T. (1999). Evaluating CSCL log files by social network analysis. In *Proceedings of the Computer Support for Collaborative Learning (CSCL) 1999 Conference* (pp. 434-442). Mahwah, NJ: Lawrence Erlbaum Associates.

Ocker, R., & Fjermestad, J. (2000). High versus low performing virtual design teams: A preliminary analysis of communication. In *Proceedings of the 33rd Annual Hawaii Conference on System Sciences*, Maui, Hawaii, USA.

Ohio State University. (2007). *PlantFacts glossary.* Retrieved December 2008, from http://140.254.84.203/wiki/index.php/PlantFacts_Glossary

Oliveira, J. M. P. d. (2002). *Adaptation architecture for adaptive educational hypermedia systems.* Paper presented at the World Conference on E-Learning in Corporate, Government, Healthcare, and Higher Education.

Oriogun, P. K., Ravenscroft, A., & Cook, J. (2005). Validating an approach to examining cognitive engagement within online groups. *American Journal of Distance Education, 19*(4), 197–214. doi:10.1207/s15389286ajde1904_2

Padilha, E., & Carletta, J. (2003). Nonverbal behaviours improving a simulation of small group discussion. In *Proceedings of the 1st Nordic Symposium on Multimodal Communications*, Copenhagen, Denmark (pp. 93-105)

Page, E. (1994). Computer grading of student prose, using modern concepts and software. *Journal of Experimental Education, •••,* 62.

Papanikolaou, K. A., Mabbott, A., Bull, S., & Grigoriadou, M. (2006). Designing learner-controlled educational interactions based on learning/cognitive style and learner behaviour. *Interacting with Computers, 18*(3), 356–384. doi:10.1016/j.intcom.2005.11.003

Park, K., & Kenyon, R. (1999). Effects of network characteristics on human performance in a collaborative virtual environment. In *Proceedings of the IEEE VR*, Houston, TX.

Park, K., Leigh, J., Johnson, A., Carter, B., Brody, J., & Sosnoski, J. (2001). Distance learning classroom using virtual Harlem. In *Proceedings of the VSMM*, Berkeley, CA.

Parkhurst, D., Law, K., & Niebur, E. (2002). Modeling the role of salience in the allocation of overt visual attention. *Vision Research*, *42*, 107–123. doi:10.1016/S0042-6989(01)00250-4

Patterson, M. L. (1982). A sequential functional model of nonverbal exchange. *Psychological Review*, *89*, 231–249. doi:10.1037/0033-295X.89.3.231

Pauleen, D. J., Corbitt, B., & Yoong, P. (2007). Discovering and articulating what is not yet known; Using action learning and grounded theory as a knowledge management strategy. *The Learning Organization*, *14*(3), 222–240. doi:10.1108/09696470710739408

Pawan, F., Paulus, T., Yalcin, S., & Chang, C. F. (2003). Online learning: Patterns of engagement and interaction among in-service teachers. *Language Learning & Technology*, *7*(3), 119–140.

Peat, M., & Franklin, S. (2002). Supporting student learning. The use of computer-based formative assessment modules. *British Journal of Educational Technology*, *33*(5), 515–523. doi:10.1111/1467-8535.00288

Peña, A., de Antonio, A., Rodríguez, F. I., & Jacobo, J. O. (2008). CoVETO: Collaborative virtual environment with interaction indicators based on nonverbal communication cues. In *Proceedings of the Workshop of Intelligent Virtual Environments (WIVE) of the Iberamia*, Lisbon, Portugal.

Persico, D., Pozzi, F., & Sarti, L. (2008). Fostering collaboration in CSCL. In A. Cartelli & M. Palma (Eds.), *Encyclopaedia of information communication technology* (pp. 335-340). Hershey, PA: Idea Group Reference.

Persico, D., Pozzi, F., & Sarti, L. (2009). Design patterns for monitoring and evaluating CSCL processes. *Computers in Human Behaviour*.

Pesenhofer, A., Mayer, R., & Rauber, A. (2008). Automating the management of scientific conferences using information mining techniques. *J. Digital Information Management*, *6*(1).

Phillips, J. J. (1998). The return-on-investment (ROI) process: Issues and trends. *Educational Technology*, *38*(4), 7–14.

Phipps, W. (1999). *Pairwork: Interaction in the modern language classroom*. London: CiLT.

Pica, T. (1987). Second language acquisition, interaction and the classroom. *Applied Linguistics*, *8*, 3–21. doi:10.1093/applin/8.1.3

Pica, T. (1994). Research on negotiation: What does it reveal about second-language learning conditions, processes and outcomes? *Language Learning*, *44*(3), 493–527. doi:10.1111/j.1467-1770.1994.tb01115.x

Pimentel, M., Gerosa, M. A., Fuks, H., & de Lucena, C. J. (2005). Assessment of collaboration in online courses. In *Proceedings of the 2005 Conference on Computer Support for Collaborative Learning: Learning 2005: The Next 10 Years!* Taipei, Taiwan (pp. 494-498). International Society of the Learning Sciences.

Pintrich, R. P., & Schunk, H. D. (1996). *Motivation in education: Theory, research, and applications*. Upper Saddle River, NJ: Prentice Hall.

Potter, R. E., & Balthazard, P. A. (2002). Understanding human interactions and performance in the virtual team. *JITTA: Journal of Information Technology Theory and Application*, *4*(1), 1–24.

Powell, A., Piccoli, G., & Ives, B. (2004). virtual teams: a review of current literature and directions for future research. *The Data Base for Advances in Information Systems*, *35*(1), 6–37.

Pozzi, F. (2006). Assessment, evaluation and monitoring in e-learning systems: A survey from the DPULS project. *Information Science for Decision Making*, *25*, 354.

Pozzi, F., Manca, S., Persico, D., & Sarti, L. (2007). A general framework for tracking and analysing learning processes in CSCL environments. *Innovations in Education and Teaching International*, *44*, 169–179. doi:10.1080/14703290701240929

Pozzi, F., Manca, S., Persico, D., & Sarti, L. (2007). A general framework for tracking and analysing learning processes in computer-supported collaborative learning environments. *Innovations in Education and Teaching International, 44*(2), 169–179. doi:10.1080/14703290701240929

Proctor, R., & Vu, K. (2005). *Handbook of human factors in Web design.* Mahwah, NJ: Lawrence Erlbaum Associates, Inc.

Rada, R. (1998). Efficiency and effectiveness in computer-supported peer-peer learning. *Computers & Education, 30*(3-4), 137–146. doi:10.1016/S0360-1315(97)00042-0

Reffay, C., & Chanier, T. (2003). How social network analysis can help to measure cohesion in collaborative distance-learning. In B. Wasson, S. Ludvigsen, & U. Hoppe (Eds.), *Designing for change in networked learning environments. Proceedings of the international conference on computer support for collaborative learning 2003* (pp. 343–352). Dordrecht, The Netherlands: Kluwer Academic Publishers.

Reichert, R., & Hartmann, W. (2004). On the learning in e-learning. In *Proceedings of the EDMEDIA 2004 – World Conference on Education Multimedia, Hypermedia and Telecommunications* (pp. 1590-1595).

Resnick, L. B. (1991). Shared cognition: Thinking as social practice. In. L. Resnick, J. Levine, & S. Teasley (Eds.), *Perspectives on socially shared cognition* (pp. 1-22). Hyattsville, MD: American Psychological Association.

Rey-Lopez, M., Dvaz-Redondo, R. P., Fernandez-Vilas, A., Pazos-Arias, J. J., Garcva-Duque, J., Gil-Solla, A., et al. (2008). An extension to the ADL SCORM standard to support adaptivity: The t-learning case-study. *Computer Standards & Interfaces.*

Rey-Lopez, M., Fernadez-Vilas, A., Diaz-Redondo, R. P., Pazos-Arias, J. J., & Bermejo-Munoz, J. (2006). Extending SCORM to create adaptive courses. In Innovative approaches for learning and knowledge sharing (LNCS 4227, pp. 679-684). Berlin, Germany: Springer.

Rezaei, A. R., & Katz, L. (2004). Evaluation of the reliability and validity of the cognitive styles analysis. *Personality and Individual Differences, 36*(6), 1317–1327. doi:10.1016/S0191-8869(03)00219-8

Richmond, V. P., McCroskey, J. C., & Payne, S. K. (1991). *Nonverbal behavior in interpersonal relations* (2nd ed.). Englewood Cliffs, NJ: Prentice Hall.

Riding, R., & Cheema, I. (1991). Cognitive styles - an overview and integration. *Educational Psychology, 11*(3), 193–215. doi:10.1080/0144341910110301

Riding, R., & Rayner, S. (1998). *Cognitive styles and learning strategies.* London: David Fulton Publishers.

Robinson, L. A. (2005). Consumers of online instruction. *Issues in Information Systems, 6,* 170–175.

Roblyer, M. D., & Edwards, J. (2001). *Integrating educational technology into teaching.* Upper Saddle River, NJ: Prentice Hall.

Rodriguez, M. A., & Bollen, J. (2008). An algorithm to determine peer-reviewers, In [*th ACM Conference on Information and Knowledge Management,* Napa Valley, CA.]. *Proceedings of the CIKM, 08,* 17.

Romero, C., & Ventura, S. (2006). Data mining in e-learning. *Advances in Management Information, 4.*

Romero, C., & Ventura, S. (2007). Educational data mining: A survey from 1995 to 2005. *Expert Systems with Applications, 33*(1), 135–146. doi:10.1016/j.eswa.2006.04.005

Romero, C., Ventura, S., & García, E. (2008). Data mining in course management systems: Moodle case study and tutorial. *Computers & Education, 51*(1), 368–384. doi:10.1016/j.compedu.2007.05.016

Roschelle, J., & Teasley, S. D. (1995). Construction of shared knowledge in collaborative problem solving. In C. O'Malley (Ed.), *Computer-supported collaborative learning.* New York: Springer-Verlag.

Rosenkrans, G. (1999). Assessment of the adult student's progress in an online environment. *The Internet and Higher Education, 2*(2-3), 145–160. doi:10.1016/S1096-7516(00)00017-8

Roth, W. M. (2001). Gestures: Their role in teaching and learning. *Review of Educational Research, 71*, 365–392. doi:10.3102/00346543071003365

Rourke, L., Anderson, T., Garrison, D. R., & Archer, W. (2001). Methodological issues in the content analysis of computer conference transcripts. *International Journal of Artificial Intelligence in Education, 12*, 8–22.

Rudner, L., & Gagne, P. (2001). An overview of three approaches to scoring written essays by computer. *ERIC Digest.*

Rumetshofer, H., & Wo, W. (2003). XML-based adaptation framework for psychological-driven e-learning systems. *Educational Technology and Society, 6*(4), 18–29.

Sadler-Smith, E. (2001). The relationship between learning style and cognitive style. *Personality and Individual Differences, 30*(4), 609–616. doi:10.1016/S0191-8869(00)00059-3

Safouris, N., Botsios, N., & Georgiou, D. (2007). Some approaches in learning style diagnosis. In *Proceedings of the ICICTE 2007*, Patras, Greece.

Sahami, M. (1996). Learning limited dependence Bayesian classifiers. In *Proceedings of the Second International Conference on Knowledge Discovery and Data Mining, KDD-96* (pp. 335-338). Menlo Park, CA: AAAI Press

Sakai Services. *Information services.* (2008). Retrieved September 2008, from http://www.nitle.org/index.php/nitle/content/view/full/1388

Sampson, D., Karagiannidis, C., & Cardinali, F. (2002). An architecture for Web-based e-learning promoting re-usable adaptive educational e-content. *Educational Technology and Society, 5*(4), 27–37.

Sánchez-Maroño, N., Fontenla-Romero, O., & Bellas, F. (2006). Aportaciones e ideas para el rediseño de la asignatura de fundamentos de informática al EEES. In *Proceedings of the Actas JENUI 2006.*

Saunders, C. S., & Ahuja, M. K. (2006). Are all distributed teams the same? Differentiating between temporary and ongoing distributed teams. *Small Group Research, 37*(6), 662–700. doi:10.1177/1046496406294323

Scardamalia, M., & Bereiter, C. (1994). Computer support for knowledge-building communities. *Journal of the Learning Sciences, 3*(3), 265–283. doi:10.1207/s15327809jls0303_3

Scheflen, A. E. (1964). The significance of posture in communication systems. *Psychiatry, 27*, 316–331.

Schlager, M., & Fusco, J. (2004). Teacher professional development, technology, and communities of practice: Are we putting the cart before the horse? In S. Barab, R. Kling, & J. Gray (Eds.), *Designing for virtual communities in the service of learning.* Cambridge, UK: Cambridge University Press. Retrieved from http://tappedin.org/tappedin/web/papers/2004/SchlagerFuscoTPD.pdf

Schrire, S. (2006). Knowledge building in asynchronous discussion groups: Going beyond quantitative analysis. *Computers & Education, 46*, 49–70. doi:10.1016/j.compedu.2005.04.006

Schroeder, R. (2007). An overview of ethical and social issues in shared virtual environments. *Futures, 39*(6), 704–717. doi:10.1016/j.futures.2006.11.009

Schümmer, T., Strijbos, J., & Berkel, T. (2005). A new direction for log file analysis in CSCL: Experiences with a spatio-temporal metric. In *Proceedings of the 2005 Conference on Computer Support For Collaborative Learning: Learning 2005: the Next 10 Years!* Taipei, Taiwan (pp. 567-576). International Society of the Learning Sciences.

Schwartzman, R. (2007). Refining the question: How can online instruction maximize opportunities for all students? *Communication Education, 56*(1), 113–117. doi:10.1080/03634520601009728

Scott, J. (1991). *Social network analysis: A handbook.* London: Sage.

Segall, N., Doblen, T. L., & Porter, J. D. (2005). A usability comparison of PDA-based quizzes and paper-and-pencil quizzes. *Computers & Education, 45,* 417–432. doi:10.1016/j.compedu.2004.05.004

Sener, J. (2007). In search of student-generated content in online education. *e-Mentor, 4*(21). Retrieved from http://www.e-mentor.edu.pl/eng

Seufert, S., Lechner, U., & Stanoevska, K. (2002). A reference model for online learning communities. *International Journal on E-Learning, 1*(1), 43–54.

Sevilla, J. (2008). The virtual campus of the Spanish Group 9 of Universities (G9). In *Proceedings of the LMAIA Final Conference*, Rome, Italy. Retrieved from http://www.lemaia.eu/PagDefault.asp?idPag=90

Shang, Y., Shi, H., & Chen, S.-S. (2001). An intelligent distributed environment for active learning. *ACM Journal of Educational Resources in Computing (JERIC), 1*(2).

Shavelson, R. J., Lang, H., & Lewin, B. (1994). *On concept maps as potential "authentic" assessments in science* (Technical Report 388). Los Angeles, CA: UCLA, Center for the Study of Evaluation (CSE/CRESST).

Shea, P., Pickett, A., & Pelt, W. (2003). A follow-up investigation of teaching presence in the SUNY learning network. *Journal of Asynchronous Learning Networks, 7*(2).

Sheard, J., Ceddia, J., Hurst, J., & Tuovinen, J. (2003). Inferring student learning behaviour from website interactions: A usage analysis. *Journal of Education and Information Technologies, 8*(3), 245–266. doi:10.1023/A:1026360026073

Shin, Y. (2005). Conflict resolution in virtual teams. *Organizational Dynamics, 34*(4), 331–345. doi:10.1016/j.orgdyn.2005.08.002

Shwarts-Asher, D., Ahituv, N., & Etzion, D. (2008). Improving virtual teams through swift structure. In T. Torres & M. Arias (Eds.), *Encyclopedia of HRIS: Challenges in e-HRM, Vol 2(I-Z)* (pp. 510-517). Spain: Rovira i Virgili University.

Siegel, J., Dubrovsky, V., Kiesler, S., & McGuire, T. W. (1986). group processes in computer-mediated communication. *Organizational Behavior and Human Decision Processes, 37*(2), 157–188. doi:10.1016/0749-5978(86)90050-6

Silva, E., & Moreira, D. (2003). WebCoM: A tool to use peer review to improve student interaction. *Journal of Educational Resources in Computing, 3*(1), 3. doi:10.1145/958795.958798

Simoff, S., & Maher, M. (2000). Analysing participation in collaborative design environments. *Design Studies, 21*(2), 119–144. doi:10.1016/S0142-694X(99)00043-5

Simonson, M., Smaldino, S., Albright, M., & Zvacek, S. (2003). *Teaching and learning at a distance.* Upper Saddle River, NJ: Merrill Prentice Hall.

Simpson, P. A., & Stroh, L. K. (2004). gender differences: emotional expression and feelings of personal inauthenticity. *The Journal of Applied Psychology, 89*(4), 715. doi:10.1037/0021-9010.89.4.715

Sims, E. M., & Pike, W. Y. (2007). Reusable, lifelike virtual humans for mentoring and role-playing. *Computers & Education, 49*(1), 75–92. doi:10.1016/j.compedu.2005.06.006

Sivunen, A. (2006). Strengthening identification with the team in virtual teams: The leaders' perspective. *Group Decision and Negotiation, 15*(4), 345–366. doi:10.1007/s10726-006-9046-6

Skrien, D. (2008). *Object-oriented design using Java.* New York: McGraw-Hill.

Slater, P., & Varney-Burch, S. (2001). *Multimedia in language learning.* London: CiLT.

Soh, L., Khandaker, N., Liu, X., & Jiang, H. (2006). A computer-supported cooperative learning system with multiagent intelligence. In *Proceedings of the Fifth international Joint Conference on Autonomous Agents and Multiagent Systems, AAMAS '06*, Hakodate, Japan (pp. 1556-1563). New York: ACM Press.

Soller, A. (2001). Supporting social interaction in an intelligent collaborative learning system. *International Journal of Artificial Intelligence in Education, 12*, 40–62.

Soller, A., Jermann, P., Muehlenbrock, M., & Martínez, M. (2004). Designing computational models of collaborative learning interaction: Introduction to the workshop proceedings. In *Proceedings of the 2nd International Workshop on Designing Computational Models of Collaborative Learning Interaction at ITS*, Maceió, Brazil.

Soller, A., Lesgold, A., Linton, F., & Goodman, B. (1999). What makes peer interaction effective? Modeling effective communication in an intelligent CSCL. In *Proceedings of the AAAI Fall Symposium on Psychological Models of Communication in Collaborative Systems*, Cape Cod, MA.

Sosik, J. J. (1997). Effect of transformational leadership and anonymity on idea generation in computer-mediated groups. *Group & Organization Management, 22*(4), 460–488. doi:10.1177/1059601197224004

Sowa, J., & Borgida, A. (1991). *Principles of semantic networks: Explorations in the representation of knowledge*. San Francisco: Morgan-Kaufmann.

Spada, H., Meier, A., Rummel, N., & Hauser, S. (2005). A new method to assess the quality of collaborative process in CSCL. In *Proceedings of the 2005 Conference on Computer Support For Collaborative Learning: Learning 2005: the Next 10 Years!* Taipei, Taiwan (pp 622-631). International Society of the Learning Sciences.

Specht, M., & Kobsa, A. (1999). *Interaction of domain expertise and interface design in adaptive educational hypermedia*. Paper presented at the Second Workshop on Adaptive Systems and User Modeling on the World Wide Web.

Spertus, E., & Stein, L. A. (1998). A hyperlink-based recommender system written in squeal. In *Proc. of the ACM CIKM '98 Workshop on Web Information and Data Management*.

Srikant, R., & Agrawal, R. (1996). Mining sequential patterns: Generalizations and performance improvements. In *EDBT: Proc. of the 5th Int. Conf. On Extending Database Technologies*.

Srivastava, J., Cooley, R., Deshpande, M., & Tan, P. N. (2000). Web usage mining: Discovery and applications of usage patterns from Web data. *SIGKDD Explorations, 1*(2), 12–23. doi:10.1145/846183.846188

Stahl, G. (2006). *Group cognition: Computer support for building collaborative knowledge*. Cambridge, MA: MIT Press.

Staples, D. S., & Webster, J. (2007). Exploring traditional and virtual team members' "best practices": A social cognitive theory perspective. *Small Group Research, 38*(1), 60–97. doi:10.1177/1046496406296961

Stathacopoulou, R., Magoulas, G. D., Grigoriadou, M., & Samarakou, M. (2005). Neuro-fuzzy knowledge processing in intelligent learning environments for improved student diagnosis. *Information Sciences, 170*(2-4), 273–307. doi:10.1016/j.ins.2004.02.026

Stein, R. T., & Heller, T. (1979). An empirical analysis of the correlations between leadership status and participation rates reported in the literature. *Journal of Personality and Social Psychology, 37*, 1993–2002. doi:10.1037/0022-3514.37.11.1993

Stevenson, W., & McGrath, E. W. (2004). Differences between on-site and off-site teams: Manager perceptions. *Team Performance Management, 10*(5/6), 127–132. doi:10.1108/13527590410556854

Straus, S. G., & McGrath, J. E. (1994). Does the medium matter? The interaction of task type and technology on group performance and member reactions. *The Journal of Applied Psychology, 79*(1), 87–98. doi:10.1037/0021-9010.79.1.87

Strijbos, J. W., Martens, R. L., Jochems, W. M. G., & Broers, N. (2004). The effect of functional roles of group efficiency: Using multilevel modeling and content analysis to investigate computer-supported collaboration in small groups. *Small Group Research, 35*(2), 195–229. doi:10.1177/1046496403260843

Sutherland, R., Armstrong, V., Barnes, S., Brawn, R., Gall, M., & Matthewman, S. (2004). Transforming teaching and learning: Embedding ICT into every-day classroom practices. *Journal of Computer Assisted Learning Special Issue, 20*(6), 413–425. doi:10.1111/j.1365-2729.2004.00104.x

Suthers, D. D., & Hundhausen, C. D. (2001). Learning by constructing collaborative representations: An empirical comparison of three alternatives. In P. Dillenbourg, A. Eurelings, & K. Hakkarainen (Eds.), *European Perspectives on Computer-Supported Collaborative Learning, Proceedings of the First European Conference on Computer-Supported Collaborative Learning* (pp. 577-584). Maastrict, The Netherlands: Universiteit Maastricht.

Sutton, L. (2001). The principle of vicarious interaction in computer-mediated communications. *International Journal of Educational Telecommunications, 7*(3), 223–242.

Sweet, R. (1986). Student drop-out in distance education: An application of Tinto's model. *Distance Education, 7*(2), 201–213. doi:10.1080/0158791860070204

Syed, M. R. (2001). Diminishing the distance in distance education. *IEEE MultiMedia, 8*(3), 18–21. doi:10.1109/MMUL.2001.939996

Tai, Y., & Ting, R. Y. (2007). Authoring tools in e-learning: A case study. In *Proceedings of the Seventh IEEE International Conference on Advanced Learning Technologies (ICALT 2007)*, Niigata, Japan (pp. 271-273).

Tan, H. H., Foo, M. D., Chong, C. L., & Ng, R. (2003). Situational and dispositional predictors of displays of positive emotions. *Journal of Organizational Behavior, 24*(8), 961. doi:10.1002/job.231

Tan, P. N., Kumar, V., & Srivastava, J. (2004). Selecting the right objective measure for association analysis. *Information Systems, 29*(4), 293–313. doi:10.1016/S0306-4379(03)00072-3

Tang, T., & Mccalla, G. (2003). Smart recommendation for evolving e-learning system. In *Proc. of the Workshop on Technologies for Electronic Documents for Supporting Learning, Int. Conf. on Artificial Intelligence in Education*, Sydney, Australia.

Tarmizi, H., Payne, M., Noteboom, C., & Zhang, c. (2007). collaboration engineering in distributed environments. *E-Service Journal, 6*(1), 76-98.

Tarpin-Bernard, F., & Habieb-Mammar, H. (2005). Modeling elementary cognitive abilities for adaptive hypermedia presentation. *User Modeling and User-Adapted Interaction, 15*(5), 459–495. doi:10.1007/s11257-005-2529-3

Taylor, P., & Maor, D. (2000). Assessing the efficacy of online teaching with the constructivist on-line learning environment survey. In A. Herrmann & M. M. Kulski (Eds.), *Flexible Futures in Tertiary Teaching. Proceedings of the 9th Annual Teaching Learning Forum*. Perth, Australia: Curtin University of Technology.

Teeler, D., & Gray, P. (2000). *How to use the Internet in ELT*. Edinburgh, UK: Pearson Education Limited.

Thompson, L. F., & Coovert, M. D. (2003). Teamwork online: The effects of computer conferencing on perceived confusion, satisfaction, and postdiscussion accuracy. *Group Dynamics, 7*(2), 135–151. doi:10.1037/1089-2699.7.2.135

Thomsen, E. (2002). *OLAP solutions: Building multidimensional information systems* (2nd ed.). New York: John Wiley & Sons.

Thoresen, C. J. (2003). Affective underpinnings of job perceptions and attitudes. *Psychological Bulletin, 129*, 914–945. doi:10.1037/0033-2909.129.6.914

Thorpe, M. (1993). *Evaluating open and distance learning*. Harlow, UK: Longman.

Timmerman, C. E., & Scott, C. R. (2006). Virtually working: Communicative and structural predictors of media use and key outcomes in virtual work teams. *Communication Monographs, 73*(1), 108–136. doi:10.1080/03637750500534396

Trenholm, S. (2007). An investigation of assessment in fully asynchronous online math courses. *International Journal for Educational Integrity, 3*(2), 41–55.

Trentin, G. (2000). The quality-interactivity relationship in distance education. *Educational Technology, 40*(1), 17–27.

Triantafillou, E., Pomportsis, A., Demetriadis, S., & Georgiadou, E. (2004). The value of adaptivity based on cognitive style: An empirical study. *British Journal of Educational Technology, 35*(1), 95–106. doi:10.1111/j.1467-8535.2004.00371.x

Triggs, P., & John, P. (2004). From transaction to transformation: Information and communication technology, professional development and the formation of communities of practice. *Journal of Computer Assisted Learning, 20*(6), 426–439. doi:10.1111/j.1365-2729.2004.00101.x

Tromp, J. G. (1995). Presence, tele-presence and immersion: The cognitive factors of embodiment and interaction in virtual environments. In *Proceedings of Conference of the FIVE Group, Framework for Immersive Virtual Environments*, London, UK.

Tromp, J., Steed, A., & Wilsonn, J. (2003). Systematic usability evaluation and design issues for collaborative virtual environments. *Presence (Cambridge, Mass.), 12*(3), 241–267. doi:10.1162/105474603765879512

Truluck, J. (2007). Establishing a mentoring plan for improving retention in online graduate degree programs. *Online Journal of Distance Learning Administration, 10*(1), 1–6.

Tyran, K. L., Tyran, C. K., & Shepherd, M. (2003). Exploring emerging leadership in virtual teams. In C. B. Gibson & S. G. Cohen (Eds.), *Virtual teams that work* (pp. 183-195). San Francisco: Jossey-Bass.

Van der Wende, M. (2000). The Bologna declaration: Enhancing the transparency and competitiveness of European higher education. *Higher Education in Europe, 25*(3), 305–310. doi:10.1080/713669277

Vanderbilt (The Cognition and Technology Group at Vanderbilt). (1991). Some thoughts about constructivism and instructional design. *Educational Technology, 31*(10), 16–18.

Vanlehn, K. (1988). Student modeling. In M. Polson & J. J. Richardson (Eds.), *Foundations of intelligent tutoring systems*. Hillsdale, NJ: Laurence Erlbaum & Associates.

Vanlehn, K., Ohlsson, S., & Nason, R. (1994). Applications of simulated students: An exploration. *Journal of Artificial Intelligence in Education, 5*(2), 135–175.

Vecchia, L., & Pedroni, M. (2007). Concept maps as a learning assessment tool. *Issues in Informing Science and Information Technology, 4*, 307–312.

Veerman, A. (2003). Constructive discussions through electronic dialogue. In J. Andriessen, M. Baker, & D. Suthers (Eds.), *Arguing to learn: Confronting cognitions in computer-supported collaborative learning environments* (pp. 117-143). Dordrecht, The Netherlands: Kluwer Academic Publishers.

Vieira, A. C., Teixeira, L., Timóteo, A., Tedesco, P., & Barros, F. A. (2004). Analyzing on-line collaborative dialogues: The OXEnTCHÊ-Chat. In J. C. Lester, R. M. Vicari, & F. Paraguaçu (Eds.), *Proceedings of the 7th International Conference on Intelligent Tutoring Systems*, Maceió, Alagoas, Brazil (pp. 315-324).

Vygotsky, L. S. (1978). *Mind in society: The development of higher psychological processes*. Cambridge, MA: Harvard University Press.

Vygotsky, L. S. (1978). *Mind in society: The development of higher psychological processes*. Cambridge, MA: Harvard University Press.

Wang, F., Chen, B., & Miao, Z. (2008a). A survey on reviewer assignment problem. In *Proc. of the New Frontiers in Applied Artificial Intelligence, 21ˢᵗ International Conference on Industrial, Engineering and Other Applications of Applied Intelligent Systems, IEA/AIE 2008,* Wroclaw, Poland.

Wang, M. (2004), Correlational analysis of student visibility and performance in online learning. *Journal of Asynchronous Learning Networks, 8*(4). Retrieved from http://www.sloan-c.org/publications/jaln/v8n4/pdf/v8n4_wang.pdf

Wang, Y. (2002). *Dynamic assignment of peer reviewers for teams.* Unpublished master's thesis, North Carolina State University, USA. Retrieved from http://www.lib.ncsu.edu/theses/available/etd-11012002-125644/unrestricted/etd.pdf

Wang, Y., Yijun, L., Collins, M., & Liu, P. (2008). Process improvement of peer code review and behavior analysis of its participants. In *Proceedings of the 39ᵗʰ SIGCSE Technical Symposium on Computer Science Education, SIGCSE '08,* Portland, OR, USA (pp. 107-111). New York: ACM Press.

Warkentin, M. E., Sayeed, L., & Hightower, R. (1997). Virtual teams versus face-to-face teams: An exploratory study of a Web-based conference system. *Decision Sciences, 28*(4), 975–997. doi:10.1111/j.1540-5915.1997.tb01338.x

Warschauer, M., & Healey, D. (1998). Computers and language learning: An overview. *Language Teaching, 31,* 57–71. doi:10.1017/S0261444800012970

Wasserman, S., & Faust, K. (1994). *Social network analysis. Methods and applications.* Cambridge, UK: University Press.

Watson, J., Ahmed, P. K., & Hardaker, G. (2007). Creating domain independent adaptive e-learning systems using the sharable content object reference model. *Campus-Wide Information Systems, 24*(1), 45–71. doi:10.1108/10650740710726482

Watts, S. S., & Lee, S. (1999). Straight talk: Delivering bad news through electronic communication. *Information Systems Research, 10*(2), 150–167. doi:10.1287/isre.10.2.150

Web, C. T. (2008). Retrieved from http://www.webct.com

Web, C. T. 4.0. (2003). Retrieved from http://www.webct.com/ce4

Webb, G., Pazzani, M., & Billsus, D. (2001). Machine learning for user modeling. *User Modeling and User-Adapted Interaction, 11*(1/2), 19–29. doi:10.1023/A:1011117102175

Webster, J., & Wong, W. K. P. (2008). Comparing traditional and virtual group forms: Identity, communication and trust in naturally occurring project teams. *International Journal of Human Resource Management, 19*(1), 41–62.

Wegerif, R. (1998). The social dimension of asynchronous learning networks. *Journal of Asynchronous Learning Networks, 2,* 34–49.

Weinberger, A., & Fischer, F. (2006). A framework to analyze argumentative knowledge construction in computer-supported collaborative learning. *Computers & Education, 46,* 71–95. doi:10.1016/j.compedu.2005.04.003

Weisband, S., & Atwater, L. (1999). Evaluating self and others in electronic and face-to-face groups. *The Journal of Applied Psychology, 84*(4), 632–639. doi:10.1037/0021-9010.84.4.632

Weiss, H. M. (2002). Conceptual and empirical foundations for the study of affect at work. In R. G. Lord, R. J. Klimoski, & R. Kanfer (Eds.), *Emotions in the workplace: Understanding the structure and role of emotions in organizational behavior* (pp. 20-63). San Francisco: Jossey-Bass.

Weiss, H. M., & Cropanzano, R. (1996). Affective events theory: A theoretical discussion of the structure, causes and consequences of affective experiences at work. In L. L. Cummings & B. M. Staw (Eds.), *Research in organizational behavior* (Vol. 18, pp. 1-74). Greenwich, CT: JAI Press.

Weiss, H., Schmidhofer, A., & Schmid, A. (2004). Animated and interactive e-learning concept and realization. In *Proceedings of the IASTED Int Conf. Web-Based Education* (pp. 151-156).

Weka. (2008). Removed from http://www.cs.waikato.ac.nz/ml/weka

Wenger, E. (1998). *Communities of practice. Learning, meaning, and identity.* Cambridge, MA: Cambridge University Press.

Weston, T. J., & Barker, L. (2001). Designing, implementing, and evaluating Web-based learning modules for university students. *Educational Technology, 41*(4), 15–22.

Wetzel, C. D., Radtke, R. H., & Stern, H. W. (1994). *Instructional effectiveness of video media.* Hillsdale, NJ: Lawrence Erlbaum Associates.

White, S., & Liccardy, H. (2006). Harnessing insight into disciplinary differences to refine e-learning design. In *Proceedings of the 36th ASEE/IEEE Frontiers in Education Conference*, San Diego, CA.

Wiley, D. A. (2000). Connecting learning objects to instructional design theory: A definition, a metaphor, and a taxonomy. In D. A. Wiley (Ed.). *The instructional use of learning object* (pp. 1-35). Bloomington, IN: Agency for Instructional Technology And Association For Educational Communications Of Technology. Retrieved July 23, 2008, from http://reusability.org/read/

Wiley, D. A. (2002). *A proposed measure of discussion activity in threaded discussion spaces* (working draft). Retrieved July 28, 2008, from http://wiley.ed.usu.edu/docs/discussion09.pdf

Winn, W. D. (2002). Current trends in educational technology research: The study of learning environments. *Educational Psychology Review, 14*(3), 331–351. doi:10.1023/A:1016068530070

Witkin, H. A., Moore, C. A., Goodenough, D. R., & Cox, P. W. (1977). Field-dependent and field-independent cognitive styles and their educational implications. *Review of Educational Research, 47*(1), 1–64.

Witten, I. H., & Eibe, F. (2000). *Data mining – practical machine learning tools and techniques with java implementations.* San Francisco: Morgan Kaufmann Publishers.

Woit, D., & Mason, D. (2000). Enhancing student learning through on-line quizzes. *ACM SIGCSE Bulletin, 32*(1), 367–371. doi:10.1145/331795.331887

Wolf, C. (2003). *iWeaver: Towards 'learning style'-based e-learning in computer science education.* Paper presented at the Fifth Australasian Computing Education Conference on Computing Education 2003.

Xenos, M., Pierrakeas, C., & Pintelas, P. (2002). A survey on student dropout rates and dropout causes concerning the students in the course of informatics of the Hellenic Open University. *Computers & Education, 39*(4), 361–377. doi:10.1016/S0360-1315(02)00072-6

Yahya, Y., & Yusoff, M. (2008). Towards a comprehensive learning object metadata: Incorporation of context to stipulate meaningful learning and enhance learning object reusability. *Interdisciplinary Journal of E-Learning and Learning Objects, 4,* 13–48.

Yair, Y., Mintz, R., & LiTVak, S. (2001). 3-D virtual reality in science education: An implication for astronomy teaching. *Journal of Computers in Science Education: An implication for Astronomy Teaching, 20*(3), 293-301.

Yang, Y., Buckendahl, C., & Juskiewicz, P. (2001). *A review of strategies for validating computer automated scoring.* Paper presented at the Midwestern Educational Research Association.

Yokomoto, C. F., & Ware, R. (1997). Variations of the group quiz that enhance collaborative learning. In *Proceedings of the IEEE Frontiers in Education Conference* (pp. 552-557).

Yoo, Y., & Alavi, M. (2004). Emergent leadership in virtual teams: What do emergent leaders do? *Information and Organization*, *14*(1), 27–58. doi:10.1016/j.infoandorg.2003.11.001

Zadeh, L. (1965). Fuzzy sets. *Information and Control*, *8*(3), 338–353. doi:10.1016/S0019-9958(65)90241-X

Zaïane, O. (2001). Web usage mining for a better Web-based learning environment. In *Proceedings of Conference on Advantage Technology for Education*, Alberta, Canada (pp. 60-64).

Zaiane, O. R. (2001). Web usage mining for a better Web-based learning environment. In *Proc. Of. The Conf. On Advanced Technology for Education*, Banff, Alberta.

Zaiane, O. R. (2002). Building a recommender agent for e-learning systems. In *Proc. of the 7th Int. Conf. On Computers in Education*, Auckland, New Zeeland.

Zaiane, O., Xin, M., & Han, J. (1998). Discovering Web access patterns and trends by applying OLAP and data mining technology on Web logs. In *Proceedings of the IEEE Forum on Advances in Digital Libraries Conference* (pp. 19-29). Santa Barbara, CA: IEEE Computer Society.

Zeller, A. (2000). Making students read and review code. *SIGCSE Bulletin*, *32*(3), 89–92. doi:10.1145/353519.343090

Zhang, D. (2005). Interactive multimedia-based e-learning: A study of effectiveness. *American Journal of Distance Education*, *19*(3), 149–162. doi:10.1207/s15389286ajde1903_3

Zhang, D., Zhou, L., Briggs, R., & Nunamaker, J. (2006). Instructional video in e-learning: Assessing the impact of interactive video on learning effectiveness. *Information & Management*, *43*, 15–27. doi:10.1016/j.im.2005.01.004

Zhang, H., Almeroth, K., Knight, A., Bulger, M., & Mayer, R. (2007). Moodog: Tracking students' online learning activities. In C. Montgomerie & J. Seale (Eds.), *Proceedings of the World Conference on Educational Multimedia, Hypermedia and Telecommunications 2007* (pp. 4415-4422). Chesapeake, VA: AACE.

Zinn, C., & Scheuer, O. (2006). Getting to know your student in distance learning context. In *Innovative approaches for learning and knowledge sharing* (LNCS 4227, pp. 437-451). Berlin, Germany: Springer.

Zirkle, C. (2003). Distance education in career and technical education: A review of the research literature. *Journal of Vocational Education Research*, *28*(2), 151–171.

Zorrilla, M. (in press). Data warehouse technology for e-learning. In. D. Zakrzewska, E. Menasalvas, & L. Byczkowska-Lipińska (Eds.), *New trends in database systems. Methods, tools, applications*. Berlin, Germany: Springer-Verlag.

Zorrilla, M. E., & Álvarez, E. (2008). MATEP: Monitoring and analysis tool for e-learning platforms. In *Proceedings of the 8th IEEE International Conference on Advanced Learning Technologies*, Santander, Spain (pp. 611-613).

Zorrilla, M. E., Marín, D., & Álvarez, E. (2007). Towards virtual course evaluation using Web intelligence. In *Proceedings of the Computer aided systems theory: EUROCAST 2007* (LNCS 4739, pp. 392-399). Berlin, Germany: Springer.

Zorrilla, M. E., Menasalvas, E., Marín, D., Mora, E., & Segovia, J. (2005). Web usage mining project for improving Web-based learning sites. In *Proceedings of the Computer aided systems theory: EUROCAST 2005* (LNCS 3643, pp. 205-210). Berlin, Germany: Springer.

Zumbach, J., Muehlenbrock, M., Jansen, M., Reimann, P., & Hoppe, U. (2002). Multi-dimensional tracking in virtual learning teams: An exploratory study. In G. Stahl (Ed.), *Proceedings of the Conference on Computer Supported Collaborative Learning CSCL-2002*, Boulder, CO (pp. 650-651).

About the Contributors

Dr. **Angel A. Juan** is an Associate Professor of Simulation and Data Analysis in the Computer Sciences Department at the Open University of Catalonia (Spain). He is also a Lecturer at the Technical University of Catalonia. He holds a Ph.D. in Industrial Engineering (UNED), an M.S. in Information Technology (Open University of Catalonia), and an M.S. in Applied Computational Mathematics (University of Valencia). His research interests include computer simulation, applied data analysis and mathematical e-learning. He has published several papers in international journals, books and proceedings regarding these fields. As a researcher, he has been involved in several international research projects. His e-mail address is ajuanp@gmail.com.

Dr. **Thanasis Daradoumis** holds a PhD in Computer Science from the Polytechnic University of Catalonia (Spain), a Master in Computer Science from the University of Illinois (USA), and a Bachelor in Mathematics from the University of Thessaloniki (Greece). He is an Associate Professor in the Dept. of Computer Sciences, Multimedia & Telecommunication at the Open University of Catalonia. His research focuses on e-learning and network technologies, Web-based instruction and evaluation, distributed and adaptive learning, CSCL, CSCW, interaction analysis, and grid technologies. He is co-director of the DPCS Research Laboratory [http://dpcs.uoc.es/]. His e-mail address is adaradoumis@uoc.edu.

Dr. **Fatos Xhafa** received his PhD in Computer Science from the Polytechnic University of Catalonia (Spain), where he currently is an Associated Professor in the Department of Languages and Informatics Systems. His research interests include parallel algorithms, combinatorial optimization, approximation and meta-heuristics, distributed programming, Grid and P2P computing. He has published in leading international journals and has served in the Organizing Committees of many conferences and workshops. He is also member of editorial board of several international journals including International Journal of Computer-Supported Collaborative Learning, Grid and Utility Computing and Autonomic Computing. His e-mail address is fatos.xhafa@gmail.com.

Dr. **Santi Caballé** has a PhD, Masters and Bachelors in Computer Science from the Open University of Catalonia (Spain). He is an Associate Professor and a Researcher at the Department of Computer Sciences, Multimedia and Telecommunication of the Open University of Catalonia, where he coordinates several online courses in the areas of Software Engineering, Computer Supported Collaborative Learning and Information Systems. His research focuses on e-learning and computer-supported collaborative learning, software engineering, and distributed and grid technologies. His email address is scaballe@uoc.edu

Dr. **Javier Faulin** is an Associate Professor of Operations Research and Statistics at the Public University of Navarre (Spain). He is also a lecturer at the UNED (Pamplona, Spain). He holds a Ph.D. in Economics from the University of Navarre (Pamplona, Spain), a M.S. in Operations Management, Logistics and Transportation from UNED (Madrid, Spain) and a M.S. in Mathematics from the University of Zaragoza (Zaragoza, Spain). He has extended experience in distance and Web-based teaching at several European universities. His research interests include logistics and simulation modeling and analysis. He has published several papers in international journals, books and proceedings. His e-mail address is javier.faulin@unavarra.es

* * *

Curtis Atkisson is Director of Marketing and Research at Idea Works, Inc. and student of Anthropology and Psychology at the University of Missouri. His research interests lie in using mathematical, statistical and computational models in evolutionary psychology, specifically in the areas of depression, learning, altruism, and homosexuality. Ongoing research involves the evaluation of learning systems, the evaluation of using computational linguistic strategies to offer real-time advice to members of work groups, the use of large scale datasets to evaluate evolutionary psychology hypotheses, and the creation of holistic evolutionary theories of depression, learning, and homosexuality. He expects to be in the field in Dominica analyzing the concurrent release of Arginine Vasopressin and Testosterone in males during the summer of 2009.

José Antonio Becerra received the B.S. and M.S. degree in Computer Science from the University of A Coruña, Spain, in 1999, and a PhD in Computer Science from the same university in 2003. He is currently a "Profesor Contratado Doctor" in the Department of Computer Science, teaching "Fundamentals of Computer Science" and "Methods in Computer Science" in Industrial Engineering, and "Artificial Life and Autonomous Robotics" in Computer Science Engineering. He is also a member of the Integrated Group for Engineering Research at the University of A Coruña, and his research activities are mainly related to autonomous robotics, evolutionary algorithms and parallel computing.

Francisco Bellas is a "Profesor Contratado Doctor" at the University of Coruña in Spain. He received the B.S. and M.S. degree in Physics from the University of Santiago de Compostela (Spain) in 2001, and a Ph.D. in Computer Science from the University of A Coruña (Spain) in 2003. He works as a professor in the department of Computer Science, teaching different subjects as "Fundamentals of Computer Science", "Methods in Computer Science", "Expert Systems" and "Artificial Life and Autonomous Robotics" in the schools of Industrial Engineering and Computer Science. Furthermore, he is a member of the Integrated Group for Engineering Research at the University of A Coruña. Current research activities are related to evolutionary algorithms applied to artificial neural networks, multiagent systems and robotics.

Edward Brent is President of Idea Works, Inc. and Professor and Associate Chair of the Department of Sociology at the University of Missouri. His research interests are in the use of intelligent computational strategies to provide tools to assist in research and teaching. He and his colleagues have also authored a program using intelligent strategies for qualitative analysis of unstructured data (Qualrus™) and a suite of programs to advise researchers in the development of research proposals (Methodologist's Toolchest™).

Ongoing research is exploring the use of the computational linguistic strategies from SAGrader to offer real-time advice to members of work groups, to automatically monitor news streams on the World Wide Web, and to detect evidence of suicidal ideation based on free-text accounts by friends.

Sotirios D. Botsios is an PhD student in Department of Electrical and Computer Engineering at Democritus University of Thrace (Greece). He is a BSc and Master holder from Chemical Engineering Department, Aristotle University of Thessaloniki (AUTH), Greece. He is Teaching Assistant as PhD candidate on Statistics and Differential Equations. In his first steps of his academic career he participated with full and short papers in international scientific conferences and published articles in Chemical Engineering and E-Learning scientific journals. His research interests are on Adaptive Hypermedia, Standards of Learning Objects Metadata, Adaptive retrieval of Learning Objects, Learning Style diagnosis, and virtual-co-learner agents. His e-mail address is smpotsio@ee.duth.gr

Dr. Dumitru Dan Burdescu is a Professor of Algorithms and Data Structures in the Software Engineering Department at the University of Craiova (Romania). He holds a Ph.D. in Industrial Engineering, and a bachelor degree in Mathematics (University of Craiova, Romania). His research interests include e-learning, data mining, knowledge management, information retrieval. He has published several papers in international journals, books and proceedings regarding these fields. As a researcher, he has been involved in several international research projects. He is director of the Multimedia Research Center [http://www.software.ucv.ro//Cercetare/CC/en/index.htm]. His e-mail address is burdescu@software.ucv.ro

Dr. Victor Cavaller holds a PhD in Information and Library Sciences from the University of Barcelona (Spain), and a Master in Applied Economic Analysis (IDEC-UPF). He is an Associate Professor of Statistics and Information Systems in the Information and Communication Sciences Department at the Open University of Catalonia (Spain). He is also an Assistant Professor of Research and Development, and Marketing, Product Innovation and Development at the International University of Catalonia (UIC). His research interests include scientometrics, informetrics, indicator systems, data analysis architecture, applied statistics, r+d+i. His e-mail address is vcavaller@uoc.edu

Oscar Fontenla-Romero received the B.S., M.S. Ph.D. degrees in Computer Science from the University of A Coruña, Spain, in 1997, 1998 and 2002, respectively. He is currently a "Profesor Contratado Doctor" in the Department of Computer Science, teaching "Fundamentals of Computer Science" in Industrial Engineering and "Formal Specification Programming Languages" in Computer Science Engineering. He is also a member of the Laboratory for Research and Development in Artificial Intelligence at the University of A Coruña, and his research activities are mainly related to machine learning, intelligent systems and neural networks.

Pietro Gaffuri is temporary research assistant at the Faculty of Psychology of the University of Bologna, and in the last two years was a scientific collaborator at the Department of Education of the University of Bologna, for the European Minerva Project "Social networks and promotion of knowledge construction in e-learning contexts". He collaborated with the Department, and with the Faculty of Psychology, in other projects and researches concerning e-learning and web communities. He has experience in learning objects production, in e-learning platforms administration and in platforms users' activity monitoring, in data mining, and also as web designer and web developer.

Dr. Edward F. Gehringer is an Associate Professor in the Department of Computer Science and the Department of Electrical and Computer Engineering at North Carolina State University. He holds a Ph.D. in Computer Science (Purdue University), a B.S. in Mathematics from the University of Detroit (now the University of Detroit-Mercy), and a B.A. in Math/Computer Science (Wayne State University). He has been a frequent presenter at education-based workshops in the areas of computer architecture and object-oriented systems. His research interests include architectural support for memory management, garbage collection, and computer-supported collaborative work. His e-mail address is efg@ncsu.edu.

Dr. Dimitrios A. Georgiou is an Associate Professor of Applied Mathematics in Electrical and Computer Engineering at Democritus University of Thrace (Greece). He is also Associate Professor of Applied Mathematics in the School of Administrative Officers of Hellenic Air Forces. He holds a Ph.D. of Mathematical Analysis (DUTH) and Post Doctoral Studies Diploma from U.C. Berkeley Mathematics Institute. His research interests focus : Qualitative behaviour of solutions of ODE, Difference Equations, PDEs, Numerical Methods for Boundary Value Problems, Intelligent Tutoring Systems, Computational Intelligence. He is director of Section of Applied Mathematics and director of Laboratory of Mathematics. His e-mail address is dgeorg@ee.duth.gr

Nathaniel Green is the Lead Systems Engineer and Chief Technical Officer at IdeaWorks, Inc. He is also a Master's student in the University of Missouri Department of Computer Science and a National Science Foundation GK-12 Fellow. Nathaniel is an alumnus of Truman State University, where he was the President of Phi Eta Sigma and the Truman State GNU/Linux Users' Group. Nathaniel has been involved in interdisciplinary research since his undergraduate days, with Dr. Kenneth Carter (chemistry), Dr. Lisa Sattenspiel (anthropology), and Dr. Marjorie Skubic (elder care).His research interests include natural language processing and understanding, sofware deployment and security, and web-scale systems. Ongoing research involves using computational linguistic strategies to offer real-time advice to members of work groups and detecting evidence of suicidal ideation based on free-text accounts by peers.

Angélica de Antonio Jimenez is associate professor at the Computer Science School of the Universidad Politécnica de Madrid, Spain (UPM) since 1990. She is also Director of the "Decoroso Crespo Laboratory for Educational Applications of Computing" since 1994, where she has lead several research and development projects both at national and international level. Her research interests include intelligent agents, virtual environments, educational software and software engineering. She received a B.S. in 1990 and a Ph.D. in Computer Science in 1994 from the UPM.

Dr. Fernando Lera-López is associate professor of Economics at the Department of Economics of the Public University of Navarra (Spain), where he lectures on the European Economy, Spanish Industry, and Strategies and Decisions within e-Enterprises. His research interests include the economic impacts of Information and Communication Technologies (ICT).

Elvis Mazzoni is researcher and social network analyst at the Faculty of Psychology of the Alma Mater Studiorum - University of Bologna. He's also founder and Executive Committee Member of the Collaborative Knowledge Building Group (CKBG) and Member of the International Society for Cultural and Activity Research (ISCAR) and of Italian Society for e-Learning (SIe-L). He has been and is involved in many national and international e-learning research projects connected to its principal research interests: the co-evolution of web technologies and human activities; web artifacts in educational and vocational training environments; web communities and web social networks in e-learning contexts.

Dr. Marian Cristian Mihaescu is a Lecturer in the Software Engineering Department at the University of Craiova (Romania). He holds a Ph.D. in Computer Science, and a M.S. in Control Engineering (University of Craiova, Romania). His research interests include e-learning, data mining, knowledge management, information retrieval. He has published several papers in international journals, books and proceedings regarding these fields. As a researcher, he has been involved in several international research projects. His e-mail address is mihaescu@software.ucv.ro

Adriana Peña Pérez Negrón received her Computer Science degree from the Universidad Vasco de Quiroga (Mexico), and her Master in Business Administration in that same university. Currently she is a PhD candidate at the Universidad Politécnica de Madrid and her research interests are in Computer Supported Collaborative Learning based on Virtual Reality, the user's avatar display of nonverbal communication and collaborative learning processes.

Marta Elena Zorrilla Pantaleón is an assistant professor in the area of Computer Science at the University of Cantabria (Spain). She earned her bachelor degree in Telecommunication Engineering and Ph. D. in Computer Science at the University of Cantabria in 1994 and 2001 respectively. She has participated and managed several research projects, and she is authoress of a database book and of several articles published in international journals and congresses. Her research interests are the design and development of information systems and intelligent systems for companies; and, inside the educational area, the application of web using mining techniques and OLAP technologies in order to analyse and improve web-based learning sites.

Donatella Persico is senior researcher at the Institute for Educational Technology of the Italian National Research Council (CNR). She has been active in the field of educational technology, theory and applications, since 1981. Her major interests include instructional design, self-regulated learning, e-learning and teacher training. She is author and editor of educational material and scientific publications of various kinds, including books, educational software, University of Genoa from 2000 to 2006. She is member of the editorial board of international and national journals on Educational Technology and has been in charge of several national and international projects.

Francesca Pozzi is presently researcher at the Institute for Educational Technology of the Italian National Research Council (CNR) and has got a Ph.D. in Cultures, Languages and ICT (University of Genoa). Her major research interests include the design and run of online courses in collaborative learning environments (CSCL), the design of strategies and techniques for fostering collaboration within these contexts, the issues related to monitoring and evaluating the learning process in CSCL field. In her work the theoretical study of models and methods has always been supported by application in real contexts as part of collaboration with a number of state schools, local and national training agencies, public bodies, etc.

Elena E. Álvarez Sáiz earned her bachelor degree and Ph. D. in Mathematics at the University of Cantabria (Spain) in 1987 and 1991 respectively. Her research focuses on Educational Computer Science.

She coordinates and develops projects concerning the use of new technologies in University teaching. She has developed multimedia educational web software for virtual environments and published several books and articles about this topic.

Noelia Sánchez-Maroño received the B.S. and M.S. degree in Computer Science from the University of A Coruña, Spain, in 2000, and a PhD in Computer Science from the same university in 2005. She is currently a "Profesora Contratada Doctora", teaching "Fundamentals of Computer Science" in Industrial Engineering and "Artificial Intelligence" and "Expert Systems" in Computer Science Engineering. She is also a member of the Laboratory for Research and Development in Artificial Intelligence at the University of A Coruña. Her research interests include functional and artificial neural networks and feature selection.

Luigi Sarti is an ITD researcher since 1982. His research interests focus on methodologies and techniques to apply ICT to learning processes from both a theoretical and a practical perspective. In particular, he is active in the field of CSCL in an attempt to adapt and re-interpret current technologies for the representation of educational data (Learning Object, metadata, Educational Modelling Languages etc.) to support collaborative learning processes framed in the social constructivism paradigm. He has bees responsible for ITD participation in a number of both EU funded and national research projects.

Daphna Shwarts-Asher is a Ph.D. student at The Faculty of Management, Tel Aviv University, Israel. Her research interests are OB and economic and behavioral aspects of the Internet. The objective of the Ph.D. research is to investigate corporate output of virtual teams, assuming team structure can compensate for the shortcomings of virtuallity. She has presented the research recently at The 3rd International e-Social Science Conference at Michigan. In addition, she teaches courses in the field of management at several institutions such as Tel Aviv University, Ort Braude College, and The Max Stern Academic College of Emek Yezreel.

Georgios Tsoulouhas is an PhD student in Department of Electrical and Computer Engineering at Democritus University of Thrace (Greece). He got hiw B.Sc. from Computer and Electrical Engineering Department at Democritus University of Thrace (DUTH). He is Teaching Assistant as PhD candidate (2007-2009) on Programming (Fortran, C and Internet Programming). He is working at Research and Innovation Centre "Athena" since 2002 and has taken part in the design and development of many of the projects of the Centre. His research interests are on Data Mining, Intelligent Tutoring Systems, Metadata Standards, Software Agents and Fuzzy Systems. His e-mail address is gtsoulou@ee.duth.gr

Bin Zou received his MA degree in Educational Studies from the University of York, UK. He completed his PhD in Computer Technology in English Language Teaching at the Graduate School of Education, the University of Bristol, UK. He has experience in teaching English as a foreign language (EFL) and English for academic purpose (EAP), particularly using computer technology in language teaching. He has interests in using ICT in education, including language teaching and learning. He has given presentations at international conferences such as BAAL, IATEFL and EUROCALL annual conferences in the UK and Ireland. He has published papers in journals such as *International Journal of Education and Development using Information and Communication Technology, International Journal of Emerging Technologies in Learning* and *TESL-EJ, etc.* He is currently an English tutor at the English Language Center, Xi'an Jiaotong-Liverpool University, China.

Index